What is the Human Being?

WITHDRAWN

The question of human nature is a question that Kant thought about deeply and returned to in many of his writings. In this lucid and wide-ranging introduction to Kant's philosophy of human nature – which is essential for understanding his thought as a whole – Patrick Frierson assesses Kant's theories and examines his critics.

He begins by explaining how Kant articulates three ways of addressing the question "what is the human being?": the transcendental, the empirical, and the pragmatic. He then considers some of the great theorists of human nature who wrestle with Kant's views, such as Hegel, Marx, Darwin, Nietzsche, and Freud; contemporary thinkers such as E.O. Wilson and Daniel Dennett, who have sought biological explanations of human nature; Thomas Kuhn, Michel Foucault, and Clifford Geertz, who emphasize the diversity of human beings in different times and places; and existentialist philosophers such as Sartre and Heidegger.

He argues that whilst these approaches challenge and enrich Kant's views in significant ways, all suffer from serious weaknesses that Kant's anthropology can address. Taking a core insight of Kant's – that human beings are fundamentally free but finite – he argues that it is the existentialists, particularly Sartre, who are the most direct heirs of his transcendental anthropology.

The final part of this book is an extremely helpful overview of the work of Richard Rorty and Alasdair MacIntyre. In this context, Frierson explains how the contemporary Kantians Christine Korsgaard and Jurgen Habermas engage with questions of naturalism, historicism, and existentialism while developing Kantian conceptions of the human being.

Including chapter summaries and annotated further reading, *What is the Human Being?* is an outstanding introduction to some fundamental aspects of Kant's thought and a judicious assessment of leading theories of human nature. It is essential reading for all students of Kant and the philosophy of human nature, as well as those in related disciplines such as anthropology, politics, and sociology.

Patrick R. Frierson is Associate Professor of Philosophy at Whitman College, Washington, USA.

KANT'S QUESTIONS

Series advisor: Allen Wood, Stanford University, USA

"The *Kant's Questions* series is thoroughly excellent. The books combine depth of philosophical treatment with a fluid, easily-readable style, offering original historical interpretations of Kant's writings with an illuminating attentiveness to issues of contemporary relevance. All in all, the series reveals the stunning depth, power, and lasting impact of Kant's writings."

—*Robert Hanna, University of Colorado at Boulder, USA*

"This is an excellently conceived series by internationally renowned Kant scholars who, unusually, focus not on individual works or sub-disciplinary fields of inquiry but engage with those questions which Kant took to be of perennial philosophical interest. Engagingly and accessibly written whilst meeting exemplary standards of scholarship, these volumes will prove an invaluable resource for students and teachers of Kant's philosophy alike."

—*Katrin Flikschuh, London School of Economics, UK*

"By providing careful and detailed accounts of Kant's answers to what he considered to be the most fundamental questions of philosophy, the books in this series constitute excellent introductions to the key aspects of Kant's philosophy. Moreover, by tracing the development of these questions and ideas to the present day, they contextualise contemporary debates within a historical narrative in a way that allows the reader to grasp the continuing relevance and significance of Kant's questions and the answers that he put forward."

—*Ralf M. Bader, New York University, USA*

"The field of philosophy ... can be reduced to the following questions: What can I know? What ought I to do? What may I hope? What is the human being? Metaphysics answers the first question, morals the second, religion the third, and anthropology the fourth."

Immanuel Kant

With the addition of his celebrated essay *An Answer to the Question: What is Enlightenment?* Kant bequeaths us five fundamental questions that continue to resonate and challenge today.

Kant's Questions explores the philosophical meaning and significance of each question. Taken individually, each book is a fresh and innovative introduction to a fundamental aspect of Kant's thought. Taken together, the series is an outstanding resource on the central questions motivating Kant's philosophical and intellectual outlook as a whole.

Each book shares a clear structure. The first part introduces Kant's question, explaining his own answer to it; the second part explores historical criticisms to the question; and the third and final part of the book places the question in a contemporary philosophical context. Also included are chapter summaries and a helpful section of annotated further reading at the end of each chapter.

The *Kant's Questions* series is essential reading, not only for all students of Kant, but those studying subjects such as ethics, metaphysics, philosophy of human nature, and the history of philosophy, as well as those in related disciplines such as religious studies, politics, and sociology.

- *What is the human being?* Patrick Frierson
- *What is enlightenment?* Samuel Fleischacker
- *What can I know?* Michelle Grier
- *What should I do?* Julian Wuerth
- *What may I hope for?* Andrew Chignell

What is the Human Being?

Patrick R. Frierson

Routledge
Taylor & Francis Group

LONDON AND NEW YORK

First published 2013
by Routledge
2 Park Square, Milton Park, Abingdon, Oxon OX14 4RN

Simultaneously published in the USA and Canada
by Routledge
711 Third Avenue, New York, NY 10017

Routledge is an imprint of the Taylor & Francis Group, an informa business

© 2013 Patrick R. Frierson

British Library Cataloguing in Publication Data
A catalogue record for this book is available from the British Library

Library of Congress Cataloging in Publication Data
Frierson, Patrick R., 1974-
What is the human being? / by Patrick R. Frierson.
p. cm. – (Kant's questions)
Includes bibliographical references (p.) and index.
1. Kant, Immanuel, 1724-1804. 2. Philosophical anthropology. 3. Human beings. I. Title.
B2798.F75 2013
128.092–dc23
2012029613

ISBN 978-0-415-55844-0 (hbk)
ISBN 978-0-415-55845-7 (pbk)
ISBN 978-0-203-07031-4 (ebk)

Typeset in Garamond and Gillsans
by Taylor & Francis Books

"Herr, was ist der Mensch, das du dich seiner annimmst?"

Psalm 144:3, Luther's translation of the Bible

"The field of philosophy ... can be reduced to the following questions: What can I know? What ought I to do? What may I hope? What is the human being? [*Was ist der Mensch?*] Metaphysics answers the first question, morals the second, religion the third, and anthropology the fourth. Fundamentally, however, we could reckon all of this as anthropology."

Immanuel Kant, from a lecture on logic (9: 25)

"I myself am a researcher by inclination. I feel the entire thirst for cognition and the eager restlessness to proceed further in it, as well as the satisfaction at every acquisition ... [but] I would feel by far less useful than the common laborer if I did not believe that this consideration could impart a value to all others in order to establish the rights of humanity."

Immanuel Kant, from private notes written in 1764–65 (20: 44)

Contents

Acknowledgments

Kant rightly notes that human beings are social beings, and he excoriates "the logical egoist" who "considers it unnecessary to also test his judgment by the understanding of others; as if he had no need at all for this touchstone" (7: 128). This book is one that could not have been written without the contributions of many generous understandings other than my own. I thank Tony Bruce for inviting me to write the book and for his valuable assistance throughout every stage of the project. Several anonymous reviewers gave very helpful comments on my proposal and two anonymous reviewers gave essential help for improving and substantially shortening the final manuscript. An earlier and much different version of Chapter 2 appeared in *Philosophers' Imprint*, and I am grateful for two anonymous commentators on that version who greatly improved it. Many thanks go to Sam Fleischacker and the University of Illinois at Chicago for hosting a conference in 2009 involving Andrew Chignell, Sam Fleischacker, Michelle Grier, Julian Wuerth, and myself, during which we had conversations that helped push my ideas forward. Very helpful comments on late drafts of particular chapters were contributed by Karl Ameriks, Andrew Cutrofello, and Rachel Zuckert. Allen Wood gave helpful comments on the penultimate version of the manuscript. My students at Whitman College have provided an invaluable intellectual stimulation that permeates this book, but I particularly thank the students in my 2009 seminar "What is the Human Being?" and two research assistants – Keefe Piper and Brian Cutter – who helped with various stages of the book and whose comments and criticisms vastly exceeded my expectations and made this a much stronger book. I thank Whitman College for two Louis B. Perry Summer Research Grants that allowed me to hire those students and for the year-long sabbatical in 2009–10 during which I wrote the majority of the book. I thank the National Endowment for the Humanities for the Summer Stipend back in 2002 that got my work on Kant's empirical psychology started and then particularly for the Research Fellowship during 2009–10 that allowed me to take a full-year sabbatical and complete my first draft of this book. Finally, I thank my partner

Katheryn and my children Zechariah, Phoebe, and Cyrus. My children patiently endured those countless occasions when my attention was divided between their needs and this book, and they made my life a constant joy during the writing of it. And Katheryn is the real reason that the book exists. She encouraged me to pursue this project, bore with me as I brought it to completion, and provided very helpful comments on my final draft. She, above all, helps me be the human being I should be.

Introduction

[W]hat is man's ultimate nature? We keep returning to the subject with a sense of hesitancy and even dread. For if ... the mind can somehow be explained as the summed activity of a finite number of chemical and electrical reactions, boundaries limit the human prospect—we are biological and our souls cannot fly free. If humankind evolved by Darwinian natural selection, genetic chance and environmental necessity, not God, made the species ... However much we embellish that stark conclusion with metaphor and imagery, it remains the philosophical legacy of the last century of scientific research. No way appears around this admittedly unappealing proposition. It is the essential first hypothesis for any serious consideration of the human condition.

(Wilson 1978–2004: 1–2)

If we want to discover what the human being amounts to, we can only find it in what human beings are: and what human beings are, above all other things, is various. It is in understanding that variousness – its range, its nature, its basis, and its implications – that we shall come to construct a concept of human nature ... To be human here is thus not to be Everyman; it is to be a particular kind of human being, and of course human beings differ ... [I]t is in a systematic review and analysis of [different ways of being human] – of the Plain's Indian's bravura, the Hindu's obsessiveness, the Frenchman's rationalism, the Berber's anarchism, the American's optimism – that we shall find out what it is, or can be, to be a human.

(Geertz 1973: 52–53)[1]

[T]here is at least one being [the human being] whose existence comes before its essence, a being which exists before it can be defined by any conception of it. ... What do we mean by saying that existence precedes essence? We mean that man first of all exists, encounters himself, surges up in the world – and defines himself afterwards. If the human being ... is not definable, it is because to begin with he is nothing. He will not be anything until later, and then he will be what he makes of himself. Thus, there is no human nature. ... The human being simply is. Not that he is simply what he conceives himself to be, but he is what he wills, and as he conceives himself after already existing – as he wills to be after that leap towards existence. The human being is nothing else but what he makes of himself.

(Sartre 1993: 15)

What *is* the human being? The three quotations with which this introduction begins lay out three alternatives: E.O. Wilson, one of the pre-eminent sociobiologists of the twentieth century, sees the parameters for the answer given by biology. Humans are animals with a particular structure that has evolved over millions of years. We are biological beings, and what we need in order to better answer the question "What is the human being?" is better biology, a more detailed description of how we, as humans, are like and unlike other animals that inhabit the earth. Clifford Geertz, five years earlier, articulated a different conception of human beings, one at the core of the "human" science of anthropology. For Geertz, there is no answer to the question "What is *the* human being?" because we are not pre-eminently *biological* organisms, but *cultural* ones; since there is not one human culture, there is not one kind of human being. What we need is not better biological description, but more widely ranging, deeply investigating studies of human variety. Rather than looking for a theory of human nature, we should seek a catalog of human ways of life. Alternatively, perhaps, as the existentialist philosopher and literary author Jean-Paul Sartre argues, human beings are "condemned to be free" (Sartre 1956: 568). Rather than trying to *discover* what human beings are, we should *make* human nature by free choices. Rather than looking as scientists or anthropologists at what human beings happen to be, we should take the role of architects of possibility, whether as artists (literary or otherwise) imagining and thereby creating new human possibilities, as political or social activists changing the social landscape, or simply as acting individuals creating human nature through our daily choices.

The world we live in today is one within which these approaches to the question "What is the human being?" cannot be ignored. Scientific knowledge about our biological nature – from the coding of the human genome to the mapping of brain activity – has made it clearer than ever that humans operate with biological constraints. As Wilson rightly points out, our knowledge of how our biology is like and unlike that of other animals cannot be ignored in any serious consideration of human nature. At the same time, as the world becomes increasingly interconnected, human diversity, even if actually diminishing, is becoming more apparent and more relevant to more and more people across the globe. Protestant Christians in the United States cannot afford to be wholly ignorant of the cultures of rural Muslims in Afghanistan or atheists in China or Buddhists in Sri Lanka. Throughout the world, diversity is literally on one's doorstep, as Catholic Filipinos work in Korea and Dubai, Muslim immigrants serve in European parliaments, and Chinese businessmen set up shop in Africa. The awareness of this diversity requires dealing with the fact that human nature is diverse. Finally, the increased power over our world and ourselves that comes from scientific, technological, and economic progress along with the awareness of the range of human possibilities that comes from seeing other cultures gives rise to an ever more acute sense that human nature really is up to us, that we can make ourselves into whatever we want to be. The current situation requires thinking carefully about what it means to be human.

But what, precisely, is one seeking when one asks "What is the human being?" What is the question that Wilson, Geertz, Sartre, and so many others are trying to answer? Strikingly, *none* of these thinkers – not even the biologist Wilson – treats the question "What is the human being?" quite like the question "What is oxygen?" or "What is a giraffe?" All of them see the question as one about our *prospects*, as one not merely about the structure of our brain or society, but about the *implications* of that structure for human choices, for what we should do with ourselves. All recognize that the question "What *is* the human being?" is also, and fundamentally, about what is *important* about us.

When we understand it in this way, we can see why this question was central for Kant, why Kant would insist, "[t]he greatest concern of the human being is ... to rightly understand what one must do in order to be a human being" (20: 41).[2] Knowing what it is to be human is – for Wilson, Geertz, and Sartre no less than for Kant – something worthy of *concern*. Thus Geertz does not simply assert that humans are different, but adds that their differences are *more important* than their similarities, more essential to what it means to be human. All of them recognize a point made by Martin Heidegger, that "The being whose analysis our task is, is always we ourselves. The being of this being is always *mine*" (Heidegger 1953: 39). They recognize that asking what a human being is really amounts to asking, "Who am I?," "What is most important about me?," "What do I value about myself?" and even "What do I aspire to be?"

The emphasis on values and aspirations, however, should not blind us to the fact that claims about human prospects and aspirations include descriptions of human beings. Even Sartre, who insists that what human beings *are* can only be answered *after* we make ourselves what we are to be, nonetheless recognizes that we are "condemned to be free," that freedom is a "human condition" from which we cannot escape. Descriptions of the human condition provide the backdrop for claims about how to act in response to them. Kant, too, recognizes the importance of accurate descriptions of human beings. In part, this is for practical reasons: "The question is which condition suits the human being, an inhabitant of the planet that orbits the sun at a distance of 200 diameters of the sun. Just as little as I can ascend from here to the planet Jupiter, so little do I demand to have qualities that are proper only to that planet ... I do not at all have the ambition of wanting to be a seraph; my pride is only this, that I am a human being" (20: 47). One needs to know what human beings *are* to know what we should aspire to be. And for Kant – as, at least, for Wilson and Geertz – human beings are also just very interesting to study. Not only must any practical account of human beings reflect an accurate description of them, but such descriptions are, in their own right, worth pursuing.

At its core, the question "What is the human being?" combines careful description of human characteristics with a normative, aspirational account of what about "us" is or would be truly valuable, an account rooted in the sense that each human questioner has of herself. Answering the question, however, involves clarifying what precisely constitutes a legitimate sort of "description" and also what structure and importance to ascribe to the normative perspective on oneself. And ultimately, as we see in the brief references to Wilson, Geertz, and Sartre, the answer to the question will combine – either implicitly or explicitly – these two aspects.

The main purpose of this book is to lay out Kant's answer to his question and to situate this answer in the context of contemporary debates about human nature and historical influences that brought us to where we are today. The first part of the book thus focuses on Kant's answer. An interlude lays out later trends that took the question in different directions. And the final part brings Kant into dialogue with the most important contemporary approaches to human nature, including those of Wilson, Geertz, and Sartre. This short book can neither fully detail Kant's answer nor survey all relevant contemporary approaches. But it introduces key Kantian and contemporary ideas, and "further reading" sections concluding each chapter suggest more detailed treatments of each topic.

Kant's "Anthropologies"

In one of his lectures, Kant is recorded as having laid out his view of philosophy as a whole:

> The field of philosophy ... can be reduced to the following questions: What can I know? What ought I to do? What may I hope? What is the human being? Metaphysics answers the first question, morals the second, religion the third, and anthropology the fourth. Fundamentally, however, we could reckon all of this as anthropology.
>
> (9: 25, cf. 11: 249)

The term "anthropology" may seem odd here for contemporary readers. We are accustomed to thinking of "anthropology" as a specific academic discipline that studies variations between people in different cultures. Kant, by contrast, uses the term anthropology in its original sense, as the study (*logos*) of human beings (*anthropos*). Thus Kantian anthropology includes comparisons between different people at different times, but it also includes – and emphasizes – general features of human beings as such. Anthropology is the discipline that answers the question "What is the Human Being?" That is how the term will be used throughout this book.

But the claim that all of philosophy can be reckoned as anthropology may seem strange for other reasons, as well. While human nature may be a *part* of philosophy, philosophy often deals with questions, such as the existence of God or the basic nature of reality, that seem to go beyond anthropology, and other disciplines deal (arguably better than philosophy) with important aspects of human nature. In equating philosophy and anthropology, Kant explicitly claims that every really important question that humans can ask, whether about God or substance or basic laws of physics or morals or aesthetics, is fundamentally a question *about* human beings, about what we can know, or should do, or may hope.

A final reason that Kant's claim to reduce all philosophy to anthropology might seem strange, especially for those accustomed to think of anthropology as an empirical discipline, is that this sort of enquiry seems inadequate to establish the normative claims embodied in the questions of what one *can* (legitimately) believe, or *should* do. Those familiar with Kant's work may be even more puzzled. At the end of his life, Kant published a book entitled *Anthropology from a Pragmatic Point of View*, but this book could hardly be said to include Kant's most important contributions to the questions of human knowledge, obligation, and hope. This *Anthropology* is striking for being deeply empirical, while Kant's answers to the questions of knowledge, obligation, and hope emphasize that these questions must be answered non-empirically. In his *Groundwork*, Kant even goes so far as to emphasize a distinction between "pure moral philosophy," which most fundamentally addresses the question "What ought I to do?," and "moral anthropology," which is secondary and merely adds empirical details. Kant's *Anthropology from a Pragmatic Point of View* relates to this secondary, empirical aspect and thus cannot articulate the most important dimensions of Kant's answers to the three questions that, supposedly, can all be "reckon[ed] ... as anthropology."

In fact Kant articulates different "anthropologies," different kinds of answer to the question "What is the human being?" Most importantly, he distinguishes between three ways in which one can ask the question and three dimensions of human life to which each of these three ways apply. The dimensions of human life arise from Kant's description of human mental states as being essentially of three kinds: cognitions (of truth), feelings (of pleasure), and volitions (for various goods). Kant does not ascribe consistent names to his three ways of inquiring, but in this book, I refer to them as "transcendental," "empirical," and "pragmatic." Put very briefly, transcendental anthropology provides normative, from-within accounts of what it is like to be human, accounts that define how one *should* think, feel, and choose based on what we take ourselves to be doing when we engage in thinking, feeling, or choosing. Empirical anthropology provides scientific (in a loose sense), observation-based descriptions and categorizations of how observable humans think, feel, and act. And pragmatic anthropology puts these two approaches together, drawing on empirical descriptions to provide advice about how best to satisfy the norms elucidated within transcendental anthropology. Part One of this book unpacks these different Kantian "anthropologies."

What is the Human Being Today?

Kant's approach to the human being cannot satisfy "the greatest concern of the human being" (20: 41) nor achieve the great goal that Kant assigned for it – "to establish the rights of humanity" (20: 44) – unless it can be brought into conversation with the dominant approaches to thinking about human beings today. After an Interlude in which I examine the accounts of human beings of five of the most important thinkers of the nineteenth and early twentieth centuries, Part III cultivates a series of interactions between Kant and the leading contemporary approaches to the question "What is the human being?"

Chapter 7 looks at scientific naturalists such as Wilson, who advocate that the question is best answered by biological or psychological studies of human beings. There are a wide range of such naturalist approaches, so this chapter gives only a relatively small sample of the ways in which philosophers and scientists have sought to use biological or psychological descriptions of human nature – what Kant would call "empirical anthropology" – to *fully* answer the question "What is the human being?" Chapter 8 looks at approaches to human beings that emphasize human diversity, whether in the context of historical changes that make the human being of today different from the human beings of other times or in the context of cotemporaneous cultural differences that make human beings in one culture different from those in another. Both of these approaches represent attempts to make what for Kant is only empirical anthropology (or even a subset of empirical anthropology) into the whole, and both approaches not only raise serious problems for Kant but also – as I hope to show – suffer from serious weaknesses that Kant's anthropology can highlight and alleviate.

Among the most important weaknesses of historicism and naturalism is their failure to take sufficiently seriously what I will call the from-within perspective of transcendental anthropology, and Chapter 9 looks at a philosophical approach to human beings that seeks to take this quite seriously, but with a different result from Kant: existentialism. Existentialists are arguably the most direct *heirs* of Kant's work in transcendental anthropology, taking a core insight of Kant's – that human beings are fundamentally free but finite beings – and radicalizing this insight in such a way that the normative weight Kant ascribes to principles of reasoning and action becomes subordinated to – rather than constitutive of – human freedom.

In the end, I argue that while existentialism can reinvigorate and even enrich certain Kantian emphases, it fails to speak to human beings because it fails to provide the right sort of normativity. Chapter 10 then takes up a small sample of contemporary approaches to normativity, beginning with some that are far removed from Kant and ending with two of the most prominent contemporary neo-Kantian philosophers writing today: Jürgen Habermas and Christine Korsgaard. These philosophers provide models for how present-day Kantians can integrate and respond to the insights of naturalism, historicism, and existentialism while still developing authentically Kantian conceptions of the human being.

Part I

KANT ON THE HUMAN BEING

1 Kant's Transcendental Anthropology

As to the subject matter with which we are concerned, we ask that people think of it ... as the foundation of human ... dignity. Each individual ... may reflect on it himself ... [Our work] claims nothing ... beyond what is mortal.
(Francis Bacon, *New Organon*, quoted by Kant in the *Critique of Pure Reason* (Bii))

"Transcendental Anthropology"

In the introduction, I claimed that Kant's answer to the question "What is the human being?" has at least three different components. Of these, I will refer to the one that made Kant famous and that he identified with "the field of philosophy" (9: 25) as "transcendental anthropology." The term "transcendental anthropology" is taken from Kant's handwritten notes, in which he refers to an "anthropologia transcendentalis," a "self-knowledge of the understanding and reason" that would critique all other sciences, including not only "geometry" and "knowledge of nature" but even "literature ... theology, law" and "knowledge of morality" (15: 395). But my use of the term arises from Kant's insistence that all of philosophy is reducible to "anthropology" (9: 25) and his description of each aspect of his philosophy as "transcendental" (see A13/B27; 4: 390; 5: 113, 266, 270; 6: 272; and 8: 381). Admittedly, Kant often uses the term "anthropology" for his *pragmatic* anthropology, and he often reserves the term "transcendental" for investigations of the conditions of possibility of *experience* (the topic of only one of his *Critique*s). But he does use both terms in broader ways throughout his works, and "transcendental anthropology" provides a useful term to contrast Kant's approach to the human being in his a priori philosophical works with empirical and pragmatic approaches elsewhere. Throughout his philosophical works, Kant answers central philosophical questions in ways that are "anthropological," but in a distinctive sense of anthropology that I call "transcendental."

While this transcendental investigation is contrasted, for Kant, with empirical study of human beings, one must be careful not to confuse "transcendental" with "transcendent" and thereby take transcendental anthropology (or philosophy) to refer to some aspect of human beings that transcends ordinary experience, or our animal nature, or something of that sort. In the same way that God might be seen as ultimately transcendent, we might want to study the transcendent aspect of human beings, through art, perhaps, or by talking about our immortal souls. Kant, however, sharply contrasts his transcendent*al* philosophy with traditional philosophies of the "transcendent." For Kant, "transcendental anthropology" is a kind of "self-knowledge of the understanding and of reason" (RA 903, 15: 395). By this he does not mean simply that in knowing human beings, we know ourselves, since this would be true for empirical investigations of human beings as well. Instead, in transcendental anthropology, one knows oneself from-within rather than looking at one's psychology from the stance of an observer. Transcendental anthropology is a most *immanent* self-knowledge, and hence sharply contrasted with both empirical sciences *and* divine-like transcendence.

The notion of transcendental anthropology as "from-within" is often described in terms of a difference between "first person" and "third person" perspectives, the perspectives of the thinking, feeling, or choosing *subject* and perspectives *on* someone as an object. This way of describing the distinction can be helpful if one avoids thinking of "introspective" states as first person, since "from-within" does not imply that transcendental anthropology is "introspective" in any traditional sense. One way of making this distinction clear can be seen in the case of choosing a course of action. Someone observing humans might say that what a person chooses in a particular case is determined by accidental environmental features of which the person is only barely conscious. Or one might introspect and suggest that one's behavior in a particular instance was caused by, say, a combination of anger and exhaustion. The next chapter shows how Kant's *empirical* anthropology focuses on these sorts of causal explanations of behavior. But when actually choosing, one doesn't consider these accidental and unconscious influences as bases for choice. One looks for various reasons for action, and even if these reasons include what one might in another context see as mere causes of action (say, one's desiring something), they have a different character when one considers them to be reasons to act; they serve not as *explanations* for behavior but as *justifications* for it. From within the context of deliberation, one's anger appears not as a necessary cause of action, but as a candidate reason for acting, a reason that one may either endorse or reject. Kant's "transcendental" anthropology characterizes the processes of thinking, judging, choice, and aesthetic appreciation from-within.

The from-within perspective involves an important evaluative or normative dimension. When explaining behavior non-transcendentally, one looks at what the causes of action are, and one need not evaluate whether these causes are "good." The question whether, say, anger is a "good" *cause* seems misguided; it either is the cause or it is not. But when thinking about behavior (or judgments, or choices) transcendentally, one looks at reasons for behavior, and reasons invite evaluation. Anger might have caused the behavior, but we can still ask whether it was a good reason for doing what one did. And this is the sort of question one asks, not merely when deciding what to do, but also when deciding what to believe, or how to judge about something, or even whether something is beautiful. The normative question – "Is this a good reason for people to do/think/feel such-and-such?" – arises within transcendental anthropology.

Along with this from-within, normative perspective on human beings, Kant's transcendental anthropology employs a distinctive style of argument. "Transcendental" arguments in Kant proceed from some "given" to the conditions of possibility of that given. Thus Kant's *Critique of Pure Reason* is an extended argument exploring the conditions of possibility of empirical cognition (what we can know). As an experiencer of the world, one can think about what must be the case for one's experience to be possible, and Kant argues that in order for humans to have the kind of experience that we have, the world must contain substances, laws of causality, and other features, and human cognition of it must be limited in various ways. Similarly, the *Critique of Practical Reason* argues from the moral law we find valid within deliberation and evaluation to various conditions of possibility of that validity.

In sum, Kant's *transcendental* anthropology focuses on what can be known about human beings a priori through an examination of basic mental faculties *"from-within"* that specifically attends to the *conditions of possibility* of *normative* constraints on human beings. The rest of this chapter takes up some details of this transcendental anthropology as it plays out in Kant's three famous *Critiques of Pure Reason, Practical Reason,* and *Judgment*. Before turning to those details, it is worth saying a bit more about the specifics of Kant's conception of the human being in order to see how the *Critiques* hang together as a whole "transcendental anthropology" and thus how "we could reckon all of [philosophy] as anthropology" (9: 25). For Kant, human mental states are divided into cognitions, volitions, and feelings. Each aspect of human beings is governed by its own a priori principles that are prescribed by a distinct higher cognitive power (5: 196). In the *Critique of Judgment*, looking back on his philosophy as a whole, Kant uses a chart (see Table 1.1) to show how his entire transcendental philosophy can be understood in terms of these different human faculties (5: 198).[1]

Table 1.1 Kant's transcendental anthropology

Core aspect of the human being	Cognitive power that prescribes principles for it	A priori principles	Application to	Relevant Critique	Relevant Question
Cognition	Understanding	Lawfulness	Nature	*Critique of Pure Reason* (1781/1787)	What can I know?
Feeling	Judgment	Purposiveness	Art	*Critique of Judgment* (1790)	What may I hope?
Desire/ Volition	Reason	Final End	Freedom	*Critique of Practical Reason* (1788)	What ought I to do?

What Can I Know? The *Critique of Pure Reason* as Transcendental Anthropology of Cognition

Kant's most famous and important work, the *Critique of Pure Reason*, focuses on a particular human capacity: "getting to the bottom of the faculty we call the understanding and ... the determination of the rules and boundaries of its use" (A xvi). Kant is not interested here in the empirical question of how the understanding operates, but in giving an account of the rules under which it must operate and the limits that these rules imply for how far we should seek to extend our knowledge. Kant starts with an interest in the status of traditional metaphysics, which involves claims that are "a priori" in that they are necessary and thus not based merely on empirical generalizations, but also "synthetic" because they put together concepts to make substantive assertions about the world. But this metaphysics raises "the general problem" of the *Critique of Pure Reason*: "How are synthetic judgments possible a priori?" (B19, cf. *Prol.* 4: 276). In answering this question, Kant aims to answer the question "What can I know?" as it applies to the "objective validity" of "a priori concepts" (A xvi), that is, "what and how much can the understanding and reason cognize free of all experience?" (A xvii). Through this transcendental anthropology of cognition, Kant defends a metaphysics that consists in a priori claims about the nature of the world and lays out an epistemology that limits the scope of such claims.

Kant's answer to the question of the possibility of synthetic a priori knowledge depends upon conceiving metaphysics as a subset of transcendental anthropology. From the beginning of his *Critique*, Kant makes his radically human-centered metaphysics clear:

> Up to now it has been assumed that all our cognition must conform to objects; but all attempts to find out something about them a priori ... have, on this presupposition, come to nothing. Hence let us once try whether we

do not get farther with the problems of metaphysics by assuming that objects must conform to our cognition.

(Bxvi)

To move human cognition into the center of metaphysics, Kant begins by isolating an assumption of prior metaphysics, the assumption that in order to know anything about the world, our judgments about the world have to conform to the way the world really is. Kant claims that this assumption has made progress in metaphysics impossible. Previous philosophers – especially during the seventeenth and eighteenth centuries – either sought philosophical systems based upon reason alone (rationalism) or sought the ultimate foundations of knowledge in experience (empiricism). Empiricists fail to account for the aprioricity of metaphysics, while rationalists fail to properly account for its synthetic status (by mistakenly overestimating what reason alone can do). Kant's Copernican turn is based on the thought that empiricists and rationalists fail because both are looking for a way to make human cognitions fit onto an independently given world of objects. There is better hope of showing how a priori synthetic judgments are possible if one assumes instead that the world of objects must conform to the structure of human cognition (B xvi). If the world conforms to our cognition, we can know about the world based on the structure of our cognition rather than by induction from experience.

Kant's next move both limits the scope of this Copernican turn and helps show how it functions to make substantive (or "synthetic") a priori knowledge possible. Kant claims that humans' thoughts about objects have two components – an active component by which we *think* about objects, and a passive component by which thoughts are *about objects*: "Thoughts without content are empty, intuitions without concepts are blind" (A50–51/B74–75). Knowledge of an objective world involves receiving "intuitions" from the world and processing them using one's concepts.

Kant's appeal to "intuitions" – a technical term for that which is given by sensibility – limits the scope of the Copernican turn. Kant does not claim, and need not claim, that *everything* about the empirical world is determined by the structure of human cognition. Because we have a receptive faculty, humans have knowledge we take *from* the world, such as that there are mountains in the Pacific Northwest of North America, that water freezes, that dogs and cats cannot interbreed, that large material objects are made of small molecules. And there are other claims that are false, but if true, would have to be discovered empirically, such as the existence of the Loch Ness monster, or fairies, or solid crystalline spheres rotating in the heavens. For such empirical knowledge, cognition must conform to the world. The world will not have fairies in it just because we believe in fairies, nor will it cease to have molecules if we cease to (or do not yet) believe in molecules. Kant's Copernican turn justifies the possibility of some substantive a priori knowledge of the world, but it does not justify claiming to know everything about the empirical world simply by reflecting on one's cognitive capacities.

But Kant also argues that the distinction between intuitions and concepts (and relatedly between sensibility and the understanding) provides for the possibility of a priori knowledge that goes beyond mere conceptual analysis. Even human receptivity has an a priori structure to which the world must conform, and so there can be an a priori science of the principles of this sensibility. Moreover, precisely because sensibility is a faculty of intuitions rather than of concepts, an a priori science of sensibility will not proceed simply by unpacking concepts, and thus may provide a way of justifying claims that are both a priori and synthetic. In particular, Kant argues that space and time are a priori intuitions that structure all humans' empirical intuitions. We can neither think of the world as non-spatial or non-temporal nor think of external objects without an already-given spatial (and temporal) structure (A22–25/B37–40, A30–32/B46–48). And given space and time as a priori intuitions, Kant can explain the success of geometry (based on space) and arithmetic (on time), both of which give synthetic a priori knowledge (A25/B40–41).

Human understanding, like sensibility, has an a priori structure, and after a lengthy, detailed, and controversial defense of a set of a priori "categories" of thought,[2] Kant turns to the way in which these two different cognitive faculties work together to structure the world of experience. By showing how humans' a priori categories work with sensibility to structure the empirical world, Kant's "system of all principles of pure understanding" provides the a priori metaphysics promised in his Preface. The specific details of the various ways in which these faculties combine are both complicated and contested, but one example (Kant's best known) is sufficient to give a sense for his general strategy. Kant defends the principle of cause and effect as one by which human beings structure the objective world: "All alterations occur in accordance with the law of the connection of cause and effect" (B232). Humans experience a changing world, so Kant's argument considers what is necessary in order for a set of perceptions to be considered perceptions of alteration (or, more generally, of something happening). Kant distinguishes merely subjective perceptions from objective experience. To have objective experience, one must organize perceptions in accordance with categories. But to have experience of objective alteration (succession), perceptions must be ordered in accordance with the category of cause–effect. If ordered using another category of connection (say, object–property or part–whole), the sequence of one's perceptions would not refer to an objective sequence, since objectively, one supposes that the properties of the thing exist at the same time as the thing and one supposes all the parts of a thing to exist at the same time. As an example of a purely subjective sequence, Kant describes the perception of a house, starting with the chimney, then the roof, then the windows, then the door. Here one does not suppose that objectively speaking there really is first a roof, then windows, then a door, and so on. By contrast, Kant gives the example of a boat, where one perceives a boat upstream, a boat midstream, and a boat downstream. Here one supposes not that these are different parts of a complicated stream-wide boat, but that in reality – that is, objectively – the boat is moving. Kant then considers what sort of concepts one would have to impose on one's set of perceptions to order them in such a way that one considers their order objective. His answer is that the perceptions would have to be thought of as though they have to occur in the order in which they do. And this necessary sequence of perceptions must be according to some rule. But necessary sequence according to a rule is just what one thinks of when one thinks of the relation between cause and effect. So if one is to think of the order of perceptions order as referring to an objective order, one must impose the concepts of cause and effect on those perceptions. But given Kant's anthropological orientation, to say that one must order perceptions in a certain way is just to say that the objects of those perceptions must in fact be ordered in that way. By imposing an aspect of the structure of the human understanding – the category of cause and effect – on the subjective flow of perceptions in inner sense, human beings are able to structure a world as a series of causally determined changes.

Throughout his proofs – for the necessity of space, time, the categories, and causation – Kant does not provide merely empirical claims about human cognition. Consistent with his insistence on transcendental anthropology, Kant looks at cognition from-within, arguing that certain cognitive presuppositions are necessary conditions of the possibility of justifying the claims that we make about the world. Because, from-within, we take mathematics to be justified, we must assume that space and time structure our world. Because we can make justified empirical claims about objects, we must be organizing and unifying the diffuse manifold of intuition into coherent cognitions. And because some of this cognition is of objective succession, we must apply categories of cause and effect to structure the world we experience.

These a priori claims about the world are "only from the human standpoint" (A26/B 42), which can be contrasted with, say, the standpoints of animals and God. Animals – according to Kant – lack "inner sense" and thereby the self-consciousness needed for reflection (see 28: 276). As a result, animals have "mere sensations" or "intuitions" and thereby no true "experience," which comes only with the addition of concepts (9: 236, 702). Animal "cognition," if we can call it that, is a mere "analogue of reason," something purely "immediate" that "cannot be described" (9: 236). While animal *intuition* may be like our own (see 28: 297, 888), animals lack the faculties of understanding and reason that give us the spontaneity to organize our representations into experience. And in the absence of this spontaneity of understanding, even animals' intuitive awareness of space and time will be markedly different from our own (not involving cognition of causal relations, for example). At the other extreme, God has a purely "intellectual intuition" with no passive sensibility at all. God's knowing is all spontaneity without finitude. From God's cognition, "one is careful to remove the conditions of time and space," and Kant claims that God's knowing will actually be a pure but creative intuition, "one through which the existence of the object is itself given" (B72). Whereas humans' forms of intuition provide a structure within which objects are given *to us*, God's intellectual intuition actually brings objects into existence. And God need not then "think" about such objects, since God fully knows them through the intuition by which they were created.

Unlike mere animals or God, human knowers are free but also finite, capable of cognizing objects given through spatial and temporal intuitions in terms of categories of the understanding applied to those objects. There could, of course, be other free but finite knowers, who would also need to understand an intuitively given world in terms of a priori categories. The categories, as basic structures of thought itself, constrain any discursive understanding of the world. But Kant seems open to the possibility that other finite rational beings could either share our forms of intuition or have different ones, saying only that "we cannot decide this" (B72).

In the end, Kant's *Critique of Pure Reason* provides a transcendental analysis of human faculties of sensibility and understanding that elucidates their a priori structure and the contributions of this structure to experience of an objective world. Human beings for whom experience and a priori synthetic judgments are possible are finite beings dependent upon sensibility and also spontaneous free thinkers. And this transcendental anthropology provides both an epistemology that delimits what we can know and a metaphysics of a world that must conform to human cognition. Metaphysics and epistemology turn out, in Kant's hands, to be reckoned as (transcendental) anthropology.

With his analysis of the way in which sensibility and the understanding combine to structure a knowable empirical world and his defense of several specific a priori principles of human cognition to which that empirical world must conform, Kant completes the first part of his answer to the question "What can I know?" But Kant's transcendental anthropology of cognition involves two further elements as well. One of these is not continued until a subsequent work. In his *Metaphysical Foundations of Natural Science*, Kant argues that "natural science presupposes ...

metaphysics of nature," which includes not only the "laws that make possible the concept of a nature in general," laid out in his *Critique of Pure Reason*, but also laws that "concern [themselves] with a particular nature of this or that kind of things" (4: 469–70). The nature of the human mind is such that if it cognizes, say, material bodies, then it will have to cognize them in particular ways, and these necessary ways of cognizing would be a priori synthetic principles of material bodies themselves. What this implies, for Kant, is that the basic principles of physics are part of transcendental anthropology. Kant even argues that given the existence of matter in motion, one can derive a priori such claims as the conservation of matter (4: 541) and Newton's laws (4: 543, 4: 554). For Kant, not only the most basic metaphysical claims about the universe but even Newtonian physics is transcendental anthropology.

The second further element comes in the second part of the *Critique of Pure Reason*. There Kant turns from human sensibility and understanding to human "reason," which presents ideals that regulate humans' pursuit of knowledge by constantly seeking the "unconditioned," that is, an answer that does not itself require a further explanation. As reason drives humans to learn more and more about their world in a search for the unconditioned, it generates illusions that an unconditioned is there to be found. The second half of Kant's *Critique of Pure Reason* focuses on the dangers of these illusions, showing how the conditions of possibility of objective cognition conflict with the nature of the unconditioned, such that these ideal goals of reason are the sorts of things that could never exist in a world structured by human forms of intuition and understanding. The details of these arguments are unnecessary in this brief account of Kant's transcendental anthropology, but one discussion is particularly important for Kant's conception of the human being.[3] Reason, in explaining causality, finds itself seeking a "free" cause that does not itself have a prior cause. Consistent with his general approach to the illusions of reason, Kant warns against assuming that any such free cause could exist in the world, but Kant's discussion of freedom also highlights a second aspect of his transcendental philosophy which is crucial to understanding Kant's answer to the question "What is the human being?"

So far, my discussion of Kant's transcendental anthropology of cognition has focused on the *positive* contribution that anthropology can make towards a robust metaphysics of nature. But Kant points out that this positive contribution entails "a very strange result ... , namely, that with this faculty [of cognition] we can never go beyond the boundaries of possible experience" (Bxx). We can establish a priori claims *about possible objects of experience*, but cannot provide any theoretical justification for any claims about unexperienceable things. Kant calls such things "things-in-themselves" or "noumena" and distinguishes them from objects of possible experience, which he calls phenomena. And throughout his transcendental account of cognition, Kant reminds his readers that the nature of human cognition determines only the way in which "objects" (of possible experience) must be, not the way in which "things-in-themselves" must be. He describes his position as "empirical realism" because its claims (e.g. about causality) are necessarily true of the empirical world but also as "transcendental idealism" because such claims are limited to the empirical world and say nothing about what "things-in-themselves" – apart from human sensibility – might be like.

In the case of freedom, this transcendental idealism does significant work. Consistent with his insights regarding causation, Kant insists that any objective alteration must be the result of causes in accordance with natural laws. But he then asks "whether it is a correct disjunction that every effect in the world must arise either from nature or freedom, or whether instead both, each in a different relation, might be able to take place simultaneously" (A336/B564). Given Kant's transcendental idealism, the law-governed causality of the empirical world does not preclude a different kind of causality – freedom – operating at the level of things-in-themselves:

> [F]or a subject of the world of sense we would have first an empirical character, through which its actions, as appearances, would stand through and through in connection with other appearances in accordance with constant natural laws ... [and] second ... an intelligible character, through which it is indeed the cause of those actions as appearances, but which does not stand under any conditions of sensibility [including causation] and is not itself [an empirical object].
>
> (A539/B567)

The distinction between empirical and intelligible character makes it possible for Kant to defend the possibility of what he calls "transcendental freedom," a power "of beginning a state from itself, the causality of which does not in turn stand under another cause determining it in ... accordance with the law of nature" (A533/B561). We cannot rule out the possibility that humans, as things-in-themselves, have an intelligible character that is transcendentally free in this sense. But this intelligible character can itself be the ground of an empirical character, and one who observes this empirical character will be able to trace empirical causes for any particular action.

The result is an initially shocking but ultimately plausible account of the relationship between freedom and natural necessity, one that distinguishes Kant's account from the dominant accounts of freedom and causal necessity both in his day and in our own. Many philosophers are "compatibilists," who argue that freedom is compatible with causal determination.

Generally, compatibilists define freedom as determination by internal, psychological causes rather than external ones, such that if an action follows from my choice, it is free, even if my choice is determined by external factors. Other philosophers defend incompatibilism, the view that freedom and natural determination conflict with one another. Such philosophers can be either "hard determinists" who believe that every event in the world, including every human choice and action, is causally determined by some set of prior conditions and therefore unfree, or "libertarians" who believe that (some) events in the world are determined by choices that are not determined by prior conditions. Kant's position has aptly been called a "compatibility of compatibilism and [libertarian] incompatibilism" (Wood 1984: 74). Like incompatibilist libertarians, Kant defines freedom in a way that excludes prior causal determination of one's choices, but, like compatibilists, Kant believes that there is a way in which one can assert both that something is freely caused and that something is the result of prior empirical causes. What makes Kant distinctive from contemporary theories is that he preserves a thoroughgoing causal necessity but at the same time an undetermined freedom. Kant's transcendental idealism allows him to see free things-in-themselves as grounds of the empirical world, while his empirical realism allows him to insist that within that empirical world causation universally proceeds according to natural laws.

There are two dominant ways that Kantians interpret this position (see Ameriks 1982b, Frierson 2010a). So-called "two-world" theorists read Kant as positing two metaphysically distinct "worlds," a noumenal world of things-in-themselves and a phenomenal world of appearances. The former includes humans insofar as we are free, the latter humans insofar as we are determined. And the former is the "ground" of the latter. Alternatively, so-called "two-standpoint" theorists claim that Kant posits only a single world that can be thought of in two different ways, as the sum of objects of possible experience or as a merely thinkable abstraction. When thinking of the world in the former way, freedom is precluded, but not when thinking of it in the latter way. Because morality requires thinking of ourselves as free (as we will see in the next section), the "merely thinkable" perspective gets content as a practical perspective from which we hold ourselves responsible. Thus insofar as human beings take an agent standpoint on the world, we must view ourselves as free. Insofar as we take a scientific-observer standpoint, we must see everything (including ourselves) as causally determined.

On either interpretation, the theory of freedom that Kant lays out in the first *Critique* is presented only as an option that metaphysics can neither establish nor rule out, an "extension" that "even if ... empty, ... we ... can fill through practical data of reason" (Bxxi, cf. A558/B586). And this sort of modesty shows an important positive aspect of Kant's limitations on metaphysics. After noting how his account of cognition precludes metaphysical proofs about things like God, humans' immortal souls, and freedom, Kant adds,

> this critique is also in fact of positive and very important utility, as soon as we have convinced ourselves that there is an absolutely necessary practical use of pure reason (the moral use), in which reason unavoidably extends itself beyond the boundaries of sensibility.
>
> (Bxxv)

Or, as he puts it more succinctly later, "I had to deny knowledge in order to make room for [practical] faith" (Bxxx). Kant used a transcendental anthropology of cognition to justify not only epistemic claims about the nature of human knowledge but even metaphysical claims about the nature of the empirical world. But precisely because such claims are limited to objects of possible experience, Kant makes room for non-empirical claims, if there is any non-cognitive access that human beings have to things-in-themselves. And Kant finds this non-cognitive access in another part of his transcendental anthropology, the transcendental analysis of volition wherein *morality* provides a non-cognitive role for reason in governing human life.

What Ought I to Do? Kant's Moral Philosophy as Transcendental Anthropology of Volition

From the question "What can I know?" Kant turns to the question "What ought I to do?" While Kant's transcendental analysis of cognition focused on human beings as free but finite *knowers*, Kant here thinks about human beings as free but finite *agents*. In some respects, Kant's foundational work in moral philosophy – *Groundwork of a Metaphysics of Morals* – might seem specifically to avoid developing ethics as a subset of anthropology: "a law, if it is to hold morally, ... must ... hold not only for human beings, as if other rational beings did not have to heed it ... [T]herefore the ground of obligation here must not be sought in the nature of the human being ... but a priori simply in concepts of pure reason" (4: 389, see also 4: 410–12, 425). Kant is deeply opposed to thinking of morality as a subset of human biology or psychology, explicitly rejecting approaches to ethics that start with "conditions of human volition ... drawn from psychology" (4: 390–91). Thus *Groundwork* discounts what Kant calls "practical" or "moral anthropology" as merely a subsidiary part of ethics (4: 388). The core of morality, Kant insists, must be "pure." But while the pure moral law would apply to other rational beings as well as to human beings, this moral law is nonetheless a central part of human beings qua rational beings, and Kant's particular applications of the moral law increasingly emphasize the nature of human being in particular. Moreover, Kant's dismissal of anthropology at the core of morals is really only a dismissal of *empirical* anthropology at that core. As in the case of cognition, Kant's transcendental anthropology focuses on human actions "from-within" rather than empirically; in particular, it explores both the norms governing human action and the conditions of possibility of being governed by those norms. Through laying out both the nature of action-guiding norms and the conditions of possibility of being bound by these, Kant offers insight – though not "knowledge" in the strict sense – into what human beings are in themselves. In particular, Kant's moral philosophy completes the argument for human freedom by showing that such freedom is not only possible, but also actual, and by laying out "laws of freedom" that govern free human agents (4: 387).

Kant's argument for humans' free agency is based on the nature of moral obligation. For Kant, the from-within standpoint of volition – where one seeks to discern what to do – has two important features relevant to human freedom. First, anyone who asks, in the broadest sense, what to do, "must regard itself ... as free" (4: 448). All choice happens "under the idea of freedom" (4: 448) because the "power of choice ... cannot be determined to action through any incentive *except so far as the human being has incorporated it into his maxim*" (6: 24). This "Incorporation Thesis" (Allison 1990: 5, 40) claims that from within deliberation, all incentives appear only as *candidate* reasons for action; one must "incorporate" them into one's plans for action before they actually motivate. From-within, one sees this incorporation as something "free."

For some contemporary Kantians, this analysis of the deliberative perspective is sufficient to establish human freedom, but Kant worries that this argument does "not prove freedom as something *real*" but only as a necessary but possibly illusory "presupposition" (4: 448–49). Kant's way of dealing with the possibility that freedom is an illusion shifts between his *Groundwork* and his *Critique of Practical Reason*. In the former, he offers an independent argument for freedom based on humans' cognition of ideas of reason, and thereby establishes our participation in an "intelligible world" and thus our susceptibility to moral norms. By the time of the *Critique of Practical Reason*, Kant rejects this argument in favor of a more straightforward regressive argument, assuming the legitimacy of moral norms in general and arguing *from* those norms to human freedom.[4] Thus Kant turns from the generic perspective of deliberation to the more specific stance of one asking the question "What *ought* I to do?", where "ought" is specifically *moral*. In the *Critique of Practical Reason*, Kant insists that this moral "ought" is ever-present within human practical deliberation: "we become immediately conscious [of the moral law] (as soon as we draw up maxims of the will for ourselves)" (5: 29). In the process of devising and considering principles to act on, we become aware of a "fact of reason" (5: 29), the fact that we are bound by a moral law, which commands obedience regardless of other incentives.

From this fact of reason, Kant aims to establish that human beings are free by showing that "a [transcendentally] free will and a will under moral laws are one and the same" (4: 447, cf. 4: 450, 5: 28–29). In order to establish this mutual implication, Kant draws on "common rational moral cognition" to "search for and establish the supreme principle of morality" (4: 392). What could the supreme principle of morality be? To answer this question, Kant focuses on two (related) features of the moral ought: its independence from inclination and its universality. Moral reasons are distinguished from other sorts of reasons in that they are not tied to things that one happens to find oneself wanting. When one decides that one "should" buy gasoline for one's car, one does so only because one thinks that such an activity will be conducive to ends that one happens to have. One can always decide to forgo those ends, and then one need not buy gasoline. But when one decides that one "ought" to refrain from falsely accusing an innocent adversary or "ought" to help a stranger in immediate pressing need, one does not see these decisions as optional in the same way. It does not matter whether the false accusation fits with other goals that one has, or whether one cares about the stranger. *Moral* obligations do not depend upon such things. Kant puts this point in terms of a distinction between what he calls "hypothetical imperatives," which are commands that one has to obey *if* one wants to achieve some particular end, and "categorical imperatives," which are (moral) commands that one simply *has to* obey *no matter what* (no "if"-clause). Relatedly, Kant argues that the moral law is *universal*: "everyone must grant that a law, if it is to hold morally … must carry with it absolute necessity," going so far as to say that "the command 'thou shalt not lie' does not hold only for human beings, as if other rational beings did not have to heed it" (4: 389). Kant's point here is not that everyone ought always to act in the same way. Someone who cannot swim need not jump into a river to save a drowning child, and someone with remarkable artistic talents may have an obligation to cultivate them that others would not have. The point, rather, is that morality itself is universal, in that when one becomes immediately conscious of obligation in general, one is conscious of it as a law that binds everyone (even if it binds different people in different ways). Another person *who is relevantly similar* to me (able to swim, or possessed of similar talents) will have the same obligations. Unlike inclinations, morality is not something that one can pick and choose. It obligates everyone.

Given these characteristics of morality, one might think that it would be impossible to derive a fundamental formula of morality. If all that we know about morality in general is that it can derive from neither particular inclinations nor contingent features of ourselves, then there seems to be nothing left from which to get a "principle" of morality at all. But in fact, Kant argues that the limitations on the content of the moral law actually give rise to a "formula" that encapsulates the fundamental principle of morality.

> [S]ince the imperative contains, besides the law, only the necessity that the maxim be in conformity with the law, while the law contains no condition to which it would be limited, nothing is left with which the maxim of action is to conform but the universality of a law as such; and this conformity alone is what the imperative properly represents as necessary.
>
> There is, therefore, only a single categorical imperative and it is this: act only in accordance with that maxim through which you can at the same time will that it become a universal law.
>
> (4: 420–21)

The moral law of which I am immediately conscious within deliberation is a law that commands me to act only in such a way that the bases for my actions – my "maxims" – could be bases for the actions of everyone. What is universally commanded to all is the practice of acting in a way that could be universal for all.

Kant goes on to redefine this categorical imperative based on a particular feature of human willing: human beings not only follow various practical laws, but also act for the sake of ends (4: 427). The moral law is not determined *by* any particular (contingent) ends, but it does determine a necessary end, "something the existence of which in itself has an absolute worth, something which as an end in itself could be a ground of determinate laws" (4: 428). And Kant finds just such an end in "the human being" (4: 428). This gives Kant a new way of describing the categorical imperative: "So act that you use humanity, whether in your own person or in the person of any other, always at the same time as an end, never merely as a means" (4: 429, see also 6: 462). This new formulation of the moral law puts human beings at the center of morals, not only in that the moral law is derived from a transcendental anthropology of volition, but also in that the ultimate end of morality, that which must at all times be respected, is nothing more (nor less) than the human being.

Precisely what Kant means by that "human being" which is a necessary end is hotly contested, with proposals ranging from Christine Korsgaard's suggestion that any being with a mere capacity for making choices is a human being (Korsgaard 1996a: 17) to Richard Dean's recent suggestion that only a person with a wholly good will counts as a human being (Dean 2006: 8). The argument for the importance of humanity in the *Groundwork* starts from the fact that "the human being necessarily represents his own existence" as an end in itself, emphasizing that this is merely "a *subjective* principle of human actions" (4: 429). But, Kant argues, since all other people have the same grounds as oneself for ascribing value to themselves, one ought to regard them as ends in themselves as well. The question, then, is what any human chooser necessarily but subjectively values in making choice, and Korsgaard's view that what is always valued in these cases is precisely the capacity for choice that is exercised in making any choice makes the best sense of Kant's position. Choosing in accordance with the moral law requires respecting the capacity for choice of other "human beings," that is, other choosers. In this context, then, "humanity" for Kant is not limited to specifically *human* choosers, but to any rational choosers. In that sense, we must respect the "humanity" of angels, extra-terrestrials, gods, or other rational animals, if there are any such beings. But even without implying that it is *uniquely* human, Kant picks out rational agency as a particularly central feature of human beings and places it at the center of his moral theory.

Finally, Kant adds another formulation of the categorical imperative that further enriches his transcendental anthropology and paves the way for his defense of human freedom: "the human being is ... subject only to laws given by himself ... and is bound only to act in conformity with his own will" (4: 432). Kant describes this independence from external laws as "autonomy" and points out that autonomy does not imply lawlessness, but rather that one is subject always only to one's own laws. This may seem to be merely a recapitulation of the Incorporation Thesis, but Kant's point here is more specific. If the moral law is to be truly universal and independent of our inclinations, then it cannot be derived from anything external to our will itself. Any *external* command would need to appeal to us for some reason, either because we feel inclined to obey it (in which case it is not truly moral) or because we *ought* to obey it (in which case its authority derives from rather than grounds morality). For moral laws to be truly one's own rather than merely the results of outside influences manipulating our contingent desires, autonomous lawgiving must proceed by means of laws that have no basis other than our own wills. But laws determined solely by our wills are categorical. So, for Kant, "autonomy of the will [is] the supreme principle of morality" (4: 440).

At this point, Kant has *nearly* proven that human beings are transcendentally free. The principle of morality is a principle of autonomy, or *self*-governance. But to make the stronger claim that this "autonomy" is identical with transcendental *freedom*, Kant goes further. He offers a quasi-geometric proof starting with the nature of moral obligation and deriving the necessity of transcendental freedom. He poses the following problem:

> Supposing that the mere lawgiving form of maxims is the only sufficient determining ground of a will: to find the constitution of a will that is determinable by it alone.
>
> (5: 28)

That is, Kant considers what sort of will could be determined by a moral law that dictates only the "form" that one's maxims must take and says only that such maxims must be universalizable, without saying anything about the "matter" of those maxims, that is, what sorts of goals one should aim for in one's actions. Kant argues,

> Since the mere form of a law ... is not an object of the senses and consequently does not belong among appearances, ... this form as the determining ground of the will is distinct from all determining grounds of events in nature ... , [so] a will [determined by this ground] must be thought as altogether independent of the law of causality.
>
> (5: 28–29)

Within deliberation, when considering whether to act on the basis of the moral law, one sees it as a law that offers nothing to one's natural inclinations. There is, in that sense, no "natural" basis for acting in accordance with it. When one chooses to act on an ordinary inclination – say, deciding to eat an appetizing cookie – one can see oneself as "giving in" to the flow of natural causes. But because its demands are fundamentally formal, the moral law is not the sort of thing to which one can merely "give in." It "presents it[self] as a determining ground not to be outweighed by any sensible conditions and indeed quite independent of them" (5: 29–30). Thus the only will that can be truly bound by the moral law is a will that is free from sensible (i.e. empirical) conditions. But freedom from determination by empirical conditions *is* transcendental freedom, so a will under the moral law is transcendentally free. Kant thus decries any traditional form of compatibilism as "wretched subterfuge," mere "psychological or comparative" freedom "no ... better than the freedom of a turnspit" (5: 96–97).

To his abstract argument and strong polemics, Kant adds a more intuitive thought-experiment to show that when we reflect on actions from-within, in terms of what we take ourselves to be capable of, even apparently irresistible temptations are eminently resistible:

> Suppose someone asserts of his lustful inclination that, when the desired object and the opportunity are present, it is quite irresistible to him; ask

him whether, if a gallows were erected in front of the house where he finds the opportunity and he would be hanged immediately after gratifying his lust, he would not then control the inclination. One need not conjecture very long what he would reply. But ask him whether, if his prince demanded, on pain of the same immediate execution, that he give false testimony against an honorable man whom the prince would like to destroy under a plausible pretext, he would consider it possible to overcome his love of life, however great it might be. He would perhaps not venture to assert whether he would do it or not, but he must admit without hesitation that it would be possible for him.

(5: 30)

The first part of this thought-experiment shows only that human beings are capable of overcoming particular sensuous desires (lust) when the fulfillment of these threatens more important sensuous desires (love of life). But the second part shows that human beings recognize in themselves an ability to overcome even love of life for the sake of the moral law. If our love of life can motivate us to overcome our everyday sensuous desires, and our respect for the moral law can motivate us to overcome even our love of life, then there is no temptation that we are unable to overcome for the sake of the moral law.

Importantly, Kant is not denying that one can observe empirical causes for actions. Even consciousness of the moral law appears as an empirical cause in a chain of mental events that gives rise to a volition to act in accordance with it. But from within volition, we become aware of a sense of responsibility, the condition of possibility of which is the transcendental freedom that, properly understood, Kant's *Critique of Pure Reason* showed to be compatible with causal-determinist explanations from-without. Through examining the moral law present within human volition, Kant shows that humans are transcendentally free and thus "fills the vacant space" (5: 49) left open by his theoretical philosophy. But Kant does more. By specifying the most fundamental principle of morality, Kant fills this vacant place "with a determinate law of ... an intelligible world ... , namely the moral law" (5: 49). That is, Kant shows not only that human beings are free, but also that human freedom is not lawless and arbitrary but a law-governed capacity to be moral. Humans' sense of moral obligation, properly understood, provides evidence of freedom and also gives rise to a specific principle of morality.

Kant's arguments for transcendental freedom as central to human nature are hardly beyond controversy, and future chapters will take up various objections to them, but the rest of this section focuses on two problems for the Kantian account of freedom and morality offered so far. First, if human beings are *really free* only insofar as we submit to the moral law,

Kant seems unable to account for the possibility of human beings ever being responsible for doing what is morally *wrong* (see, e.g., Sidgwick 1901 and Reinhold 2006). If the moral law is the law of freedom, then whenever human beings act contrarily to the moral law, they must not really be free. But freedom is a condition of possibility of moral responsibility, so whenever human beings act wrongly, they are seemingly not morally responsible for their actions. Kant does claim that human beings can be held responsible for acting badly, but how can he do this? Second, Kant's transcendental anthropology of desire is intended not merely to lay out the conditions of possibility of moral responsibility but also to clarify precisely what, from the standpoint of deliberation, humans find them-selves obligated to do. But if Kant's moral philosophy is supposed to answer the question "What ought I to do?," the mere formula of universal law (FUL) – *"act only in accordance with that maxim through which you can at the same time will that it become a universal law"* (4: 421) – seems too abstract to provide real guidance for action.

Regarding the first problem, as important as freedom is to his trans-cendental anthropology, Kant recognizes that human choosers are not *merely* morally free beings. Even from within the perspective of human volition, we find ourselves *both* free beings subject to the moral law *and* subject to empirically informed desires and inclinations. Even Kant's "pure moral philosophy" articulates what morality means for beings like us, who participate in both an intelligible world governed by laws of freedom and a sensible world governed by laws of nature. Thus while *Groundwork* begins with the "good will" in general, Kant quickly specifies the nature of this will such that it applies more particularly to wills "under certain subjective limitations and hindrances" (4: 397). Because of our sensible nature, human beings have natural inclinations that can conflict with moral demands in particular circumstances. Because we have such non-moral inclinations, morality takes the form, for humans (unlike for God), of "duties" and "imperatives," commands that we *ought* to obey rather than a moral law that we simply *do* obey (4: 413).

In that context, Kant distinguishes between "positive" and "negative" freedom. Negative freedom is a "property in us ... of not being necessitated to act through any sensible determining grounds" (6: 226, cf. 4: 446), while positive freedom is the property of acting through a non-sensible determining ground, the moral law (4: 446–47, 6: 213–14). Negative freedom is necessary in order to hold human beings morally *responsible*, while positive freedom constitutes the full-blown autonomy of a morally *good* agent. But there is an intrinsic link between negative and positive freedom. Insofar as negative freedom is a freedom from having one's actions governed by anything external to oneself, the only way to remain free is to make one's law, the law of freedom, the categorical imperative.

As one commentator has put it, "by making the [categorical imperative] its principle, the free will retains the position of [freedom]" (Korsgaard 1996a: 166, cf. 6: 227). By contrast, "the free will that puts inclination above morality sacrifices its freedom for nothing" (Korsgaard 1996a: 167). Human beings are always negatively free, in that we *need not* let our actions be determined by forces external to us, but we are not always positively free, since we often relinquish autonomy in the face of temptation.

The second problem, as Hegel classically put it, accuses Kant's categorical imperative of being an "empty formalism," an "abstract universality, whose determination is ... without content" (Hegel 1991: 162). Precisely because this "specific principle of morality" is purely formal, it gives only the most abstract account of what is required of human beings. In order to complete his account of the norms that ought to govern human volition, Kant must deliver a more complete framework of normative constraints on human volition. Hegel and others have argued that this will require "bringing in material *from outside* [to] arrive at *particular* duties [because] it is impossible to make the transition to ... particular duties ... from the determination of duty as *absence of contradiction ... with itself*" (Hegel 1991: 162). Kant's abstract moral law seems insufficient to provide moral content from within.

Kant has a two-fold response to this objection. First, even if the categorical imperative is, in itself, formal, it is still action-guiding. Hegel suggests that the categorical imperative would only prohibit stealing, for example, if one has independent bases for thinking that property rights are good. But insofar as one tests *maxims* for action, one can evaluate those maxims based on the values implicit within them, without ascribing any independent normative weight to those values. Thus the thief who acts on the maxim "I will steal my neighbor's car in order to have it for myself" commits herself to the value of private property by virtue of her end (having it *for herself*), and thus her maxim conflicts with the categorical imperative. The child's "I will take this (other child's) crayon to draw a picture" does not directly violate the categorical imperative because while this maxim implies crayons' value for drawing, it does not directly commit the child to institutions of private property. Even if the categorical imperative is insufficient for evaluating the moral status of *actions*, it does seem to be an important way of picking out certain *maxims* that, because they require making an exception of oneself, are morally wrong.

Second, Kant's emphasis in *Groundwork* on pure moral philosophy is explicitly only a *foundation* for a complete "metaphysics of morals." Just as the empirical concept of matter is needed to move from the metaphysics of the *Critique of Pure Reason* to the basic principles of physics, empirical attributes of human beings are needed to move from a general principle of morals to specific moral duties. As the particular kinds of embodied, finite agents that human beings are, we have talents, needs, strengths, and limitations that give rise to specific duties. The normative force of these duties comes from their connection to the fundamental moral principle by virtue of which human beings are free rational agents. But the specific content comes from the way that we must act in order for our empirically discoverable needs and desires to be satisfied through acting on maxims that conform to that fundamental moral principle (6: 217). The result, when Kant turns to his *Metaphysics of Morals*, is a detailed account of human obligations in the face of our finite natures, both a "doctrine of right" laying out the rules governing human actions in the context of an empirical world where conflict is possible and a "doctrine of virtue" laying out particular ends human beings need to pursue given our particular predispositions, talents, and needs.

In the end, Kant's transcendental anthropology of desire offers a detailed answer to the question "What ought I to do?" and in the process further expands on the conception of human beings as free and finite beings that Kant began in the *Critique of Pure Reason*. Not only are we free and finite *doers* as well as *knowers*, but because transcendental freedom is a condition of possibility of the moral obligation under which we find ourselves within the standpoint of choice, we can justifiably believe that humans are transcendentally free things-in-themselves, even though we can never strictly "know" this. Kant's promise in the first *Critique* that he would "deny knowledge to make room for faith" (Bxxx) is fulfilled in his moral philosophy. In the process, the "faith" for which he held out hope in the *Critique* is shown to be not a *blind* faith, but a solid conviction grounded in rational arguments based on the conditions of possibility of moral responsibility.

Before closing this section, it is worth attending to one further, dramatic aspect of Kant's transcendental anthropology of desire. In the *Critique of Pure Reason*, Kant had highlighted *three* traditional problems of metaphysics that would be stricken from the realm of knowledge – "God, freedom, and immortality" (Bxxx, A3/B7) – and in his transcendental anthropology of volition, Kant comes back not only to freedom but also to the issues of God and immortality. As in the case of freedom (though to a different degree), Kant argues that belief in God and immortality are practically necessary. Neither God nor immortality are conditions of the possibility of moral responsibility per se, but when Kant considers what the ultimate goal of a virtuous agent must be, he argues that while the "supreme end" will be virtue alone, the "complete" end – that end from which nothing good is absent – must include both virtue and "happiness distributed in … proportion to morality" (5: 110). Insofar as virtuous agents seek this highest good, they must believe in whatever is necessary in order for their activity to reasonably be held to contribute to this highest good. For

Kant, immortality is necessary because virtue can never be fully realized in one's finite life but only in endless progress (5: 122). God is necessary in order to ensure that happiness is doled out in proportion to virtue (5: 124ff.). Only by believing in both God and immortality can our efforts toward virtue be reasonably taken to be efforts toward the complete highest good.

Kant's arguments for God and immortality are more complicated than I have suggested here, and their validity is widely disputed. For the purposes of understanding Kant's conception of human beings, the details of these arguments are less important than the overall implication of Kant's approach. Just as *The Metaphysical Foundations of Natural Science* makes Newtonian physics a subset of a transcendental anthropology of cognition, Kant here makes traditional *theology* a subset of a transcendental anthropology of volition. By the end of his transcendental anthropology of cognition, Kant had shown that the a priori structure of human cognition establishes (among other things) our ability to know an empirical world as consisting of substances in causal relationships with one another, and he offers a priori foundations for natural science. Having added a transcendental anthropology of volition, Kant has laid out the a priori laws governing the realm of free human agents and defended even God's existence as part of philosophical *anthropo*logy.

What May I Hope? The *Critique of Judgment* as Transcendental Anthropology of Feeling

Given the results of the previous two sections, Kant's transcendental anthropology might seem complete. Human beings are free, finite knowers and doers, governed within each realm by a priori laws that we give ourselves. We exist as both fully free things-in-ourselves and finite, embodied appearances in the empirical world. Within the empirical world, we see ourselves and everything else as governed by natural laws. As free, we are governed by moral laws. Kant's first and second questions – about knowledge and obligation – have been answered, and the question "What may I hope?" seems answered by Kant's practical postulates of God and immortality. Nonetheless, shortly after finishing his *Critique of Practical Reason*, Kant set to work on a third *Critique*, which would eventually become the *Critique of Judgment* and would provide the a priori laws of feeling that could complete his transcendental anthropology. By this time, Kant had made three realizations that required a rethinking of the nature of this anthropology.

First, Kant came to see feeling as capable of a priori, transcendental investigation. Kant saw the pleasures humans take in what is merely "agreeable" – food, sex, reputation – as empirically rooted and thus incapable of a priori investigation. But as he continued to teach and study aesthetics, he came to see that judgments about beauty are at once sub-jective because they are rooted in feeling and taken to be universal and normative; to claim that something is beautiful is to claim that *all* others *should* find it beautiful. Normativity, perhaps even of an a priori sort, is applicable to aesthetic feeling. Second, Kant recognized that his account of the cognition of nature was incomplete in its application to the empirical world. His *Critique of Pure Reason* ensured that the world would conform to certain general structures of human cognition, but it provided no assurance that humans would be able to expand the scope of their knowledge in any systematic way. Finally, Kant's moral philosophy was incomplete in its application to the empirical world. The *Critique of Practical Reason* provided an a priori argument to show that the end human beings are obligated to promote – the highest good – is possible, but it provided no basis for this possibility in the observable order of nature. Kant's attempt to "deny knowledge in order to make room for belief" was insufficient to explain *how* nature and freedom relate to each other. He needed a *Critique of Judgment* to provide a "mediating concept between the concepts of nature and the concept of freedom" (5: 196, cf. 5: 176). These realizations led Kant to complete his transcendental anthropology with a *Critique of Judgment* that would investigate the faculty of feeling and the power of judgment.

The general structure of the *Critique of Judgment* can seem perplexing, since it is divided into two halves that seem unrelated.[5] The first half – a "Critique of Aesthetic Judgment" – explores conditions of possibility of making justified aesthetic judgments about beauty or sublimity. The second half – a "Critique of Teleological Judgment" – lays out Kant's philosophy of biology, within which Kant argues that for the study of living things, one must make use of teleological principles in addition to the laws of mechanical causation defended in his *Critique of Pure Reason* and *Metaphysical Foundations of Natural Science*. While the "Critique of Aesthetic Judgment" lays out an a priori principle governing feeling, there is no direct reference to feeling in the "Critique of Teleological Judgment." And while the "Critique of Teleological Judgment," especially with its discussion of the ultimate and final ends of nature, provides a transcendentally grounded framework for answering the question "What may I hope?," Kant's aesthetics seems irrelevant to that question. All of this can make it seem that, however helpful this book might be in other respects, it cannot provide the unified transcendental anthropology of feeling that would complete Kant's philosophy.

In fact, however, the book as a whole is unified by the principle of the purposiveness of nature. As transcendental anthropology, this a priori principle of the *human* power of judgment provides a basis for universal norms governing feeling. Purposiveness emerges as an a priori principle for aesthetic feeling (20: 244), but once established as an a priori principle, Kant use purposiveness to supplement insufficiencies in his transcendental accounts of cognition and volition. What starts in a transcendental anthropology of (aesthetic) feeling becomes the unifying principle of Kant's transcendental anthropology as a whole and a partial basis for answering the final question of Kant's philosophy: "What may I hope?"[6]

Before unpacking the details of this account, we should address the question of whether a transcendental anthropology of feeling is even appropriate. Recall that *transcendental* anthropology has at least three distinctive features: it is a priori, investigates humans from-within, and emphasizes normative constraints. Human *feelings* seem ill-suited to any of these sorts of analyses. Of all aspects of human life, feelings seem to be the most empirically contingent. And even though we can introspectively examine our feelings, there does not seem to be the sort of "from-within" relationship to feeling that we have with cognition and desire. And normativity does not seem appropriate to feeling; it is at least a bit odd to say that a person *felt* wrongly. And even if there is *some* sort of normativity governing feelings, it does not seem a priori.

Kant raises many of these concerns himself. He points out that while there are "empirically knowable" connections between objects and natural feelings of pleasure that give rise to desires for those objects, such connections are "not grounded in any principle a priori" and thus do not provide suitable material for a transcendental anthropology of feeling (20: 206, cf. A21). (Kant calls the objects of these pleasures "agreeable.") Other objects might give rise to pleasure because they are useful in some way, and one takes pleasure in their suitability to some end. Such objects please because they are "good-for" something and their pleasure will be based in empirically knowable connections between those objects and the ends for which they are good. There is also respect for the moral law, which is both a feeling and required a priori, but it is required only by virtue of its connection with volition. The necessity of respect does not require a "special … critique of the feeling of pleasure and displeasure" but can be subsumed under a transcendental anthropology of volition (as Kant does in the *Critique of Practical Reason*). In fact, pleasure in *both* the agreeable *and* the good (whether useful or moral) can be explained by reference to the faculty of desire (or volition). Agreeable objects are the goals of hypothetical imperatives; the gratification we find in them "arouses inclination" (5: 207). Useful objects are the necessary or helpful means to some given ends, so they provide satisfaction "only as a means" (5: 207). And the morally good is the object of the categorical imperative; we feel satisfaction in the morally good because of its connection to volition.

But Kant claims that some pleasures are due to neither agreeableness nor goodness in their objects. These pleasures, for Kant, are judgments of "taste" or of "aesthetic pleasure" and have for their objects things that are "beautiful" (or "sublime"). Kant structures his transcendental analysis of beauty around several key claims about how pleasure in the beautiful presents itself to us from-within: it is *disinterested* (5: 204–11), it is non-conceptually *universal* and *necessary* (5: 211–19, 5: 235–40), and it presents its object as *purposive without a purpose* (5: 219–35). For these sorts of pleasures, Kant argues, an a priori principle is both needed and available.

Kant's first claim – that aesthetic pleasure is disinterested – merely emphasizes that beautiful objects are neither agreeable nor good and thus cause pleasure without connection to "interest" (i.e. without arousing volition). The second claim brings up the central dilemma that drives Kant's analysis, the "reason why judgments of taste are subject to a critique with regard to their possibility" (5: 191). Aesthetic judgments involve "a feeling of pleasure ... which ... is nevertheless ... expected of everyone" (5: 191). Like other key claims in Kant's transcendental anthropology, this insistence that human beings take pleasure in the object is not an empirical–psychological claim; one does not claim that all others *will* or *do* feel this pleasure, but rather that they *should*. Aesthetic judgments present a normativity that is reducible neither to epistemic norms (since epistemic norms apply to the formation and application of concepts) nor moral–practical norms (both because aesthetics is disinterested and because practical norms require an appeal to concepts).

The final key claim about pleasure in the beautiful provides Kant's solution to his central dilemma, but it is also the most confusing of Kant's claims about the beautiful. Beautiful objects incite pleasure because they are "purposive without a purpose" (see 5: 220). In explaining what this means and how the purposiveness of beautiful objects can ground universal pleasure, Kant connects his transcendental anthropology of *feeling* with a critique of the power of *judgment*. The normative universality of aesthetic feeling is explicable in terms of purposiveness as an a priori principle of human judgment that governs both experiences of beauty and our investigation of nature. By showing the connection between aesthetic feelings and purposiveness as a principle of judgment, Kant also solves the problems of incompleteness in the first and second *Critiques*.

The *Critique of Judgment* deals with an incompleteness in Kant's transcendental anthropology of cognition that arises because while the *Critique of Pure Reason* showed that changes in the world must happen according to causal laws, it failed to show that the set of causal laws governing the world is finite, much less that these laws fit into anything like a systematic whole within which diverse particular laws are explicable in terms of more general laws (5: 183, but cf. A642–68/B670–96). But human beings seek just such systematic interconnections, so while it would be consistent with the conditions of possibility of experience in general for each change to be governed by its own causal law, we cannot actually think that this is the case. Our principles for investigating the world assume uniformity that, strictly speaking, we are not justified in assuming. Kant refers to "pronouncements of metaphysical wisdom" that are "scattered about in the course of science" such as that "Nature takes the shortest path" or "the great multiplicity of its empirical laws is nevertheless unity under a few principles" (5: 182, cf. 5: 185). Without such cognitive rules of thumb, we could never get anywhere in terms of a systematic empirical science; we would be left with the abstract metaphysical foundations of science laid out in Kant's earlier transcendental philosophy. For Kant, the "power of judgment" provides the transcendental basis for these scientific rules of thumb, and the transcendental principle of reflective judgment is purposiveness: "Nature specifies its universal laws in accordance with the principle of purposiveness for our faculty of cognition" in that natural laws are suited "for human understanding in its necessary business of finding the universal for the particular that is offered to it by perception and then further connection in the unity of the principle for all that is different" (5: 186). The otherwise happy accident that nature is suited to be understood as a systematic whole is required, a priori, as a "purposiveness in relation to the cognitive faculty of the subject" (5: 185) that is assumed in every act of the regulative power of judgment. The *Critique of Judgment* thus fills in an important gap in the *Critique of Pure Reason*.

But Kant goes on to connect the purposiveness of nature for cognition with humans' faculty of feeling pleasure. The connection is, at first, fairly straightforward: for human beings, "the attainment of every end is combined with the feeling of pleasure," so if reflective judgment gives an a priori aim valid for every human being, "then the feeling of pleasure is also determined through a ground that is a priori and valid for everyone" (5: 187). Specifically, since understanding particulars in terms of general laws and "bringing heterogenous laws of nature under higher ... laws" are demands of reflective judgment made possible through an assumed "purposiveness of nature for our understanding," "if we succeed in this accord of such laws ..., pleasure will be felt" (5: 187–88). When the paleontologist studying a strange fossil is finally able to classify that fossil as a distinct species falling under some more general genus, she experiences pleasure at this success. The a priori principle of reflective judgment that makes possible the search for systematicity in our understanding of nature thus provides the first guide to a transcendental anthropology of feeling, since it proposes a necessary *end* for all human beings – unifying particulars under increasingly general laws – the attainment of which is a necessary and universal basis of pleasure for human beings. The presumption of purposiveness in nature grounds a necessary pleasure in actually discovering such purposiveness.

This pleasure is not aesthetic because it is both interested and conceptual, and in principle, objects in the world might be purposive only in that they possess a general conduciveness to be understood. But Kant uses the dilemma of aesthetic feeling to show the nature and necessity of aesthetic representations of purposiveness. Along with his contemporaries, Kant takes for granted that there *are* normative judgments of feeling ("good taste"). Kant's transcendental anthropology looks for conditions of possibility of such judgments. They are problematic, he argues, because they must be both subjective and universal. But given the role of purposiveness in reflecting judgment that aims for systematic, empirical knowledge, Kant presents an account of what an immediately felt, non-conceptual representation of an object's purposiveness would have to be. And it turns out that such representations are precisely what would make possible normative claims that are both universal and subjective.

In particular, for Kant, an immediately felt, non-conceptual representation of an object's purposiveness would have to be a recognition of the suitability of an object not to any particular concept or concepts, but simply to humans' cognitive faculties *in general*. In the form of the beautiful, one's cognitive powers are "in free play," in contrast both with the *work* that such powers do when, for example, reflecting judgment develops empirical concepts or unifies diverse laws under more general ones, and with a possible *conflict* between such powers, such as when one's perceptions *resist* being brought under general concepts. For the feeling of beauty, the relevant cognitive powers are the imagination and understanding; when these powers play freely together, one feels aesthetic pleasure.

While there is substantial disagreement amongst commentators about the nature of this free play,[7] the general idea can be gleaned from Kant's examples of beautiful objects:

> Flowers are free natural beauties. Hardly anyone other than the botanist knows what sort of thing a flower is supposed to be; and even the botanist ... pays no attention to this natural end if he judges the flower by means of taste. Thus the judgment is not grounded on any kind of perfection, any internal purposiveness to which the composition of the manifold is related. Many birds (the parrot, the hummingbird, the bird of paradise) and a host of marine crustaceans are beauties in themselves, which are not attached to a determinate object in accordance with concepts ... but are free and please for themselves. Thus designs *à la grecque*, foliage for borders or on wallpaper, etc., signify nothing by themselves: they do not represent anything, no object under a determinate concept, and are free beauties. One can also count ... musical fantasias (without a theme), indeed all music without a text.
>
> (5: 229)

All of these examples refer to objects that inspire continuous reflection without any determinate knowledge. Unlike clearly conceptualizable forms – such as an equilateral triangle (see 5: 241) – that give no room to the imagination to examine them in new ways, a flower stimulates a constant redirection of attention from one aspect of its form to another, a constant attempt to reassemble the visually presented material with different emphases. But in contrast to a merely chaotic mish-mash of stimuli, the diverse perspectives that one can take on a flower are all orderly; the understanding is given constant encouragement to find patterns and generalities in the representations of the object. Moreover, the activities of imagination and understanding do not merely take place side-by-side; they are "reciprocally expeditious" (20: 224). Finding patterns in one way of looking at a flower facilitates the re-presentation of the flower in yet another way, which leads to the recognition of a new order, and so on. One can continuously contemplate beautiful flowers, birds, and musical improvisations, constantly reinterpreting them in the light of new "imaginative" ways of pulling together one's impressions.

The purposiveness of beautiful objects is not toward *goals* of our cognitive powers (increasing knowledge of the empirical world) but toward the *activity* of those powers. For Kant, pleasure is a feeling of "the agreement of an object with the productive power[s] of the soul" (29: 894); the "animation of [the] cognitive powers" of imagination and understanding gives rise to a pleasure, which "is itself" the consciousness of the purposiveness of the beautiful object (5: 222). Beautiful objects are *pleasurable*, and because this pleasure lies in the *mere* animation of one's cognitive powers, and not any *end* brought about by those powers, it is *disinterested*. This animation of cognitive powers is the effect of the mere representation of the object, not dependent upon any determinate cognition of the object, so one's judgment that the object is beautiful is *non-conceptual* and thus *subjective*. But – and this is Kant's key move – because the subjective basis of one's judgment is the free play of cognitive powers *that all human beings share*, one can legitimately expect that *any* human being *should* feel pleasure at the representation of the beautiful object. Because the judgment that an object is beautiful is a judgment that the object is *purposive for one's cognitive powers*, and because human beings share those cognitive powers, an aesthetic judgment carries universality. (Of course, one might still get aesthetic judgments *wrong*. One's pleasure in an object might only *seem* to be due to disinterested, non-conceptual contemplation. In that case, one might mistakenly call beautiful what is really agreeable or good.)

The purposiveness that grounds the subjective universality of aesthetic judgments of beauty also provides the basis for truly *free* pleasure: "among all ... kinds of satisfaction only that of the taste for the beautiful is a disinterested and *free* satisfaction; for no interest, neither that of the senses nor that of reason, extorts approval" (5: 210, cf. 5: 354). As is typical for Kant's transcendental anthropology, *freedom* in the context of pleasure is normatively governed. Just as free cognition is governed by a priori categories and forms of intuition, and free volition is governed by a categorical imperative, so the free experience of pleasure is governed by a principle of purposiveness by which one judges objects as beautiful and hence worthy of pleasure. Moreover, the free pleasure in beauty is a particularly *human* sort of pleasure: "Agreeableness is also valid for nonrational animals; beauty is valid only for human beings ...; the good is valid for every rational being in general" (5: 210).

In an important sense, then, Kant's account of the feeling of pleasure in beautiful objects completes his transcendental anthropology. With this "critique of aesthetic judgment," Kant presents the entirety of human mental life – cognition, volition, *and feeling* – as susceptible to transcendental investigation. Like cognition and volition, human feeling is normative, and one can investigate the conditions of possibility of this normative structure from-within. While cognition is governed by a priori principles of the understanding and volition by an a priori principle of reason, feeling is governed by an a priori principle of *judgment*: the principle of purposiveness. Moreover, Kant uses his account of beauty to bridge the gap between nature and freedom in both the cognitive and volitional dimensions. With respect to cognition, the experience of beautiful objects involves reflectively judging about objects in the world and feeling the purposive suitability of this world to our cognitive capacities. This purposiveness regulates the investigation of nature, bridging the gap between the *Critique of Pure Reason*'s assurance that the world would conform to certain general structures of human cognition and the need to be able to expand the scope of knowledge systematically. With respect to volition, the experience of beautiful objects reveals, in the most subjective dimension of human existence, a universality and autonomy that are analogous to and preparatory for moral choice.

Kant *could* have ended his transcendental anthropology with his account of the beautiful, but he added two important dimensions to his *Critique of Judgment*: a theory of the sublime, and an account of teleological judgment. The account of the sublime is a natural addition to Kant's critique of aesthetic judgment. Without going into the details, the account of the sublime completes Kant's account of aesthetic pleasure and supplements his treatment of the beautiful in three important ways. First, because Kant aims to give a complete transcendental anthropology, he must account for all of the ways in which humans' feelings of pleasure can be governed by a priori norms. Since humans' experience of the sublime is governed by such norms, it must be discussed. Second, the sublime provides an important balance to the contribution of the beautiful to Kant's anthropology of cognition. In the beautiful, we feel the conduciveness of the world to human understanding; in the experience of the sublime, we feel how reason imposes demands that transcend the world. Finally, and most importantly, the sublime provides a bridge between nature and freedom that is importantly different from that of the beautiful. With the beautiful, humans' experience of fitness between themselves and nature makes us aware of a free, disinterested, universal capacity for pleasure that is analogous to moral demands. With the sublime, especially the dynamically sublime, humans directly feel their moral dignity. The experience of the sublime involves feeling the same sort of respect for oneself that is constitutive of moral motivation. Kant claims, "true sublimity must be sought only in the mind of the one who judges, not in the object in nature ... That is sublime which even to be able to think of demonstrates a faculty of mind that surpasses every measure of the senses" (5: 256, 250). In reflecting on certain objects, one comes to recognize a disharmony caused by the superiority of one's humanity over the sensible, natural world. While this disharmony initially provokes displeasure, the *source* of the disharmony – one's transcendent reason – inspires an ambivalent, but nonetheless intense and pleasurable, feeling of self-esteem. Thus while the sublime reflects the disconnect between oneself and nature, it also marks a bridge from an experience of nature that is not itself moral to a respect for oneself that plays a central role in moral motivation.

The rest of the *Critique of Judgment* does not directly address humans' faculties of feeling. But it extends Kant's account of judgment into biology in ways that are important for understanding Kant's account of human beings. In particular, Kant argues for what he calls an "objective purposiveness" in nature, according to which the "natural laws" under which we subsume given phenomena (organized beings) depend upon thinking of causes of those phenomena as *for the purpose of* their effect. Because one can make sense of an organized being only as "a thing ... [that] is cause and effect of itself" (5: 370), such a being is a "natural end." When one understands the motion of a heart in terms of its functional role in promoting the circulation of blood, and the circulation of blood in terms of promoting the life functions of an animal, and these life functions as in turn ensuring the continual motion of the heart, one interprets an animal in terms of purposiveness. When, further, one sees an individual animal as both the effect of its species and the cause of the continuation of the species, one interprets the animal purposively; it exists *for* the propagation of the species (and vice versa).

In theory, there might not be "natural ends," but in fact one finds self-propagating organized beings in the world "which cannot be explained through [mechanism] alone" (5: 374). The result is that human beings are entitled, and even required, to posit a principle for judging organized (biological) beings: "*An organized product of nature is that in which everything is an end and reciprocally a means as well.*" Or, in less technical language, "Nothing is in vain, purposeless, or to be ascribed to a blind mechanism of nature" (5: 376). Importantly, for Kant, while "indispensibly necessary," these principles are purely "regulative," mere heuristics "for guiding research into objects of this kind" (5: 376). For Kant's transcendental anthropology, the addition of these teleological principles has two important implications. First, it allows a limit to the causal explanation that the first *Critique* justified. While Kant insists that *in principle* everything in nature is explicable in terms of efficient causes and even that we are required to explain nature mechanically – that is, in terms of basic properties of matter – as much as possible (5: 379, 429), he concedes that for humans studying the living world, such explanations will often not be possible. Second, Kant shows here a willingness to introduce new principles for judgment on the basis of empirical discoveries. The principle of objective purposiveness *precedes* and *guides* empirical research; biologists *assume* purposiveness prior to finding the specific purposes of particular aspects of organized beings. But this assumed purposiveness is itself the result of discovering *through experience* that certain beings in nature can only be understood (by us) in this way.

The need to investigate living things in accordance with a principle of purposiveness gives rise to two further implications that will prove important for Kant's anthropology as a whole. The first is discussed in the next chapter. Briefly, just as Kant's *Critique of Pure Reason* created a space for an empirical anthropology that views human beings as empirical objects subject to natural laws, his *Critique of Judgment* makes clear that, like other living things, humans require teleological explanations of some basic biological powers. The second implication is discussed in detail in the *Critique of Judgment* and constitutes the most important contribution of that work to the third key question of philosophy: "What may I hope?" After explaining that organized beings in general must be understood as natural ends, Kant introduces "the idea of the whole of nature as a system in accordance with the rule of ends" (5: 378–79). This yields fruit in a scientific ecology studying organisms' interdependence, and Kant insists that such study naturally leads one to think about what could be the "final end" of nature as a whole.

In his transcendental anthropology of volition, Kant has already shown that humanity is a final end-in-itself. But this end-in-itself requires a transcendental freedom that cannot be an end *of nature*. Once we know that human beings as transcendentally free choosers are *final* ends, however, we can look for an "*ultimate*" end, "that which nature is capable of doing in order to prepare [the human being] for what he must himself do in order to be a final end" (5: 430). Identifying this "ultimate end of nature" provides the basis for a rational hope that nature will cooperate with our moral vocation. For Kant, this *ultimate* end is humans' "aptitude[s] for setting ends at all and ... using nature as a means appropriate to the maxims of free ends in general" (5: 431). The *details* of Kant's account of human beings as the ultimate end of nature, including the empirical evidence that emerges from (and in turn supports) his regulative principles, are elsewhere and will be discussed in Chapter 3. But Kant's *Critique of Judgment* shows how purposiveness as the principle of regulative judgment not only grounds aesthetic judgments but also leads, through its application to biology and ecology, to a conception of human beings as ultimate ends of a purposively ordered nature.

Kant's *Critique of Judgment* is a transcendental anthropology of the faculty of feeling and the power of judgment that provides that faculty with its regulative principle. As an analysis of feeling from-within, the *Critique* shows how there can be non-conceptual normative standards for judgments of taste, and it reveals an analogy to morality in the most sensuous aspect of human nature: our feelings of pleasure. In its further analysis of purposiveness in the study of nature, this *Critique* not only justifies the assumption of order in nature but even shows the necessary role of purposiveness in regulating humans' study of living things. These human principles of judgment provide a foundation for answering the question "What may I hope?" both affectively and rationally. In aesthetic pleasure, we legitimately feel hopeful in our cognitive strivings for systematic understanding of the world and in our moral aspirations for disinterested, universally justifiable choices. And in our understanding of nature as a teleologically ordered whole, we look for (and find) evidence that nature as a whole cooperates with our highest moral vocation.

Summary

Kant's three *Critiques* present a picture of human beings as finite but free knowers, actors, and feelers. Human knowledge is constituted by passively received intuitions that are conceptualized by an understanding that spontaneously (freely) imposes categories to cognize objects. Human action involves subordinating subjective and therefore finite maxims to an autonomous (free) moral principle. And aesthetic pleasure arises from the free play of faculties that testify to our finitude. Moreover, the transcendental anthropology of volition in particular provides a (practical) proof that one is a *transcendentally* free "homo noumenon," capable of acting on grounds that are undetermined by empirical causes. The transcendental anthropology of cognition ensures that the empirical *expression* of one's transcendentally free choices will always be a "homo phenomenon," susceptible to empirical description in terms of natural laws (6: 417–18). And the transcendental anthropology of feeling shows how the empirically given world supplies material that provokes pleasurable aesthetic feelings that, in different ways, reveal our freedom to us.

Insofar as humans are homo phenomena, they must be understood in terms of categories of the understanding and forms of intuition. But even as homo phenomena, humans are still distinct from merely physical nature in that we are teleologically ordered biological organisms with particular features, many of which have important implications for applying the moral law in practical life. Insofar as human beings are free homo noumena, we are both negatively free, in that our (noumenal) choices are not determined by any particular empirical causes, and positively free, in that we are subject to the moral law as the law of our own will (autonomous). By virtue of our freedom, we are worthy of respect and hence the proper "end" of moral choice, and we are worthy of "awe" and hence proper objects of sublime feeling.

The transcendental anthropology in Kant's critical works not only sets up the general framework of phenomenal–noumenal humanity but also specifically addresses the *non-causal* laws that govern human beings, providing a normative account of the human being from-within: an epistemology, an ethics, and an aesthetics. However, "transcendental anthropology" is incomplete as an overall answer to the question "What is the human being?" Because human beings appear in the empirical world, transcendental anthropology must be supplemented with an empirical anthropology that describes what humans look like "from-without." And Kant's a priori moral philosophy requires supplementation by an "empirical part" that will involve "judgment sharpened by experience" to know how the moral law should be applied and how "to provide [it] with access to the human will" (4: 388–89). Finally, while the practical postulates of God and immortality and the general teleology revealed through beauty and biology give *some* basis for moral hope, "experience and history" provide further reasons that "we should not despair about our species' progress toward the better" (7: 329). While developing his *transcendental* anthropology, then, Kant also pursued *empirical* studies of human beings, to further answer the question "What is the human being?" and thereby better answer his remaining questions: "What can I know [including empirically about human beings]?," "What ought I do [to human beings with the empirical features that we have]?" and "What may I hope [based on the progress human beings have made historically so far]?" It is to this *empirical* anthropology, then, that we now turn.

Further Reading

Kant's transcendental philosophy is among the most widely studied topics in the history of philosophy. The following is only a very partial list of key works covering what I call his transcendental anthropology.

Kant's most influential interpreter in recent years is Allison. His *Kant's Transcendental Idealism* (Yale University Press, 1983) helped make two standpoint theories of Kant's transcendental idealism widely accepted. *Kant's Theory of Freedom* (Cambridge University Press, 1990) was influential for thinking about Kant's practical philosophy. And *Kant's Theory of Taste* (Cambridge University Press, 2001) covers Kant's aesthetics.

For good general overviews of Kant's philosophy, see Guyer and Wood. Guyer offers his influential but critical reading of Kant and includes further reading on each aspect of Kant's philosophy. Wood's much shorter book discusses Kant's transcendental philosophy but includes helpful chapters on empirical and historical aspects of Kant's thought.

Paul Guyer, *Kant* (London: Routledge, 2006)
Allen Wood, *Kant* (Oxford: Wiley-Blackwell, 2004)

For Kant's transcendental anthropology of cognition (his *Critique of Pure Reason*), see works by Grier, Guyer, Heidegger, Kitcher, and Strawson. Grier discusses Kant in relation to contemporary approaches to what I can know. Guyer's book is a highly critical reading of the first *Critique*. Heidegger's book is the most important work on Kant by one of the most significant philosophers of the twentieth century, but it is a very difficult read. Kitcher's volume helpfully brings Kant's transcendental philosophy into conversation with contemporary issues in the philosophy of mind. And Strawson's classic reconstruction of Kant's metaphysics helped (re)introduce Kant to mainstream analytically oriented philosophy.

Michelle Grier, *Kant's Questions: What Can I Know?* (Abingdon: Routledge, forthcoming)
Paul Guyer, *Kant and the Claims of Knowledge* (Cambridge: Cambridge University Press, 1987)
Martin Heidegger, *Kant and the Problem of Metaphysics* (trans. R. Taft, Indianapolis: Indiana University Press, 1997)
Patricia Kitcher, *Kant's Transcendental Psychology* (Oxford: Oxford University Press, 1993)
P.F. Strawson, *The Bounds of Sense* (Abingdon: Routledge, 1966)

Kant's moral philosophy is one of the most influential moral theories today and generates a voluminous literature. Korsgaard combines exegetical essays with others that bring Kant's philosophy into dialogue with other contemporary moral theories. Wood provides an excellent and anthropologically informed study of Kant's moral theory. Wuerth situates Kant's moral philosophy in the context of his faculty psychology and applies that philosophy to contemporary moral issues.

Christine Korsgaard, *Creating the Kingdom of Ends* (Cambridge: Cambridge University Press, 1996)

Allen Wood, *Kant's Ethical Thought* (Cambridge: Cambridge University Press, 1999)

Julian Wuerth, *Kant's Questions: What Ought I Do?* (London: Routledge, forthcoming)

For discussion of Kant's *Critique of Judgment*, see Allison's *Kant on Taste* above, as well as Makreel's classic hermeneutical reading, Zammito's situations of the book in its historical context, and Zuckert's recent book, which offers the best overview of the *Critique of Judgment* as a whole and many references to further works.

Rudolph Makreel, *Imagination and Interpretation in Kant: The Hermeneutical Import of the Critique of Judgment* (Chicago: Unversity of Chicago Press, 1990)

John Zammito, *The Genesis of Kant's Critique of Judgment* (Chicago: University of Chicago Press, 1992)

Rachel Zuckert, *Kant on Beauty and Biology: An Interpretation of the Critique of Judgment* (Cambridge: Cambridge University Press, 2007)

2 Kant's Empirical Anthropology

In the previous chapter, we examined Kant's "transcendental" anthropology, his examination of the cognitive, volitional, and affective dimensions of the human being from the standpoint of a priori, normative, autonomously given laws governing those faculties. But Kant also engaged in empirical debates about human beings. The next three chapters focus on different dimensions of Kant's empirical anthropology. In this chapter, I examine Kant's overall empirical anthropology of the human mind, that is, his empirical psychology. This psychology includes Kant's accounts of the different faculties of human beings, the causal laws that describe the activity of those faculties, and the bases of such faculties in "natural pre-dispositions" found in humans' biological nature. In Chapter 3, I turn to two more specific aspects of Kant's empirical anthropology: his treatments of human evil and of the historical nature of the human species. In Chapter 4, I examine Kant's accounts of human diversity.

The Possibility of Empirical Psychology

Given the importance of Kant's transcendental anthropology, he might seem merely to dismiss empirical anthropology. But in fact, one of the key claims that Kant establishes in his transcendental account of cognition is that human beings are capable of having empirical knowledge of their world, and he emphasizes that such knowledge *includes* empirical knowledge *of human beings*. Although a human being cannot cognize itself "in accordance with what it is in itself," Kant adds "that through inner sense we intuit ourselves ... as we are internally affected by ourselves ... [and thus] we cognize our own subject ... as an appearance" (B156, cf. B69, 153). Like everything else we cognize, human beings can be cognized as appearances, as "homo phenomenon" (6: 418). Even where the *Critique of Pure Reason* most emphasizes the possibility of human freedom, Kant insists that "all actions of a human being are determined in accord with the order of nature ... [I]f we could investigate all the appearances ... there would be no human action we could not predict with certainty"

(A549/B577, cf. 20: 196). Kant gives a striking example to illustrate this general point:

> Let us take ... a malicious lie. ... First, we endeavor to discover the motives to which it has been due, and secondly, we proceed to determine how far the action ... can be imputed to the offender. As regards the first question, we trace the empirical character of the action to its sources, finding these in defective education, bad company, in part also in the viciousness of a natural disposition insensitive to shame. ... *We proceed in this enquiry just as we should in ascertaining for a given natural effect the series of its determining causes.*
>
> (A554–55/B 582–83, emphasis added)

In the *Groundwork*, too, Kant reiterates that "everything which takes place [is] determined without exception in accordance with laws of nature" (4: 455), and in the *Critique of Practical Reason*, he goes so far as to say that if we knew the relevant preconditions, "we could calculate a human being's conduct for the future with as much certainty as a lunar or solar eclipse" (5: 99).

Despite Kant's insistence on empirical study of human beings, many call into question whether Kant can really allow for empirical anthropology. First, it seems impossible for Kant to admit that humans are susceptible to truly "scientific" study, since any such study must provide *universal* claims about its objects: "The empirical doctrine of the soul can ... never become ... a science of the soul, nor even a psychological experimental doctrine" (4: 471). Moreover, a completely empirical anthropology might seem to conflict with Kant's very strong claims about human freedom (see pp. 26–28). Finally, empirical anthropology just seems fraught with practical problems. Kant discusses epistemic challenges such as the fact that "if a human being notices that someone is ... trying to study him, he ... either ... cannot show himself as he really is or ... does not want to be known as he is" (7: 121) and moral dangers of self-study: "self-observation ... is the most direct path to illuminism or even terrorism, by way of a confusion in the mind of supposed higher inspirations and powers flowing into us ... from who knows where" (7: 133). These comments suggest that even if empirical human science is possible in principle, it is unreliable and dangerous in practice.

In fact, however, none of these concerns preclude an empirical anthropology suitably construed. To start with the first point, Kant rejects the possibility of an empirical human science in the very strict sense of "science" that refers only to a priori knowledge (4: 471). Newton's laws count as science, for Kant, because "outside of what lies in [the empirical] concept [of matter], no other empirical principle is used" (4: 470). By contrast, even if one starts with empirical, psychological concepts – such as the existence of a mind – one cannot derive further substantive claims about the mind a priori. And unless one can derive claims about human psychology a priori, one cannot make *strictly* universal claims (A1–2, B3–4, A91/B124, A196/B241). But Kant's rejection of a scientific and strictly universal status for empirical anthropology does not preclude what he calls a "historical systematic natural doctrine of the inner sense" (4: 471), a "natural science … improperly so called, … [which] would treat its object … according to laws of experience" (4: 468; cf. 25: 472–73, 577). Empirical anthropology will not be a science precisely like physics, since it will lack a mathematical, a priori foundation for strictly necessary claims. But even in the first *Critique*, Kant admits that "empirical rules … can acquire through induction … comparative universality, that is, extensive applicability" (B124/A91). While not "science" strictly speaking, empirically grounded laws of human beings constitute a comparatively universal, systematic presentation of human mental and social life.

A second concern arises from Kant's account of human freedom. Many commentators have rightly pointed out that the account of free action in Kant's transcendental anthropology of volition offers a different conception of moral psychology from the traditional empiricist belief–desire model according to which human beings are simply motivated by their strongest active desire. But those who take this insightful alternative approach to conflict with Kant's empirical account of human action (e.g. Reath 1989: 290–91) are misguided. As noted in Chapter 1, Kant's transcendental idealism aims to show how an empirical and even causal model of human behavior leaves room for real freedom, not within the empirical model but as something distinct from (and grounding) humans' empirically knowable characters. Kant's transcendental anthropology of cognition shows that humans experience everything – including themselves – in terms of a structure of cognition that interprets change in terms of causal relationships. But this metaphysics of the empirical world leaves room for a different standpoint from which freedom is possible, and Kant's transcendental anthropology of desire – his moral philosophy – makes clear that human agents must see themselves as free causes of their actions. This implies, of course, that Kant's empirical anthropology is only empirical: it does not provide access to what Kant will call the human being as it is in itself, the "homo noumenon" (6: 418, cf. 7: 397–400). It is possible to have access to what the human being is like in itself (as we saw in Chapter 1), but empirical anthropology provides no such access.

The final challenge for rigorous empirical investigation of human beings is the set of specific difficulties with self-study that make empirical anthropology – as Kant put it at the opening of his first course in anthropology – a "hard descent into the Hell of self-knowledge" (25: 7). In his published *Anthropology*, Kant presents several "difficulties … inherent in human nature itself" (7: 120–21) and in a draft of his anthropology even adds that "psychology has plenty to do in tracing everything that lies hidden in it" such that it "may not ever hope to complete this task and answer satisfactorily the question: 'What is the human being?'" (7: 398–99). For Kant, empirical study of human beings proceeds by introspection and observation of others, both of which face serious problems: mental life is intrinsically complex, human beings typically act differently when being observed, self-observation is inhibited by the fact that many of the most interesting and important activities in human life preclude the calm and attentive work of introspection, and human beings can develop contingent characteristics – habits of time and place – that seem essential. The result of all of this can be desperation about ever answering the question "What is the human being?"

Despite these cautions, Kant insists that "an anthropology ... that is systematically designed" is possible and "yields an advantage for the reading public," including the promotion of "the growth of [this] science for the common good" (7: 121–22). Kant maintains that anthropology begins with a "general knowledge of human beings" (7: 120) that "is provided ... by inner sense" (7: 398, cf. 25: 252, 863–65) and enriched by good literature (e.g. Shakespeare, Montaigne, and Fielding), travel and travel literature (7: 120), and careful "observ[ation] of human beings and their conduct" (25: 472). While Kant doubts the possibility of a wholly satisfactory empirical anthropology, he aims to develop as full an empirical account as possible, or at least a sufficient account "from which a prudent use in life can ... be drawn" (25: 472, cf. 7: 119).

Kantian empirical anthropology, then, is general rather than strictly universal, and thus a science only in a loose sense. Even as such a science, it is vulnerable to error given humans' tendencies to get ourselves wrong. But a fallible quasi-science laying out empirically justified general laws of human beings is, for Kant, possible, interesting, and useful. The rest of this chapter lays out the overall framework of this empirical anthropology.

Kant's Faculty Psychology

When Kant began working on empirical anthropology, the dominant empirical approach to human beings in Germany (promoted by Christian Wolff and Alexander Baumgarten) involved laying out different human mental states in terms of various "faculties of soul" and then showing how these faculties could be reduced to a single faculty of "representation." The idea was that rational cognitions were the clearest and most distinct representations of the world, and sensory cognitions, feelings, and desires were representations with varying degrees of obscurity and indistinctness. Against this view, many philosophers and emerging psychologists (most prominently,

Moses Mendelssohn, Johannes Tetens, and August Crusius) argued that mental states were irreducibly distinct; the main alternatives suggested were either a very wide diversity of human mental states, a bi-partite model within which belief and desire are irreducible to each other, or some combination of these within which irreducibly distinct mental states can be classified broadly into beliefs and desires. Although he lectured from a textbook (Baumgarten's) that promoted the single-faculty approach, Kant's own work defended mental state pluralism. Unlike his compatriots, however, Kant insisted upon combining a broad mental state pluralism with a fundamentally tri-partite structure. For Kant, there are a large number of irreducibly distinct sorts of mental states that can be grouped into three irreducible types: cognition, feeling, and desire.

Kant's argumentative strategy for this view is two-fold. First, he develops a general philosophy of science according to which one should seek to "deriv[e] diverse powers, which we know only through observations, as much as possible from basic powers" (28: 564, cf. A648–49/ B676–77). One should assume as many basic powers as are really necessary, a point Kant emphasizes by comparing Descartes, who "explains all [physical] phenomena from the shape and the general motive power of bodies," with Newton's "more satisfactory" method that allows the assumption of "certain basic powers ... from which the phenomena are derived" (29: 935–36). The phenomena one finds in both the physical and the mental worlds require more than a single basic power. So while Kant seeks to reduce powers as much as possible (for instance by showing that memory is a form of imagination), his focus is on not overly reducing mental powers. Second, Kant lays out specific arguments to show that particular mental powers are irreducible to one another. For example, Kant emphasizes his isolation of feeling as a state distinct from both cognition and desire, noting that feeling is not merely a confused cognition of a thing, and emphasizing that aesthetic pleasures, no matter how intense, do not give rise to volitions (29: 877–78). He points out that while cognition is "related merely to the object and the unity of the consciousness of it," a volition is "the cause of the reality of this object" (20: 206). More generally, Kant argues that one can only reduce distinct powers if one can find a power from which they "could be derived" (8: 181n). In the end, Kant insists, "there must be several [basic powers] because we cannot reduce everything to one" (29: 773–822).

For Kant, the set of distinct basic powers includes each of the five senses; an "inner sense" by virtue of which we are aware of our own mental states; the imagination; higher cognitive powers of reason, understanding, and judgment; a power of feeling pleasure and displeasure; and various powers of volition. Kant groups these distinct powers into the general faculties of cognition, feeling, and desire, and further sub-divides

Table 2.1 Faculties of soul

	Cognition	Feeling	Desire/Volition
Higher	Judgment, understanding, reason	"satisfactions or dissatisfactions which depend on the manner in which we cognize the objects through concepts" (28: 254)	"Motives" based on practical principles
Lower	Sight, hearing, taste, smell, feeling, inner sense, imagination (including memory)	"satisfactions and dissatisfactions which depend on the manner in which we are [sensibly] affected by objects" (28: 254)	"Stimuli," impulses rooted in instinct or inclination

them between "higher" and "lower" faculties. "Lower" faculties are primarily receptive, while "higher" faculties are "self-active" (28: 228, 29: 880), by which Kant does not mean the transcendental freedom of the homo noumenon but a "comparative concept of freedom" according to which "actions are caused from within" (5: 96). We can lay out Kant's overall taxonomy of mental powers as shown in Table 2.1.

Causal Laws Governing Human Beings

Kant did not discuss the structure of human mental faculties simply to argue against Wolff's reduction of the mind to a single faculty of representation. Getting clear on different mental faculties is crucial for developing a full empirical anthropology because "the concept of cause lies in the concept of power" (28: 564), and in empirical human science we seek "natural laws of the thinking self" based on "observations about the play of our thoughts" (A347/B405). Each distinct mental power is governed by its own causal laws (including laws governing how it relates to other mental powers), and a complete empirical anthropology describes these laws.

For Kant, faculties of soul are causally ordered such that "pleasure precedes the faculty of desire, and the cognitive faculty precedes pleasure" (29: 877–78). Moreover, "all desires have a relation to activity and are the causality thereof" (25: 1514); desire plays the same role in psychology that motive forces like momentum play in physics (25: 577). In fact, desire is defined as a representation that is the ground of an action that brings about some state of affairs (6: 211, 399), so there are no actions not preceded and caused by desires, and no desires that do not lead to actions (in the absence of external impediments). For any human action, a sequence of causes can be traced as follows:

Cognition $\rightarrow$ Feeling of pleasure (or pain) $\rightarrow$ Desire $\rightarrow$ Action

At any step along this progression, the causal chain could be cut off. For example, when a normal human being tastes a mango (cognition), that taste gives pleasure (feeling), that pleasure causes a desire for the mango, and that desire leads one to eat (or continue eating) the mango. But one's mango might be snatched away, preventing one from eating (or continuing to eat) the mango. Or one might see a beautiful flower (cognition) and experience a "disinterested" pleasure that gives rise to no subsequent desire. Or one might learn that the capital of Iceland is Reykjavik and thus have a cognition, but without this cognition giving rise to any pleasure or desire.

This sketch requires filling in. Kant needs to explain what gives rise to cognitions in human beings, how and when those cognitions give rise to pleasures, and how and when those pleasures give rise to desires. As Kant offers the details of these causal laws, his account gets extremely detailed, so here I only highlight aspects of his account. With respect to the lower faculty of cognition, Kant distinguishes between the five traditional senses, "inner sense" (our ability to "observe" our own inner mental states), and imagination (including memory). About the five senses, Kant lays out only the most general descriptions, such as that "the sense of touch lies in the fingertips and the nerve endings (papillae) and enables us to discover the form of a solid body by means of contact with its surface" (7: 155) and that sight, touch, and hearing are "mechanical," while taste and smell are "chemical" (25: 495). Kant speculates about "a faculty of the nerves [that] underlies the mind" and even suggests some "water of the brain" encountered by the "ends" of the "stimulated optic nerve" or "auditory nerve" (12: 34). But Kant's dominant approach is not to try to explain how light, for instance, causes a visual sensation by stimulating the optic nerve, but simply to classify what physical causes bring about this mental state. Just as Newton does not solve the "problem" of gravitational action at a distance but instead names and classifies the phenomenon, Kant does not try to "solve" the so-called "mind–body problem" of how states of the brain cause mental states, instead merely classifying the basic powers that underlie these connections.

The most extensive psychological discussion of lower cognitive faculties comes with the imagination, which is governed by three fundamental laws: affinity, forming intuitions in space, and association. Association, for example, is the principle that "empirical ideas that have frequently followed one another produce a habit in the mind such that when one idea is produced, the other also comes into being" (7: 176). Hearing a particular song may trigger thoughts of the person with whom one often listened to that song, or the thought of a certain book may cause one to think of the place where one read that book. The imagination also figures centrally in Kant's account of language: it is by virtue of customary association between sounds and thoughts that those sounds (and eventually written words) come to stand as symbols for those thoughts.

The higher faculty of cognition is subdivided into three basic powers: reason, the understanding, and judgment. Most generically, "Understanding draws the general [i.e. concepts] from the particular. ... Reason draws the particular from the general. ... The power of judgment is the subsumption of one concept under others [or of particulars under concepts]" (29: 890). The power of judgment operates according to the principles governing analogy – "things ... which ... agree in much, also agree in what remains" – and induction – "what belongs to many things of a genus belongs to the remaining ones too" (9: 133, see also 24: 772). The understanding generates certain concepts as an immediate consequence of sensory perceptions, but most concepts of the understanding are generated through chains of comparison, reflection, and abstraction. With respect to the former, Kant argues that "on the occasion of experience" certain "concepts have arisen through the understanding, according to its nature" (28: 233), such as the basic concepts of causation and substance that make it possible for our experience to be intelligible as experience of an objective world. In other cases, sensory cognition leads to empirical concepts, such as when seeing "a spruce, a willow, and a linden" leads one to

> compare these objects with one another [and] note that they are different from one another in regard to the trunk, the branches, the leaves, etc.; but next ... reflect on that which they have in common among themselves ... and ... abstract from the quantity, the figure, etc. of these; and thus ... acquire a concept of a tree.
>
> (9: 95)

Reason, finally, operates through principles of logic: the cognition of the premises of an argument gives rise to a cognition of the conclusion of that argument. When I think about the facts that "Socrates is a human" and "All humans are mortal," I am led to the thought that "Socrates is mortal."

Thus far, Kant's account of how higher faculties work tracks how they ought to work, but Kant knows that people's higher faculties often do not function according to these ideal laws, and he develops an account of how "other activities of the soul ... are connected with the judgments of the understanding" to generate a "mixed effect" that can be mistaken for "a judgment of the understanding" (16: 283–84). Such mixed effects result from what Kant calls "prejudices," which primarily arise from "imitation, custom, and inclination" (9: 76) and function as alternative principles by which some cognitions give rise to others according to causes distinct from the understanding strictly speaking. For example, "the prejudice of the prestige of the age" leads some to favor the writers of antiquity more than they should, thereby "elevating the relative worth of their writings to an absolute worth" (9: 79). For those affected by this prejudice, cognitions of claims associated with a particular ancient writer will immediately give rise to affirmation of those claims, a transition inexplicable in terms of properly functioning higher cognitive powers alone. Prejudices do not wholly displace higher cognitive faculties, but they provide a way for Kant to make sense causally of transitions between beliefs that are not actually justified, and thus cannot be explained in terms of the higher cognitive faculties alone. This account of prejudice, supplemented with detailed accounts of various prejudices and an account of how the higher and lower faculties of cognition relate, completes Kant's empirical account of the faculty of cognition.

Kant's account of the faculty of the feeling of pleasure and displeasure is the most original, complex, and confusing aspect of his faculty psychology. The originality lies in Kant's claim – based on his account of aesthetic pleasure – that the faculty of feeling can be reduced to neither cognition nor volition. Even those who argued against Wolff's attempt to reduce all the basic powers of the soul to a single one generally ended up describing pleasure either as a subjective form of cognition like color or scent or as a constitutive part of desire. But for Kant,

> We have pleasure or displeasure without desiring or abhorring, e.g. if we see a beautiful area, then it enchants us, but we will not on that account wish at once to possess it. Pleasure or displeasure is thus something entirely different from the faculty of desire.
>
> (29: 877)

The difference between pleasure and volition cannot be explained merely in terms of strength. Even a mild pleasure in the thought of a sweet treat brings with it a desire to eat (more of) that treat, while the most intense purely aesthetic pleasure gives rise to no volition at all. Because there can be pleasures unconnected with volition, Kant argues, pleasure cannot be seen as merely a component of volition. But pleasure is also not mere cognition. Someone could understand everything there is to know about an object that pleases me and still not find pleasure in it. Pleasure indicates something about *me*, not necessarily anything about the object. So while many feelings might be linked with cognitions and volitions, feeling in general cannot be reduced to cognitive-volitional aspects.

On Kant's general account of feeling, there can be very different kinds of feelings, but all feelings are, in some sense, feelings of satisfaction (pleasure) or dissatisfaction (displeasure). Because pleasure is not a kind of cognition, Kant rejects the dominant Leibnizian–Wolffian definition of pleasure as "the [obscure] sensible representation of the perfection of an object" (20: 226). Instead, Kant offers two "definitions" of pleasure:

1. The consciousness of the causality of a representation with respect to the state of the subject for maintaining it in that state can here designate in general what is called pleasure.

(5: 220)

2. Pleasure is the representation of the agreement of an object or of an action with the subjective conditions of life.

(5: 9n)

First, pleasure is defined simply as a mental state (a "representation") oriented toward preserving itself. But Kant relates this feeling oriented to persisting in one's state with the concept of "life," which he connects with self-activity and sometimes defines as a "faculty of a being to act in accordance with laws of the faculty of desire" (5: 9n). For human beings, "life" involves the full set of mental powers of cognition, feeling, and desire. When something seems to promote the activity of one's powers, a distinctive mental state – "pleasure" – arises that reflects this advancement of activity. In a lecture on metaphysics, Kant connects his two definitions:

The feeling of the promotion of life is pleasure, and the feeling of the hindrance of life is displeasure. Pleasure is when a representation contains a ground for being determined, for producing again the same representation, or for continuing it when it is there.

(28: 586)

When one feels pleasure, one feels like continuing in one's state because one's state seems conducive to the activity of one's powers. When one feels displeasure one feels like ending one's state because one's state feels like an inhibition of activity.

Given his definition(s) of pleasure, Kant divides possible objects of pleasure into different categories. Most fundamentally, and central to Kant's insistence that pleasure is not merely an aspect of desire, Kant claims that pleasures can be distinguished into those that give rise to desires and those that do not. Generally, preserving pleasurable states involves acquiring objects or objective states of affairs that bring pleasure. Pleasure in a mango depends upon actually eating the mango. Such pleasures, in order to "produce again the same representation or … continue it" (28: 586), give rise to desires, mental states that actually affect the world by causing one to act (e.g. eat the mango). Kant calls such pleasures "interested" or "practical." Other pleasures – aesthetic ones – are not interested: "[A] judgment about beauty in which there is mixed the least interest is very partial and not a pure judgment of taste" (5: 205). Kant takes this point quite far, claiming that if "the palace that I see before me [is] beautiful" I will feel a distinct pleasure in the contemplation of it, even if "were I to find myself on an uninhabited island ... and could conjure up such a magnificent structure through my mere wish, I would not even take the trouble of doing so" (5: 204–5, cf. 29: 878). Aesthetic pleasures arise from reflection, and the actuality of the object of one's reflection is not necessary in order to promote the "free play of the powers of representation" (5: 217) that grounds the feeling of pleasure. Kant's aesthetics (discussed in Chapter 1) focuses on a transcendental account of these disinterested pleasures. For the purpose of his empirical account, his main purpose is to show that there are such pleasures and thereby distinguish the faculty of feeling from that of desire.

With the exception of aesthetic feelings, pleasures sustain themselves by means of the faculty of desire. The faculty of desire is the most complicated faculty in terms of its causal laws, and explaining it fully requires a discussion of the biological roots of causal laws in Kant's account. In general, though, the faculty of desire is "the faculty to be, by means of one's representations, the cause of the objects of those representations" (5: 9n, 6: 211). That is, desire is a mental state by which one becomes a cause of the objects of that mental state. Whereas cognition merely thinks about its objects and feeling merely enjoys its objects, desire actually brings about what it represents. To desire something is to have the requisite mental state for bringing that thing about. Even when desire is not fully self-conscious (as in animals, or as with bare urges) or when it is merely a response to sensory stimuli, it is still a mental state directed toward an object as a cause of bringing that object about. When desire is more deliberate and self-conscious, following from the higher faculty of cognition such that we want something because we understand it, then such desire is "a faculty to do or to refrain from doing as one pleases" (6: 213). A desire, for Kant, always involves a volitional commitment to an object, but when one is committed to bringing about the object while still recognizing that one lacks the power to actualize that commitment, one's desire is called a mere "wish" (6: 213). When one desires an object and is also aware of one's power to bring about that object, one "chooses" it (6: 213). It should be clear, here, that "desire" is in some ways closer to what we consider "choice" than it is to what we typically consider "desire." When a person "desires" something in Kant's sense, it means that they have the sort of mental state that will bring about its object if it can. Thus what we might consider a mere "desire" would for Kant be an inactive *ground* for a possible desire. "Concupiscence (lusting after something) must be distinguished from desire itself, as a stimulus to determining desire.

Concupiscence is always a sensible modification of the mind but one that has not yet become an act of the faculty of desire" (6: 213).

Beyond this general description of desire, Kant must explain why it is that desires arise for certain objects and not others. Given a cognition that gives rise to a practical pleasure, one will experience a desire for the object of that pleasure. The problem is explaining why certain cognitions give rise to practical pleasures while others do not. Kant's solution to this problem is, justifiably, extremely complex. He distinguishes between higher and lower faculties of desire based on whether they are moved by pleasures in higher cognitions (principles informed by concepts or ideas) or lower cognitions (brute sensations or imagination). But within these classifications, Kant must explain the variety of forms of human desire, and he articulates that account in the context of a description of biological and environmental factors that characterize human beings. To get a fuller empirical anthropology, then, we need to turn to Kantian human biology.

Natural Predispositions

A central claim of Kant's biology is that "it would be absurd ... to hope that there may yet arise a Newton who could make comprehensible even the generation of a blade of grass according to natural laws that no intention had ordered" (5: 400). In rejecting a Newton of a blade of grass, Kant denies theories of mechanistic "epigenesis" that explained life in terms of purely physical forces. But Kant also rejects the dominant alternative, "preformationism," which assumed that all humans (and other animals) pre-existed in the egg or sperm of their most distant ancestors, formed in miniature and waiting to emerge. The dominant concept in Kant's biology is the "natural predisposition," which combines important aspects of both epigenesis and preformationism. Natural predispositions are "grounds of a determinate unfolding which are lying in the nature of an organic body" (2: 434). Kant argues that "chance or universal mechanical laws could not produce such agreements [adaptive homologies], [so] we must consider such arrangements as preformed," but "outer things can well be occasioning causes" for the development of these predispositions (2: 435, cf. 2: 126). Like epigenesists, Kant wants to explain natural variety using the smallest number of explanatory principles, but, like preformationists, he allows that some elements of biological structure cannot be explained by mechanism alone. Moreover, the way in which Kant suggests that outer things affect the development of natural predispositions ends up being selective rather than purely mechanical. That is, natural predispositions "lie ready ... to be on occasion either unfolded or restrained, so that [an organism] would become suited to his place in the world" (2: 435). For Kant, organisms are born with a set number of predispositions that develop in response to various environmental conditions based on what is needed to thrive within those conditions.

Kant's appeal to "predispositions" does not commit him to any particular metaphysical conception but rather effects an epistemic and methodological shift. Unlike epigenesist attempts to account for the emergence of biological structures from simpler processes, Kant argues that investigation of living beings proceeds best when one seeks to discover the minimal number of predispositions from which one can best explain the full range of biological phenomena one finds in the world. Kant's pessimism about a Newton of a blade of grass is not a denial that the generation of a blade of grass may in fact be causally determined according to mechanistic laws, but only an admonition to distinguish biology from physics and allow forces in the former that might be inadmissible in the latter (see 5: 411, 415, 422). This distinction from physics supports a further aspect of Kant's biology that we highlighted in Chapter 1. Given that organic predispositions serve purposes within organisms, Kant can employ a "heuristic" "principle of final causes" (5: 411, 387). In Kant's biology, one can legitimately ask, about any biological structure, what purpose that structure serves, and answers to such questions are legitimate parts of biological investigation.

Kant's preformationism has several important implications for his empirical anthropology. First, it allows Kant to forego describing how human predispositions came into existence: "we begin with something that human reason cannot derive from prior natural causes – that is, with the existence of human beings," including all of their natural predispositions (8: 110). Kant's empirical anthropology reduces given powers to as few natural predispositions as possible, explaining environmental factors that allow certain predispositions (but not others) to flourish in (certain) human beings and using this small number of natural predispositions to explain what we observe of human beings. Second, Kant's emphasis on teleological explanation of these predispositions gives him additional resources for "explaining" predispositions without mechanistically explaining them. Kant gives teleological explanations of phenomena as diverse as sleep (7: 166, 175, 190), laughter (7: 261), and distinctions between the sexes (7: 305). Third, Kant's preformationism contributes to his general disinterest in giving materialist explanations of psychological predispositions. Kant contrasts his approach to the empirical anthropology of his contemporary Ernst Platner, which Kant identified with "subtle, and … eternally futile inquiries as to the manner in which bodily organs are connected with thought" (10: 145). Through positing predispositions as fundamental concepts in biology, Kant's empirical anthropology can focus on explaining diverse mental phenomena in terms of as few basic powers as

possible, tracing these basic powers back to purposive natural predispositions and the environmental influences that cause these predispositions to
unfold, without being preoccupied with finding the physical structures
that underlie those predispositions.

In his empirical anthropology, then, basic powers are developed forms
of natural predispositions. We can describe the connection between any
two mental states in terms of a causal law that is grounded in a basic power,
which is itself the determinate unfolding of a natural predisposition.

Mental State 1 → Mental State 2
↑
Actualized Natural Predisposition

The concept of natural predisposition allows Kant to expand the sense
of "basic power" beyond the limited and abstract structure of his empirical psychology. Especially in the context of the faculty of desire, Kant
develops a vocabulary for natural predispositions that provides the flex-
ibility and variety needed to make sense of the myriad different ways in
which human beings are motivated.

With respect to the faculty of cognition, Kant's treatment of natural
predispositions is fairly straightforward. The senses, inner sense, the imagination, and the higher faculties of judgment, understanding, and reason
are all different natural predispositions in the human being (A66, 6:
444–45). Humans have natural predispositions to sense, imagine, and
think in accordance with the laws described in the previous section. Thus
in explaining the connection between one cognition and another, one
appeals to the natural predispositions active in effecting that transition.
For example, when the transition from the thought of one's dog to the
thought of dog food is effected by the imagination, one can describe this
transition as follows:

Thought of dog → Thought of dog-food
↑
Imagination (the predisposition governed by the law of association)

By contrast, the transition from the thought of one's dog to the
thought "animal" would be effected by the understanding, a different
predisposition. In both cases, however, a complete explanation of the
origin of a particular cognition must include, for Kant, not only the prior
state that caused the cognition and the causal law according to which that
state caused that transition, but also the natural predisposition that is the
ground of that law.

Human beings vary in terms of the exercise of natural cognitive predispositions. Some variations are in predispositions themselves, such as

certain forms of mental illness. Others involve a deficiency in the development of natural predispositions. And others, including all prejudices, involve circumstances in which some predispositions (linked either to imagination or to the faculty of desire) override the understanding and reason, leading to erroneous judgments. There are also positive variations in cognitive powers, such as wit or originality of thought, which Kant calls "talents," a sort of "excellence of the cognitive faculty which depends not on instruction but on the subject's natural predisposition" (7: 220). Altogether, Kant's account of cognitive predispositions identifies basic powers of cognition as predispositions and accounts for variations in cognitive abilities through either hereditary or acquired defects in predispositions or their expression.

Predispositions become more important and complex with respect to faculties of (practical) pleasure and desire. As noted in the last section, the causal structure that determines whether particular cognitions give rise to desires or aversions can be exceedingly complex. Many things that give rise to desires in one person do not do so in others, things can give rise to desires at some times and not others, and humans – even as objects of empirical study – seem capable of a kind of freedom of choice that might seem to preclude causal explanations. In every case, desires are preceded by cognitions that provoke feelings of pleasure. But to explain why some cognitions can cause pleasure, others displeasure, and others no feelings at all, Kant traces our volitional structure to two kinds of natural predispositions: instincts and propensities.

Instincts

The nature and role of instincts is fairly straightforward. Among natural predispositions present in human beings are a set of instincts that ground connections between various cognitions and practical pleasures (or pains) that give rise to desires (or aversions) for objects of those cognitions. Given the distinctness between the faculties of feeling and desire, there would be, strictly speaking, separate predispositions underlying the connection between, on the one hand, a particular cognition and subsequent feeling, and, on the other hand, that feeling and its consequent desire. But because all practical pleasures give rise to desires and Kant offered an account of non-practical desires that explains how they cause feelings without subsequently generating desires, his detailed account of human motivation conflates the power that grounds a connection between cognition and feeling and the power that grounds the connection between the feeling and desire. Kant ascribes the transition from cognition to desire to a single basic natural predisposition. (For ease of presentation, I often drop the reference to the intermediary practical feeling in Kant's account and simply describe the role of natural predispositions as relating cognitions to desires.) In the case of instinct, Kant's model of motivation maps straightforwardly onto his account of predispositions in general. For example:

$$\text{Cognition} \rightarrow \text{Pleasure} \rightarrow \text{Desire}$$
$$\uparrow \qquad\qquad \uparrow$$
$$\text{Instinct}$$

$$\text{Sweet smell of a ripe mango} \rightarrow \text{Pleasure} \rightarrow \text{Desire for that mango}$$
$$\uparrow \qquad\qquad \uparrow$$
$$\text{Instinct for sweet foods}$$

Often, instincts become operative when one is in the presence of the object that one's instinct predisposes one to desire (or avoid): "little chicks already have from nature an instinct of aversion to the hawk, of which they are afraid as soon as they merely see something fly in the air" (28: 255). With respect to human beings, Kant explains how smell, by means of "its affinity with the organ of taste" and "the latter's familiar sympathy with the instruments of digestion," serves as an "instinct" that "guided the novice ... allow[ing] him a few things for nourishment but for[bidding] him others" as though it were a kind of "faculty of pre-sensation ... of the suitability or unsuitability of a food for gratification" (8: 111). Central to these operations of instinct is that instincts ground connections between cognitions and anticipatory pleasures that give rise to desires. And these connections occur even before any experience of pleasures that might follow from the satisfaction of the desire. In cases where the objects of instincts are not present, Kant even suggests that instincts can be "directed to an indeterminate object; they make us acquainted with the object" (25: 584), such as the sucking instinct or even, in some cases, the sexual one (25: 584).

Moreover, the power of imagination can greatly expand the scope of instinct. Kant describes a scene where "a fruit which, because it looked similar to other available fruits which he had previously tasted, encouraged him to make the experiment" of eating it (8: 111). Given an association between a particular visual experience and a particular olfactory experience, a similar visual experience will – by virtue of the laws that govern the imagination – give rise to an imaginative idea that corresponds to that olfactory experience. Given a sufficiently strong instinctual connection between that olfactory experience and practical pleasure, the mere sight of a similar fruit will give rise to a desire to consume that fruit.

Inclination

Even with this expanded conception of instinct, however, most of human desire is not instinctual, for two important reasons. First, human desires for things like the company of one's friends, wearing fashionable clothes, resting on comfortable sofas, watching one's favorite television programs, attending baseball games, and even for things like smoking cigarettes and eating fine foods, cannot be explained by appeal to brute instincts. These are all, in varying degrees, connected with *habits* that give rise to desires for certain objects. Second, even when we pursue objects for which we have instincts, humans typically do not pursue those objects *directly* from instinct. Instincts give rise to what we might call a desire, but we have a capacity to reflect on whether or not to pursue the object of that desire. Humans frequently decide not to follow through on instinct for the sake of something else, often something for which they do not have particularly strong instinctual desires at that moment. When I decide not to eat delicious icecream, I do not act from any instinctual desire for long-term health. If humans acted only from instinct, the task of explaining human motivation would require merely a catalog of relevant instincts and careful descriptions of environments in which those instincts play out. But human behavior is, as Kant recognized, much harder to explain.

One might be tempted, at this point, to appeal to human freedom as a reason for the difficulty of explaining human behavior. And many have thought that the complexity of human motivation provides some support for Kant's account of freedom. But within his empirical anthropology, Kant takes the complexity of human action not as a reason to posit transcendental freedom, but rather as a basis for a more complicated but still empirical anthropology. Kant adds the requisite complexity through a generous use of the category of "propensity." In one lecture, Kant defines a propensity as a "natural predisposition" that provides "the inner possibility of an inclination" (25: 1111–12; cf. 7: 265). More generally, a propensity is a natural predisposition that does not itself provide a ground for connections between cognitions and practical pleasures, but that makes it possible for the human being, in the context of environmental factors, to develop a ground for such connections. Having introduced this notion of a propensity, Kant uses it to address the two problems mentioned in the previous paragraph.

First, Kant focuses on propensities for "inclinations," which he identifies as "habitual grounds of desire" (25: 1114) and which, for the purposes of his empirical anthropology, are distinguished from instincts. Like instincts, inclinations provide bases for connections between cognitions and desires. Unlike instincts, however, inclinations are not natural predispositions but tendencies brought about through certain experiences. For example,

[S]avages have a propensity for intoxicants; for although many of them have no acquaintance ... with intoxication, and hence absolutely no desire for the things that produce it, let them try these things but once, and there is aroused in them an almost inextinguishable desire for them.

(6: 29; cf. 25: 1112, 1339, 1518)

Sometimes one needs only a single experience of an object for an inclination to be awakened. Generally, however, inclinations require "frequent repetition" (25: 1514). There is also a generic propensity to develop habits, such that when one experiences something consistently over a long period of time, one develops an inclination for it (cf. 9: 463–64). In any case of inclination, however, it is not enough to simply have exposure to something to develop an inclination for it. Experiences give rise to inclinations only when human beings already have requisite propensities. The model for explaining human action in those cases looks like:

$$
\begin{array}{ccc}
\text{Sensory cognition} & \rightarrow & \text{Feeling/Desire} \\
\text{(sight or smell of intoxicant)} & & \text{(desire to consume intoxicant)} \\
& \uparrow & \\
\text{Past experience (with intoxicants)} & \rightarrow & \text{Inclination (for intoxicants)} \\
& \uparrow & \\
& \text{Propensity (for intoxicants)} &
\end{array}
$$

In these cases, the immediate explanation for why a particular cognition gives rise to a practical pleasure and thereby a desire will be similar to the case of instinct, but because inclinations are not themselves innate, the account requires an extra level of complexity. And this complexity provides for much of the richness and diversity that one finds in human desires. Fancy clothes, comfortable sofas, cigarettes, and baseball are all possible objects of inclination, even when we have no instinctual desire for them. And because humans differ in their experiences, even those with the same propensities (and Kant allows for some, but not much, variation in basic human propensities[1]) end up with very different patterns of desire. A general propensity for competitive sport (or, even more generally, for esteem and physical exertion) leads to widely varying inclinations depending on the particular sports to which one is first exposed. Because propensities are natural predispositions, Kant does not give mechanical accounts for them, but he does aim to reduce the number of posited propensities to as few as possible; ideally, he would also provide teleological explanations for each propensity.

Kant also suggests that inclinations generally involve pleasure in ways that differ from instinct. For both instinct and inclination, experience of the object of desire brings a subsequent pleasure distinct from the practical pleasure that causes the desire. For instincts, this subsequent pleasure plays no explanatory role in the development of the instinct. The instincts for nursing or for sex motivate human beings to seek milk or sex innately, not because one has experienced their pleasures already. Instincts ground pre-sensations (8: 111) of pleasure. But in the case of inclinations, the anticipatory practical pleasure that gives rise to desires generally follows from past experiences of the pleasure that one experienced upon attaining the objects of desire. One accidentally experiences some object, gets pleasure from the experience, and forms an inclination that grounds future connections between the cognition of that object and the desire to experience it. One might taste an intoxicating beverage out of thirst or conformity (rather than a desire for intoxicants) or might literally fall into a pleasantly cool pool of water on a hot day. When the experience of such objects brings pleasure, one will seek intoxicating beverages even when one is not thirsty, or one will intentionally seek out and immerse oneself in cool pools of water. In these cases, we might specify the past experience as an experience of pleasure in the objects. One need not always experience pleasure in order to form an inclination. One who has started smoking can find herself craving cigarettes even while the actual experience of smoking is still generally unpleasant, and one who develops a habit of acting in a particular way can develop an inclination to continue acting in that way, even if it is not, in itself, particularly pleasurable. Generally, however, a propensity brings about a corresponding inclination at least in part through pleasure in attaining its object.

Character

The addition of inclinations to Kant's account of human motivation greatly enriches that account, and it makes it possible to explain why there is such a wide range of divergent human interests. But inclinations, like instincts, still do not involve the reflective desires that characterize much human action. Kant captures this limitation by ascribing both instinct and inclination to the "lower" faculty of desire. Both affect human beings insofar as we are motivated by sensory or imaginative mental states, but not insofar as we govern our actions by means of concepts, principles, or maxims (the "higher" faculty of desire). For Kant, the higher faculty of desire, to which Kant assigns the term "choice" (6: 213), "cannot be determined to action through any incentive except so far as the human being has incorporated it into his maxim" (6: 24).[2] To explain how "maxims" give rise to volitions and thereby actions, Kant cannot merely appeal to instincts or inclination. Instead, he appeals to yet another propensity, a propensity to what he calls "character."

Kant uses the term character in several senses throughout his writings. In the broadest sense, a thing's character is the "law of its causality, without which it would not be a cause at all," such that "every effective cause must have a character" (A539/B567, cf. 25: 634). In this sense, gravity reflects the "character" of matter, and one's instincts are part of the "character" of one's lower faculty of desire. In a quite different sense, Kant uses "intelligible character" to refer to the free ground – "which is not itself appearance" – of one's appearances in the world (A539/B567). Character in this sense has no role to play in empirical explanations of action, although Kant argues that intelligible character grounds the empirical character of the higher faculty of desire. The character that plays an important role in Kant's empirical theory of the higher faculty of desire is distinct from though grounded in intelligible character, and more specific than the character of an efficient cause in general. Kant defines this sense of character as "that property of the will by which the subject has tied himself to certain practical principles" (7: 292) or "a certain subjective rule of the higher faculty of desire" (25: 438, cf. 25: 277). This character plays the same role for the higher faculty of desire that instincts and inclinations play for the lower. As Kant explains, "the man of principles, from whom we know for sure what to expect, not from his instinct … but from his will, has character" (7: 285, cf. 25: 1514). One can describe such motivations as follows:

Cognition (of a practical principle) → Pleasure/Desire
↑
Character

"Character" involves commitment to principles or "maxims" of action. Thus, one may have a commitment to the principle "early to bed, early to rise." In such a case, one's actions might be explained as follows:

"Early to bed …" → Desire to go to bed
↑
Fixed commitment to "Early to bed, early to rise"

Of course, this example is too simple in several respects. For one thing, the cognition of the principle "Early to bed, early to rise" is not in itself sufficient to generate the desire to go to bed, since one must also have awareness of the fact that it is evening – time for bed – rather than morning or afternoon. In order for one's character to ensure that the principle will be efficacious in generating its corresponding action, one requires both perception of one's situation and consciousness of the relevant principle.

Moreover, commitment to the principle "early to bed … " is itself the result of other causes. Kant needs an account of the causes of character as such, that is, the ability to act in accordance with principles at all, and an account of the origins of the particular principles upon which individuals act. Regarding the first, Kant's account of character development is similar to his account of the development of inclinations. There is a "propensity to character" (25: 1172) that is actualized by various experiences (7: 294, 25: 1172). In the case of character, habit plays no positive role. Instead, Kant emphasizes education (25: 1172), examples (7: 294), and "moral discourses" (25: 1173n1), and he gives specific recommendations regarding the kinds of education that are most effective, such as avoiding "imitation" (25: 635). Beyond direct influences, Kant suggests oblique factors that support character cultivation, such as stable and just political regimes, peace, and even progress in the arts and sciences. And finally, Kant points out how other natural predispositions (especially temperament) facilitate character development (cf. 7: 285, 290). All these elements work together to transform a mere propensity into an active ability to govern oneself with conscious principles rather than reactive instincts and inclinations.

Many of the influences responsible for the development of character as such also foster specific practical principles, but Kant emphasizes that most of these principles still "rest on sensibility, and … merely the means for arriving at the end are presented by the understanding" (28: 589). For example, one might learn "early to bed … " through instruction, but this instruction is effective because it proposes a plausible principle for satisfying instincts and inclinations. Even in the absence of specific instruction, one with experience forms principles of action based on what best promotes desired ends. Such principles are intellectual rather than sensible, but they still "rest on sensibility" because one formulates them for the sake of "lower" (i.e. sensible) inclinations and instincts. Even actions described in Kant's moral philosophy as following "from inclination" are generally grounded in a character committed to principles that make objects of inclination its ends. Generally, inclinations for sweets do not directly cause one to eat them; rather, one understands that eating this food will satisfy a felt inclination, and (because of one's character) this thought causes one to eat it.

Actions motivated by these "impure" principles of character are explained by an extremely complicated motivational picture. Through natural higher cognitive powers, sensory data are transformed into a conceptual understanding of one's situation. At the same time, by virtue of instincts and inclinations, sensory awareness of one's situation gives rise to various lower desires (or, more strictly, proto-desires). The understanding then provokes the thought of one or more practical principles based on how reason connects its conception of one's situation with one's felt lower desires. Thus one who recognizes the darkening sky under the concept of "early evening" might be led to think of the principle "early to bed … " by virtue of understanding this as the time at which going to bed will best facilitate the satisfaction of various inclinations over the long term. These practical principles give rise to practical pleasures and thereby desires – which Kant, in these cases, calls "choices" – by means of a character that has been formed through education, social–cultural influences, one's own past behavior, and the cooperating or hindering influence of inclinations and instincts. Both character in general and the inclinations that largely determine the content of the principles on which one acts are grounded in natural propensities. Thus human beings, due partly to different natural predispositions but largely to different past experiences, are motivated by similar sensory data to behave in different ways.

As complicated as this picture is, Kant thinks that human motivation is even more complicated, for three important reasons. First, the account given above assumes that for any given set of sensory data, there is only one way in which one's natural powers can conceptualize that content and, more importantly, that this conceptualization only lends itself to a single practical principle. But it might well be that the recognition of the darkening sky is conjoined with a recollection of an invitation to a social gathering that promises to be particularly enjoyable. Here one may be led to think of the principle "early to bed, early to rise" but also "don't forgo opportunities for enjoyable social gatherings" (cf. 6: 473, 7: 277–82), when one cannot in fact follow both principles. Even one with a well-formed character can have conflicting grounds of action. From within practical reflection (transcendental anthropology), what one does is a matter of free choice. But empirical anthropology must provide a psychological explanation. Kant first insists, "in empirical psychology, wholly equal incentives cannot be thought" (28: 678) because in the case of equal incentives, there would be no choice and thus no action (29: 902). As a result, Kant distinguishes "living" and "dead" grounds of desire, where one acts on the "living" ground, while the "dead" ground results in what Kant calls a "wish," where the "ground determining one to action … is [not] joined with one's consciousness of the ability to bring about its object" (6: 213). Thus one goes to bed because one's overall character subordinates the principle of socialization to that of prudent rest, but one falls to sleep wishing that one could somehow both go to bed early and partake of the enjoyable party.

The second added complication is that very few people have character in the fully developed sense that requires commitment to *consistent* principles. In a lecture, Kant specifically mentions difficulty with the maxim to rise early:

[one] who is not steadfast in this, often lays hold of a resolve, of which he knows for sure that nothing will come, because he knows that he has already often broken resolutions. Then the human being is in his [own] eyes a

wind-bag. He no longer has any confidence in himself ... This is how it is with things for which one wants to break one's habit ..., such as sleeping in; for it is always said, just one more time, but then no more, and thus one again philosophizes oneself free of one's plan.

(25: 624)

Sometimes inclinations directly overpower one's higher faculty of desire, such that in the strict sense, one acts on the inclination alone, without the reflection that characterizes choice. But such cases are rare. More often, inclination corrupts grounds of choice and one "philosophizes oneself free of one's plan" by acting on a maxim that differs from what one had resolved. For Kant, this tendency is quite common. Truly firm character "is fixed very late," only "com[ing] at a ripe old age" (25: 654, 1385). Most people have a kind of "bad" or "flawed" character (25: 650, 1172). Such "character" is a "constitution of one's higher powers" (25: 227) according to which, rather than acting from fixed principles, one allows principles of choice to vary based on inclinations active at the time of choice. Here inclinations and instincts not only affect to which practical principles one commits oneself but also determine whether and to what extent those principles affect deliberation at particular moments. One with a firmly established character decides, by assessing the impact of various principles on her life as a whole, how to prioritize such principles. When the time comes for action, which practical principles determine action are set by this prioritization. One with flawed character might similarly rank practical principles, resolving, for instance, to prioritize an early start to the day over satisfying the inclination to sleep in, but inclinations of the moment, rather than resolved-upon rankings, determine which principles become effective.

A final, crucial component of Kant's account is that humans are capable not only of "impure" principles of action that are "intellectual ... in some respect," but also of purely intellectual principles of action. Human beings have a "predisposition to the good" (6: 26), a "moral predisposition" (7: 324) that gives motivational force to a principle that is "purely intellectual without qualification" because it is an "impelling cause" that "is represented by the pure understanding" (28: 589). A purely intellectual principle is not based in any way on instincts or inclinations but proceeds solely from practical reason. Like other natural predispositions, the predisposition to the good is simply posited in human nature. Like instincts, this predisposition is innate in human beings (6: 27–28, 7: 324), and Kant even offers empirical evidence for it (7: 85). But like all predispositions of the faculty of desire (including instincts), experiential factors determine the extent to which the moral predisposition is living and efficacious or amounts to mere wish. Thus, for example, when one person "confronts [another] with ... the moral law by which he ought to act ..., this confrontation [can] make an impression on the agent, [so that] he determines his will by an Idea of reason, creates through his reason that conception of his duty which already lay previously within him, and is ... quickened by the other ... [to] determine himself accordingly to the moral law" (27: 521). And Kant discusses various ways in which, for instance, moral education (5: 155, 6: 479), polite society (6: 473, 7: 151), and moral–religious communities (6: 94ff.) can enliven one's innate moral predisposition.

From the standpoint of the environmental and predispositional bases of moral motivation, Kant's account of moral motivation thus fits well into his general empirical anthropology. Because of the importance of moral motivation for his transcendental anthropology, however, and especially the importance of making sense of how a finite, empirically situated being can be motivated by a pure moral law, Kant adds detailed specific accounts of the nature of the "feeling of respect" that serves as the anticipatory "pleasure" causing choice in accordance with the moral law. Kant's account of respect for the moral law is notoriously difficult to interpret. Kant says that "there is indeed no feeling for this [moral] law" (5: 75), but he proceeds to give a detailed analysis of the "feeling of respect for the moral law," the "moral feeling" that is "produced solely by reason" (5: 75–76). Understandably, then, readers of Kant are largely split into those that favor a "cognitivist" reading of respect – for whom mere cognition of the moral law, independent of feeling, motivates action in accordance with it – and those that favor a "sentimentalist" reading of respect within which the feeling of respect plays an essential motivational role.[3]

Given that Kant posits both a transcendental and an empirical anthropology, it is understandable that he might give different accounts of the role of pleasure in moral motivation. From the standpoint of transcendental anthropology, pleasure cannot play any role in grounding decisions to act in accordance with the moral law. If I choose to do what is right because it is pleasurable, I do not choose autonomously and hence do not really choose to do what is right (5: 71). Kant rightly adds that, from this transcendental perspective, "how a law can be of itself and immediately a determining ground of the will ... is ... insoluble ... and identical with ... how a free will is possible" (5: 72). But the fact that one must see oneself as free, and as bound to freely adopt the moral law as the law of one's will, does not preclude an empirical analysis of what such a free choice "effects ... in the mind insofar as it is an incentive" (5: 72). That is, Kant can still explain how it appears when a person freely chooses to follow the moral law. And in this context, Kant posits an "intellectual pleasure" that arises from "representation of the [moral] law" (29: 1024) and that serves as the motivational transition from cognition of that moral law to action in accordance with it. Kant thus provides a framework for empirically describing what, from the standpoint of transcendental anthropology, are free choices of a morally good will.

Summary

As objects of empirical study, humans are biological beings with complex mental lives. As biological beings, we have predispositions best discussed in terms of purposes they serve, and these predispositions ground causal laws that determine how our environment shapes our three faculties of cognition, feeling, and desire. The result is a complex causal account of mental powers and prejudices, instincts, inclinations, and characters, all of which allows for significant differences between individuals while still situating these differences in the context of universal laws of human psychology.

So far, this account of human beings has been relatively free of moral implications. As a strictly *empirical* anthropology, there is no direct basis for ascribing moral value to any particular psychological structures over others. But Kant uses his empirical anthropology to argue for an important moral claim about human beings. As we will see in the next chapter, Kant argues that there is good empirical evidence that human beings have a predispositional structure that can rightly be called "radically *evil*." Moreover, this chapter has emphasized humans' empirical nature as both universal and fixed. But Kant's empirical anthropology also includes accounts of the *historical change* of the human species and of significant *diversity* in humans' make-up. The next chapter investigates Kant's account of human historicity, and we turn to Kant's account of human diversity in Chapter 5.

Further Reading

Kant's empirical anthropology is not widely discussed by English-language scholars. Watkins is particularly useful for two chapters (by Sturm and Makkreel) that specifically focus on Kant's empirical psychology. Cohen, Jacobs and Kain, Louden and Wilson discuss empirical psychology in the context of broader accounts of Kant's pragmatic anthropology. McCarty and Guevara offer specific accounts of Kant's theory of choice and action.

Alix Cohen, *Kant and the Human Sciences* (London: Palgrave Macmillan, 2009)
Daniel Guevara, *Kant's Theory of Moral Motivation* (Boulder, CO: Westview Press, 2000)
Brian Jacobs and Patrick Kain, *Essays on Kant's Anthropology* (Cambridge: Cambridge University Press, 2003)

Robert Louden, *Kant's Impure Ethics* (Oxford: Oxford University Press, 2000)

Richard McCarty, *Kant's Theory of Action* (Oxford: Oxford University Press, 2009)

Eric Watkins, *Kant and the Sciences* (Oxford: Oxford University Press, 2001)

Holly L. Wilson, *Kant's Pragmatic Anthropology: Its Origin, Meaning, and Critical Significance* (Albany, NY: SUNY Press, 2006)

3 Kant on Human Evil and Human History

In the last chapter, we saw Kant's detailed empirical anthropology. While this anthropology does not rise to the level of a "science" in Kant's strict sense, it is a highly systematic account of universal human characteristics. This chapter looks at two further and related aspects of Kant's empirical account of human beings that flesh out Kant's empirical anthropology and complete unfinished business left by the *Critique of Judgment* regarding what we may hope for humanity (see 11: 429). First, we look at Kant's account of human evil. For Kant, human beings are "radically" evil "by nature." Despite this apparently glum assessment, however, Kant endorses a realistic hope for human goodness. Second, we look at one component of this hope, Kant's philosophy of human history, beginning with the emergence of human beings as a new kind of animal with a rational nature and progressing toward a future of perpetual peace amongst nations and increasingly cosmopolitan political, ethical, and social lives.

Radical Evil in Human Nature

"The Human Being is Evil by Nature"

Kant discusses human evil in his *Anthropology* (7: 324f.) and in various lectures and notes on ethics, anthropology, and religion, but his most sustained discussion of it takes place in *Religion within the Boundaries of Mere Reason*, a work in which Kant aims "to make apparent the relation of religion to a human nature partly laden with good dispositions and partly with evil ones" (6: 11). Kant's argument for human evil is complicated because of apparently contradictory claims. At times, Kant seems to rule out knowing anything about one's moral status at all, saying that "we can never, even by the strictest examination, completely plumb the depths of the secret incentives of our actions" (4: 407; see also 6: 36–37, 63; 8: 270). But Kant does argue for human evil, and when he does so, he claims both that evil "can only be proved [by] anthropological research" and "experiential demonstrations" (6: 25, 35) and that "the judgment that an agent is an evil human being cannot reliably be based on experience" (6: 20). Insofar as he does appeal to experience, Kant sometimes seems to argue directly from "the multitude of woeful examples that the experience of human deeds parades before us" (6: 32–33), but elsewhere insists that his claim that "the whole species" is evil can be justified only "if it transpires from anthropological research that the grounds that justify us in attributing ... [evil] to human beings ... are of such a nature that there is no cause for exempting anyone from it" (6: 25). From a quick look at these passages, it becomes unclear whether there can even be an argument for human evil, and among Kantians who find such an argument, there is a vibrant debate between those who think that this argument is a priori (e.g. Allison 1990 and 2001) and those who think that it is empirical (see Wood 1999: 287, Frierson 2003).

Fortunately, things are not as hopeless as they seem, and Kant's various statements can be put together into a complicated but plausible anthropological defense of human evil. The key to putting together Kant's argument comes at the beginning of *Religion*:

> We call a human being evil ... not because he performs actions that are evil..., but because these are so constituted that they allow the inference of evil maxims in him ... In order ... to call a human being evil, it must be possible to infer a priori from a number of consciously evil actions, or even from a single one, an underlying evil maxim.
>
> (6: 20)

Kant's argument for evil involves both an empirical component (the experience of "evil actions") and an a priori component that justifies the inference from these to the "evil maxim" that underlies them. The rest of this section unpacks this argument.

The quotation above implies that one can infer maxims from actions. While this might seem to contradict the claim above about the impossibility of self-knowledge, Kant is actually remarkably consistent. Whenever Kant emphasizes the inscrutability of humans' motives, he emphasizes only that we can never know that our maxims are *good*. With moral evil, the case is different. While there are no actions that cannot be done from bad motives, there are some actions that cannot be done from good motives. Kant's reference, in the above quotation, to "actions that are evil," and his specification of these as "contrary to law," is important. Generally, maxims rather than actions are good or evil. But there are "actions ... contrary to duty" (4: 397), and in his *Metaphysics of Morals*, Kant articulates a political theory based on the intrinsic wrongness of actions that cannot "coexist with everyone's freedom in accordance with a universal law" (6: 231). Because these actions are wrong regardless of their ends, one can legitimately infer bad underlying maxims from the performance of such actions. Moreover, because moral inscrutability comes partly from humans' tendency to self-flattery, it is implausible that one would pretend to a motive less noble than one's actual motive, so when one finds an evil motive, one can reasonably trust that there is no underlying righteous motive. Motivational inscrutability is asymmetrical: one can never know that a person – including oneself – is morally good, but one can know that people are evil.

Even if Kant's claims about inscrutability do not preclude knowledge of human evil, though, how can Kant make inferences from experience to the existence of human evil given that "the judgment that an agent is an evil human being cannot reliably be based on experience" (6: 20)? Neither experience nor a priori arguments alone are sufficient for Kant's proof of evil. Experience of actions contrary to duty would not be sufficient for ascribing an evil will to human beings without an argument that links those actions to evil maxims. But given evil actions, one knows that if those actions are grounded in freely chosen maxims, then the maxims are evil. So to connect evil actions and evil maxims, all that is needed is an argument that human beings are free agents who choose in accordance with maxims that can ground evil actions such as those found in experience. Kant's transcendental anthropology has already shown that human actions are phenomenal expressions of noumenal, free choices. In *Religion*, Kant adds an account of the specific structure of the fundamental maxim that grounds evil actions.

In particular, *Religion* makes two important additions to the account of free choice found elsewhere in Kant's Critical philosophy. First, he argues that human choices must be grounded in a basic maxim that is either fundamentally good or fundamentally evil; no middle ground is possible.

> [I]f [someone] is good in one part [of life], he has incorporated the moral law into his maxim. And were he ... to be evil in some other part, since the moral law ... is a single one and universal, the maxim relating to it would be universal yet particular at the same time: which is contradictory.
>
> (6: 24–25)

Because morality requires unconditional and universal compliance (4: 416), one who only sometimes acts morally never really makes the moral law his ultimate motive, since any law whose application depends upon circumstances cannot be the moral law.

Second, Kant connects his transcendental account of humans' free finitude with his empirical account of human predispositions. As we saw in the last chapter, Kant's conception of a "predisposition" has wide application, covering all basic human powers and the instincts and propensities that direct the faculty of desire. In *Religion*, Kant employs this notion of a predisposition to discuss a fundamental "predisposition to the good" that consists of three distinct "elements of the determination of the human being" – animality, humanity, and personality (6: 26–27). The predisposition to animality includes instincts for self-preservation, sex, and "community with other humans" (6: 26). The predisposition to humanity includes innate tendencies to compare ourselves with others and "inclination[s] to gain worth in the opinion of others" (6: 27). Finally, the predisposition to personality is "susceptibility to respect for the moral law as of itself a sufficient incentive in the power of choice" (6: 27).

By subsuming human volitional predispositions under the general category "predisposition to the good," Kant emphasizes that no natural instincts or inclinations are themselves evil: "the ground of evil cannot ... be placed ... in the sensuous nature of the human being" (6: 34). But because the good predispositions of human beings include some that are not unconditionally or morally good, there is a basis in human nature for evil.

> The human being (even the worst) does not repudiate the moral law ... The law rather imposes itself on him irresistibly, because of his moral predisposition; and if no other incentive were at work in him, he would also incorporate it into his supreme maxim as sufficient determination of his power of choice ... He is, however, also dependent upon the incentives of his sensuous nature because of his equally innocent natural predisposition, and he incorporates them too into his maxim ... Hence the difference, whether the human being is good or evil, must not lie in the difference between the incentives that he incorporates into his maxim ... but in their subordination ...: which of the two he makes the condition of the other. It follows that the human being (even the best) is evil only because he reverses the moral order of his incentives in incorporating them into his maxims.
>
> (6: 36, see also 6: 32)

In this important passage, Kant lays out the essence of his account of human evil. Importantly, the account can be read both in terms of transcendental freedom and in terms of empirical anthropology. The transcendental reading is crucial since in the absence of a transcendental perspective on the subordination of moral to non-moral incentives, no empirical claim can imply anything about human evil: "In freedom alone is evil" (18: 212). From the perspective of freedom, when one looks at one's action from-within, what Kant claims here is that in all choices we have concern both for morality and for well-being (animal and social inclinations), but that ultimately we subordinate one concern to the other. Our free (noumenal) nature is constituted by whether we unconditionally prioritize the moral law to non-moral concerns or whether we allow non-moral concerns of sufficient weight to trump the moral law. This aspect of Kant's account depends crucially upon the account of morality from Kant's transcendental anthropology, within which Kant shows that human beings are both transcendentally free and morally obligated. Here, Kant uses these claims to argue that because morality requires *unconditional* obedience from a transcendentally free will, *any* subordination of moral to non-moral concerns is wholly evil.

But Kant's argument for human evil is not merely directed toward helping readers recognize evil from-within. He also makes an empirical–anthropological point – that human beings are evil *by nature*. The quotation above thus helps complete Kant's empirical anthropology. Human beings have various predispositions that can be classified in terms of animal instincts, social inclinations for recognition, and moral interests. But a complete empirical account of human beings must discern how these needs interact in cases when more than one is active. And Kant sees empirical evidence suggesting that the empirical character of human volition is structured such that moral grounds are inactive when they conflict with sufficiently strong non-moral grounds. Kant finds such evidence in the "multitude of woeful examples" of human misdeeds, which shows not only that humans have predispositions that make evil possible but also that we have a volitional structure in which the moral predisposition is made inactive by sufficiently strong sensuous incentives. Given our transcendental freedom (established by Kant's transcendental anthropology), human beings are thus evil. Transcendentally speaking, there is no necessity for human beings to have this volitional structure; it is contingent upon transcendentally free choice. But empirically speaking, when one seeks to discern human nature based on empirical evidence, there is good reason to think that human volition subordinates *pure* higher volition to *im*pure higher volition. And given that Kant's transcendental anthropology shows this empirical character to be grounded in free choice, there is reason to describe this subordination as "evil."

In the end, Kant's argument for human evil is simple in outline and rich in detail.

1. In widely varying circumstances, human beings perform actions that contradict the moral law and/or consciously perform actions that are immoral.
2. Human actions result from the influence of empirical causes through ordered predispositions that determine how empirical causes effect particular actions.
3. Human beings have both a moral predisposition and non-moral predispositions to pursue natural and social goods.
4. The moral law is essentially unconditional, requiring stable and pure adherence.

5. Thus, human behavior is characterized by a prioritization of non-moral predispositions over the moral predisposition.
6. Humans' empirical behavior and character express their transcendentally free choices.
7. Thus, human beings are morally evil.

The first three premises are empirical generalizations, of different levels of complexity. The first is a straightforward generalization of observations about human beings. The second and third generalize an empirically grounded anthropological explanatory model. These premises are developed in much greater empirical detail, as we showed in Chapter 2. The fourth premise is a moral premise, a part of Kant's a priori, transcendental anthropology of volition. The evidence for this claim is thus a priori. If this a priori premise is taken as stipulative, the preliminary conclusion at (5) could be taken as an empirical–anthropological conclusion. That is, if prioritizing the moral predisposition involves consistency (by definition), it is clear from premises (1)–(3) that human beings act according to a complex structure of predispositions within which the "moral" predisposition is subordinated to others. In that sense, (5) is an empirical fact. But premise (6) is essentially transcendental; there is no empirical evidence for humans' status as free grounds of their empirical characters. Given this premise, however, the prioritization of non-moral predispositions over the moral predisposition that was shown to be a part of human nature is also revealed as an expression of moral evil. The conclusion, which is both transcendental and empirical, is that human beings are evil by nature, that is, that moral evil can be ascribed to every member of the human species.

The Nature of Radical Evil

Having shown that human beings are evil, Kant elaborates on the nature of evil. Most importantly, Kant emphasizes that human evil is "radical" in that "it corrupts ... the subjective supreme ground of all maxims" (6: 37). The "maxim" by which humans subordinate moral to non-moral incentives is their most fundamental maxim. In general, humans act in accordance with various principles (maxims) of action, which can be ordered hierarchically. To take one of Kant's own examples, one might act on the maxim "when I believe myself in need of money I shall borrow money and promise to repay it, even though I know that this will never happen" (4: 422), but this maxim is merely a particular application of more general maxims such as "I will trust my own assessments of my needs" and "whenever I can make use of others to satisfy my needs, I will do so," and this latter maxim is a more specific application of an even more general maxim that

Kant explains in terms of the relative subordination of inclinations and morality, something like "I will obey the moral law only insofar as doing so is compatible with satisfying other desires, and I will seek to satisfy some non-moral desires." This last maxim is the fundamental guiding maxim of an evil human being, and all other maxims are merely applications to particular cases where inclinations and/or the moral law are in play. Because this corrupt maxim lies at the root of all one's choices, Kant refers to human beings as "radically evil."

In laying out this account of radical evil, Kant clarifies important details about the nature of evil. For one thing, radical evil is not only "itself morally evil, since it must ultimately be sought in a free power of choice" (6: 37), but is also tied to a "natural propensity to evil" that structures particular evil choices that human beings make. Many commentators see this propensity to evil as a *precondition* of radical evil (e.g. Allison 1990, Wood 2000), but I see Kant as portraying the propensity to evil both as a *consequence* of humans' radical evil and as a *ground* of further evil choices (see Frierson 2003). Moreover, the source of radical evil in choice implies that radical evil "cannot be placed, as is commonly done, in the sensuous nature of the human being and in the natural inclinations originating from it" (6: 34–35). For one thing, evil cannot be in the human being qua object of empirical investigation but must be traced to the free, noumenal agent that grounds empirically observable behavior. But even the empirical expression of radical evil is not in the lower faculties – the senses and inclinations – but in the higher faculties, especially in the higher faculty of desire. Human agents, even as empirically observed, have a capacity to act from principles, and the way this capacity is used gives empirical evidence of freely chosen evil.

Kant also describes three ways evil might express itself in one's choices: frailty, impurity, and depravity. The first involves merely a lack of character, an "inability to act according to principle" (25: 650). Here the principles of one's higher faculty of desire are good, but when it comes to acting, these principles do not actually determine one's actions. As we noted in the last chapter, there can be conflicting underlying grounds of action, and often one or more powers are "dead" or "inactive" while others are active in effecting a transition to a new mental state or an action. Those with frail wills understand the principles according to which they should act, and the character of their higher faculty of desire is such that "they incorporate the good (law) into the maxim of my power of choice, but this good … is subjectively the weaker (in comparison with inclination) whenever the maxim is to be followed" (6: 29). In the paradigm cases of frailty, one's higher faculty of desire is properly oriented such that, if active, it would cause one to do what is right. But when the relevant moment comes, the higher faculty of desire is weaker than inclination (the lower faculty of desire) and hence inactive.

The other two forms of evil involve acting in accordance with corrupted principles. "Impurity" occurs when one's "maxim is good with respect to its object ... [but] has not ... adopted the law alone as its sufficient incentive" (6: 30). One who is impure generally chooses what is morally required, but always only because it is both morally required and conducive to satisfying other desires. Such conditional adherence to the moral law is not real adherence. The final form of radical evil, "depravity," involves a specific "propensity of the power of choice to maxims that subordinate the incentives of the moral law to others (not moral ones)" (6: 30). The depraved person might often act in seemingly moral ways, but his power of choice is structured by a fundamental commitment to non-moral desires, regardless of whether these are morally permitted or not.

Importantly, Kant rejects the possibility of what he calls "diabolical" evil, the "disposition ... to incorporate evil qua evil ... into one's maxim" (6: 37). For Kant, even the most evil person is not motivated by evil as such. Thus Kant does not allow the possibility of cases like St. Augustine's famous theft of pears "not to eat for ourselves, but simply to throw to the pigs[, where] our real pleasure consisted in doing something that was forbidden" (Augustine 1961: 47). For Kant, Augustine's self-diagnosis must be mistaken; human beings do not have a desire to do what is morally forbidden per se. Evil arises only from putting non-moral desires ahead of our innate moral predisposition.

Finally, in all of these cases, radical evil need not imply that one always chooses contrary to the moral law. To be evil is to be disposed to allow the moral law to be overridden given a sufficient sensuous incentive. Frailty, impurity, and even depravity all involve, in different ways, a subordination of the moral law to non-moral desires. But one can be radically evil and still often do what is good, if one does what is good only because the price of doing good is, in a particular case, not too high (see 6: 39).

The Problem of Radical Evil

Kant's claim that human beings are radically evil raises a serious problem at the intersection of transcendental and empirical anthropology, a problem that Kant spends the rest of his *Religion* trying to solve. Put simply, because this evil "corrupts the grounds of all maxims" it seems that it cannot "be extirpated through human forces, for this could happen only through good maxims – something that cannot take place if the subjective supreme ground of all maxims is presupposed to be corrupted" (6: 37). We cannot extirpate evil from our power of choice through that same (evil) power of choice. Radical evil is a consequence of humans' use of their transcendental freedom. But given that we freely choose evil *as the basis of all of*

our other choices, it seems impossible to use that same freedom to rid ourselves of evil. The problem of radical evil is made even worse by the fact
that human beings not only choose in evil ways but also cultivate themselves
and their environment (especially their social environment) to promote
the easy exercise of evil tendencies. Finally, the problem is even more acute
because no matter how good one might be able to become, one has chosen
badly, so one can never be a person who *always* chooses in accordance with
the moral law (6: 72). Altogether, not only is one's choice oriented in
such a way that one rejects moral reform (*radical* evil), but even if one
were somehow to begin such a process of reform, one would have to
contend with self-wrought influences that make morally upright action
difficult (a *propensity* to evil), and even if one somehow overcame these
influences, one would never have a life that was wholly good from start to
finish (one *started from* evil).

Nonetheless, Kant defends moral hope, the possibility of reforming
oneself morally despite one's radical evil. But this commitment to hope
generates a problem: how can one reconcile moral rigorism, radical evil,
and moral hope? At one level, Kant does not even try to explain how
moral reform is possible given radical evil. He points out that evil cannot
be extirpated "through human forces" (6: 37) and adds, "Some supernatural cooperation is also needed" (6: 44). This "supernatural cooperation"
is ultimately beyond rational comprehension and even practical use (see
6: 117–18, 191; 7: 43–44). The main role of this "grace" is to reinforce
humans' need to do their part to "make themselves antecedently worthy
of receiving it" (6: 44). Kant emphasizes that the inscrutability of grace is
no greater than the inscrutability of freedom and even that humans'
continuing recognition of their moral obligations reveals an enduring
"germ of goodness … that cannot be extirpated or corrupted" (6: 45–46).
The enduring germ of goodness shows that all people still have a capacity
for goodness, and one's freedom gives an enduring but inexplicable hope
that this capacity can still be used well. Of course, none of these claims
about inscrutability actually address the central problem of radical evil.

But Kant's theoretically inadequate discussion of radical evil highlights
the proper stance toward the problem.[1] Given his transcendental anthropology of cognition, Kant is correct that the metaphysical mechanisms by
virtue of which radical evil might be overcome will never be understood
by human beings. But the problem of radical evil is not, fundamentally, a
metaphysical problem but a practical one. What ought one do in light of
radical evil and what may one hope with respect to it? If evil is a free
choice to subordinate the moral law to non-moral desires, one must
simply subordinate non-moral desires to the moral law. But radical evil is
also a self-wrought tendency to act immorally, and it is, moreover, a
tendency evident in humans by nature. And these aspects of radical evil

require some grounds for moral hope in the human species as a whole as well as an account of how one can work to undo and arm oneself against self-wrought evil tendencies. Kant deals with the former task in his sophisticated philosophy of human history, a history situated in the context of radical evil but one that justifies hope in humanity's future. Kant deals with the second task in his "moral anthropology," which deals with "the subjective conditions in human nature that hinder people or help them in fulfilling [moral] laws ... , with the development, spreading, and strengthening of moral principles" (6: 217). The rest of this chapter focuses on Kant's philosophy of history. Kant's moral anthropology will be discussed in Chapter 5.

Human Beings as a Historical Species

While Kant's conception of human evil draws from and leads to a historical conception of human beings, Kant is not generally known for his philosophy of history, and a historical conception of human beings can seem to be at odds with other important aspects of Kant's philosophy. Nonetheless, during the height of work on his transcendental philosophy, Kant wrote a series of papers on human history that develop his empirical anthropology through, among other things, the claim that human "predispositions ... develop completely only in the species [and over history], but not in the individual" (8: 18). The rest of this chapter lays out this historical conception of humanity.

Methodology

Like the anthropology discussed in the last chapter, Kant's historical methodology is primarily empirical. Kant begins his essay "Idea for a Universal History with a Cosmopolitan Purpose" by emphasizing that "human actions" as "appearances ... are determined just as much as every other natural occurrence in accordance with universal laws of nature" and "History ... concerns itself with the narration of these appearances" (8: 17). But history is not "mere empirical groping without a guiding principle" (8: 161), and Kant's account of predispositions provides this principle. While the empirical anthropology of the previous chapter focused on predispositions as bases of causal powers, Kant's history studies predispositions teleologically. In his *Critique of Judgment*, Kant argued that organic life could be interpreted via purposive predispositions (5: 376). In writings on history, Kant adds that "all natural predispositions of a creature are determined sometime to develop themselves completely and purposively" (8: 18). For most animals, this teleological assumption has implications only for the study of individual organisms. To identify a feature of an organism as a physical or behavioral predisposition, one must assume a purpose for it, which implies that at some point in the normal development of the organism, the feature will develop in the way needed to serve that purpose. For human beings, however, some predispositions are not fully realized in the life of any single person. The full development of human reason in arts, sciences, and politics happens only over the history of the species. But insofar as one still treats capacities such as reason as natural predispositions, one must apply the same regulative principles to them as to other predispositions; one assumes that they develop toward their end. And this assumption provides an "Idea" that can underlie a rationally guided but empirically based history of ways humans' natural predispositions unfold over time.

The Beginning of Human History

Kant's treatment of the earliest human history is laid out in "Conjectures on the Beginning of Human History," which offers a quasi-scientific commentary on the story of humans' creation from Genesis. While some philosophers and anthropologists in the eighteenth century sought to show how human beings developed from other primates – the issue of the relationship between the upright posture and reason was a hot topic of the day – Kant starts with "the existence of the human being ... in his fully formed state ... [and] in a couple" (8: 110, see also 8: 179). By "fully formed" Kant means only that humans have all of their natural predispositions, not that these are all fully developed, but even this assumption means that Kant does not explain, as his student Herder aimed to do, how "*psychology*" arises from "determinate *physiology*," how higher cognitions arise from the contractions and expansions of "irritated little fiber[s]" (Herder 2002: 196, 189). Instead, Kant starts with primitive rational and sexual beings and shows how humans developed from that stage. In this essay, the key development that inaugurates truly human history is "the first development of freedom from its original predisposition in the nature of the human being" (8: 109). In his "Idea," Kant argued that "Nature has willed that the human being should produce everything that goes beyond the mechanical arrangement of his animal existence entirely out of himself" (8: 19), and "Conjectures" shows how an animal with the mere potential for this sort of free species-development comes to have actual freedom.

Kant outlines four steps into actualized human freedom. Blending Genesis with Rousseau, Kant first describes how human beings come to desire objects that are not natural objects of instinct: "Instinct ... allowed ... a few things for nourishment but forbade ... others ... Yet reason soon began to stir and sought, through comparison ..., to extend his knowledge of the means of nourishment beyond the limits of instinct"

(8: 111–12). Humans' cognitive faculties become capable of modifying desires and human beings decide to try "a [new] fruit whose outward look, by its similarity with other pleasant fruits …, invited him to the attempt" (8: 112). Humans' faculties of desire are no longer wholly at the mercy of their lower, sensory faculties of cognition, but become capable of control by the higher faculty of cognition, by conceptual awareness and principles for action.

This first step into freedom is not wholly beneficial. The ability to generate new desires includes an ability to generate unhealthy desires, "desires not only without a natural drive … but even contrary to it" (8: 111). Moreover, freedom over desires causes a new problem, "concerning how he … should deal with this newly discovered faculty" (8: 112). Once capable of generating new desires through reasoning, one must decide which objects are worth pursuing among an apparently infinite expanse of possibilities. But one still lacks any framework for making such determinations.

While the first stage in human freedom transformed desires in general, the second stage transforms the most intense and powerful social instinct in human beings: the sexual instinct. Following Rousseau, Kant sees a fundamental difference between the raw desire for sex and the way in which sexuality plays out in human life. Human beings overlay onto their desire for sexual gratification an interest in the beauty and even personality of the sex object. Reason "make[s] an inclination more inward and enduring by withdrawing its object from the senses," which "shows already the consciousness of some dominion of reason over impulse" (8: 113). The third step involves the "deliberate expectation of the future" (8: 113), which requires still higher and more organized interactions between reason and desire. Like the first steps, the effects of this are ambivalent: it "is the most decisive mark of the human advantage of preparing himself to pursue distant ends … – but also simultaneously it is the most inexhaustible source of cares and worries" (8: 113).

Finally, in the last stage the human being "comprehended (however obscurely) that he was the genuine end of nature" (8: 114). Human beings come to see the products of nature as possible instruments for their own use, but they also recognize – albeit obscurely – that every other human being is an "equal participant in the gifts of nature" and thus can rightly make "the claim of *being himself an end*, of also being esteemed as such …, and of being used by no one merely as a means to other ends" (8: 114). Kant does not think that the earliest human beings had worked out theories of human rights, nor that they actually treated all other human beings as equals. Kant is well aware that human beings seek to dominate each other and treat others as mere instruments. But domination among human beings has, according to Kant, a fundamentally different character from the struggle with the rest of nature. Among beings who are all capable of forming plans for themselves on the basis of "a faculty of choosing ... a way of living" (8: 112), influence takes a form either of blameworthy domination or of cooperation.

The Development of Human History

The emergence into freedom marks only the beginning of Kant's historical anthropology. Before emerging into freedom, human beings were distinguished from animals only by latent predispositions to higher cognitive and volitional faculties. But upon becoming free, humans could become a truly historical species. The claim that "human ... predispositions ... develop completely only in the species" (8: 18) comes to the fore, and Kant adds a further claim central to his account of human history: "Nature has willed that the human being should ... participate in no other happiness or perfection than that which he has procured for himself free from instinct through his own reason" (8: 19). Humans' faculties of choosing for themselves generate the structure of human history, according to which all development of human predispositions occurs by humans' own deliberate work.

Kant almost immediately adds an important caveat to this emphasis on freedom. While human history progresses by means of human choices, Nature uses human choices to achieve ends that diverge from the immediate ends of the choices themselves. In particular, nature uses humans' "unsocial sociability ..., i.e., their propensity to enter into society, ... combined with a thoroughgoing resistance that constantly threatens to break up this society" (8: 20). For Kant, this "unsocial sociability" is the primary driving force of human progress: "it is this resistance that awakens all the powers of the human being [and] brings him to overcome his propensity to indolence" (8: 21). Humans' merely natural needs for food, rest, and sex are sufficiently limited that they do not require much development of human capacities. But the capacity to develop new desires, especially in the context of a need to prove oneself superior to others, requires that one cultivate the full range of human capabilities. "Thus happens the first true steps from crudity toward culture ...; thus all talents come bit by bit to be developed, taste is formed, and even, through progress in enlightenment, a beginning is made toward [forming society] into a moral whole" (8: 21). At first, this might happen on a purely individual level, as human beings cultivate speed, strength, and dexterity, and then increasingly the ability to imagine and reason, along with the effort to make progress not only in sciences but in the arts. These steps are motivated primarily by "ambition, tyranny, and greed" (8: 21), which are sufficient to bring people out of indolence and into the hard work of becoming more and more perfect (though not *morally* perfect) human beings. Through humans' unsocial sociability, nature achieves the great goal of bringing to fruition what are at first mere latent potentials for reasoning, character, scientific development, and artistic creativity.

The story does not end with individual progress, however. The ultimate end of nature includes not merely culture, within which human predispositions are developed, but also a form of society as a moral whole: "the greatest problem for the human species, to which nature compels him, is the achievement of a civil society administering right" (8: 22). Nature aims for just relations among humans, a "society in which freedom under external laws can be encountered ..., a perfectly just civil constitution" (8: 22). This "civil constitution" involves unions of people under "republican" forms of government and governments at peace with each other. Human history tends toward a condition within which all human societies will be organized under just, republican forms of government united into a "pacific league" of nations, a "federative union" that can "secure a condition of freedom of states conformably with the idea of the right of nations" (8: 356).

Within his moral philosophy, Kant argues that just government and peace among nations are morally required ends for human beings. Thus Kant sometimes "rests [his] case" that history can progress toward such a state "on [his] innate duty ... so to influence posterity that it becomes always better" (8: 309). But Kant's philosophy of history also emphasizes empirical evidence that moral interest in political right is a real force in human affairs. For example, in the response of spectators to the French Revolution, "the mode of thinking of the spectators ... manifests a universal yet disinterested sympathy [that] demonstrates ... a moral character of humanity, at least in its predisposition, which ... permits people to hope for progress toward the better" (7: 85). But Kant's primary basis for hope in political progress is not based on humans' moral interests. Instead, as in the case of the development of human culture, Kant argues that humans' unsocial sociability provides grounds for progress toward more and more just institutions. Even "a nation of devils" could solve "the problem of establishing a just state ... in order to arrange the conflict of their unpeaceable dispositions ... so that they themselves ... constrain one another to ... bring about a condition of peace" (8: 366). Like Hobbes, Kant argues that even without any moral interests, conflicts among humans will lead them to find laws to which they can subordinate themselves and others in order to achieve the peace and stability necessary for the satisfaction of their desires.

Finally, Kant insists that political progress be supplemented by an ethical community, "a society in accordance with, and for the sake of, laws of virtue" (6: 94). While political community is established by "external legal constraint," ethical community depends upon mutual encouragement toward virtue; the only "constraint" applicable here is through a supposed divine lawgiver "who knows the ... most intimate parts of the dispositions of each and everyone and ... give[s] to each according to the worth of his action" (6: 99). Even with God as "moral ruler of the world," Kant insists that an ethical community have "purity: union under no other incentives than moral ones (cleansed of ... superstition ...)" (6: 102). As in the case of political and cultural progress, Kant suggests that progress toward this community depends upon the cooperation of nature (6: 100–1) but Kant insists particularly strongly that "each must ... conduct himself as if everything depended upon him. Only on this condition may he hope that a higher wisdom will provide the fulfillment of his well-intentioned effort" (6: 101). Whereas political and even cultural progress happens through unsocial sociability, progress toward *ethical* community occurs only in conjunction with properly motivated cooperation.

Moral Progress?

For Kant, human beings are historical. Humans progressively develop innate talents and predispositions, contributing toward a culture within which arts and sciences flourish. We progress toward more just political structures, both within and among states. Educational progress contributes to bringing about enlightenment, a state in which humans think for themselves. And ethical community contributes to moral development. Precisely how far this moral development goes is unclear. Given his transcendental anthropology of desire, according to which each human being is free and responsible for her own moral status, Kant seems committed to the view that fundamental moral character is an individual affair. In some of Kant's works on human history, he emphasizes that historical progress is "not ... an ever increasing quantity of *morality* [but only] ... an increasing number of actions governed by duty, ... i.e. ... the external phenomena of man's moral nature" (7: 91). Elsewhere, though, Kant suggests that historical progress does have an effect on human beings at their deepest moral level. Ethical community seems oriented toward making human beings morally good, and Kant suggests that "since the human race is continually progressing in cultural matters (in keeping with its natural purpose), it is also engaged in progressive improvement in relation to the moral end of its existence" (8: 308–9).

One way to think about moral progress in history is in terms of the *Critique of Judgment*'s aim of bridging the gap between nature and freedom. The final end of nature is good human wills actually expressed in concrete human lives. Progress in arts and sciences makes it possible for humans who aim for the happiness of others to more effectively promote that happiness, and the good will that seeks its own perfection requires a cultural context within which the resources for that pursuit are available. Moreover, given the necessity of external freedom for the full expression of one's choices, political rights are needed for good wills to fully express themselves in the world.

Radical evil poses deeper problems for the concrete expression of goodness in human lives. Because human beings "started from evil" (6: 72), the final end of nature cannot be perfect human wills but only wills that unendingly progress toward goodness. And given that radical evil involves an ongoing propensity to evil facilitated through self-deception, even this ongoing progress involves struggle against self-wrought evil tendencies. Finally, since human evil is both fundamental and rooted in the human *species*, it is not clear how one could ever begin to progress beyond one's fundamental commitment to prefer happiness to morality.

Kant's account of historical progress can address at least the first two issues, and may be able to address the third. We saw in Chapter 1 that Kant postulates immortality as a condition of the possibility of fully satisfying the moral law, but Kant's philosophy of history provides a naturalistic, secular way of understanding immortality. A human life can be considered a good life as a whole insofar as it not only gradually improves in its own individual pursuit of virtue but also works toward an unending progress in the expression of morally good deeds through reforming the society of which it is a part. The historicity of human nature makes it possible for one's own struggle against evil to be part of an enduring struggle of humanity as a species. In particular, and this aligns the first issue with the second, part of one's struggle against radical evil involves enacting social conditions that strengthen virtue rather than evil propensities. "Ethical community" is a community of people constantly reminding one another of their moral obligations, holding one another accountable in ways that, without being judgmental, make it increasingly difficult to ignore the demands of morality in self-deceptive ways. In the context of human beings as initially radically evil but potentially in revolution against that evil, even not-strictly-moral cultural and political progress can profoundly affect the extent to which one's revolution expresses itself in concrete improvements. Those whose fundamental moral disposition is one of struggle against evil might, in early phases of human history, be largely dominated by evil tendencies and show only the slightest glimmers of success in the struggle against it, while those at later stages of historical progress, being increasingly armed against the evil principle through social structures that facilitate morality, will express their good wills more and more fully in their concrete, embodied lives.

These sorts of moral progress in history still leave open the question of whether historical progress can go all the way down, actually enabling or facilitating the revolution in fundamental maxims. And here one might take a clue from Kant's discussion of supernatural influence. Just as "the concept of a divine concursus is quite appropriate and even necessary" "so that we should never slacken in our striving toward the good" (8: 362), but we should not use appeals to divine cooperation to excuse moral complacency; so we might appeal to moral progress in history as encouragement that our struggle against evil will bear real fruit, but must appeal to this progress only in such a way that it prevents rather than justifies complacency. Kant's philosophy of history can thereby provide empirical support for the moral hope that is justified religiously by appeal to God's grace and our immortality.[2]

Summary

Because of humans' misdeeds, we can posit a motivational–predispositional structure in human beings that subordinates moral incentives to non-moral ones. Because we are transcendentally free, this predispositional structure can be ascribed to moral evil. Thus human beings are evil by nature, and because this evil is "radical," it seems ineradicable. Still, Kant has hope for human beings. Partly, this hope is tied to the possibility of supernatural grace. But Kant's hope is also reflected in his historical conception of human beings. Kant's philosophy of history has three main elements: humans' emergence from a pre-rational to a rational condition; the development of art, science, culture, and political justice through humans' unsocial sociability; and the hope for the emergence of an ethical commonwealth for the sake of fostering virtue.

In Chapter 1, we saw how Kant's transcendental anthropologies of volition and feeling contribute to answering the question "What may I hope?" through the postulates of God and immortality and through the recognition of human beings as ultimate and final end of nature. But when Kant introduced his questions, he associated "What may I hope?" with *religion* and claimed that *Religion within the Boundaries of Mere Reason* is where he tried to answer that question (11: 429). While Kant's transcendental anthropology provides an overall framework within which hope can be justified, his religion and history give this framework an empirical content and flesh out his transcendental philosophy by providing assurance that the empirical world is conformable to the moral demands of freedom for radically evil beings like us.

Further Reading

Kant's account of human evil has recently been the topic of vibrant debate between Allison, who defends an a priori argument for humans' radical evil, and Wood, who defends an empirical–anthropological argument. Anderson-Gold, like Wood, connects Kant's theory of evil with human history. Grenberg situates Kant's theory of evil in the broader context of an ethics of "humility." Michaelson discusses evil in relation to philosophy of religion. Frierson relates evil to Kant's anthropology and theory of freedom.

Henry Allison, *Kant's Theory of Freedom* (Cambridge: Cambridge University Press, 1990, see especially chapter 8) and *Idealism and Freedom* (Cambridge: Cambridge University Press, 1996, especially chapter 12).

Sharon Anderson-Gold, *Unnecessary Evil* (Albany, NY: SUNY Press, 2001)

Patrick Frierson, *Freedom and Anthropology in Kant's Moral Philosophy* (Cambridge: Cambridge University Press, 2003)

Jeanine Grenberg, *Kant and the Ethics of Humility* (Cambridge: Cambridge University Press, 2005)

Gordon Michaelson Jr., *Fallen Freedom: Kant on Radical Evil and Moral Regeneration* (Cambridge: Cambridge University Press, 1990)

Allen Wood, *Kant's Ethical Thought* (Cambridge: Cambridge University Press, 1999, see especially chapter 9)

Full-length books dealing with Kant on history include Yovel, Galston, and Kleingeld. Rorty collects essays by top scholars on Kant's "Idea" essay. Significant portions of recent books by Wood (above) and Louden deal with Kant's philosophy of history, and Louden nicely outlines the range of views about the extent to which Kant's history of progress is a history of *moral* progress.

William Galston, *Kant and the Problem of History* (Chicago: The University of Chicago Press, 1975).

Pauline Kleingeld, *Fortschritt und Vernuft: Zur Geschichtsphilosophie Kants* (Würzburg: Königshausen & Neumann, 1995)

Robert Louden, *Kant's Impure Ethics* (Oxford: Oxford University Press, 2000)

Amelie Oksenberg Rorty, *Kant's Idea for a Universal History with a Cosmopolitan Aim: A Critical Guide* (Cambridge: Cambridge University Press, 2009)

Yirmiahu Yovel, *Kant and the Philosophy of History* (Princeton: Princeton University Press, 1980)

4   Kant on Human Diversity

Much of Kant's anthropology emphasizes universality and uniformity. His *transcendental* anthropology implies proper ways of cognizing, acting in, and even feeling about the world that are universally applicable to all people. Even Kant's empirical anthropology describes general properties of human nature; while Kant recognizes that "circumstances of place and time ... produce *habits* which, as is said, are second nature," he insists that anthropology should aim to overcome this "difficulty" in order to "rise to the rank of a formal science" (7: 121). And Kant's claim that "the human being is evil by nature" is supposed to be based on "anthropological research that ... justif[ies] us in attributing ... [evil] to human beings" in such a way that "there is no cause for exempting anyone from it" (6: 25).

Throughout his life, however, Kant was also preoccupied with human differences. Kant lectured more on "physical geography" than any other subject, and especially during its early years, this course included substantial attention to cataloging differences between different types of human beings. He describes the content of this course in 1765, saying, "The comparison of human beings with each other, and the comparison of the human being today with the moral state of the human being in earlier times, furnishes us with a comprehensive map of the human species" (2: 312–13). Moreover, from the start of his anthropology course in 1772, Kant included discussion of differences between human beings based on variations in temperament, nationality/ethnicity, and sex. In his published *Anthropology*, Kant emphasizes "an advantage for the reading public" in offering "headings under which this or that observed human quality ... can be subsumed," giving "readers many occasions and invitations to make each particular into a theme of its own, so as to place it in the appropriate category" (7: 121–22). Among these "headings" one finds different sorts of talents and inclinations, mental illnesses, temperaments, and ethnic and gender differences.

This chapter focuses on Kant's account of human variation. I start with a brief treatment of individual differences, including mental disorders. I then turn to human temperaments, the four basic affective-volitional structures into which every human being can be classified. Finally, I turn to the two most controversial aspects of Kant's account of diversity, his discussions of sexual and racial/ethnic difference.

Individual Variations

Within Kant's empirical anthropology, human beings are unique in their particular configurations of predispositions and powers. Chapter 2 noted that human beings have universal, natural predispositions that govern cognition, feeling, and desire, but the precise way in which these predispositions unfold is not universal. Many differences between individuals are ascribable to environmental differences, such as why one person plays cricket while another plays baseball or why individuals have different beliefs and tastes. But other differences are, to varying degrees, innate.

The most extreme individual differences are found in Kant's accounts of mental disorders.[1] For Kant, mental disorders affect each of the three fundamental human psychological faculties: cognition, feeling, and desire. Because cognition is subdivided into different powers (imagination, judgment, etc.), Kant distinguishes cognitive disorders according to which mental power is affected and how. For example, dementia (*Wahnsinn*) is "deranged" imagination, while craziness (*Aberwitz*) is deranged reason. Kant also distinguishes mere deficiencies from positive forms of derangement, such that, for instance, stupidity is a deficiency of judgment whereby one simply lacks the ability to figure out whether a particular case falls under a general rule, while insanity (*Wahnwitz*) is a derangement of judgment whereby one groups together disparate particulars under false universals. Further, Kant adds melancholia and hypochondria as cognitive disorders distinct from those that fall under more general groupings. Regarding feeling and desire, Kant treats all disorders of feeling under the general name of "affects" and disorders of desire under the general name of "passions." Both are states wherein a particular feeling or desire overpowers the reflection needed to compare that feeling or desire with others, so a single feeling or desire motivates action without (sufficient) reflection. Finally, Kant describes origins of mental disorders and ways of treating them. Madness is ascribed to a biologically inherited "germ" that sets on at a particular time and takes on its particular character due to circumstances present when it sets on (7: 217). Hypochondria results from a "natural predisposition" (7: 104) that has the form of a propensity and can be resisted through "intentional *abstraction*" (7: 212).

While interested in "bringing a systematic division" into mental disorder, Kant also classifies differences between ordinary, mentally healthy human beings. Such people have the same mental powers that operate by the same general rules, but there are differences in the details of their operation and the relative weight of different influences on thought and action. Kant classifies these human differences into two general categories, those that "indicate what can be made of the human being" and those that "indicate what he is prepared to make of himself" (7: 285). The latter is identified by Kant with "character purely and simply" (7: 285) and has been discussed in Chapter 2. The former, including talents, natural aptitudes, and temperaments, involve variations "founded upon ... [different] natural predisposition[s]" (7: 286) and describe degrees to which various natural powers are capable of being exercised or improved. Talents refer to "excellence[s] of the cognitive faculty" (7: 220), natural aptitude "has more to do ... with feeling" (7: 286), and temperament "has ... to do ... with the *faculty of desire*" (7: 286). All these natural variations "must ... be distinguished from ... habitual disposition (incurred through habit) because a habitual disposition is not founded upon any natural predisposition but on mere occasional causes" (7: 286). Beyond humans' shared mental powers and the differences acquired through different lives and experiences, there are also innate differences in the degrees to which and ways in which mental powers can be exercised.

Temperament

Amongst the natural variations that constitute "what nature makes of the human being," the most important is temperament. Whereas talents and natural aptitudes are highly individual, Kant follows a long tradition in holding that one can classify people into precisely four "temperaments": sanguine, choleric, melancholic, and phlegmatic. While these categories were originally developed within ancient medicine, Kant brackets medical and physiological conceptions of temperament (see 7: 286). Acknowledging that "temperaments we attribute merely to the soul may have corporeal factors ... as covertly contributing causes" (7: 286), Kant divides the four temperaments into sanguine and melancholic "temperaments of feeling" and choleric and phlegmatic "temperaments of activity" (7: 286–87, 289). The sanguine "is carefree and of good cheer" and lives in the moment (7: 288). The melancholic is serious, thoughtful, and tends toward misanthropy (7: 288). The choleric is "*hot-tempered* ... [and] *rash* [and] his ruling passion is ambition" (7: 289). Just as the sanguine *feels* quickly and easily but is also quickly distracted, so the choleric *acts* quickly but is quickly appeased. As the sanguine has an excess of (cheerful) feeling, the choleric has an excess of activity. Finally, the phlegmatic has "*lack of emotion*" and "the quality of not being moved easily" (7: 289–90).

Although generally dismissed today, Kant's discussion of temperament is important for several reasons. First, in the absence of some accounts of temperaments, Kant might rightly be accused of failing to recognize the important natural (even biological) differences between human beings. Kant's doctrine of temperaments, like more contemporary psychological investigations and classifications of human psychological variations, provides his universal and historical anthropology with a necessary supplementary account of human difference. Second, Kant's account of temperaments is important as part of a specifically *pragmatic* anthropology. I discuss pragmatic anthropology in more detail in the next chapter, but here it is important to note that Kant does not *merely* classify different temperaments. He also emphasizes their characteristics in ways relevant to moral and practical assessments and deliberations. For example, when Kant claims that the sanguine person "makes promises in all honesty, but does not keep his word because he has not reflected deeply enough beforehand" (7: 288), his advice not only provides needed warning to the sanguine about their own morally pernicious tendencies but also helps others know how to deal with sanguine companions and even how to properly evaluate the moral status of the sanguine's broken promises (as flightiness, not deception).[2] Finally, Kant's discussion of temperament provides an important "hinge" (Larrimore 2001: 270) between Kant's general and universal anthropology and his discussions of differences between human sexes, nationalities (or ethnic groups), and races. Given the offensive nature of Kant's views about sex and race, this calls for thinking about what, if anything, distinguishes Kant's practice of subdividing people according to "temperament" – shared, for example, by those who favor psychological personality tests as a way of improving interpersonal relationships – and his practice of subdividing people according to sex and race.

Differences between the Sexes[3]

Kant's discussion of temperament marks the start of his attempt to classify human beings in terms of generic *types* of human. Throughout his anthropological writings, Kant follows his discussion of human temperaments with an account of "The Character of the Sexes" (7: 303). Consistently, and in perfect conformity to feminist characterizations of Western discourse as fundamentally patriarchal, Kant's discussion of differences between men and women focuses exclusively on the unique character of *women*. Kant takes men to be paradigmatic of human beings in general, such that a characterization of "the sexes" involves only showing how the previous characterization of human beings in general must be modified for the "special case" of women.

Kant's *Observations*, his earliest (1764) and most popular anthropological discussion of the sexes, includes both perfect sound-bites of Kantian misogyny – "A woman who has a head full of Greek ... might as well have a beard" (2: 229) – and apparent mantras of egalitarianism – "the fair sex has just as much understanding as the male" (2: 229). The core of Kant's account of the sexes in *Observations* is that women are primarily beautiful, while men are primarily sublime:

> it is not to be understood that woman is lacking noble [sublime] qualities or that the male sex must entirely forego beauties; rather one expects that each sex will unite both, but in such a way that in a woman all other merits should only be united so as to emphasize the character of the *beautiful* ... while by contrast among the male qualities the *sublime* should clearly stand out.
>
> (2: 228)

Kant's distinction is both descriptive – women *are* generally more beautiful and men more sublime – and normative: "To this [distinction] must refer all judgments of these two sexes, those of praise as well as those of blame" (2: 228) such that "what is most important is that the man become more perfect as a man and the woman as a woman" (2: 242–43).

Unless one keeps both the descriptive and the normative dimensions of Kant's distinction in mind, Kant's account might seem to preclude virtue in women. Kant says both "It is difficult for me to believe that the fair sex is capable of principles" (2: 232, see also 27: 49), and "true virtue can only be grafted upon principles" (2: 217). This might require, as Jean Rumsey claims, that "women ... are in Kant's view less than ... full moral agents" (Rumsey 1997: 131). But such attention to the merely descriptive aspect of Kant's distinction misses Kant's insistence in *Observations* that women *are* capable of virtue, but "The virtue of the woman is a *beautiful virtue*" (2: 231). And whereas the principles of which women are incapable "are also extremely rare among the male sex" (2: 232), the "love [of] what is good" that serves as the foundation of beautiful virtue is grounded in "goodly and benevolent sentiments" that "providence has implanted ... in [woman's] bosom" (2: 232). Whereas few men will attain sublime virtue, women are well equipped for beautiful virtue.

By the time of *Anthropology* (1798), Kant's thought underwent several changes that affected his discussion of women. Some of these reflect Kant's interest in courtship and marriage. So, for example, Kant's personal notes and lectures in anthropology increasingly emphasize that it is "an essential condition of nature, that woman must be sought" (25: 708), so that "the woman *refuses*, the man *woos*; her surrender is a favor" (7: 306). This characterization of "natural" courtship practices contributes to Kant's attention to a womanly "art of appearing" or "art of illusion" (20: 61, 69, 121, 140) that provides a way to "govern ... men and use them for their own purposes" (7: 304).

Kant also reconceived of the difference between the sexes in terms of an overall natural teleology. From his earliest discussions of women, Kant had referred to their "innate" characteristics (2: 229) and insisted that women not only are but also ought to be different from men (2: 229–30). But his later anthropology takes this further. First, Kant clarifies the extent to which these differences are natural. He recognizes substantial differences between eighteenth-century European relations between sexes and those in "uncivilized conditions" (7: 303), where one sees no significant differences between men and women. But, Kant claims, this greater sameness between men and women is hardly a boon to women, who find themselves, without distinctively feminine sources of strength, in conditions like "domestic animal[s]" (7: 304). Consistent with his account of predispositions in general, Kant sees feminine character traits as propensities that require the right conditions to flourish: "culture does not introduce these feminine qualities, it only allows them to develop and become recognizable under favorable conditions" (7: 303). Kant also offers specific arguments against those who "dispute this [account of sex differences] in the way one disputes something from the speaker's lectern [to show that they are not inherent to] nature and [they] believe it to be a matter of fashion" (25: 709). Kant appeals to "universal and constant" facts about the sexes, including not only that women bear children while men to not, but also that for humans as well as "animals ..., one sees the female is the refusing, but the male the courting party" (25: 709). From such universal characteristics, further characteristics of human females – their abilities to please through illusion, a desire to dominate men through charm, and so on – can be explained.

The most important part of Kant's account of women is his treatment of "nature's end in establishing womankind" (7: 305). There are two natural purposes for women's distinctive characteristics: the preservation of the species [and] the cultivation and refinement of society (7: 305–6). "Nature entrusted to woman's womb its dearest pledge, namely, the species, in the fetus," so women's "fear of physical danger" (7: 306) combined with an ability to "demand male protection" ensures that the fetus (and thus species) will be threatened neither by excessive boldness on the part of the woman nor physical dangers (against which the man will protect her). The second great end of nature is the cultivation of society: "nature wanted to instill the finer feelings that belong to culture – namely, ... sociability and propriety" (7: 306). As we saw in the previous chapter, the development of culture is the great natural end for human beings as a species. There Kant emphasized unsocial sociability as the driving force behind this development. Here he highlights that unsocial sociability has a gendered structure. Men and women are attracted into society with one another but manifest their superiority in different ways. Women's power over men depends upon increasingly polite and refined social interactions; her direct power is exercised through "modesty and eloquence in speech and expression" (7: 306). In order to gain equality, women become adept at social interaction. But as women become more capable of coaxing men, they "claim ... gentle and courteous treatment by the male," who finds himself "fettered ... through his own magnanimity, and led by her, if not to morality itself, to that which is its cloak, moral decency" (7: 306, see also 2: 241). The apparent weakness and timidity of women ends up becoming one of the driving forces behind cultural and even proto-moral progress in the human species.

Unfortunately, Kant's increased interest in women as a driving force behind progress in history, even to the point of helping develop a moral decency "which is the preparation for morality" (7: 306), was accompanied by profound changes in his overall moral theory, changes that effectively preclude women from virtue. Whereas *Observations* emphasizes the importance of "beautiful" or "adopted" virtues even for men and devotes significant attention to spelling out the details of "the virtue of women" (2: 231), Kant's mature moral theory not only does not include but also seems to exclude anything that could *genuinely* be called feminine *virtue*. Kant shifted from an empirical and sentimentalist moral theory in the 1760s that allowed different sorts of moral worth based on different aesthetic feelings to more rigorous rationalist morals in his *Groundwork* and later works that emphasized a "good will" as the only thing "good without limitation" (4: 393). This shift precludes taking seriously as "virtue" anything that does not involve acting out of respect for a pure moral law. Thus when he refers to "feminine virtue" (7: 307) in his *Anthropology*, the claim seems to be a mere remnant of an earlier view, a remnant that no longer makes sense in the context of Kant's mature moral theory.

At the same time, Kant's anthropological characterization of women as incapable of male virtue (which becomes the only real virtue) is unchanged. The early claim that "It is difficult for me to believe that the fair sex is capable of principles" (2: 232) blossoms into a more technical (and more problematic) claim that certain "feminine principle[s are] hard to unite with a *character* in the narrow sense of the term" (7: 308). This "narrow sense" of character is the capacity to act on consistent principles of one's own, a capacity that not only "has an inner worth" of its own (7: 293) but is also a necessary condition of a good will (Rumsey 1989, Frierson 2006). Given that woman's distinctive art is an art of appearing, it is perhaps unsurprising that character, which depends upon "not dissembling" (7: 294), is unavailable to them. And given that women naturally focus on "pleasing others" (7: 305), it is unsurprising that they lack the self-governance required by the moral law.

Given his apparent indifference to treating women as capable of moral worth, Kant's moral and political theory unsurprisingly fails to accord women the same rights as men. Within political theory, women show up in the contexts of citizenship and marriage. Kant defines citizens as "the members of a society who are united for giving law" and insists that "all women" are "passive citizens" not "fit to vote" but nonetheless with "freedom and equality *as human beings*" (6: 314–15). And whereas, in general, society's laws must allow that "anyone can work his way up from this passive condition to an active [citizenship]" (6: 315), his insistence that *all* women are passive excludes them from this condition. For Kant, women must remain forever dependent upon husbands for public representation.

In *Anthropology*, Kant adds two important nuances to this account. First, he makes clear that while "woman regardless of age is declared to be immature in civil matters," this is a specifically civil declaration; a wife is, if anything, "over-mature" in her ability to "represent both herself and her husband." But "just as it does not belong to women to go to war, so women cannot personally defend their rights and pursue civil affairs by themselves." Second, Kant suggests that women *do* defend their rights and pursue civil affairs *indirectly*, since "legal immaturity with respect to public transactions makes women all the more powerful in respect to domestic welfare; because here the *right of the weaker* enters in, which the male sex by its nature already feels called on to respect and defend" (7: 209). For Kant, women are excluded from public politics not because of a genuine incapacity, but in order to empower them at home, where they can control their husbands and ensure that husbands take care of the family's public affairs.

Kant discusses marital rights in the general context of *property* rights, in a section illuminatingly entitled "on rights to persons akin to rights to things" (6: 277). There are three ways to acquire "a person akin to a thing," when "a *man* acquires a *wife*; a *couple* acquires *children*; and a *family* acquires *servants*" (6: 227). Of these three, Kant insists that both children and servants are acquired only for a specified period of time, after which they must be granted complete freedom from their parents/masters (6: 281, 283). Only women are capable of being "acquired" for life. To be fair, Kant's account of the husband's ownership right over the wife is carefully described not as a right to a person *as a thing*, which would blatantly contradict the obligation to respect all others as an end and not a mere means, but only as a right *akin* to rights to things. In fact, Kant's discussion of the marriage right is one of the clearest places where he articulates the view that women, despite whatever limitations they may have anthropologically, are nonetheless ends in themselves who have a "duty … to humanity in [their] own person[s]" (6: 280). It follows, for Kant, that marriage rights – unlike rights over children and servants – must include entire reciprocity and "equality of possession," such that just as the husband entirely owns the wife, so the wife in turn entirely owns the husband (6: 278). Thereby Kant rules out polygamy, concubinage, and prostitution; and he even insists on "equality in their possession of material goods" (6: 278). Consistent with accounts of differences between sexes in *Anthropology* and elsewhere, Kant does not think that husband and wife play identical roles within marriage. In the *Metaphysics of Morals*, where legal rights are at stake, Kant insists that the husband "is to be [the wife's] master" (6: 279). However, consistent with his view that women hold power primarily through charming manipulation of their husbands, while the *law* recognizes the husband as head of household, the wife – through her relational adeptness – "dominates" the husband through his own will.

In the end, Kant's account of sex difference comes down on the "wrong side" of the most important issues of the day, such as women's education and citizenship. And while he "gallantly" (e.g. 7: 310) praises women's distinctive charms, his overall account sees them primarily as means to the civil and moral development of *men*. Even Kant's explicit endorsements of women's equality (or superiority) fit within an overall attempt to defend and entrench patriarchal political structures. Saying that women have soft power that flourishes in contexts where they lack explicit and formal power is an excellent way to justify denying them political equality. And drawing attention to women's ability to control men through charm is a good way of discounting the role of rational argument and dialogue at the level of intellectual equals. This discounting can have profound effects not only within marriages – where husbands will expect wives to be charming rather than wise – but also in the education of girls, which education would, for Kant, properly emphasize learning social graces rather than intellectual pursuits (including not only abstract metaphysics but also disciplines that involve more obvious uses of power, like physics, engineering, and politics).

Simply accepting Kant's views about women is unacceptable not only because they conflict with contemporary assumptions, but also because they conflict with Kant's own transcendental anthropology.[4] Through all the particular anti-feminist and misogynistic claims in Kant's eventual account of women's nature, it is the inability for women in their own right to have the unconditional worth of a good will that is the most morally and philosophically problematic. Moral responsibility, worthiness to be considered an end-in-oneself, and the capacity for a good will are inextricably connected in Kant's transcendental anthropology. Kant explicitly claims that women must be treated as ends-in-themselves (6: 278, 280). And there is no evidence that he denies them moral *responsibility*. So Kant needs to provide an account of how women can be capable of moral worth. And doing this will require substantial revisions in his anthropology.

Today, there are two major and opposing responses to Kant's characterization of women. The dominant response among those sympathetic to Kant "is to say that Kant's views on women are mistaken, that one should instead concentrate on his more important philosophical achievements, and that one can simply leave his theory about the sexes behind" (Kleingeld 1993: 140). This response rejects Kant's anthropological characterization of women and extends his general anthropology to include women. Within such an approach, one would affirm – with Kant – that character and rationality are crucial to virtue, but add – against Kant – that women are no less capable of these traits than men. A second response, dominant amongst feminist critics of thinkers like Kant, is to argue that Kant's philosophy as a whole reflects his masculinist bias. Such critics typically agree with Kant's general anthropological claim that there are important differences between men and women, but reject his identification of what is universal and normative for "human beings" with what is universal and normative for men. Carol Gilligan, for example, suggests – with Kant – that for women "morality is conceived in interpersonal terms and goodness is equated with ... pleasing others" rather than in an "understanding of rights and rules" (Gilligan 1982: 2). While she rejects the view that this difference is either universal or essential, Gilligan – like the Kant of *Observations* – takes the "different voice" women bring to moral deliberation to be legitimate and needed to balance masculine emphasis on rule-following and personal autonomy (Gilligan 1982, see also Noddings 1984). While Gilligan focuses on differences in moral perspectives, other feminist thinkers have made similar points about Kant's transcendental anthropology more generally. His emphasis on reason and understanding over sensibility has been taken to reflect a masculinist bias in epistemology, one that puts "the Enlightenment conception of a universal, rational subject" above "feminist notions that the self is embedded in social relations, that the self is embodied, and is thus historically specific and partial" (Schott 1997: 8).

This divided response to Kant's thought highlights in contemporary form the problem that arises within Kant's own anthropology. Philosophers who find Kant's transcendental anthropology convincing have sought to jettison empirical–anthropological accounts of women than make them seem ill-suited for fulfilling requirements of that transcendental anthropology. But philosophers and empirical psychologists who study sex and gender often end up supporting, if not Kant's specific claims, at least accounts of gender differences that raise similar philosophical problems for a broadly Kantian account of moral and epistemic norms. What seemed to be a tension internal to Kant, one that he lamely resolved by simply settling into misogyny and ignoring the problems this raised for his transcendental anthropology, appears as a real problem for anyone who finds plausible both Kant's arguments for universal norms governing thought, choice, and feeling and the importance of empirical sensitivity to human differences in thinking about how those norms play out in the world.

One important way to deal with the tension would be through more careful and fine-grained approaches to both transcendental and empirical anthropology. These might find that women and men are not different in ways that have moral relevance. Even if, say, morality requires acting on principles and women tend to be more situational, this does not *necessarily* mean that they lack what is necessary for morality. Morality might *also* require situational sensitivity (see e.g. Herman 1993), and women might also be capable of morally principled action, even if not in the same way or to the same degree as men.

Another middle ground would accept both Kant's philosophical defense of norms that seem more masculine than feminine and empirical evidence of differences between sexes, but reject the teleological essentialism underlying Kant's explanation of those differences. The recent emphasis on distinguishing "sex" and "gender" fits into this general approach. Insofar as one's gender can be distinguished from one's biological sex, one need not identify biological sex (male/female) with the characteristics associated with particular genders (masculine/feminine), and one can largely ascribe gender characteristics to social factors. As Carol Gilligan emphasizes, "differences arise in a social context where factors of social status and power combine with reproductive biology to shape the experiences of males and females and the relations between the sexes" (Gilligan 1984: 2). Kant himself recognizes that the sex differences he discusses arise only in particular social and political contexts (7: 304) and his discussion of women's civil inequality (6: 314, 7: 204) remains at least open to the idea that women's civil immaturity is socially created rather than natural. Differences between men and women that inhibit women from fully realizing Kantian ideals of autonomy may be due to unjust social conditions that can and should be remedied. This approach could support increased attention to social and political reforms to create a world within which women would have as good a chance as men at measuring up to universally human moral (and other) norms. Kant, unfortunately, rejected this middle ground both in his anthropology – where he insists that differences between men and women are natural and not merely social (e.g. 25: 709) – and in his politics – where his explanation of the passive citizenship of "all women" is combined with both complacency and an account of marriage that seems to reinforce this civil inequality.

Finally, even if it does turn out that there are essential differences between men and women *and* that these differences make it considerably more difficult for women to attain to a good will, one might still – and

Kant certainly should — insist that it *is* possible for women to have unconditional moral worth. Modifying Kant's claim from *Religion* (see Chapter 3), we might say "In spite of [one's sex], the command that we ought to become better human beings still resounds unabated in our souls; consequently, we must also be capable of it" (6: 45). In this context, the difference between men and women would be akin to differences between temperaments, not a denial of the *possibility* of virtue for women, but a detailed attention to the fact that women will face greater and different challenges in progress toward virtue than men.

In the end, Kant's treatment of women, in the context of his anthropology as a whole, raises problems and tensions that continue even today to affect thinking about relations between the sexes, and between empirical and transcendental philosophy. But Kant not only rejects the most natural ways of dealing with these problems, but his infatuation with the "charming difference that nature sought to establish between the two human sexes" (2: 228) seems to have made him blindly and complacently unaware of them.

Racial and Ethnic Differences

Sex differences are not the only offensive and provocative part of Kant's anthropology. When Kant discusses racial and national character, he makes statements about other races that are, from our contemporary standpoint, outrageously racist. Moreover, Kant develops a complicated *theory* of race, one that played a role in the development of nineteenth-century scientific racism and thereby continues to affect the way in which races are conceived today. Finally, Kant's moral and political theory at times specifically addresses the relationships between people of different racial and ethnic groups. Precisely how these elements fit together is not always clear; and at least the first, and probably the second, share with Kant's views on women both immediate offensiveness and serious tension with his transcendental philosophy.

Throughout this section, I focus on racial rather than ethnic (or what Kant calls "national") differences.[5] Kant was (one of) the first thinker(s) to develop a scientific concept of "race," and many of his most outrageous comments about other peoples are comments about non-European races. The emphasis of this section on different races is due both to the presence of a systematic race theory in Kant's own writings and to the importance of "race" today. For Kant, however, differences amongst Europeans were at least as important as differences between Europeans and others. His published *Anthropology* includes a major section on differences amongst European nations but only two short paragraphs on the character of the races, and even his *Observations on the Feeling of the Beautiful and Sublime* devotes only a "quick look" to "other parts of the world" (2: 252) after offering a substantial discussion of differences between European people groups (French, Spanish, English, etc.) (2: 243–52).

Kant's Descriptions of Other Races

Kant's most disgraceful (published) claims about races are found in his *Observations on the Feeling of the Beautiful and Sublime*. After describing a conversation about the nature of women between an African carpenter and a European missionary, Kant writes of the African's comments, "There might be something here worth considering, except for the fact that this scoundrel was completely black from head to foot, a distinct proof that what he said was stupid" (2: 254–55). Kant's general characterization of black Africans in *Observations*, though painfully offensive, is also worth quoting:

> The *Negroes* of Africa have by nature no feeling that rises above the ridiculous. Mr. *Hume* challenges anyone to adduce a single example where a Negro has demonstrated talents, and asserts that among the hundreds of thousands of blacks who have been transported elsewhere from their countries, although very many of them have been set free, nevertheless not a single one has ever be found who has accomplished something great in art or science or shown any other praiseworthy quality, while among the whites there are always those who rise up from the lowest rabble and through extraordinary gifts earn respect in the world. So essential is the difference between these two human kinds, and it seems to be just as great with regard to the capacities of mind as it is with respect to color. The religion of fetishes which is widespread among them is perhaps a sort of idolatry, which sinks so deeply into the ridiculous as ever seems to be possible for human nature. A bird's feather, a cow's horn, a shell, or any other common thing, as soon as it is consecrated with some words, is an object of veneration and of invocation in swearing oaths. The blacks are very vain, but in the Negro's way, and so talkative that they must be driven apart from each other by blows.
>
> (2: 253)

This text does not represent the limit of Kant's offensive comments. In notes from his lecture course on *Anthropology*, Kant claims, in terms reminiscent of his comments about women:

> If we compare the character of the Oriental nations with the character of the Europeans, we here thus find an essential difference ... A capacity to act in accordance with concepts and principles is required for character. All Oriental nations are completely incapable of judgment in accordance with concepts ... All Oriental nations are not in the position to explain a single

property of morality or of justice through concepts; rather all their morals are based on appearance.

(25: 655)

And in his *Physical Geography*,[6] Kant offers a sort of summary of his views of the different races of the world:

> Humanity is at its greatest perfection in the race of the whites. The yellow Indians do have a meager talent. The Negroes are far below them and at the lowest point are a part of the American peoples.
>
> (*Physical Geography*, 9: 316, see also 25: 843[7])

These comments offer but a sample of the dismissive and demeaning views about non-Europeans scattered throughout Kant's writings and lectures.

Kant is not always *entirely* dismissive of other races. In *Observations*, he has some admiration for the "sublime cast of mind" of the "*savages ... of North America.*"

> *Lycurgus* probably gave laws to such savages, and if a law-giver were to arise among the six [Native American] nations, one would see a Spartan republic arise in the new world; just as the undertaking of the Argonauts is little different from the military expeditions of these Indians, and *Jason* has nothing over *Attakakullakulla* except the honor of a Greek name.
>
> (2: 253–54, though cf. 25: 1187)

Elsewhere Kant says that "Hindus ... have a strong degree of composure, ... they all look like philosophers, ... [and] they acquire culture in the highest degree" (25: 1187). On the whole, however, Kant's informal "observations" about other races reflect the prejudices of a European satisfied with the superiority of his own race and ready to believe the worst and most degrading claims about others.

To those who know Kant through his moral philosophy or the universal claims of his transcendental and empirical anthropology, these deeply disdainful comments about other races are disturbing to say the least. How should we respond to comments that seem so out of line with the respect for humanity that Kant emphasizes elsewhere in his work?

Unlike Kant's comments about sex, where many continue to argue that there are important differences between men and women that may be relevant to moral or epistemic issues, the notion that there are serious innate differences between races that would inhibit members of a particular race from being able to satisfy the demands of Kant's transcendental anthropology cannot be taken seriously. To those who know of Toni Morrison, Jacob Lawrence, Benjamin Banneker, or Wangari Maathai, Kant's reference to Hume's claim that "not a single [African] has ever been found who has accomplished something great in art or science" (2: 253) would display little more than laughable ignorance if it were not so appalling. With respect to race, the issue is not whether to accept Kant's racial distinctions and adjust his transcendental philosophy or vice versa. No serious thinker today can affirm Kant's racial observations. But two issues remain: first, whether Kant's views on non-white races taint the rest of his philosophy such that his claims about, say, moral norms or cultural progress must be abandoned because they are inextricably linked with racism, and second, how Kant – that champion of universal human dignity – could espouse views that seem to deny that dignity to most of the world.

One response to the first issue involves simply dismissing or ignoring Kant's racially offensive comments. While there are glimmers of Kant's views of other races in his more well-known writings – for example his reference in *Groundwork* to "the South Sea Islanders ... [who] let talents rust and are concerned with devoting life merely to idleness, amusement, [and] procreation" (4: 423) – by and large Kant's best read texts give little explicit indication of his racial views. It seems easy to excise these offensive texts from Kant's corpus, ignore them, and focus on the parts of Kant's thought that can and should be candidates for serious consideration today.

The advantages of this approach should be clear. Kant's philosophy has had profound impacts on metaphysics, epistemology, ethics, aesthetics, philosophy of religion, political theory, and so on. Kant's moral philosophy, in particular, continues to play important roles in safeguarding human rights and individual autonomy. Throwing out Kant's insights in these areas because of his personal views about other races is a waste. Moreover, Kant himself provides an important justification for leaving his racially offensive comments behind and focusing on the rest of his anthropology. For Kant, transcendental anthropology (epistemology, ethics, and even aesthetics) must be developed a priori; empirical insights – including observations about human differences – are relevant only later, in thinking about how to apply a priori norms to empirically situated human beings. Given Kant's own discipline in isolating his transcendental philosophy from his empirical observations, one seems justified in ignoring the latter and reaping the insights of the former.

That said, simply ignoring Kant's comments on race brings important dangers. One danger is that one risks misunderstanding those parts of Kant that one chooses to accept. Kant's apparently off-handed reference to the South Sea Islanders, for example, takes an important stand in eighteenth-century debates about the moral status of so-called "primitives." Most travelers' accounts, especially of Tahiti (rediscovered by Europeans in 1767), were both "morally provocative" – contrasting Europeans morals with those of the natives – and "complimentary," in that travelers to these places typically presented the lives of at least the Tahitians (and often other "savages" as well) as idyllic not only in terms of pleasures but also of morals (Wilson 1998: 317). Kant's insistence on the obligation to cultivate one's perfections (including non-moral talents) is an important part of his moral philosophy, one for which Kant offers an apparently universal justification. But in the context of Kant's claims about other races, this claim can be situated into a general Kantian defense of the superiority of the progressive historical self-conception of a European comparing himself to the rest of the world. In itself, this added insight does not give a reason to *reject* Kant's claim that humans ought to cultivate their talents. But it does force one to look more carefully at the justification and implications of that claim. Precisely how to understand claims that might otherwise seem to be universal, especially when these arise in Kant's transcendental anthropology, cannot be easily settled simply by pointing to Kant's views about races. But paying attention to these views can encourage more nuanced attention to Kant's philosophical views.

This point highlights other risks of simply ignoring Kant's views on race. Kant's claims about other races at least *seem* to conflict with other aspects of Kant's anthropology. At the very least, they raise questions about how Kant could have reconciled his universal anthropology with a view that "Negroes" are irredeemably stupid and "Orientals" incapable of concepts. Trying to figure out how Kant could have held together what seem to be such disparate views can open up new insights into the meaning, limits, and dangers of what might otherwise seem benign aspects of his philosophy (see Eze 1994, Larrimore 1999, Louden 2000). Alternatively, showing precisely the way in which, say, Kant's moral theory conflicts with these claims can reveal that moral theory as an important resource for overcoming racism today (Boxill and Hill 2001, Louden 2000). Finally, failing to pay attention to Kant's negative views on race can mark a missed opportunity to more fully understand the limits of philosophy itself. Investigating how Kant, who claims, "I would feel by far less useful than the common laborer if I did not believe that [my philosophy] could impart a value to all others in order to establish the rights of humanity" (20: 44), could hold such offensive views about other races can help reveal some of the causes that continue to prolong racism today.

Despite the dangers of simply *ignoring* Kant's racially offensive comments, however, dismissing Kant's whole philosophy as tainted by racism is worse. For one thing, Kant's transcendental anthropology has played an extremely important role in helping philosophers – and societies – see racism as unacceptable. Kant's moral emphasis on respect for each and every person is still one of the most powerful philosophical tools for combating racism. And as we will see in Chapter 8, even Kant's epistemological claim that our world is constructed in terms of imposed a priori categories has helped cultivate awareness of how *non*-universal categories of thought can shape experiences, an awareness crucial for cross-cultural understanding. And although Kant's interest in transforming the study of other cultures into a serious academic discipline was tainted, his conviction that being an educated world citizen requires understanding of not only universal characteristics of human beings but also human differences remains an important insight today. Finally, a considerable amount of Kant's philosophy, at least as that philosophy has been taken up and influences philosophers, can be freed of Kant's racist views. The mere fact that most readers of Kant – including those whose interpretations are most influential – are virtually (and often completely) unaware of his views on races shows that those views can, at least to a considerable degree, be understood and appreciated independently. As philosophers and scholars continue to explore the implications and impact of Kant's racial views on his philosophy as a whole, some interpretations of Kant will have to change, and some aspects of his views that might have seemed plausible will now raise more suspicion. But there is at present no reason to think that his philosophy as a whole will need to be dismissed simply because most of his claims about other races must be.

When we turn to how Kant could have held these views, one obvious response – simply ascribing Kant's racial stereotypes to his eighteenth-century background – is insufficient. On the one hand, his racist views are largely informed by popular prejudices. The contexts in which Kant's comments occur are almost entirely contexts in which Kant is deliberately seeking to write (or teach) in ways that will be "popular," "entertaining" for his readers and students (10: 146). *Observations*, in which his most outrageous claims occur, was Kant's most popular book during his lifetime and was written in part to attract students to his lectures. Because negative attitudes toward non-white racial groups were widely shared, Kant's demeaning comments would likely have enhanced his works' popularity. His working-class background may have encouraged him to draw divisions between people that would put himself and the upper-class students that he needed to attract to his lectures on the same side. Being a relatively poor intellectual who never went more than 90 miles from home, Kant was limited in his data about other races to accounts written by merchants, explorers, and missionaries. In fact, Kant's courses in Physical Geography and Anthropology were, at least in part, designed "to make a more certain knowledge of believable travel accounts and to make this into a legitimate course of study" (Wilson 2006: 3). Thus Kant was, to a considerable degree, limited by the biases and prejudices of the travel accounts to which he had access and the culture of which he was a part.

On the other hand, however, it is also clear that eighteenth-century thinking about non-white people was not *uniformly* negative. Kant's empirical sources were often much more generous in their observations than Kant, being written by travelers influenced by a moral ideal of simplicity that seemed well-exhibited in the exotic peoples they observed (Wilson 1998). Among the most important alternative theoretical ways of thinking about races were those of Kant's own student Herder, who, drawing from similar travel logs and empirical sources, developed a much less patronizing view of non-European nations, and Georg Forster, who not only published travel accounts of his own that emphasized much more positive views of non-Europeans but also specifically criticized Kant's own race theory as being insufficiently egalitarian. In both cases, Kant fought *against* more generous portrayals of other races. In his review of Herder's *Ideas*, Kant even wrote:

> [F]rom a multiplicity of descriptions of countries one can prove, if one wants to, that Americans, Tibetans, and other genuine Mongolian peoples have no beard, but also, if it suits you better, that all of them are by nature bearded ...; that Americans and Negroes are each a race, sunk beneath the remaining of the human species in their mental predispositions, but on the other side by just as apparent records that ... they are to be estimated equal to every other inhabitant of the world; so it remains to the choice of the philosopher whether he wants to assume differences in nature or wants to judge everything in accordance with the principle "Everything is as it is with us."
>
> (8: 62)

This self-awareness about the process of picking and choosing amidst empirical data shows how Kant *could* – even with his sources and his cultural baggage – have developed a different view of non-white races. And Kant should have seen the inconsistency of his dismissal of other races with his own personal and philosophical trajectory. In the end, while one can point to reasons for Kant's demeaning views of other races in his cultural context, Kant's own words require him to acknowledge "the choice of the philosopher." And while one might understand this choice in terms of pleasing the crowd (especially given the public purpose of his *Observations*) or even in terms simply of making his best attempt at getting things right (given the pedagogical purpose of his physical geography and anthropology lectures), one must also admit that Kant, despite his acuity in some areas of philosophy, was neither sufficiently thoughtful nor sufficiently courageous in thinking about other races.

Kant's Race Theory

Kant's most extreme claims about race come in early or informal works, largely disconnected from any formal theory about races. But over a decade after the publication of *Observations*, Kant wrote an essay entitled "Of the different races of human beings" that marked the beginning of a series of papers in which Kant "invented the concept of race" (Bernasconi 2001: 11) or at least became "a leading proponent of the concept of race at a time when its scientific status was still far from secure" (Bernasconi 2002: 146). Kant's racially offensive but informal remarks bear a greater superficial similarity to present-day racism. But his race *theory* arguably played a more significant role in creating conditions for present-day racism by giving "the concept [of race] sufficient definition for subsequent users to believe that they were addressing something whose scientific status could at least be debated" (Bernasconi 2001: 11).

In one respect, Kant's theory of race was deeply *anti*-racist, in that Kant was a staunch defender of "monogenesis" – the view that human beings are a single species derived from a common ancestor – during a period in which polygenesis – the view that, for instance, black Africans and white Europeans are different *species* – was gaining prominence. The different behavior and physical appearance of distant peoples challenged the limits of the European imagination to the point that postulating different species seemed a natural response to the discomforting possibility that "we" and "they" were the same sort of being. At the same time, biological science lacked a universally accepted criterion for determining commonality of species.

In response to the growing interest in polygenesis, Kant sought a scientific account of the human species that would reconcile monogenesis with Europeans' desire to distinguish between people with recognizable and heritable differences. The essence of Kant's account is to distinguish "species" from "race." For "species," Kant adopts from his contemporary Buffon what has come to be the standard account in contemporary biology: "animals that produce fertile young with one another ... belong to one and the same physical species" (2: 429). Thus, "all human beings on the wide earth belong to one and the same natural species because they consistently beget fertile children with one another" (2: 430). Because interfertility does not *necessarily* imply common ancestry, Kant makes his mono*genesis* explicit: "[H]uman beings belong not merely to one and the same *species*, but also to one *family*, [since otherwise] many local creations [of members of the same species] would have to be assumed – an opinion which needlessly multiplies the number of causes" (2: 430).

Having settled on monogenesis, Kant explains heritable diversity with his concept of a race:

> Among ... the hereditary differences of animals which belong to a single [species], those which persistently preserve themselves in all transplantings (transpositions to other regions) over prolonged generations among

themselves and which also always beget half-breed young in the mixing with other variations of the same [species] are called *races*.

(2: 430)

To distinguish racial characteristics from merely environmental differences, Kant insists that racial differences must persist over many generations even after the relevant "race" is transplanted to a different place. Racial differences must also *blend* when members of different races interbreed to distinguish racial differences from what Kant calls "strains" (2: 430).

> In this way, *Negroes* and *whites*, while not different kinds of human beings ..., are still two *different races* because each of the two perpetuates itself in all regions and both necessarily beget ... *blends* (mulattoes) with one another. By contrast, *blondes* and *brunettes* are not difference *races* of whites, because a blond man can have entirely blond children with a brunette woman.
>
> (2: 431)

As this example suggests, Kant argues that *skin color* "is especially suited" for dividing races (8: 94–95). He thus divides humans into "four classificatory differences ... with respect to skin color ...[:] the *whites*, the *yellow* Indians, the *Negroes*, and the *copper-red* Americans" (8: 93).

For Kant, merely defining the concept of race is insufficient. Kant also aims to show how the concept of race can be illuminated by his overall philosophy of biology, and in particular by the role of natural teleology in empirical anthropology. Thus Kant uses his account of natural predispositions to explain both *how* and *why* human beings became differentiated into different races. Starting with the *purpose* of racial differentiation, Kant claims, "The human species was destined for all climates and for every soil; consequently, various germs and natural predispositions had to lie ready in him to be on occasion either unfolded or restrained" (2: 435). Different racial characteristics are well-suited for different climates. Given Nature's end – for humans to settle the entire globe – human beings had a variety of predispositions that could develop in accordance with different local conditions "so that he would become suited to his place" (2: 435). For Kant, however, variability with local conditions is not *merely* an ability to adapt; it has a hereditary component:

> Once a race ... had established itself ... this race could not be transformed into another one through any influences of the climate. For only the [original representatives of the species] can degenerate[8] into a race; however, once a race has taken root and suffocated the other germs, it resists all transformation just because the character of the race has then become prevailing in the generative power.
>
> (2: 442)

What begins as a mere lack of expression of certain natural "germs" (proto-predispositions) becomes, over time, a "suffocation" of those germs. It is unclear whether Kant intends to say that the germs literally die out, or – more likely – that a propensity for them not to express themselves becomes hereditary. In either case, individual adaptations to climate become fixed characteristics. And this, too, has a natural purpose, so that human beings, "over the course of generations … appear to be … made for that place" in which they reside (2: 435). Nature intends not only for human beings to spread all over the globe, but also for humans to fit well wherever they find themselves. Kant thus charts a middle path between those who claim that human beings are biologically distinct and those who claim that differences are environmental. Differences between human beings are caused by environmental factors, but at least some of these differences become hereditary.

In many respects, Kant's formal theory of race is less problematic than his informal negative comments about various races. With rare exceptions, Kant's race essays refrain from describing moral or intellectual qualities as hereditary, and the claim that skin color is necessarily hereditary is not, in itself, particularly offensive. Arguably, Kant's account of race is even an important step toward a broadly Darwinian account of the possibility of environmentally caused hereditable changes in given populations. But Kant's race theory raises three new problems for assessing Kant's philosophy as a whole. First, the stagnation of various natural predispositions within Kant's race theory raises the stakes of his disparaging comments. If other races have literally lost the *capacity* for moral or intellectual advancement, this poses problems for Kant's moral theory and philosophy of history that are similar to those raised in the context of the sexes (where women seemed incapable of moral worth). Second, whatever its relationship to his moral theory, Kant's race theory seems deeply intertwined with the account of natural teleology in his *Critique of Judgment*, which provides the capstone of transcendental anthropology. Even if Kant's transcendental anthropology could be isolated from Kant's informal comments about races, it seems harder to isolate his race *theory*. Finally, even if Kant's race theory is not as immediately offensive as the comments discussed in the last section, by contributing to the development of a scientific, skin-color-based conception of race, Kant arguably played a real historical role in the development of modern racism.

With respect to the first issue, Kant's works provide mixed evidence about the extent to which he conceived of moral and intellectual attributes as irremediably fixed in races. In *Observations*, the early essay with Kant's most atrocious claims about races, Kant adds a crucial footnote:

> My intention is not at all to portray the characters of the peoples in detail; rather I will only outline some features … [O]nly a tolerable level of

accuracy can be demanded in such a depiction, ... and no nation is lacking in casts of mind which unite the foremost predominant qualities. ... For this reason the criticism that might occasionally be cast on a people can offend no one, as it is like a ball that one can always hit to his neighbor.

(2: 243n)

Later, Kant reiterates,

In each people the finest portion contains praiseworthy characters of all sorts, and whoever is affected by one or another criticism will, if he is fine enough, understand it to his advantage, which lies in leaving everyone else to his fate but making an exception of himself.

(2: 245n)

Here differences between peoples are like those between temperaments, natural advantages or disadvantages that can be overcome. Readers should take negative characterizations of their nation or race as exhortations to moral strength rather than signs of inextricable inferiority. Moreover, although Kant refers to differences between Europeans and Africans as "essential" (2: 253), his early comments on racial differences stick to the level of "observations." Kant even claims,

I will not investigate here whether these national differences are contingent and depend upon the times and the type of government, or whether they are connected with a certain necessity with the climate.

(2: 243n)

Because this section focuses on "The Character of the *Nations*," including non-European races as an afterthought, the footnotes *might* be restricted to Europeans. But they show a way that Kant could reconcile claims about races with his universalist moral theory. And even when Kant develops his formal race theory, in which he argues for essential and hereditary racial characteristics, he insists that "no characteristic property other [than skin color] is *necessarily hereditary*" (8: 94). Thus in anthropology lectures delivered the year Kant published his "Of the different races of human beings," he insists that the "savage Indian or Greenlander ... has the same germs ... as a civilized human being" (25: 694). In these and other passages, Kant seems to endorse the view that whatever moral and intellectual differences there are between races can be overcome.

However, Kant's racial comments often imply heritable and unchangeable moral and intellectual inferiority. Kant's rankings of various races (e.g. 2: 441), and his claim that differences between Africans and Europeans are "essential" and "just as great with regard to the capacities of mind as ... with respect to color" (2: 253), imply as much. And although his formal race essays emphasize skin color, the last of these essays describes Native Americans as *"incapable* of any culture" (8: 176, emphasis added, cf. 10: 239), and the first ascribes to them a "half-extinguished life power" while describing Africans as "lazy, soft, and trifling" (2: 438). Perhaps the most systematic-sounding claim comes in a footnote of Kant's last race essay. Here, in the context of a discussion of whether African slaves could be used as free laborers, Kant writes:

> Should one not conclude ... that in addition to the *faculty* to work, there is also an immediate drive to activity (especially to the sustained activity that one calls industry), which ... is especially interwoven with certain natural predispositions; and that Indians as well as Negroes do not bring any more of this impetus into other climates and pass it on to their offspring than was needed for their preservation in their old motherland ... [where t]he far lesser needs ... demand no greater predispositions to activity.
>
> (8: 174n)

Strictly speaking, Kant does not claim that Negroes or Indians are *incapable* of activity or industry, but he does suggest a biological basis for the "laziness" ascribed to them in earlier essays, which brings motivational characteristics into the realm of biologically fixed racial differences. In the end, Kant does not strictly commit himself to race differences with moral implications as profound as those of sex, but even insofar as he approaches these sorts of views, Kant's moral philosophy gives decisive reasons to treat Kant's characterizations of various races the way Kant suggests in *Observations*, as a catalogue of traits to which individuals can and should make exceptions of themselves. Even this way of reading Kant is hardly without danger. Members of racial groups classified as having particular defects can come either to be demoralized through Kant's theory or to overcompensate, trying to "prove themselves" in ways that go beyond the actual demands of moral and cultural life. Even interpreted in the most generous way, Kant's race theory brings problems, and taken too far, it could license the worst racist abuses, as Kant's seeming support of slavery in the footnote above might forebode.

On the second issue – the relationship between Kant's race theory and his *Critique of Judgment* – it would be nice to say, as we did with Kant's informal observations about race, that one can insulate his Critical philosophy from his race theory. In fact, however, as Robert Bernasconi has rightly pointed out, "Kant's understanding of race is at stake in the discussion of teleology in the *Critique of Judgment*" (Bernasconi 2002: 147). But the relationship between race theory, teleology, and the central aspects of Kant's Critical philosophy (and with it, transcendental anthropology) is not as problematic as some commentators (e.g. Eze 1994) have suggested because it tends to be unidirectional. Race theory supports Kant's philosophy of biology by showing a particularly interesting way in which it can be applied, but the general points Kant uses in his race theory – such as the distinction between natural history and mere description of nature (2: 434n, 8: 153f) or the legitimacy of teleological principles in biology (8: 157–84) – are, as Kant recognizes, compatible with different empirical accounts depending upon the empirical details to which they are applied. Where Kant's race theories go astray is not at the level of these general methodological principles but in their specific and misguided application. Thus while problems with the accounts of judgment and teleology in the *Critique of Judgment* could undermine Kant's race theory, abandoning his race theory altogether, if done for empirical and not methodological reasons, would not jeopardize his *Critique*. Kant's more general philosophy of biology does not *preclude* scientific racism, which may be an indictment of a sort, but it also does not *imply* it.

The final issue – the role of Kant in the development of modern racism – is complicated. Kant's defense of monogenesis and emphasis on physical rather than moral or intellectual characteristics is what one might expect a thoughtful, cosmopolitan humanitarian to develop in the eighteenth century. As a way of making sense of the confusing array of anthropological discoveries faced by Europeans coming into greater contact with the rest of the world, Kant's race theory might have seemed well-suited to his moral ideals. All human beings are a single species and hence – one would think – equally worthy of respect. But there are real, hereditary, biological differences between people that manifest in their physical appearance. So far, so good.

But Kant's racial views were not *in fact* limited to physical characteristics. We have seen this in Kant's own life, where he combined a scientific account of race with an intensely negative characterization of non-Europeans. But the same held true for those who appropriated the concept of race as a scientific concept in the nineteenth and twentieth centuries. Given the role that "scientific racism" came to play in the entrenchment of racist ideology, especially in Europe and the Americas (see Gould 1981), Kant's role in making this science possible implicates him in those racist ideologies, even if only indirectly. Kant's concept of race was not, of course, the most important influence on racism (even scientific racism) in the twentieth century; Darwin was more important. And if Kant's personal views were different, his overall place in the history of racism might well be that of the well-intentioned but naïve humanitarian attempting to combat proto-racist tendencies through science, whose science ended up working to promote racism. But given Kant's personal views about race and the fact that his race theory *did* in fact end up playing a real role in the development of what has come to be modern-day racism, Kant must – unfortunately – be given a prominent a place in the history of racism as he has in the histories of human rights, aesthetics, theology, and other fields where his impact has been more positive.

Political Issues: Slavery and Colonialism

When Kant turns from *descriptions* of different races to *prescriptions* for how to deal with members of other races, the merits of his moral philosophy overwhelm his empirical anthropology. The two most important issues facing Europeans in their interactions with other races were the closely connected issues of colonialism and race-based slavery. And Kant's later political writings involve detailed and impassioned rejections of both. With respect to slavery, Kant's published writings are clear and direct.[9] He refers to West Indian slavery as "the cruelest and most calculated" (8: 359) and insists in his *Metaphysics of Morals* not only that no one may sell himself into slavery (6: 270) but also that *any* relationship between master and servant can be "at most only for an unspecified time, within which one party may give the other notice" and "children … are at all times free" (6: 283). Whatever forms of indentured servitude might be allowed, the chattel slavery associated with the slave trade and European (especially British) colonialism are excluded.

Regarding colonialism in general, Kant is eloquent:

> If one compares [the duty to universal hospitality] with the *inhospitable* behavior of civilized, especially commercial, states in our part of the world, the injustice they show in *visiting* foreign lands and people (which with them is tantamount to conquering them) goes to horrifying lengths. When America, the negro countries, … and so forth were discovered, they were, to them, countries belonging to no one, since they counted the inhabitants as nothing. In the East Indies (Hindustan), they brought in foreign soldiers under the pretext of merely proposing to set up trading posts, but [brought] with them the oppression of the inhabitants, incitement of the various Indian states to widespread wars, famine, rebellions, treachery, and the whole litany of troubles that oppress the human race.
>
> (8: 358–59)

Kant not only vehemently rejects "counting [non-white peoples] as nothing," but he shows a surprisingly degree of insight into the deceptive justifications for standard practices of European colonialism. In his *Metaphysics of Morals*, Kant returns to the issue of colonialism. Kant claims that "all nations stand *originally* in a community of land" but emphasizes that this does *not* give anyone the right to possess any land they find. Instead, Kant emphasizes the right of first possession (6: 263) and specifically applies this to the case of "newly discovered lands":

> If the settlement [of these lands] is made so far from where [the local] people reside that there is no encroachment on anyone's use of his land, the right to settle is not open to doubt. But if these people are shepherds or hunters (like the Hottentots, the Tungusi, or most of the American Indian nations) who depend for their sustenance on great open regions, this settlement may not take place by force but only by contract, and indeed by a contract that does not take advantage of the ignorance of those inhabitants with respect to ceding their lands. This is true despite ... it [being] to the world's advantage ... [A]ll these supposedly good intentions cannot wash away the stain of injustice in the means used for them.
>
> (6: 353)

Again, Kant not only rejects the practice of seizing land in the "New" World, but specifically addresses two of the main ways in which this practice is justified, through appeals to the greater good and through spurious "contracts." Despite his personal views about the capacities of non-white peoples, Kant has no tolerance for failing to afford them the rights consistent with our common humanity, and he eloquently defends those rights against encroaching European colonial practices.

There are at least two important ways of reading Kant's moral and political stances toward other races, both of which partially redeem Kant. First, one might rightly point out that Kant's moral theory emphasizes the importance of respect for the humanity of others, where humanity primarily involves the mere capacity for choice. Just as Kant insists that a person's (radical) evil does not justify denying them respect, so he should equally insist that whatever differences there are between Europeans and non-Europeans, as long as non-Europeans are human beings with a capacity for choice, they must be respected. In that sense, Kant's moral arguments against slavery and colonialism are not only consistent with his overall moral theory but also show the power of that moral theory even in the face of extreme personal prejudice. Second, one might find in Kant's political writings some hint that Kant's views on other races changed in response to criticisms by Forster, Herder, and others (see Kleingeld 2007). The comments in which Kant is disparaging of other races gradually cease after 1792, such that Kant's *Anthropology* (published in 1798), while in other respects following the general outline of his *Observations*, refrains from making any mention of his views on race, instead referring readers to a text by another author. This has led at least one scholar to argue that "Kant changed and improved his position [on race] during the 1790s" (Kleingeld 2007: 3).

Neither of these ways of reading Kant's later work justifies his racially offensive comments. The fact that in his later years Kant did not use negative characterizations of other races to justify slavery or colonialism does not take away the real harm of depicting them as naturally inferior to whites, and Kant was well aware of the damage to one's personhood that comes from damaging the way that one is perceived in the eyes of others. Even changing his views eventually does not justify Kant's holding them for as long as he did. But just as Kant's other writings on race show the limits of Kant's moral philosophy, these later texts show some of its power. At the very least, the emphasis on universal human dignity in his moral philosophy helped prevent Kant from drawing the worst practical implications of his early views on other races. At best, his philosophy may have even helped him see the errors of those views.

Summary

Kant's anthropology has been criticized for being excessively universal, for painting all humans with the same brush and ignoring the differences between them, for being insufficiently attentive to the idiosyncratic, masculine, or European perspective from which Kant writes. Kant himself was deeply attuned to these concerns. Even before he started developing an a priori transcendental anthropology, Kant insisted on teaching a course in physical geography to "make good [his students'] lack of experience" and equip them to function in the world. An important part of this course was exposing his students to the variety of manners and types of people in the world, and from his early *Observations* to his eventual courses (and book) in anthropology, Kant expanded this part of his geography course to include detailed accounts of human difference.

This attention to human difference as important for being an active world citizen is an admirable aspect of Kant's overall anthropology, but the details of Kant's accounts reveal a darker side to such attention. Kant's resources for understanding human diversity were limited. He never married and his primary knowledge of women was through formal dinner parties and English novels. He never traveled, so his primary knowledge of non-Europeans (and even most Europeans) was from books written by others. Kant made the most of books, voraciously reading travel logs, novels, scientific and medical treatises, and other accounts of human difference. But even with this background, Kant recognized that ultimately "the choice of the philosopher" plays a significant role in how such data is interpreted. And Kant's choices, with respect to both women and non-Europeans, were generally reprehensible. With respect to both women and other races, Kant not only gave isolated disparaging remarks, but also developed theories rooted in his natural teleology that essentialized sexual and racial differences. What could have been a significant *improvement* to Kant's anthropology now serves as a *warning* about the dangers of supplementing a transcendental anthropology with an empirical one, and especially of supplementing a universal anthropology with an account of diversity. Despite its errors and dangers, however, Kant's account of human diversity is an important part of his overall account of human beings, and his insistence that human difference is an important part of what makes us who we are is an insistence that continues to resonate today.

Further Reading

Very little has been written about Kant's views on forms of diversity other than race and gender, but Louden and Cohen both discuss diversity (including temperament, women, and race) in their more general treatments of Kant's anthropology.

Alix Cohen, *Kant and the Human Sciences* (London: Palgrave Macmillan, 2009)
Robert Louden, *Kant's Impure Ethics* (London: Oxford University Press, 2000)

Schott 1997 has the fullest collection of articles discussing Kant's views on women, and Schott 1993 is a general discussion of what she sees as a dangerous Kantian overemphasis on pure reason. Louden has further references in his brief discussion of Kant on women in Louden 2000 (above). Shell discusses Kant's shifting views on women especially during the 1760s.

Robin May Schott, *Feminist Interpretations of Immanuel Kant* (University Park, PA: Pennsylvania State University Press, 1997)
Robin May Schott, *Cognition and Eros: A Critique of the Kantian Paradigm* (Pennsylvania State University Press, 1993)
Susan Meld Shell, *The Embodiment of Reason* (Chicago: University of Chicago Press, 1996)

Commentators on Kant's view of race divide between those who think that these views taint the rest of Kant's philosophy (Eze, Larrimore) and those who think the rest of his philosophy can be saved (Boxill and Hill). Louden 2000 (above) gives a good overview of this debate. Eigen and Larrimore 2006 has a significant and helpful set of essays on Kant. Kleingeld (see especially chapter four) has reshaped debate by suggesting that Kant's views on race changed. Bernasconi is the most important and sophisticated writer on the subject.

Robert Bernasconi, "Kant as an Unfamiliar Source of Racism" in J. Ward and T. Lott (eds.) *Philosophers on Race: Critical Essays* (Oxford: Blackwell, 2002)
Robert Bernasconi, "Who Invented the Concept of Race?" in R. Bernasconi (ed.) *Race* (Oxford: Blackwell, 2001)

Bernard Boxill and Thomas Hill Jr., "Kant and Race" in B. Boxill (ed.) *Race and Racism* (Oxford: Oxford University Press, 2001)

Sara Eigen and Mark Larrimore (eds.) *The German Invention of Race* (Albany, NY: SUNY Press, 2006)

Emmanue Eze, "The Colour of Reason: The Idea of 'Race' in Kant's Anthropology" in K.M. Faull (ed.) *Anthropology and the German Enlightenment* (Lewisburg, PA: Bucknell University Press, 1994)

Pauline Kleingeld, *Kant and Cosmopolitanism: The Philosophical Ideal of World Citizenship* (Cambridge: Cambridge University Press, 2012)

5 Kant's Pragmatic Anthropology

The previous four chapters examined the transcendental and empirical "anthropologies" expressed in various written works and unpublished lectures composed by Kant over his lifetime. At the end of his life, however, when Kant wrote the only published work he entitled *Anthropology*, this book was neither *Transcendental Anthropology* nor *Empirical Anthropology* but *Anthropology from a Pragmatic Point of View*. And throughout his life, Kant taught "Anthropology" courses that cannot be described as either transcendental or empirical. Instead, what Kant sought to do, throughout his life and especially in *Anthropology from a Pragmatic Point of View*, was to develop a *new* approach to thinking about human beings, one that combined theoretical insight into human nature with humans' fundamental practical concerns, and one that avoided stale, metaphysical debates about such things as the relationship between mind and body, while providing a useful, philosophically sophisticated, systematic answer to the question "What is the human being?" In his "pragmatic" anthropology, Kant pulls together his transcendental and empirical anthropologies into a coherent whole that can help his readers "properly fulfill [their] station in creation" (20: 41). While not the arena within which Kant answers all the questions of philosophy, pragmatic anthropology marks a culmination of Kant's anthropology where he most fully combines philosophical insights with empirical–psychological observations of human beings in order to *improve* humans' cognition, feelings, and actions.

The Scope of Pragmatic Anthropology

Kant discusses "anthropology" in various published works, most famously in his *Groundwork* and *Metaphysics of Morals*, where he explains that "ethics" will have an "empirical part" called "practical anthropology," which will "deal ... with the subjective conditions in human nature that help or hinder in fulfilling the laws of a metaphysics of morals" (6: 217). Kant's discussion of humans' radical evil also requires some explanation for how one can work to undo and arm oneself against self-wrought evil

tendencies, an explanation that one would expect from moral anthropology. One might think, then, that Kant's *Anthropology from a Pragmatic
Point of View* would provide this much-needed supplement for his pure
moral philosophy.

Anthropology from a Pragmatic Point of View provides this moral supplement,
but goes further, aiming to "disclose the basis of … everything that pertains
to the practical" (10: 146). This broad understanding of pragmatic as "practical" shows up early in Kant's published *Anthropology*. Kant distinguishes
"pragmatic" anthropology from "physiological" ones because whereas the
latter emphasize "what nature makes of the human being," pragmatic
anthropology attends to "what *he* as a free-acting being makes … or can
and should make of himself" (7: 119). More specifically, while the physiological anthropologist looks at the neurophysical bases of mental powers,
"he must admit that in this play of his representations he is a mere
observer and must let nature run its course, for he does not understand
how to put [these neurophysical bases] to use for his purposes" (7: 119).
In contrast, the pragmatic anthropologist focuses on that "knowledge of
the human being" that is *useful* for, say, improving memory; this anthropologist "uses perceptions concerning what has been found to hinder or
stimulate memory in order to enlarge it or make it agile" (7: 119).

Kant's particular example of memory is important for clarifying what
exactly is meant when Kant refers to the subject matter of pragmatic
anthropology as something that "concerns … the investigation of what he
as a free-acting being … can and should make of himself." In particular,
pragmatic anthropology need not take the free subject of transcendental
anthropology as its *topic*. In the rest of Kant's *Anthropology*, not only
through his stated methodology (7: 120–22) but also in practice, the
information about human beings that makes up the content of pragmatic
anthropology is empirical.[1] In an important sense, then, pragmatic
anthropology has no distinctive content of its own. Elsewhere, Kant even
refers to its principles as mere "scholia" of empirical "knowledge of [human]
nature" (20: 199). But pragmatic anthropology is concerned with free-
acting human beings in that it is *addressed to* human agents who can *make
use* of empirical knowledge for accomplishing (freely chosen) goals.

When one asks where the ends served by pragmatic anthropology arise,
one must look to transcendental anthropology in the broadest sense. It is
only from within the standpoints of thinking, feeling, and willing that one
comes to discover – at least in outline – what the human being *should*
make of himself. As freely acting beings, human beings find themselves
with two main orienting principles of volition: happiness and duty. And
from the start, Kant recognized that these orienting principles require
considerable empirical knowledge for their application. Happiness is
"such an indeterminate concept that although every human being wishes

to attain this, he can still never say determinately and consistently with himself what he really wishes and wills" (4: 418) and even moral laws require "a judgment sharpened by experience ... to distinguish in what cases they are applicable and ... to provide them with access to the will of the human being" (4: 389). Kant's pragmatic anthropology fills in the empirical knowledge of human nature that is required to discern not only the means for pursuing one's ends but even to what ends free but finite human agents should devote attention.

Moral Anthropology

For Kant, the one end "good without limitation" (4: 393) is the good will, so Kant's pragmatic must include *moral* anthropology. This "moral anthropology" is a necessary empirical supplement to "pure" moral philosophy. Precisely what moral anthropology contributes is disputed and even seems to shift between Kant's earlier *Groundwork* and later *Metaphysics of Morals*. We can distinguish two ways empirical anthropology might supplement moral philosophy. First, and most obviously, we might need what Kant, in *Groundwork*, refers to as a "judgment sharpened by experience ... to distinguish in what cases [moral principles] are applicable" (4: 389). For generating specific principles from the categorical imperative, we need empirical information about human beings. For example, the obligation not to make false promises applies to only beings like ourselves, not, for instance, to the extra-terrestrials Kant imagines in his *Anthropology*, "who could not think in any other way but aloud" (7: 332). We might also use empirical facts about human desires to specify and apply our general obligation to promote others' happiness, and we can use facts about human limitations to set boundaries for various human interactions. As we will see at the end of the next section, Kant does see pragmatic anthropology as playing important roles in this sort of application of moral principles to human life. But this role is not the role of "moral anthropology" strictly speaking.

Instead, "moral anthropology" is concerned with a second way of putting empirical anthropology to use for moral philosophy: "Moral anthropology ... deal[s] with the development, spreading, and strengthening of moral principles" (6: 217). Empirical insight is needed to "make human beings ready to follow [moral laws]" (27: 244) and even to "give duties the power of inclinations" (25: 1437, cf. 25: 471–72, 734–35). That is, one can use empirical knowledge about how human volition actually works in order to help human beings – both oneself and others – act on the basis of the moral law. This task of putting empirical knowledge to use for moral improvement is particularly important, for Kant, because of the problem of radical evil diagnosed in Chapter 3. Human beings not only perform evil acts but also cultivate tendencies to do more evil. In response to the problem of human evil, Kant proposes both a theological solution – God's grace – and a new practical orientation. In Chapter 3, we emphasized Kant's practical focus on human *historicity* and *ethical community*. But this focus is supplemented by moral anthropology. Given radical evil, the best human beings can do with respect to morality is to "remain forever armed for battle," "under the leadership of the good principle, against the attacks of the evil principle" (6: 93). This arming involves an unending effort to *strengthen* the good principle and *weaken* the evil principle in one's empirical character, an effort facilitated through empirical knowledge of how human volition actually works.

Thus Kant develops moral anthropology, which applies empirical anthropology to the problem of how to cultivate virtue in human agents. Throughout his moral philosophy, Kant emphasizes the *practical–pedagogical* importance of presenting the moral law in all its purity (e.g. 4: 390, 5: 156), and not only offers a "moral catechism" (6: 480), but sketches a model of how to use stories of moral heroes to bring a "ten-year old boy ... to a lively wish that he himself could be such a [virtuous] man" (5: 155–56). Kant's lectures on pedagogy discuss how to cultivate the moderation and self-discipline that support virtue. And Kant's lectures on ethics attend to how "a person may be compelled to duty by others" (27: 521) through careful articulation of moral responsibilities. Unsurprisingly, then, Kant's *Anthropology from a Pragmatic Point of View* includes substantial attention to empirical features of human beings that are particularly salient for the cultivation of moral virtue and even ends with an impassioned reiteration of humans' moral vocation (see 7: 330–33). The rest of this section highlights four examples from *Anthropology* that show Kant's moral emphasis: politeness as an aid to virtue, passions and affects as hindrances to virtue, character as a necessary ground for virtue, and understanding diversity to cultivate morals properly.

For Kant, politeness is a "duty to oneself as well as to others" (6: 473), but also a "permissible moral illusion" (7: 151). Against philosophers like Hume and Smith, Kant emphasizes how politeness is significantly different in kind from truly moral action; it is a "mere external ... which give[s] a beautiful illusion [merely] resembling virtue" (6: 473). But against Rousseau, Kant insists that this merely external show of virtue can, over time, "promote a virtuous disposition" (6: 474). *Anthropology* uses empirical facts about human beings – such as the "tendency to willingly allow himself to be deceived" – to demonstrate how engaging in shows of virtue can, over time, help a person combat the evil principle and cultivate genuine virtue (see Frierson 2005).

While politeness aids virtue, passions and affects are prime examples of moral hindrances. Both are "illness[es] of mind" (7: 251), degrees of emotional agitation that prevent reflection. Both preclude a good will, since the reflection necessary to be motivated by the moral law is absent, but how they preclude the good will is different. Affects, such as sudden rage or shock, are an extreme and passing form of weak or frail will, where one is simply overcome by feeling and engages in no reflection at all. Fortunately, affects are passing, and one afflicted by affect can, during cool, calm hours, take steps to prevent further outbursts. Passions, such as vengeful hatred or lust for power, are akin to depraved wills but focused, not on overall happiness, but solely on a single end. Kant's taxonomy of mental faculties and overall empirical account of human action explain the difference between these mental illness and why passions are "incurable" (7: 266) and "properly evil" (6: 408) while affects are merely a passing "lack of virtue" (6: 408).

Kant follows his discussion of affects and passions with an account of "character" that pulls together his empirical treatment of character with his moral philosophy. Character – the "property of the will by which the subject binds himself to definite practical principles" (7: 292) – is the surest antidote to passions, affects, and even ordinary human emotional fluctuations that can be problematic to moral life. And character is necessary in order to have a will that is stably and purely bound to the moral law as its principle. Thus Kant's *Anthropology* devotes considerable attention to cataloging measures that one can take to cultivate genuine character.

After discussing individual character – the sort so prominent in his empirical theory of the higher faculty of desire – Kant also discusses other sorts of "character," including the character of different nations and races, and various "influences on character," including temperament. Kant's moral anthropology, especially when it comes to the matter of character, absorbs his interest in diversity. And in this context, his treatments of diversity take on a special moral importance. In particular, Kant often highlights the diverse "struggles against the evil principle" that different people will have. In describing the sanguine as "not ... evil ... but ... a sinner hard to convert [because] he regrets ... much but quickly forgets this regret" (7: 288) or the phlegmatic as one who "proceeds from principles" even when lacking "wisdom" (7: 290), Kant highlights different emphases for moral cultivation in these two sorts of people. And Kant's claims that French "vivacity is not sufficiently kept in check by considered principles" (7: 313) or that Germans "have a tendency to imitation ...[,] a mania for punctiliousness and ... a need for methodical division" (7: 318–19) show that these two nations face different challenges in the cultivation of (moral) character (7: 293). Kant's pragmatic attention to empirical differences between human beings often focuses on just those "subjective conditions" relevant for moral anthropology.

Of course, nothing in Kant's anthropology dictates empirical causes of good wills since a good will cannot be empirically caused. But Kant lays out empirical causes of and practical advice for cultivating character, highlights particular moral challenges that will be faced by those of varying temperaments and national origins, and describes resources for progress in the species as a whole. Because all of these considerations are empirical, they cannot ultimately determine whether one's free, noumenal choice is for good or evil. But a person who recognizes radical evil and earnestly seeks every resource to combat the "evil principle" within her knows that merely choosing rightly in a particular case is insufficient for moral progress. For radically evil human beings, virtue requires taking one's life as a whole to be a battlefield between one's evil tendencies to self-deceptive moral complacency and one's moral struggle to revolt against those tendencies. Knowing that one's friendliness or even principled actions are merely matters of temperament can help one focus on those areas of life that require greater moral attention (being more principled if one is naturally sanguine, or being less imitative if one is naturally phlegmatic). And given how lack of character leads to moral failings, knowledge of how to cultivate character, properly used, can arm one against the evils of frailty and impurity of will. Even if moral anthropology does not teach how to effect a noumenal revolution against radical evil, it gives one tools to live out that revolution in a life of constant progress toward greater and greater conformity to morality's demands.

Pragmatic Anthropology

While Kant's emphasis on the good will in his moral writings might lead some to think that there is little more to life than doing one's duty, Kant's pragmatic anthropology encompasses "everything that pertains to the practical" (10: 146). Kant is adamant that excellent human lives include not only duty but also happiness and the increasing perfection of the whole range of human predispositions. In fact, while moral anthropology is an important part of Kant's pragmatic anthropology, Kant consistently downplays the moral importance of his anthropological claims. Politeness is important not merely for moral ends but for the sheer pleasure of polite company. Affects and passions are dangerous, and character beneficial, not merely for virtue but also for happiness. Kant discusses how an *"evil character"* can inspire "admiration" (7: 293) and his main examples of affects and passions show how these prevent people from reflecting on "sum of all feelings of pleasure" (7: 254) or the "sum of all inclinations" (7: 265). Even Kant's account of diverse national characters is oriented toward discerning "what each can expect from the other and how each could use the other to his own advantage" (7: 312). Anthropology is full of applications of Kant's empirical anthropology toward helping human beings cultivate skills and capacities or become happier through better knowledge of human nature (both one's own and those of others). For this chapter, four examples of this non-moral "pragmatic" anthropology suffice: memory, distraction, "the highest physical pleasure," and "the highest ethico-physical good."

Kant's discussions of memory and distraction highlight his application of empirical anthropology to the perfection of predispositions that are neither moral nor a direct part of human happiness. With respect to memory, Kant advocates "*judicious* memorizing [of] a *table* of the *divisions* of a system" and various mnemonic "tricks" such as "maxims in verse" (7: 184). Distraction, which Kant warns can lead to "forgetfulness" (7: 185) or even "dementia" (7: 207) if overused, is recommended in moderation as a sort of mental cleansing agent:

> [O]ne can also *distract oneself*, ... as, for example, when the clergyman has delivered his memorized sermon and wants to prevent it from echoing in his head afterwards. This is a necessary and in part artificial precautionary procedure for our mental health. Continuous reflection on one and the same object leaves behind it a reverberation, so to speak (as when one and the very same piece of dance music that went on for a long time is still hummed by those returning from a festivity ...). Such a reverberation ... molests the mind, and it can only be stopped by distraction and by applying attention to other objects; for example, reading newspapers.
>
> (7: 207)

While both good memory and the "mental health" referred to here may be helpful for happiness and/or virtue, Kant emphasizes using empirical anthropology for the "pragmatic" purpose of perfecting cognitive powers *as such*, regardless of moral or hedonic purposes to which these might be put. These examples also elegantly show the interplay of empirical–causal description with pragmatic purposes. With distraction, for instance, Kant assumes that people are free in that he directs this advice to someone he takes to be capable of acting upon it. But the advice is based on a picture of human cognition that traces empirical causes of cognitive changes, from the way continuous reflection on a single object causes "reverberation" to ways one can undo this reverberation by reading newspapers.

From his long and detailed "pragmatic" discussion of cognition (which takes up more than half of his published *Anthropology*), Kant turns to the faculties of feeling and desire, and there devotes attention to "pragmatic" advice about how to make human beings happy. Those familiar with Kant's moral philosophy may recall his periodic despair about the possibility of "imperatives of prudence" ever "presenting actions ... as practically necessary" because "the concept of happiness is such an indeterminate concept" (4: 418, cf. 5: 36). One might not expect Kant to offer empirically rooted rules of prudence, but his *Anthropology* not only lays out a general discussion of pleasure and pain (7: 231), but also gives detailed analyses of inclinations that reveal how they are often self-defeating from the standpoint of human happiness. Even while discussing the cognitive faculty, Kant emphasizes implications for happiness. For example, after distinguishing "attention" from "abstraction," Kant notes, "Many human beings are unhappy because they cannot abstract. The suitor could make a good marriage if only he could overlook a wart on his beloved's face, or a gap between her teeth ... But this faculty of abstraction is a strength of mind that can only be acquired through practice" (7: 131–32). Kant diagnoses a source of unhappiness and suggests means for cultivating cognitive powers to have a happier life. The peak of *Anthropology*'s emphasis on happiness comes in specific accounts of "the highest physical good" and "the highest moral-physical good," *both* of which, despite the terms "good" and "moral," are suggestions for how to best be *happy*.

The "highest physical good" is that "greatest sensuous enjoyment" found in *"resting after work"* (7: 276). Kant identifies psychological features that interfere with this enjoyment, especially "laziness" ("the propensity to rest without having first worked" (7: 276)) and he uses his account to explain phenomena as diverse as the appeal of "a game," the tendency of "a love story [to] always end with the wedding," and the nature of "boredom" (7: 232–33). The "highest moral-physical good" is the way to unify "good living with virtue in *social intercourse*" and is found in *"a good meal in good company"* (7: 277–78). Kant details the importance of such dinner parties and how they should be conducted, including advice about the number of guests (ten), the order of conversation, and even the proper roles of "small ... attacks on the [female] sex" (acceptable as long as they are "not shameful") and dinner music ("the most tasteless absurdity that revelry ever contrived") (7: 277–82, cf. Cohen 2008). Such dinner parties please by virtue of humans' innate sociability, and they even channel unsociability into conversation and "dispute ... which stirs up the appetite" but which, because it avoids excessive seriousness, is consistent with "mutual respect and benevolence" (7: 280–81). Unlike vain luxury and chasing after superiority over others, "the art of good living" is a skillfulness of choice in social enjoyment, which "mak[es] pleasure mutually beneficial, and is calculated to last" (7: 250). The end result is a "stimulating play of thoughts" that "promotes sociability" and thereby "dresses virtue to advantage" (7: 279–82). While seemingly "insignificant ... compare[d] to pure moral laws," the graces of "social good living" are not only enjoyable in themselves but also serve virtue by preventing it from becoming distorted into a cold "mortification of the flesh" (7: 282), and the social interactions of a well-run dinner party help pave the way for polite and enjoyable moral exhortations amongst members of an ethical commonwealth. In the end, *Anthropology* enriches the austere conception of human life one might find in Kant's transcendental anthropology with details that are not moral, epistemic, or aesthetic.

Why does Kant devote so much attention to how human beings can be happier? In part, Kant may be using empirical anthropology to specify duties required by pure moral philosophy. Since the two "ends that are also duties [are] *one's own perfection* and *the happiness of others*" (6: 386), learning what makes people happy and best facilitates the perfection of "natural powers" (6: 444) specifies, in empirically informed and concrete ways, how to work toward these obligatory ends. But Kant also emphasizes that human beings "unavoidably want" happiness (6: 386) because of "predispositions to animality ... [and] humanity" that are ultimately parts of our more general "predisposition *to good*" (6: 26). Even the perfection of non-volitional capacities is "pragmatic" (6: 444) because these capacities "serve and are given ... for all sorts of possible purposes" (4: 423). In contrast to monkish moralists who decry basic desires and Rousseauian moralists who decry socially created inclinations, Kant endorses *as good* a wide range of human inclinations – for food, sex, social life, fine wine, good conversation, and so on. While not "good without limitation" (4: 393), these important if "limited" goods should be pursued well. So an important part of pragmatic anthropology is discerning, through careful empirical investigation, what sorts of activities best satisfy and delight human beings over the long term. *Groundwork's* apparent despair about rules of prudence is mitigated in *Anthropology* by a serious effort to provide the best, empirically informed, practical advice for improvement and well-being.

Empirical, Transcendental, and Pragmatic Anthropology

So far, this chapter has focused on details of Kant's pragmatic anthropology, but it is time to ask how Kant saw his pragmatic anthropology in relation to his empirical and transcendental anthropologies. In other words, it is time to answer Kant's question – "What is the human being?" – in an integrated way. Throughout his life Kant distinguished what I have called "transcendental" from "empirical" anthropology, particularly insisting that the latter not corrupt the former. But Kant's pragmatic anthropology brings the two sorts of investigation together, into what is at once "knowledge of the world" and "the investigation of what [the human being] as a free-acting being ... can and should make of himself" (7: 119). While this might seem to compromise Kant's distinction, pragmatic anthropology actually offers a coherent and plausible model for how empirical and transcendental anthropologies should be integrated, and thus a model for a complete "doctrine of the knowledge of the human being" (7: 119).

As we saw at the beginning of this chapter, Kant's claim that pragmatic anthropology attends to the human being as a "free-acting being" distinguishes his "pragmatic" anthropology from the "physiological" anthropology of his contemporary Ernst Platner in that Kant's (unlike Platner's) focuses on knowledge of human beings that can be put to use. Kant uses the case of memory to explain that what makes an anthropologist pragmatic is that he "uses perceptions concerning what has been found to hinder or stimulate memory in order to enlarge it or make it agile" rather than dwelling over purely theoretical claims about memory that are "a pure waste of time" (7: 119). And so when he turns to discuss memory in detail in *Anthropology*, Kant uses his empirical anthropology to discern the best mnemonic strategies, rather than merely explaining the "nature" of memory as such. Similarly, when Kant recommends distracting oneself to avoid reverberation in imagination (7: 207), he directs this advice to someone capable of freely acting on it, but the advice is based on various empirical causes of cognitive changes. And Kant's accounts of how politeness cultivates good character, the nature of affects and passions, and even the general role of character in action are all *empirical*–anthropological claims, but ones that can be put to use. Kant *addresses* free agents, teaching empirical facts about human nature in order to show what free *human* beings can make of themselves, and how.

But pragmatic anthropology is not *merely* usable empirical anthropology. Kant also implicitly recommends *how* to use this empirical knowledge. Pragmatic anthropology teaches both what human beings *can* make of themselves and what they *should* make of themselves. And these *norms* cannot be justified merely empirically but depend upon the from-within perspective that is the focus of Kant's *transcendental* anthropology. The molestation of mind that calls for distraction appears only from-within, in one's response to one's cognitive state. And Kant's discussion of cognition even ends with a series of "unalterable commands" that "lead to wisdom," including the need "to think *for oneself*" and "Always to think *consistently*" (7: 228), and with an exhortation to "exit from his self-incurred immaturity" (7: 229). By providing free human thinkers with empirical knowledge about how cognition works, Kant can cultivate the autonomy of thought that is a normative requirement of thinking. Similarly, as we saw earlier, Kant's pragmatic anthropology puts empirical anthropology to use to cultivate *good character* in human beings. By understanding the aspects of our natures that tempt and lead us astray and by understanding how to cultivate character, we can better engage in the struggle toward the good will that Kant's transcendental anthropology of desire reveals as the only thing good without limitation. Pragmatic anthropology thus unifies transcendental with empirical anthropology; transcendental analyses provide a priori normative principles for our human powers, and empirical anthropology shows how to cultivate powers that conform to those norms.

One aspect of Kant's pragmatic anthropology, however, goes beyond the mere application of empirically given means to transcendentally given ends. Kant's discussions of happiness, which play a particularly important role in his "pragmatic" anthropology, make use of empirical anthropology to specify ends for human beings. Happiness is a universal end, one we observe all humans seeking and that we can discover, from-within, to be naturally necessary for ourselves. But happiness is "such an indeterminate concept" (4: 418) that it requires empirical content to be action-guiding *at all*. Whereas there can be a priori cognitive and moral principles, the best that humans can do regarding the pursuit of happiness is to carefully study, through introspection as well as the investigation of others, what actually gives the most pleasure over the long term. In that sense, the pursuit of happiness is the special domain of pragmatic anthropology, the domain within which pragmatic anthropology specifies not only means but also – because "happiness" is *so* indeterminate – the end itself.

There is one further important aspect of Kant's "pragmatic" anthropology that has not yet received sufficient attention. So far, this chapter focused on the importance of pragmatic anthropology for fostering *one's own* capacities, happiness, and virtue. But for Kant, one of the primary reasons for developing a pragmatic anthropology is to learn how *others* respond to various empirical conditions in order to appropriately navigate within a world defined largely by other people. Thus Kant claims "all pragmatic instruction is instruction in prudence" (25: 471), and in *Groundwork* identifies "prudence" with "the skill of ... influencing others so as to use them for his own purposes" (4: 416n., see also 7: 322). Thus in laying out characteristics of different nationalities, Kant claims, "In an anthropology from a pragmatic point of view, ... the only thing that matters to us is to present the character of [each] ... in some examples, and, as far as possible, systematically; which makes it possible to judge what each can expect from the other and *how each could use the other* to his own advantage" (7: 312, emphasis added). By understanding human nature, one not only knows how to influence *oneself* in order to improve memory, attain happiness, or cultivate character, but one also knows or can quickly assess the strengths and weaknesses of others in order to influence their development and behavior.

This way of approaching others can sound sinister when Kant speaks of "using" others "to one's own advantage," but Kant's point is more benign, and, properly understood, even an affirmation of human dignity. Regardless of how free people might be from-within, human beings have empirically knowable tendencies that enable prediction of how different people respond to various situations. One *might* put this knowledge to use to manipulate others as *mere* means to one's ends. But one might also put this knowledge to use in order to best achieve one's ends *without* treating others as mere means. If I know that the sanguine "attributes a great importance to each thing for the moment, and the next moment may not give it another thought" (7: 287–88), while the melancholy "finds cause for concern everywhere" (7: 288), I know to treat social commitments with these two types of people differently. If I have agreed to go to a movie with someone but feel like going to a concert instead, I will suggest this change to my sanguine friends (who are likely to be thrilled by my spontaneity, and in any case will tell me if they still want to go to the movie) but not to my melancholic ones (who are likely to silently take offense while reluctantly agreeing to the change of plans). Knowing how others are affected by empirical conditions can make me *more* respectful of their humanity, rather than less. Thus "we are taught anthropology" so that, as we seek to influence others, "we are neither too hard nor too offensive" (25: 1436). One uses anthropological knowledge *rather than* manipulation or force to accomplish one's ends in relation to others while still respecting their humanity.

Even this level of interest in others, of course, might still focus merely on *not* offending others while pursuing "one's own advantage." But Kant makes clear that his ambitions with respect to others are higher. In one lecture, Kant laments that "the reason that morals and preaching that are full of admonitions ... have little effect is the lack of knowledge of man" (25: 471–72). In another, he explains the "great uses" of anthropology as including "pedagogy ... morals and religion" (25: 1437). And Kant's published *Anthropology* ends with an inspiring allusion to the ethical commonwealth of Kant's *Religion*:

> [Anthropology] presents the human species not as evil, but as a species of rational beings that strives among obstacles to rise out of evil. ... In this ..., achievement is difficult because one cannot expect to reach the goal by the free agreement of *individuals*, but only by a progressive organization of citizens of the earth into and toward the species as a system that is cosmopolitically united.
>
> (7: 333)

Learning how other people are affected by empirical influences is crucial for "morals and preaching," "pedagogy ... [and] influences on morals," and ultimately "a progressive organization of citizens are earth." In these ways, pragmatic anthropology is the science needed to actively promote an ethical commonwealth.

Summary

In a sense, Kant's *Anthropology from a Pragmatic Point of View* provides his answer to the question "What is the human being?" For Kant, the question is a pressing practical one about humans' place in the universe, about who we are and also, crucially, about what we can and should make of ourselves. Many aspects of Kant's answer to this question come in his transcendental anthropology, where he develops his metaphysical account of humans' free and finite natures and lays out norms that should govern cognition, feelings, and volitions. Many aspects of Kant's answer show up in his empirical anthropology, where he provides detailed descriptions of how human beings actually think, feel, and choose. But Kant's pragmatic anthropology integrates these two sets of answers to help human beings better satisfy norms of cognition, feeling, and volition and live happier, more virtuous, and more socially beneficial lives. This chapter has looked at some examples of this integration, in the roles of politeness, passions and affects, and character on promoting the achievement of both moral and prudential norms, and in the concrete recommendations Kant makes for improving our cognitive powers and making ourselves happier.

Pragmatic anthropology also helps complete Kant's accounts of human evil and human history, showing what we can do here and now, given the natures that we actually have, to improve ourselves and others. Human beings get into moral trouble both by prioritizing non-moral incentives over moral ones, and by simply being inconsistent, foolish, excessively passionate, and inept. The second problem can rise to the level of a genuinely moral problem, especially given our evil tendency to cultivate ineptness to excuse our failings. But it is also a broader problem for living well. And Kant's pragmatic anthropology provides specific suggestions for overcoming general problems that make us both vicious and miserable. This approach also puts Kant's accounts of diversity in a new light, showing tools to *improve* humanity, rather than excuses for dismissing or exploiting others.

This model of pragmatic anthropology provides a useful model for how philosophical investigation of human nature might interact with human sciences today. Transcendental philosophy articulates and provides conditions of possibility for norms governing human life. Empirical sciences show the best ways to cultivating human beings who can achieve those norms, and they specify the one human end – happiness – that is genuinely empirical. In the end, the answer to the question "What is the human being?" is provided by philosophical accounts of the from-within, norm-governed perspectives of free and finite beings like us engaged in thinking, feeling, and choosing, along with empirical–scientific accounts of the characteristics and causal laws governing *homo sapiens*, combined into pragmatic knowledge that helps us become better-functioning, happier, more virtuous citizens of the world.

Further Reading

Kant's pragmatic anthropology is increasingly studied and discussed. The best general treatments are Cohen, Frierson, Jacobs and Kain, Louden,

Munzel, Wilson and Zammito. Wood's book, while focusing on Kant's ethics, does so with an eye toward pragmatic anthropology. Moran discusses moral cultivation with a particular focus on moral community.

Alix Cohen, *Kant and the Human Sciences* (London: Palgrave Macmillan, 2009)

Patrick Frierson, *Freedom and Anthropology in Kant's Moral Philosophy* (Cambridge: Cambridge University Press, 2003)

Brian Jacobs and Patrick Kant, *Essays on Kant's Anthropology* (Cambridge: Cambridge University Press, 2003)

Robert Louden, *Kant's Impure Ethics* (Oxford: Oxford University Press, 2000)

Kate Moran, *Community and Progress in Kant's Moral Philosophy* (Washington, DC: Catholic University of America Press, 2012)

G. Felicitas Munzel, *Kant's Conception of Moral Character: The "Critical" Link of Morality, Anthropology, and Reflective Judgment* (Chicago: University of Chicago Press, 1999)

Holly L. Wilson, *Kant's Pragmatic Anthropology: Its Origin, Meaning, and Critical Significance* (Albany, NY: State University of New York Press, 2006)

Allen Wood, *Kant's Ethical Thought* (Cambridge: Cambridge University Press, 1999)

John Zammito, *Kant, Herder, and the Birth of Anthropology* (Chicago: University of Chicago Press, 2002)

Part II

INTERLUDE: FROM KANT TO THE TWENTIETH CENTURY

6 Hegel, Marx, Darwin, Nietzsche, and Freud

Kant had high hopes for his philosophy of the human being. He claimed that his Critiques, especially the *Critique of Pure Reason*, "completely specified [reason's] questions according to principles, and, after discovering the point where reason has misunderstood itself, ... resolved them to reason's complete satisfaction" (Axii). He wrote of his course in anthropology that he would make this "very pleasant empirical study" into "a proper academic discipline" that could, "distinct from all other learning, ... be called knowledge of the world" (10: 146). Kant's account of God, immortality, and human evil would, he hoped, put religion "within the boundaries of reason alone."

But while Kant did inaugurate a Copernican turn in philosophy, this turn did not take the form he expected. Within a generation after publication of the *Critique of Pure Reason*, Kant's philosophy was superseded by that of G.W.F. Hegel, who sought a much more comprehensive philosophical knowledge than Kant's modest system allowed. Within a hundred years, philosophy itself had lost its privilege of being the dominant discipline for answering the question "What is the human being?" Through the influence of Marx, Darwin, Nietzsche, and Freud, the social and biological sciences, along with art, literature, and politics, became dominant ways of addressing Kant's question. This chapter takes up five key post-Kantian figures who reflected on human nature in ways quite different from Kant's own. The next part of the book turns to the state of Kant's question in contemporary discussions influenced by those figures.

Philosophy's Climax: Hegel's Absolute Knowledge

The years following the publication of Kant's *Critique of Pure Reason* saw a host of responses to Kant's account of the human being, most of which sought an account of human beings that would better integrate aspects of human nature that Kant had divided: reason and feeling, the transcendental and the empirical, duty and inclination. "German Romantics" typically emphasized the importance of art and literature and resisted excessive systematization by appealing to the ultimate philosophical inscrutability of reality (including human reality).[1] "German Idealists," by contrast, sought ever more foundationalist and comprehensive philosophical systems, seeking to overcome Kant's strictures against knowledge of things-in-themselves and to develop coherent and well-grounded philosophies of everything. Among these post-Kantian developments, the most important was the philosophy of G.W.F. Hegel, the pre-eminent German Idealist. By the time Hegel became the dominant voice in German philosophy, Kant's role in German philosophy had become largely symbolic, and Hegel pulls together many early criticisms of Kant's philosophy. Thus Hegel rejects Kant's distinction between appearances and things-in-themselves and seeks "Absolute Knowledge." In his *Phenomenology of Spirit*, Hegel says, "if ... Science, ... in the absence of [Kantian] scruples [about Absolute Knowledge], gets on with the work itself and actually cognizes something, it is hard to see why we should not turn around and mistrust this very mistrust" (Hegel 1979: 47). Hegel aims to undermine Kant's idealism about knowing things-in-themselves by actually establishing that knowledge.

In order to gain such knowledge, Hegel develops a new philosophical methodology, a "logic" that moves through positions revealed as "one-sided" in such a way that one first moves from, say, an overly subjective approach to an overly objective approach, and then moves forward by rejecting the common one-sided assumption underlying both approaches. The general strategy is to start from a naïve conception of some reality and "negate" this conception by showing its immanent conflict with itself, but to negate it in a way that "determinately" gives rise to a more sophisticated conception of reality (see especially Hegel 1979: §§77ff.).

Hegel's dialectical arguments criticize Kant's "one-sided" dualist conception of human beings in favor of a more holist conception. Hegel objects to distinguishing empirical objects from things-in-themselves and incorporates various Kantian dichotomies into a single, coherent conception of the self (and world) that combines objective and subjective, volition and cognition, understanding and sensibility. Hegel rejects the unknowable "thing-in-itself" and appropriates from Schiller (an early Romantic) a critique of Kant's separation between duty and inclination, insisting that "what is rational becomes actual and what is actual becomes rational" (Hegel 1991: viii). For human motivation in particular, "it is an empty assertion of the abstract understanding to require that only a [moral] end shall appear [autonomously] willed ... , and likewise to take the view that, in volition, objective and subjective ends are mutually exclusive" (Hegel 1991: 151). Hegel finds unity between subjective inclinations and moral duties first in love but eventually also in the feelings of honor, trust, and patriotism that lead one to do one's duties in society and the state. Like Kant, Hegel insists that human particularity must be subordinated to universal principles, but his conception of "universality" is concrete and social rather than abstract. Kant's conception of the categorical imperative as an "abstract universality" makes morality an "empty formalism." Without "material from outside," the categorical imperative gives no particular duties, since *anything* can be universalized if one does not care about any particular consequences: "the fact that no property is present is in itself no more contradictory than is the non-existence of this or that individual people ... or the complete *absence of human life*" (Hegel 1991: 162). Hegel proposes that "ethics" – as opposed to abstract Kantian "morality" – must be situated in particular social and political contexts.

For Hegel, human insight into the legitimacy of the existing world emerges from the unfolding of the world itself. Art and religion are important sources of this insight, but *ultimate* knowledge is provided by philosophy. Moreover, human nature must be understood historically such that human rationality is a gradually unfolding historical achievement rather than an eternal condition or a transcendental fact. But this historical development is rationally comprehensible; world history *justifies* its stages. Human beings arise out of nature through an inevitable process of Spirit, or the Absolute, coming to know itself. And particular ethical and epistemic norms not only arise out of the concrete historical situations in which one finds oneself but are ultimately conducive to Absolute Knowledge. Hegel ends up with a conception of humans as agents and knowers situated in terms of a nature, history, and social life that are rationally comprehensible through a Science of dialectical reason. Likewise, freedom is not an abstract metaphysical concept, not an "uncaused cause" or noumenal thing-in-itself grounding an empirical world, but a historical and social accomplishment. Human beings are free because (or insofar as) we are self-knowing members of well-ordered communities at the right moment(s) in world history.

At the time of his death in 1831, Hegel was the pre-eminent philosopher in Germany (and arguably the world) and philosophy, at least in Germany, was the most important discipline in the academy. Within a decade, German philosophy had largely moved beyond Hegel, but without an obvious replacement. Since Hegel's death, no single philosopher has dominated the philosophical scene in any part of the world, and philosophy has seen its role increasingly diminish. Hegel's philosophical system – like Kant's – included a detailed logic, an account of the nature of being, an investigation of the basic principles of physics and biology, explanations of political and social organization both historically and in his own day, an account of the proper role of the state, a detailed aesthetics (including, in Hegel's case, a history of art), interpretations of the French Revolution and the rise of the nation-state, and so on. For many of these questions, it is hard to imagine that *philosophers* provide the best answers today, and for none of them is it clear to *which* philosopher one should turn. Many even suspect that any questions for which one needs a philosopher are likely to be those for which there cannot be any real answer. Whereas many in Hegel's time hoped philosophy could provide solid, lasting, and comprehensive answers to all-important questions, today the most plausible "Theories of Everything" seem to come from physics, biology, or social sciences. This shift is particularly dramatic in terms of the question "What is the human being?" For Kant, this question was simply *equivalent* to philosophy as such. Even for Kant's immediate successors, the question was a properly philosophical one. Today, however, most would be more likely to turn to the sciences for a rigorous answer to the question. And even those who worry that the sciences might miss something essential about human beings are more likely to turn to art or literature than embrace philosophy.

In the rest of this chapter, I look at four episodes in the development of this contemporary perspective. In each case, I point out both the ways in which these developments pose significant problems for Kant's conception of human beings and the ways in which they draw from (or mesh with) important dimensions of Kant's thought. I start with Marx, the most direct successor to Hegel. Marx's historical materialism and conception of human beings as socially and materially determined beings reflected an important response to earlier philosophical accounts and helped set the stage for the emergence of the social and historical disciplines that are so important today. Second, I turn to Darwin, whose theory of evolution offered a theoretical structure for a new biological account of human beings. Third, I look at Friedrich Nietzsche, and especially his genealogical revaluations of values. Finally, I discuss the emergence of scientific psychology and the work of Sigmund Freud.

Marx and the Rise of Human Sciences

Marx (1818–83) was one of the dominant intellectual figures of the nineteenth century, and Marxism was one of the greatest political influences on the twentieth century. Marx is typically thought of more in connection with his revolutionary *Communist Manifesto* than with his close analysis of Hegel's *Philosophy of Right* or even his own magnum opus, *Capital*. In this brief section, however, my emphasis is on Marx's philosophical conception of human beings, which emerged from issues and debates in German philosophy after Kant and Hegel. During his university years, Marx even invoked Kant's political theory to explain his shift from jurisprudence to philosophy (Marx 1997: 46). After engaging in a course of philosophical study, Marx wrote a now-lost philosophical dialogue that moved from "Cleanthes, or the Starting Point and Necessary Continuation of Philosophy" through Kant, Fichte and Schelling, but whose "last proposition was the beginning of the Hegelian system" (Marx 1997: 47). In that sense, as Marx puts it, he was "deliver[ed] into the arms of the enemy" at the outset of his philosophical work (Marx 1997: 47). As a close reader of Hegel, Marx took the core ideas that human beings are essentially constituted by historically situated social interactions and that human freedom requires embodiment in the world through socially recognized work. But Marx rejects what he saw as Hegel's "uncritical" political conservatism that teaches a mere "restoration of the existing empirical world" that justifies the world in thought rather than *changing* it (Marx 1963: 201, Marx 1994: 83). Similarly, in one of his few direct criticisms of Kant, Marx describes him as the "whitewashing spokesman" of "the German middle class," who settled for mere "good will," separating "theoretical expression from the interests which it expressed" and replacing "materially motivated determinations of the will" with "purely ideological conceptual determinations and moral postulates." While the French were engaged in "the most colossal revolution that history has ever known" and the English were "revolutionizing industry and subjugating ... the world," Kant gave the Germans abstractions and a "horror [at] the practice of ... energetic bourgeois liberalism as soon as this practice showed itself ... in the Reign of Terror and in shameless bourgeois profit-making" (Marx 1970: 97, 99).[2] The result of Marx's praxis-oriented Hegelianism is a conception of human nature as a historical accomplishment that depends upon certain economic conditions, conditions not yet realized under the current capitalist economic system. In this short section, then, I start with Marx's human ideal, then turn to how this ideal is not yet achieved because of the alienation in capitalist (and pre-capitalist) forms of life, and then end with Marx's dialectical materialism and revolutionary, change-oriented approach to philosophy.

Marx's Human Ideal

For Marx, humans are relational, and our most important relationships are with nature, society, and ourselves. Regarding nature, Marx follows Hegel in emphasizing that what it means to be human is in part to make the world in our own image, not merely in the Kantian sense that we see it through human categories, but in the more practical sense that we *work* on nature – whether physically or intellectually or both – to make it into a human world. "The human being ... begins to distinguish himself from the animal the moment he begins to *produce* his means of subsistence ... By producing food, the human being indirectly produces his material life itself" (Marx 1970: 42). Put another way, "It is just in his work upon the objective world that the human being really proves himself ... By means of it nature appears as *his* work and reality. The object of labor, therefore, is the *objectification of man's species-life*" (Marx 1963: 128). By working on nature, human beings make real their "species-character," the sort of beings they are. Ideally, humans "create the human being by human labor" that effectuates "free, conscious activity [which] is the species-character of human beings" (Marx 1963: 128, 166). While the species character of animals need involve nothing more than perpetuating the physical and instinctive characteristics of their species, human engagement with the world should bring about expressions of the freedom that is characteristically human. Thus in contrast to animals, "man produces when he is free from physical need and only truly produces in freedom from such need," such as when one "constructs ... in accordance with laws of beauty" (Marx 1963: 128).

The emphasis on *work* as our proper relationship with nature is combined, in Marx, with a strong emphasis on humans' *social* nature. The human being "is in his existence ... a social being" (Marx 1963: 154). Marx takes as an example his own "scientific work," since science – as the pursuit of truth about the world – might seem to be something that could be carried on in isolation from others. But Marx insists that this activity is "social, because human" (Marx 1963: 157), in that even "the material of my activity – such as language itself" – is a social contribution to that activity, and "what I myself produce I produce for society, and with the consciousness of acting as a social being" (Marx 1963: 158). To be truly human, one must live and work in the context of relationships to society.

Finally, our proper relationship with ourselves takes place through actualizing free, conscious activity of socially situated work in our own particular way. Marx emphasizes that one's individuality is the individuality of a "unique ... individual communal being" (Marx 1963: 158). Particular strengths and weaknesses are relevant only within social contexts. Just as Marx's unique social theorizing depends upon his context, so too does the activity of any human individual. One becomes who one is when one "makes the community ... his object both practically and theoretically, [and] also ... treats himself as the present, living species, as a *universal* and consequently free being" (Marx 1963: 128). As an individual communal being drawing from society to contribute to society, our labor helps define and expand the parameters of human possibility. One relates to oneself properly, as a "species being," when one's individual life becomes a means for expressing the goods of the species in free and creative ways.

Alienation

For Marx, then, humans engage in free, conscious, social activity. Unfortunately, according to Marx, one living in a capitalist society "exists only as a *worker* and not as a human being" (Marx 1963: 137). What's worse, "the worker sinks to the level of ... a most miserable commodity" (Marx 1963: 120). The dehumanization of workers takes place through what Marx calls "alienation." In general, alienation occurs when what should be an essential aspect of one's humanity is made "alien" to oneself. Marx diagnoses four key forms of alienation within capitalism: alienation from the products of one's labor, from other people, from oneself, and from humanity.

Alienation from the products of one's labor is the simplest to comprehend: "the alienation of the worker in his product means not only that his labor becomes an object, assumes an *external* existence, but that it exists independently, *outside himself*, and alien to him, and that it stands opposed to him as an autonomous power" (Marx 1963: 122–23). *Any* product, simply by virtue of being a product, stands independent of its maker in some sense. When Marx develops a scientific theory or when an artist makes a work of art or when a good cook makes a delicious meal, the theory or art or meal are independent of their creators. But in these cases, the work remains the concrete *expression* of its maker's free activity. Insofar as the theory is studied or the artwork contemplated or the meal eaten, its maker accomplishes his own ends and the activity is merely completed in the external existence of the product. But within capitalist economies, workers no longer produce for the sake of their products but for the sake of *wages*. (This emphasis on wage-labor, though not alienated labor per se, is distinctive of capitalism.) In such a system, the worker's *goal* is wages for sustaining (animal) life; the independent product – the automobile or blue jeans or artwork marketed to wealthy collectors or meal sold to paying customers – is *alien*, something that does not express the free and conscious activity of its *human* maker but merely the mechanical operations of a worker. The result, for Marx, is devastating: "The more the worker expends himself in work the more powerful becomes the world of objects which he creates in the face of himself, the poorer he becomes in his inner life, and the less he belongs to himself" (Marx 1963: 121). Rather than taking an alien nature and transforming it in the light of free human activity, the workers in a capitalist economy imbue alien nature with their own labor in order to make it even more powerful and more alien. One ends up alienated not only from the immediate products of labor, but – because labor is how the *world* becomes one's own – from the entire "sensuous external world" (Marx 1963: 125).

Moreover, within capitalism, human relationships become increasingly corrupt. People are valued for their profitability, not only by employers but also in more intimate contexts, where one increasingly regards friends and neighbors, and even parents and children, in terms of how much they help or hinder economic interests. Even more subtly, human relationships end up being crafted around communities of common interest, where "interests" are largely a matter of one's situation within the labor market.

As Marx puts it, "every man regards other men according to the standards and relationships in which he finds himself placed as a worker" (Marx 1963: 129).

The alienation from one's products and others leads to alienation from one's *self*. For one thing, alienation from *products* of labor quickly becomes alienation from *activity*:

> the work is *external* to the worker ... [I]t is not a part of his nature; and ... consequently he does not fulfill himself in his work but denies himself ..., does not develop freely his mental and physical energies but is physically exhausted and mentally debased ... His work is not the satisfaction of a need, but only a *means* for satisfying other needs ... This is the relationship of the worker to his own activity as something alien and not belonging to him, ... This is *self-alienation*.
>
> (Marx 1963: 124–26)

What starts as selling the products of labor transforms activity as such into something that is not part of who one *is*, but something to be traded *away* in exchange for satisfying basic needs. But because life *is* activity, who one is *is* what one does and one's place in society, alienation from one's *activity* is alienation from one*self*.

The result of this three-fold alienation from the sensuous world, other people, and oneself, is an alienation from true humanity. "[T]he human becomes animal" as people find fulfillment not in work and relationships but in food, sex, and at best "decorating and personal adornment" (Marx 1963: 125). Rather than the activity of the individual contributing to defining the species, one puts one's distinctively human traits – one's language, reason, relationships with nature and others – to the service of merely animal ones:

> alienated labor ... makes *species-life* into a means of individual life ... For labor, *life activity, productive life*, now appear to man only as *means* for the satisfaction of a need, the need to maintain his physical existence.
>
> (Marx 1963: 128)

Even if, say, one constructs a home in accordance with aesthetic ideals, in a capitalist economy one does so only so that one can get better wages and thereby more food, sex, and entertainment. In the end, "alienated labor ... alienates from man his own body, external nature, his mental life, and his *human* life" (Marx 1963: 129).

Dialectical Materialism

Given this account of alienation, Marx sees "the human being" as the end of a not-yet-finished process: "world history is ... the creation of the human being" (Marx 1963: 166–67) and "the *human level* ... will be the ... *future* of [currently capitalist] nations" (Marx 1963: 52). This conception of humanity as not-yet-realized has at least two important implications. First, like Hegel, Marx endorses a form of historicism according to which the actual lives of human beings are characterized differently at different times in history. Marx is well known for his "dialectical materialism" or "historical materialism," according to which *material* conditions of people at different eras determine forms of "human" life at those stages, shape the philosophies and "ideologies" that dominate them, and also – inevitably – set the stage for a transition to a different stage in world history. Second, unlike Hegel, Marx sees the historical process as far from finished, which leads him to emphasize *action* over mere thought, revolution over mere philosophizing.

Marx's dialectical materialism involves two central claims: first, that historical changes are results of an "inevitable" or "necessary" development (Marx 1963: 115, 120), and, second, that the fundamental basis for these changes are *material* conditions, where "material" here primarily refers to the control over the means for putting human work to use, whether these be physical factories or institutions or knowledge. Marx specifically distinguishes his philosophy of history from Hegel's in emphasizing not the unfolding of rational ideas into material relations but how material conditions generate the ideas of a particular epoch: "[c]onceiving, thinking, and the intellectual relationships of men appear here as the direct result of their material behavior ... In contrast to German philosophy, which descends from heaven to earth, here one ascends from earth to heaven" (Marx 1970: 47).

Marx's materialism is opposed to both Hegel and many still-popular conceptions of historical change. For Marx, ideas do not change the world, but vice versa. Only as material conditions of production change can ideas change, since ideas merely reflect those conditions: "Humans are the producers of their conceptions, ideas, etc., but these ... humans ... are conditioned by a definite development of their productive forces" (Marx 1970: 47). Similarly, historical change is not fundamentally a matter of *political* change. Because "legal relations [and] political forms ... originate in the material conditions of life" (Marx 1994: 210), any *fundamental* shift must always be in material conditions. Real political change is the *consequence*, not the cause, of this material change.

Importantly, Marx's "materialism" is not the *physical* materialism of atoms in a void, but the *economic* materialism of concrete productive activities. Human beings must labor to survive and express their species-being. And because labor is social,

> men inevitably enter into definite relations, which are independent of their will, namely relations of production appropriate to a given stage in the development of their material forces of production. The totality of these

structures of production constitutes the economic structure of society, the real foundation, on which arises a legal and political superstructure and to which correspond definite forms of social consciousness … It is not the consciousness of men that determines their existence, but their social existence that determines their consciousness.

(Marx 1994: 211)

Explaining the evolution of the material forces of production gets extremely detailed, and it is largely the effort to detail the important shift to a capitalist economy and the forces driving a shift *from* that economy that pre-occupy Marx's intellectual life. But Marx's overall focus is on associations of producers and those who exploit them, that is, on *classes*. Thus not only are ideas in a given period shaped by that period's material conditions, but, more specifically, "In every epoch, the … class that is the ruling *material* power of society is at the same time its ruling *intellectual* power" (Marx 1994: 129). In general, "The history of all hitherto existing society is the history of class struggles" (Marx 1994: 158). Ultimately, while Marx defends historical materialism in general, he focuses on applying it to his own capitalist society, within which all class struggles of previous ages are simplified into a single class antagonism between bourgeoisie and proletariat. The bourgeoisie own the (increasingly industrial-scale) means of production, while the proletariat work. We have already seen Marx's analysis of workers' alienation. In the context of dialectical materialism, Marx emphasizes how capitalism generates contradictions that will give rise to its own downfall. "The bourgeoisie not only has forged the weapons that bring death to itself; it has also called into existence the men who are to wield those weapons – the modern working class – the proletarians" (*Communist Manifesto*, in Marx 1994: 164).

Marx's Revolutionary Philosophy

Marx's philosophy would not, in itself, have made him one of the defining figures of the nineteenth and twentieth centuries. But Marx's philosophy was not the complacent thought-experiment of an armchair philosopher. Instead, Marx and others used his ideas to mobilize, organize, and inspire concrete activities of communists seeking to change the world. For Marx, "the chief defect of all hitherto existing materialism," and of all previous philosophy, is that it "does not grasp the significance of 'revolutionary', of 'practical-critical', activity": "The philosophers have only interpreted the world in various ways; the point is to change it" (Marx 1994: 99, 101). In a thinly veiled autobiography of his role in historical progress, Marx describes how "a portion of the bourgeoisie goes over to the proletariat, and in particular, a portion of the bourgeois ideologists, who have raised themselves to the level of comprehending theoretically the historical movement as a whole" (Marx 1994: 167).

This practical focus manifested itself in Marx's writing style, which tended to be polemical rather than philosophical, and in his active involvement in worker's movements around Europe. The ultimate result was that Marx's ideas – albeit in warped and incomplete forms – shaped the ideology of two of the three most powerful nations in the world during the twentieth century, and even today over a billion people live under (nominally) "Communist" rule. Today, after the fall of the Soviet Union and the increasingly capitalist economic structure in China, Marxism in its Leninist–Stalinist–Maoist form is increasingly discredited. But the end of these *supposed* communist systems opens the possibility for a reappraisal of the contributions that *Marx* – as opposed to Marx*ism*[3] – can make to our conception of human beings. While Marx's strictly *political* influence may be waning, his *intellectual* influence is still significant in disciplines such as history and sociology, where not only Marx's general emphasis on material conditions of human life but also many of his specific analyses continue to exercise significant influence. More generally, although Marx is widely disclaimed by professional economists, it was Marx who most forcefully argued that economics is *the* science of human nature, and the increasing dominance of economic ways of conceiving of human beings can trace much of its origin to Marx. Finally, even if Marx's utopian vision is overstated, his conception of human beings as needing a fulfillment that capitalist economic structures inhibit needs to be taken seriously.

Darwin and the Rise of Biology

When Kant was working through his philosophy of biology, scientific biology was still in its infancy. The new physics gave hope to mechanistic accounts of biology, but in Kant's day, these approaches had given way to various forms of "preformationism" or vitalism. Preformationism posited that each species was separately created and that individual members of those species were present in their ancestors. (Its crudest version claimed that every human being was present, in miniature, in the eggs of Eve.) Vitalist explanations were closer to mechanist ones, positing that complex forms of life emerge from simpler material interactions, but that matter itself is "alive." The challenge for all of these forms of biological explanation was how to make sense of the apparent *purposiveness* of living things; such as that hearts are needed to pump blood. Kant's philosophy of biology affirms purposive explanations in biology while according them merely "regulative" status. But while Kant is open in principle to synthesizing purposive explanations with mechanistic accounts, he doubts the real possibility of a "Newton of a blade of grass."

Arguably, Charles Darwin (1804–82) is just such a Newton. He provided the basis for a new sort of mechanism in biology that showed how purposive structures of organisms emerge from natural and not intrinsically purposive causal processes. Over time and under various environmental influences, random variations in organisms give rise to increasingly refined and even purposive structures through a process of "natural selection." This new approach put biology on scientific footing by establishing an intuitively plausible and rigorous methodology for explaining organisms' origins and variations. Darwin's theory of evolution by natural selection all-too-clearly applied to human beings. As natural organisms, our characteristics must have emerged from a natural process of evolution. For many, this offered new hope of finally and decisively answering the question "What is the human being?" For others, it offered reason for despair, seemingly making humans no more than animals.

Darwin's theory of evolution by natural selection, as described in *The Origin of Species*, is fairly simple. Biological reproduction has two important characteristics: first, descendants tend to share most of the traits of their ancestors; and second, organisms tend to reproduce in sufficiently large numbers that there is a "struggle for existence," by virtue of which many descendants die early or are unable to reproduce. Darwin argues,

> Owing to the struggle for life, any variation, however slight and from whatever cause proceeding, if it be in any degree profitable to an individual of any species, ... will tend to the preservation of that individual, and will generally be inherited by its offspring. The offspring, also, will thus have a better chance of surviving ... I have called this principle, by which each slight variation, if useful, is preserved, by the term of Natural Selection.
>
> (Darwin 1859/1982: 115)

Over long spans of time, preserved variations tend to become more prevalent within a population, and the species "evolves." Given that there is often more than one way members of a species can thrive, "the greatest amount of life can be supported by the greatest diversification of structure" (Darwin 1859/1982: 157). If different members of a population have different variations that are valuable for different purposes, the species diverges, eventually becoming two or more distinct species.

The power of this approach is evident in the title of Darwin's work: *On the Origin of Species*. Over the course of the eighteenth and early nineteenth centuries, the idea that one could provide an account of the origin of biological entities in terms of mechanical forces had increasingly lost ground against biological theories that took for granted an original creation of the full range of biological species, each with their distinctive traits firmly established. In part, this view in biology was religiously motivated, but in part, it was due to the apparent failure to find clear mechanisms to explain complex biological features. But Darwin's straightforward account made sense of how species could evolve, change, and diverge through selection processes that are not, in themselves, purposive. In that sense, it revolutionized biology, making both special creations and inherent teleology obsolete.

In his *Origin of Species*, Darwin barely mentions *human* evolution, saying only:

> In the distant future I see open fields for far more important researches. Psychology will be based on a new foundation, that of the necessary acquirement of each mental power and capacity by gradation. Light will be thrown on the origin of man and his history.
>
> (Darwin 1859/1982: 458)

Still, implications of *The Origin of Species* for human beings were immediately obvious to Darwin and his contemporaries. In notebooks containing writings from a period during which he was first developing his theory of evolution, Darwin points out that "Man ... is not a deity," challenges those who "dare boast of [humans'] preeminence," considers "What circumstances may have been necessary to have made man," and compares human beings to orangutans (Darwin 1987: 263–64). And in 1863 – just five years after the first edition of *Origin* – T.H. Huxley began his *Evidence as to Man's Place in Nature* with a diagram of the human skeleton juxtaposed to the apes to which Huxley argued he was related.

Darwin directly entered the fray with publication of *The Descent of Man* in 1871. In this work, Darwin makes use of the increasingly wide acceptance of the notion that there are homologous structures in man and the lower animals: "man is constructed on the same general type or model with other mammals" (Darwin 1871/1902: 10). Like dogs and even pigeons, human beings have a heart, two lungs, a skeletal structure including vertebrae, ribs, and even distinct radius and ulna in the fore-arm/leg/wing. Darwin uses this physical similarity between man and other animals for two important and related purposes. First, it is "evidence of the descent of man from some lower form" (Darwin 1871/1902: 9). Second and more importantly, homologous *physical* structures provide an analogy for homologous *mental* structures. Darwin argues both that "there is no fundamental difference between man and the higher mammals in their mental faculties" (Darwin 1871/1902: 35) and that therefore the human mind is descended from some lower form just as much as the human body. This shift from physical to mental homology is radical: Descartes, long before Darwin and without raising any significant threat for religion, had argued that the human *body* could be explained as the natural result of evolution by means of natural, mechanical interactions of matter in motion. But Descartes reserved a special place for the human *soul*, which, he claimed, was uniquely able to explain humans' rational superiority over animals. Likewise today, many are comfortable with humans' physical nature as naturally evolved but nonetheless argue for something special about humans requiring a different explanation.

Darwin had no patience for this idolizing of human beings. While acknowledging the "immense" "difference in mental power between the highest ape and the lowest savage," he insisted that animals share such supposedly "human" traits as reason, abstraction, and even ennui (Darwin 1871/1902: 34, 109, 117f., 102, 99). More importantly, he offered an evolutionary account of the origin of humans' most distinctive traits, including language, higher cognitive faculties, morals, and even religious belief. Darwin quotes, at the beginning of his discussion of human morals, *Kant's* description of our moral predisposition: "Duty! Wondrous thought ... before whom all appetites are dumb" (Darwin 1871/1902: 134–35). Rather than taking this as an inexplicable human given, though, Darwin explains its origin through evolution:

> any animal whatever, endowed with well-marked social instincts ... would inevitably acquire a moral sense or conscience, as soon as its intellectual powers had become as well ... developed, as in man. For, firstly, the social instincts lead an animal to take pleasure in the society of its fellows, to feel a certain amount of sympathy with them, and to perform various services for them ... Secondly, as soon as the mental faculties had become highly developed, images of all past actions and motives would be incessantly passing through the brain of each individual: and that feeling of dissatisfaction, or even misery, which invariably results, as we shall hereafter see, from any unsatisfied instinct, would arise, as often as it was perceived that the enduring and always present social instinct had yielded to some other instinct, at the time stronger, but neither enduring in its nature, nor leaving behind it a very vivid impression ... Thirdly, after the power of language had been acquired ... , the common opinion how each member ought to act ..., would naturally become in a paramount degree the guide to action.
> (Darwin 1871/1902: 135–36)

As in the rest of his account of human beings, Darwin emphasizes similarities between humans and other animals, noting that humans are one of many social animals, and appealing to dogs in particular as examples of animals with social instincts like love, sympathy, self-command, and "something very like a conscience" (Darwin 1871/1902: 142). Having shattered the uniqueness of humans' social affections, Darwin offers a general account of the advantages of social instincts for groups whose members have them, and thus of the likelihood that those instincts will be passed on to offspring.

The implications of Darwinism have been profound. Darwin provided a methodology for an empirical biology that marginalized many sorts of reflections on human nature that had dominated philosophy. The scope of Darwin's theory seemed to include every aspect of human nature, apparently leaving nothing for philosophers of human nature to do except engage in Darwinian biological research.

For Kant, Darwinism might seem particularly problematic. At the most mundane and direct level, Darwin seemingly provided a refutation of Kant's philosophy of biology. Kant presumed that teleology was intrinsic to the study of biological entities as such, but Darwin showed how *apparent* teleology is merely the effect of a process of evolution by natural selection. But Darwinism seems to pose even more serious problems, since it suggests that Kant's transcendental anthropology is secondary to a revamped empirical anthropology. And even within empirical anthropology, Darwin suggests that the most important part of any such anthropology is precisely the part that Kant ignored: the description of how humans' "predispositions" (in Kant's language) evolved from more primitive structures.

Nietzsche, Art, and Literature

While Darwin and Marx helped shift the question "What is the human being?" outside of the field of philosophy, Friedrich Nietzsche (1844–1900), though trained as a philologist rather than a philosopher, has become the most well-known and widely read nineteenth-century *philosopher* of human nature. Unlike Darwin and Marx, Nietzsche refuses to advance a particular answer. His philosophy of human nature can be seen as a continuation of the Romantic response to Kant mentioned earlier in this chapter. Like the Romantics, Nietzsche is anti-systematic and anti-metaphysical. Thus at the end of one important articulation of his philosophy, Nietzsche laments,

> Alas, what are you after all, my written and painted thoughts! It was not long ago that you were still so colorful, young, and malicious, full of thorns and secret spices ... and now? You have already taken off your novelty, and some of you are ready, I fear, to become truths: they already look so immortal, so pathetically decent, so dull!
>
> (Nietzsche 1966: 236)

While Nietzsche articulates provocative and important claims about humans, his writings resist settling on any particular "theory" of human "nature." Nonetheless, important claims about human beings can be gleaned from his writings, claims that he repeats, develops, and reiterates, even if we should resist classifying them as "Nietzsche's answer" to Kant's question.

Nietzsche stresses creativity and individuality over abstract rationality and universal duty, and develops a historicism that emphasizes the contingency and a-rationality of systems of thought and morals. And Nietzsche situates all of this in the context of an optimistic conception of "will to power" as an underlying creative force in the universe that seeks ever higher forms of expression through a self-overcoming that, at its best, involves a *creative* suffering "like pregnancy" (Nietzsche 1967: 88). In relation to Kant, it is helpful to emphasize four Nietzschean contributions: (1) his genealogical methodology, whereby human cognition and morals are seen as contingent historical–cultural perspectives; (2) his opposition to certain metaphysical conceptions of the self, especially those involving a coherent and unified "I" or a Kantian conception of human "freedom"; (3) his perspectivism, which draws from but radicalizes Kant's anthropological turn; and (4) his conception of the "overman," the idea that our current configuration of moral and philosophical perspectives can and should be overcome and that a new, higher type of human being can emerge.

Genealogy

Nietzsche's impact has been most influential in thinking about morals, and the title of his *Genealogy of Morals* – much like Darwin's *Origin of Species* – highlights the profound shift he inaugurates. Unlike the "stiff seriousness that inspires laughter" of "all our philosophers" who "wanted to provide a *rational foundation* for morality," Nietzsche will "own up in all strictness to what is still necessary here for a long time to come ... : to ... arrange a vast realm of subtle feelings of value and differences of value which are alive, grow, beget, and perish ... all to prepare a *typology* of morals" (Nietzsche 1966: 97). Just as natural scientists required Darwin to shake confidence in the fixity of species, so moral philosophers can thank Nietzsche for shattering their assumption of a given, fixed morality for which they could provide the "conditions of possibility." As Nietzsche puts it, "my curiosity as well as my suspicions were bound to halt quite soon at the question of where our good and evil really *originated* ... [U]nder what conditions did man devise these value judgments good and evil" (Nietzsche 1967: 17).

It is not necessary to get into the details of Nietzsche's account of the origin of nineteenth-century European values here. Throughout, he appeals to social and natural forces in explaining shifts in human values, such as how "the change which occurred when [man] found himself finally enclosed within the walls of society and of peace" gave "old instincts" a new – inward – direction (Nietzsche 1967: 84). The most important shift, for Nietzsche, involved turning away from a "noble morality" that was fundamentally self-affirming, active, and strong through a "slave revolt" where the weak and oppressed turned against their oppressors in a subtle "revaluation of values" that rejected as "vices" the strengths of the nobles and affirmed as "virtues" the characteristics of the weak. "Weakness is being lied into something *meritorious* ... and impotence which does not requite into 'goodness of heart'; anxious lowliness into 'humility'; subjection to those one hates into 'obedience'" (Nietzsche 1967: 47). Kant's emphasis on autonomy is recast by Nietzsche as an "instinct of obedience" to "formal conscience" (Nietzsche 1966: 110), a slavish and herdlike "morality as timidity" (Nietzsche 1966: 109). Against Kant's "bad taste of wanting to agree with many," Nietzsche proclaims, "My judgment is *my* judgment; no one else is entitled to it." "How," he asks, "should there be a 'common good' ... [W]hatever is common always has little value" (Nietzsche 1966: 53). But as important as these descriptions of Kant's morality as common, timid, and slavish are, Nietzsche's shift from *justifying* a timeless morality transcendentally to *describing* the emergence, changes, and possibilities of contingent moralities is – as we will see in more detail in Chapter 8 – Nietzsche's most lasting and influential "criticism" of Kant.

Metaphysical Objections

For Nietzsche, the shift from justification to genealogy is not limited to morality. Philosophy itself is built on contingent and historically emergent prejudices. In criticizing these "philosophical truths," Nietzsche offers general criticisms of metaphysical systems, such as that "every great philosophy so far has been ... the personal confession of its author and a kind of unconscious and involuntary memoir ... [in which] the moral (or immoral) intentions ... constitute [its] real germ of life" (Nietzsche 1966: 13). And Nietzsche also takes aim at concepts particularly important for Kant's philosophy. About the fundamental question of Kant's *Critique of Pure Reason*, Nietzsche says,

> [I]t is high time to replace the Kantian question, "How are synthetic judgments a priori possible?" with another question, "Why is belief in such judgments *necessary*?" – and to comprehend that such judgments must be *believed* to be true, for the sake of the preservation of creatures like ourselves, though they might, of course, be *false* judgments for all that!
> (Nietzsche 1966: 19)

Rather than a transcendental justification of the legitimacy of judgments, Nietzsche challenges his readers to think of the interests served by them. With respect to freedom, Nietzsche's opposition to Kant is more specific. He argues that while "[p]hilosophers are accustomed to speak of freedom as if it were the best-known thing in the world," this approach only "adopt[s] a *popular prejudice* and exaggerate[s] it" (Nietzsche 1966: 25). "Freedom" is "a sort of rape and perversion of logic" and "nonsense" (Nietzsche 1966: 28). Against this empty, formal, nonsensical notion of freedom, Nietzsche offers an alternative, wherein the "will" is a "complex of sensation, thinking, and above all *affect*," such that "freedom" is always the freedom of one aspect of human nature to dominate others (Nietzsche 1966: 25). Rather than a freedom from domination by instinct altogether, Kant's "transcendental freedom" is the domination of a particular instinct over others.

Perspectivism

For Nietzsche, this general unmasking of philosophical pretensions to "absolute truth" or "universality" was only part of a more general effort to radicalize and relativize Kant's anthropological turn toward a perspectivism that would pave the way for more creative approaches to human existence. Nietzsche asks, "under what conditions did man devise value judgments good and evil?" only to go on to ask, *"and what value do they themselves possess?* Have they hitherto hindered or furthered human prosperity?" (Nietzsche 1967: 17). What Kant saw as necessary conditions of possibility of any human experience become, in Nietzsche's hands, particular prejudices of particular ages, embodied in language and shared prejudices.

> Kant ... ma[d]e everything that has ... been esteemed so far easy to ... think over, intelligible and manageable ... *Genuine philosophers, however, are commanders and legislators*: they say, *"thus* it *shall* be*!"* ... With a creative hand they reach for the future, and all that is and has been becomes a means for them, an instrument, a hammer.
>
> (Nietzsche 1966: 136)

Unlike Kant's helpful transcendental analyses of present realities, Nietzsche's genealogies pave the way for truly creative *revaluings of values*.

Becoming conscious of the historical contingency of values and prejudices opens a new sphere of freedom, a recognition that values and prejudices are precisely *not* an a priori that constrains us but a set of tools to be utilized *as we see fit*. And insofar as we live – as Kant argues – in a world that is in part the product of our presuppositions and values, our power *over* these presuppositions is a power to create *new worlds*: "it is enough to create new names and valuations to create new 'things'" (Nietzsche 1974: 122). There is, of course, something frightening about this freedom. Having seen the contingency of all values, it is no longer possible to go back to the naïve "a priori" to which we had only to submit (see Nietzsche 1974: 180–81). But homesick nostalgia for unreflective naïveté is not the only possible reaction to the death of our old prejudices and values, our old "God."

[A]t hearing the news that "the old god is dead", we philosophers and "free spirits" feel illuminated by a new dawn; our heart overflows with gratitude, amazement, forebodings, expectation—finally the horizon seems clear again, even if not bright; finally our ships may set out again, set out to face any danger; ... the sea, *our* sea, lies open again; maybe there has never been such an "open sea".

(Nietzsche 1974: 280)

For Nietzsche, the bases for our old values and morals are gone. Some will respond to this loss with despair. Most will respond with a self-deception that refuses to admit the loss. Pretending that old values still live, they throw themselves into business and "commonsense" to avoid the reality of living on an open ocean. But this openness gives rise to a new sort of ideal, an ideal of the true "philosopher" and "free spirit," the one who can respond to the loss of naïveté with honesty, courage, and the strong creativity needed to form *one's own* values.

Der Übermensch

This emphasis on creativity, on the possibility of new possibilities for human beings, makes Nietzsche a philosopher "of the future."[4] For Nietzsche, "the human being is something that shall be overcome," a mere "rope" between "beast" and what Nietzsche calls *der Übermensch*, literally that which is over, or beyond, the human being (Nietzsche 1978: 12, 14). Given Nietzsche's condemnation of universality, there is not – and cannot be – a formula for what an *Übermensch* is. But Nietzsche offers a few general visions of a future, better, humanity. The *Übermensch*, unsurprisingly, is creative and self-confident, not seeking to accommodate his views to those of the masses but willing to strike out on his own. This self-confidence goes further in Nietzsche's doctrine of the "eternal recurrence," which he calls "the highest formula of affirmation that is at all attainable" (Nietzsche 1967: 295). The thought that the world will repeat itself infinitely, that "whatever was and is" will be "repeated into all eternity" (Nietzsche 1967: 68) at first terrifies Zarathustra (the protagonist of *Thus Spake Zarathustra*), but ends up being embraced in moments when Zarathustra is most akin to the *Übermensch*. The *Übermensch* is an "ideal of the most high-spirited, alive, and world-affirming human being ... shouting insatiably *da capo* [repeat] – not only to himself but to the whole play and spectacle, [and] who makes [this whole play] necessary because again and again he ... makes himself necessary" (Nietzsche 1978: 68). The ideal person is so self-affirming that he affirms – again and again – all the pettiness, misery, and evil in the world, because it went into making a world that included *himself*.

But this self-affirmation also implies that the *Übermensch* live her life in such a way that it *can* justify the world. While "once one said 'God' when one looked upon distant seas," Nietzsche now invites us to say *"Übermensch"* (Nietzsche 1978: 85). And for Nietzsche, there is a crucial difference between these ideals: "God is a conjecture, but I do not wish your conjecturing to reach beyond your creating will. Could you *create* a God? – Then, I pray you, be silent about all gods! But you could well create the *Übermensch"* (Nietzsche 1978: 85). Nietzsche is ambivalent about the *full* extent to which one can bring about the *Übermensch* – the preceding quotation continues "Not perhaps you yourselves ... but into ... forefathers of the *Übermensch* you could transform yourselves" – but the *Übermensch* is, at least, a goal that is attainable in principle, something toward which we can orient our active, creative powers rather than Someone to whom to submit. Thus Nietzsche (in the guise of Zarathustra) asks, "What have *you* done to surpass humankind?" (Nietzsche 1978: 12, my emphasis).

Unlike Darwin, Marx, and (as we will see) Freud, whose legacies are clearly identifiable in contemporary biology, psychology, and social sciences, Nietzsche did not leave behind a discipline distinct from philosophy. But Nietzsche's legacy lingers today not only in the discipline of philosophy itself, where he continues to be one of the most widely read philosophers, but also in the ever increasing emphasis on art, literature, and now film as sources for answering the question "What is the human being?" Just as some turn to biology or psychology as *sciences* that can answer that question, those who sense more to being human than what science captures are likely to turn to literature and art. And this emphasis on literature for thinking about humanity reflects deeply Nietzschean impulses. For one thing, literature refuses to simplify human behavior into simple formulae or universal rules; "common" literature is bad literature, and that which is truly great is something particular, individual, *extra*ordinary. Moreover, good literature exposes its readers to a range of human possibilities, opening new vistas and perspectives rather than simplifying perspectives into a taxonomy. And good literature (or art) is precisely the literature worth reading and rereading, literature depicting the lives that meet Nietzsche's vision of the *Übermensch* who can reflect with pleasure on the eternal return of all things because these are vindicated in her own interesting, original, dynamic, and creative life.

Freud and the Rise of Psychology

Sigmund Freud (1856–1939) is best known for various popular theories and expressions such as "Freudian slips" and the Oedipal Complex. But Freud played an important part in the emergence of modern empirical psychology. He insisted that psychology should be an empirical science, emphasizing that "the psycho-analytic view is ... empirical – either a direct expression of observations or the outcome of a process of working them over" (Freud 1920/1963: 302) – and comparing psycho-analysis with astronomy, as two subjects in which "experimentation is particularly difficult" but which can nonetheless make inferences based on observations (see e.g. Freud 1933/1964: 27). Freud emphasized the distinction between psychology and physiology (see Freud 1920/1963: 23–24) and thereby helped provide a realm of its own to scientific psychology. Freud also emphasized clinical and therapeutic applications of psychology.

Freud's most important contribution, not only to modern empirical psychology but also to conceptions of the human being more generally, was his emphasis on *unconscious* mental processes and structures. Freud insisted that the most important mental phenomena were *unconscious* and thus that empirical psychology would have to be *indirect*. Thus, for example, slips of the tongue and dreams "have a sense ..., meaning, intention, [and] purpose" (Freud 1920/1963: 74). But "To whom?" (Freud 1920/1963: 267). For Freud, we can best interpret actions and conscious mental processes as expressing aims and purposes of which one is not conscious or even which one consciously rejects. But then the psychologist must posit *unconscious* aims and purposes. Today, even if relatively few psychologists are strictly "Freudian," virtually all empirical psychologists agree that inner sense is often unreliable, that one must use indirect means to discern what is really going on in the mind of a human being, and that the analyst/experimenter can often know what is going on in a person's mind better than the person herself.

Freud was well aware of the importance of his emphasis on the unconscious: "the hypothesis of their being unconscious mental processes paves the way to a decisive new orientation in the world and science" (Freud 1920/ 1963: 26). As Freud puts it in his *Introductory Lectures on Psychoanalysis*:

> In the course of two centuries, the naïve self-love of men has had to submit to two major blows at the hands of science. The first was when they learnt that our earth was not the center of the universe ... This is associated in our minds with the name of Copernicus. ... The second blow fell when biological research destroyed man's supposedly privileged place in creation and proved his descent from the animal kingdom and his ineradicable animal nature. This revaluation has been accomplished in our own days by Darwin ... But human megalomania will have suffered its third and most wounding blow from the psychological research of the present day which seeks to prove to the ego that it is not even master in its own house, but must content itself with scanty information of what is going on unconsciously in its mind.
>
> (Freud 1920/1963: 352–53)

Freud – like Copernicus and Darwin – undermines humans' centrality, but Freud's revolution goes further than either Copernicus or Darwin because Freud challenges our centrality in *our own lives*. For Freud, much of who "I" am is not up to me. Not only am I not the center of the universe, nor even the pinnacle of life on earth; I am not even the most important force in my own soul.

As the preceding passage shows, Freud did not limit his conception of "unconscious" to rare and relatively unimportant mental processes of which one might not be aware at the moment. Freud shifts from "unconscious" as "the name of what is latent at the moment" to a whole theory of *the* unconscious as "a particular realm of the mind with its own wishful impulses, its own mode of expression, and its particular mental mechanisms" (Freud 1920/1963: 262). As his thought develops, he refines the structure of this realm of the mind, such that in his mature theory the human mind can be seen as structured along two axes. On the one hand, there is a distinction between the conscious, the pre-conscious, and the unconscious. The "preconscious" is an "unconscious that is only latent and thus [that] easily becomes conscious" (Freud 1933/1964: 89, cf. Freud 1920/1963: 366–68), while the unconscious strictly speaking is further from consciousness. The "transformation" of what is truly uncon-scious to consciousness is difficult, requiring for its possibility something like psycho-analysis, and this transformation is always incomplete (Freud 1933/1964: 89). One the other hand, cutting across the divide between conscious and unconscious processes is a three-fold distinction between the id (literally *das Es*, or "the it"), the ego (literally *das Ich*, or "the I"), and the super-ego.[5] The ego is what one normally considers one's self, the generally conscious, self-aware, decision-making regulator of one's life, the "reason and good sense" that must "guide the powerful movement" of the id (Freud 1933/1964: 95–96). The super-ego performs the functions of "self-observation, conscience, and [maintaining] one's ideals" (Freud 1933/1964: 83). What Kant calls the "predisposition to personality," the conscience against which one measures one's activities and evaluates them morally, is, for Freud, the "super-ego."

The id is Freud's most important contribution to the theory of human nature: "The space [in the mind] occupied by the unconscious id [is] incomparably greater than that of the ego or the preconscious" (Freud 1933/1964: 98); in fact, *all* of the parts of the mind are really just mod-ifications of the id, such that, for instance, the ego is "the better orga-nized part of the id, with its face turned toward reality" (Freud 1933/1964: 116). The id is "the dark inaccessible part of our personality ... , a chaos, a cauldron fully of seething excitations ... [It] knows ... no good and evil, no morality ... [but only] instinctual cathexes seeking dis-charge" (Freud 1933/1964: 91). The ego is subject to a "reality principle" that requires that it moderate its desires so that they are consistent both with each other and with what is achievable in the world. But in the id, "contrary [and unrealistic] impulses exist side by side" (Freud 1933/1964: 92). The law of non-contradiction and even "the philosophical theorem that space and time are necessary forms of our mental acts" do not apply to the id, where "no alteration ... is produced by the passage of time." The fundamental principles of the id are the pleasure principle, which Freud associates pre-eminently with sexual desire, and a principle of self-destruction and aggression (see Freud 1920/1961, Freud 1933/1964: chs. 32 and 34). The particular fixations and excitations of the id arise partly from innate natural instincts, partly from unconscious cultural inheritances, and largely from events – especially in infancy and childhood – that structure one's sexual and aggressive desires but that one refuses, for various reasons, to admit to consciousness. Thus the famous Oedipal Complex arises from innate sexual desires in infancy that focus on the mother as a desire-object. Particular and forgotten details of one's infantile relationship with one's mother can then exercise powerful but unconscious influences on one's later life.

In relation to Kant, Freud's most important challenges relate to the general problem of self-knowledge and to the specific issue of the origin and nature of morality. With respect to self-knowledge, Freud is arguably even more modest that Kant's own claim that "we can never, even by the most strenuous self-examination, get entirely behind our own covert incentives" (4: 407). In Kant, this strong claim implied only a fairly straightforward humility about self-knowledge and was conjoined with what remained a fairly naïve approach to psychological investigation, one that privileged introspection and straightforward inferences of motives from actions. Freud's complex psychic architecture, his willingness to posit unconscious forces radically at odds with what we experience in conscious life, and his development of a specific psychoanalytic methodology for unlocking the secrets of this unconscious all take him very far from Kant.

Far more important than his particular Copernican turn, however, is Freud's revaluation of the value of conscience. For Kant, what it ultimately means for a human being to reach his potential is for him to live autonomously, in accordance with normative principles of thought, feeling, and action that arise from participation in an intelligible world. In Freudian terms, Kant advocates a complete subordination of one's id (or "untamed passions," Freud 1933/1964: 95) and even one's ego to one's super-ego, one's conscience. But while Freud shares with Kant a commitment to articulate "rational explanations" for moral requirements rather than ascribing them to divine decree (Freud 1927/1961), he does not see the super-ego as the unconditionally good expression of human autonomy. Freud's "rational explanation" is ultimately in terms of the realistic satisfaction of desires rather than a defense of a categorically valid imperative governing humans as members of an intelligible realm. Even the super-ego, which arguably issues categorical imperatives, is seen by Freud as an internalization of one's infantile fear of parental punishment and Oedipal desire to please one's mother (Freud 1933/1964: 77f.). It is a "vehicle of tradition" (Freud 1933/1964: 84) and largely responsible for repressions and neuroses that haunt people in their adult lives. In sharp contrast to the moral–prudential goals of Kant's pragmatic anthropology, "the therapeutic efforts of psychoanalysis have [the] intention ... to strengthen the ego, to make it more independent of the super-ego ... so that it can appropriate fresh portions of the id" (Freud 1933/1964: 99).

While Freud's specific insights have waxed and waned in terms of their importance for contemporary psychological practice (see e.g. Kramer 2006: 10), his legacy continues to influence contemporary thinking about the human being in at least four important ways. First, Freud brought the unconscious mind to center stage for psychological explanation of human thought and action. Today, even those who distance themselves from Freud's specific theories often continue to think of mental life on the model of competing (or cooperating) psychic forces of which one is only rarely conscious. Second, there continue to be vibrant psychoanalytic practices, and psychoanalytic techniques for diagnosing and treating mental disorders continue to be used in contemporary psychiatry. Third, near the end of his career, Freud applied his general models of explanation to historical and cultural analysis, where they continue to be widely appropriated by anthropologists and cultural critics. And finally and most importantly, Freud's Copernican Revolution continues to exercise a profound influence on general human self-conceptions. The sort of naïve assertions of self-awareness that dominated earlier attempts to know and express oneself have been replaced by suspicion of our self-awareness and a willingness to accept that who we are is largely the product of uncontrolled psychological forces of which we are often unaware.

Summary

This chapter surveyed five of the most important figures who came after Kant and shaped debates about human beings. In very different ways, Hegel Marx, Darwin, Nietzsche, and Freud helped open new vistas for understanding ourselves. Even within contemporary philosophy, many of the most important ways of addressing the question of human beings go back to one or more of these five thinkers. But they also helped shift Kant's question out of philosophy, into biology, psychology, other human sciences, and the arts. In the next chapter, we will take up the contemporary philosophical heirs of Darwin and Freud, who seek answers in the sciences of biology and psychology. Chapter 8 turns to thinkers who emphasize the contingency, historicity, and diversity of human natures, drawing from the historical and genealogical approaches of Hegel, Marx, and (especially) Nietzsche. And in Chapter 9, we look at existentialist approaches to the self, approaches that in many respects trace themselves to Nietzsche's movement "beyond good and evil," toward a radically self-affirming conception of the (super-)human self.

Further Reading

For the general post-Kantian philosophical scene in Germany, see Ameriks, Beiser, and Bowie. Beiser focuses on the immediate reception of Kant's philosophy (pre-Hegel), Ameriks gives an account of the reception of Kant up to and including Hegel that is sympathetic to Kant, and Bowie gives a good general overview of German philosophy from Kant to the present. In addition, diGiovanni and Sassen provide helpful primary sources for Kant's early reception.

Karl Ameriks, *Kant and the Fate of Autonomy: Problems in the Appropriation of the Critical Philosophy* (Cambridge: Cambridge University Press, 2000)

Frederick Beiser, *The Fate of Reason: German Philosophy from Kant to Fichte* (Cambridge, MA: Harvard University Press, 1993)

Andrew Bowie, *Introduction to German Philosophy from Kant to Habermas* (Cambridge: Polity, 2003)

George diGiovanni (ed.), *Between Kant and Hegel: Texts in the Development of Post-Kantian Idealism* (2nd edn., Indianapolis: Hackett, 2000)

Brigitte Sassen (ed.), *Kant's Early Critics: The Empiricist Critique of the Theoretical Philosophy* (Cambridge: Cambridge University Press, 2000)

For Hegel, Taylor is a classic by a leading contemporary neo-Hegelian. Pinkard, Pippin, and Wood provide helpful introductions with different emphases (Pinkard on philosophy as a whole, Pippin and Wood on ethics), and Pinkard's biography is well-written and philosophically rich. Hegel's own works are notoriously difficult, but works below are relatively readable and include some engagement with Kant.

G.W.F. Hegel, *Introduction to the Philosophy of History* (Indianapolis: Hackett, 1998)

G.W.F. Hegel, *The Philosophy of Right* (ed. Allen Wood, Cambridge: Cambridge University Press, 1991)

Terry Pinkard, *Hegel: A Biography* (Cambridge: Cambridge University Press, 2001)

Terry Pinkard, *Hegel's Phenomenology: The Sociality of Reason* (Cambridge: Cambridge University Press, 1996)

Robert Pippin, *Kant's Practical Philosophy: Rational Agency as Practical Life* (Cambridge: Cambridge University Press, 2008)

Charles Taylor, *Hegel* (Cambridge: Cambridge University Press, 1977)

Allen Wood, *Hegel's Ethical Thought* (Cambridge: Cambridge University Press, 1990)

Marx, Freud, Darwin, and Nietzsche have generated more scholarly commentary than Kant, so lists below are extremely selective. Wood provides a general introduction to Marx. Rockmore is helpful for distinguishing Marx's thought from Marx*ist* thought. For investigating Marx's conception of human nature, Sayers provides a helpful introduction, and Schmidt and Cohen provide important and influential readings of key concepts. The Marx reader below includes many of Marx's most important writings relevant to human nature.

G.A. Cohen, *History, Labor, and Freedom: Themes from Marx* (Oxford: Clarendon, 1988)

Karl Marx, *Selected Writings* (ed. Laurence Simon, Indianapolis: Hackett, 1994)

Tom Rockmore, *Marx after Marxism* (London: Wiley-Blackwell, 2002)

Sean Sayers, *Marxism and Human Nature* (London: Routledge, 1998)

Richard Schmitt, *Alienation and Freedom* (Boulder, CO: Westview Press, 2002)

Allen Wood, *Karl Marx* (2nd edn., London: Routledge, 2004)

Darwin's classic work is the *Origin of Species*, but *The Descent of Man* is more important for Kant's question. Desmond and Moore's biography is excellent on both Darwin's life and his thought. Mayr and Dennett provide introductions to Darwinism, with Dennett's focusing on philosophical implications of evolutionary theory. Depew and Weber highlight the development of evolutionary biology from Darwin's own theory to the late twentieth century.

Charles Darwin, *The Origin of Species* (intro. by Ernst Mayr, Cambridge, MA: Harvard University Press, 1964)

Charles Darwin, *The Descent of Man, and Selection in Relation to Sex* (Princeton: Princeton University Press, 1991)

Daniel Dennett, *Darwin's Dangerous Idea* (New York: Touchstone, 1996)

David Depew and Bruce Weber, *Darwinism Evolving: Systems Dynamics and the Genealogy of Natural Selection* (Cambridge, MA: MIT Press, 1995)

Adrian Desmond and James Moore, *Darwin: The Life of a Tormented Evolutionist* (New York: W.W. Norton, 1991)

E. Mayr, *Evolution and the Diversity of Life* (Cambridge, MA: Harvard University Press, 1976)

Ernst Mayr, *One Long Argument: Charles Darwin and the Genesis of Modern Evolutionary Thought* (Cambridge MA: Harvard University Press, 1991)

Nietzsche has been an inspiration to countless recent philosophers. Allison (1985) provides an excellent collection of essays by prominent recent continental philosophers (including Heidegger, Deleuze, and Derrida). For more accessible introductions to Nietzsche, Kaufman and Nehamas are helpful. Leiter and Sinhababu (2009) collect essays showing recent trends toward appropriating Nietzsche for contemporary analytic philosophy. Nietzschean texts to start with are *Beyond Good and Evil* and *On the Genealogy of Morals*, the former with a broader focus than the latter.

David Allison (ed.), *The New Nietzsche* (Cambridge, MA: MIT Press, 1985)

Walter Kaufmann, *Nietzsche: Philosopher, Psychologist, Antichrist* (Princeton: Princeton University Press, 1950)

Brian Leiter and Neil Sinhababu (eds.), Nietzsche and Morality (Oxford: Oxford University Press, 2009)

Alexander Nehamas, *Nietzsche: Life as Literature* (Cambridge, MA: Harvard University Press, 1995)

Friedrich Nietzsche, *Beyond Good and Evil* (trans. Walter Kaufman, New York: Random House, 1989)

Friedrich Nietzsche, *On the Genealogy of Morals* (trans. Walter Kaufman, New York: Random House, 1967)

Freud's introductions to his thought are helpful and readable. Gay's biography excellently introduces both Freud and his views of human nature. Lear provides a good philosophical introduction with advice on further readings.

Sigmund Freud, *Introductory Lectures on Psychoanalysis* (trans. James Strachey, New York: W.W. Norton, 1966)

Sigmund Freud, *New Introductory Lectures on Psychoanalysis* (trans. James Strachey, New York: W.W. Norton, 1964–65)

Peter Gay, *Freud: A Life for Our Time* (New York: W.W. Norton, 1998)

Jonathan Lear, *Freud* (New York: Routledge, 2005)

Part III

WHAT IS THE HUMAN BEING TODAY?

7 Scientific Naturalism

When Kant answered the question "What is the human being?," biologists still took seriously that species were eternal creations and every human being might literally and physically have "pre-existed" in Eve's womb. Kant despaired of finding a "Newton ... of a blade of grass" (5: 400) and emphasized that scientists "do not know cranial nerves and fibers, nor do [they] know how to put them to use" (7: 119). Empirical psychology was largely based on introspection and was not distinguished from philosophy.

Things have changed. Consider just a few highlights of our scientific knowledge about human beings:

- The Human Genome Project has successfully mapped humans' genetic code, and we increasingly understand both where we came from and how genes direct our development.
- PET and fMRI scans can track brain activity of human beings involved in specific mental tasks.
- Studies on non-human primates show possible origins of human altruism, language, and culture.
- Psychologists have developed models of unconscious motivation, and new methodologies (such as neural mapping, controlled correlational studies, and double-blind experiments) have begun to transform empirical psychology into a rigorous science.

In addition to these very general developments, scientists have recently made some counter-intuitive claims that would dramatically change our sense of what it is to be human. For example,

- Benjamin Libet and others argue that unconscious physical processes in the brain precede and cause conscious choices.
- A biases and heuristics program in contemporary psychology offers evidence that irrationality is widespread and unrecognized even in the most careful and thoughtful human beings.

- Situationist psychology shows that much human behavior is determined by context rather than character.

These developments cover only a small fraction of recent progress in human biology and psychology, without even mentioning contributions by economics, sociology, anthropology and history to understanding human beings.

Taken together, this scientific progress not only calls into question fundamental aspects of Kant's anthropology but also offers some people hope that the question "What is the human being?" can be answered by science rather than philosophy. In other words, scientific progress provides hope for scientific naturalism about human beings. Scientific naturalism is the view that everything that is real is part of the world investigated by natural sciences (including biology and scientific psychology). Generally, people think that questions such as "What is the monarch butterfly?" or "What is oxygen?" are sufficiently answered, in principle at least, by fully developed scientific accounts of butterflies or oxygen. Many suggest that human beings are not fundamentally different, that the best answer to "What is the human being?" is whatever our best biological and/or psychological theories say the human being is. Philosophy has nothing distinctive to contribute except to "clarify and unify" what is given by science (Dennett 2003: 15).

This chapter explains and critiques scientific naturalists' answers to Kant's question. Given the breadth of empirical research and range of naturalist approaches, this chapter limits itself to a few highlights. By the end of my brief survey, I hope simplistic reactions to naturalism will become more complicated. Naturalism does not flow as neatly from the progress of science as its proponents hope, but it does have more adequate resources for dealing with important aspects of our self-conception than many opponents fear. Moreover, the value of science is greatest for actually helping us be better human beings when incorporated into a broadly Kantian anthropological framework.

Because scientific naturalism often involves a commitment to "materialism" (the view that there is nothing non-material such as a soul) and "reductionism" (that non-physical processes such as cognition can be understood in terms of, or "reduced to," physical processes), I start with the most thoroughly materialist and reductionist approach to human beings: cognitive neuroscience, which investigates human reasoning, emotion, decision-making, and even creativity from the standpoint of physical processes in the brain. I then turn to evolutionary biology, which describes how human beings have developed from more primitive biological ancestors, and opens the door to a different sort of naturalist explanation of cognition, consciousness, culture, morals, and even freedom. Finally, I examine some current trends in empirical psychology that philosophers have increasingly used to develop naturalistic approaches to epistemology and ethics.

Human Brains: Neuroscience and the Philosophy of Mind

In 1848, fifty years after the publication of Kant's *Anthropology*, an accidental explosion sent an iron rod through the head of Phineas Gage, a railroad worker in Vermont. After recovering from the initial shock, Gage arose, rode into town awake and alert, and saw a doctor. Within two months, Gage was said to be cured, and by all indications was perfectly functional. But whereas Gage before the accident had been polite, well-balanced, and self-disciplined, Gage after the accident was "fitful, irreverent ..., capricious and vacillating" (Valenstein 1986: 90, cf. Damasio 1994). A physical alteration to Gage's brain seems to have engendered a wholesale transformation in his character.

Gage's case is not unique; physical brain injuries have long caused mental and dispositional changes in human beings. And recent years have brought increasingly fine-tuned accounts of the parts of the brain responsible for different mental functions. At first, such scientific developments occurred primarily through careful analyses of victims of accidents like Gage's. But since the mid-1970s, PET and fMRI scans have made it possible to scan brains of normally functioning adults performing mental tasks. This brought increasingly fine-tuned maps of different control centers in the brain. Scientists have identified specific parts of the frontal and temporal lobes as loci of linguistic activity, a primary projection area in the parietal lobe that controls most motor activity, and C-fibers in peripheral nerves of the somatosensory area that are instrumental in feeling pain. At the same time, studies of neurons and glial cells at the cellular level help scientists understand brain activity and development, and new theoretical frameworks increasingly allow modeling of the brain as a complex neural network.

Applying these neuroscientific discoveries to thinking about the human mind and its relationship with the brain has become a central problem within the "philosophy of mind." One view of the mind, which might seem to be the most intuitive implication of the close correlation between brain-states and mental states, is "eliminativist materialism" about mental properties, the "identification of mental states with physical states," such that what seems to be mental is really physical. Paul Churchland compares the case with that of color: "In discriminating red from blue ... our external senses are actually discriminating between subtle differences in intricate electromagnetic ... properties of physical objects ... The same is presumably true of our 'inner' sense: introspection" (Churchland 1984: 29).

Such a view represents a strong scientific naturalism, in that there is nothing more to human beings than our (neuro)physiology. It also implies materialism and reductionism: what seems mental is really physical, and psychology is wholly reducible to neurobiology. As Daniel Dennett has put it, "there is only one sort of stuff, namely matter – the physical stuff of physics, chemistry, and physiology – and the mind is somehow nothing but a physical phenomenon. In short, the mind is the brain" (Dennett 1991: 33).

Some important problems with eliminativism are related to qualia, multiple-realizability, and intentionality/normativity. The term "qualia" refers to the subjective feel of particular mental states. In his "What is it Like to be a Bat?," Thomas Nagel argues that the subjective character of an organism's mental states entails that "there is something that it is like to be that organism – something it is like for the organism" (Nagel 1974: 476, cf. Tye 2007). Many philosophers have come to think that this subjective character of our mental states makes the mind irreducible to brain-states investigated by neurobiology. The problem of multiple-realizability arises for many attempts at reductionism, including the reduction of the mind to the brain. The problem is that phenomena that appear at one level of explanation (e.g. pain) are realizable in different ways at a different level of explanation (e.g. in different neurobiological configurations, see Putnam 1967). The problems of intentionality and normativity come from the fact that many mental states seem to be *about* something and/or to have the potential of being right or wrong. One is not merely afraid, but afraid *of* a lion. One does not merely have a belief-state, one believes (rightly or wrongly) that the lion is going to attack. One does not merely have a volitional state, one decides (rightly or wrongly) to run away from the lion. But while a brain state can be *caused* by something else (say, the perception of a lion), it is not clear how it can be *of* something else, nor how it could be true or false or right or wrong.

These considerations have led many philosophers of mind to develop alternatives to eliminative materialism. One alternative is Descartes's substance-dualism, which described the mind–brain connection as a mutual influence between two distinct substances: a non-material soul, or mind, and a material part of the brain. The soul experiences qualia and engages in intentional, normatively governable mental activity. The body is purely material and acts on other material things. These two substances are capable of interaction, so that changes in one can cause changes in the other, but neither is reducible to the other and either could in principle persist without the other.

Currently, most philosophers of mind reject both substance-dualism and eliminativism in favor of a more complex view that can be called functionalist property-dualism (Botterill and Carruthers 1999). Property-dualism is way of responding to the problems with crude materialism without falling into a full-blown substance-dualism. It posits two irreducibly distinct sorts of *properties* of human beings: physical and mental. These are not different substances, but they are irreducible to one another, such that one could make true claims about the mind – say, claims about qualia or connections between mental states – that could not be translated into claims about the brain. Functionalism is a way of making sense of what one refers to when one describes a particular type of mental state: "functionalists characterize mental states in terms of their [functions or] causal roles, particularly, in terms of the causal relations to sensory stimulations, behavioral outputs, and other mental states" (Block 1980: 172, cf. Putnam 1967).

To some, Kant's view on the relationship between mental states and brain-states might seem similar to Descartes's substance-dualism. Kant distinguishes between the noumenal thing-in-itself and phenomenal appearances, and Kant applies this distinction to human beings, who are both transcendentally free things-in-themselves and embodied appearances. But this apparent parallel with Cartesian dualism is misleading. While Kant makes use of the distinction between transcendental and empirical anthropology to make sense of some of the problems that lead philosophers of mind toward various dualisms, his own account of Cartesian dualism locates this dualism within the realm of appearances (see e.g. 28: 680–81). In fact, since the category of "substance" is a category that structures the empirical world, Kant's distinction between things-in-themselves and appearances cannot, except in an analogical sense, be considered a "substance-dualism." For Kant, the "mind" is an empirical object available to inner sense, and Kant must therefore ask to what extent this empirical mind is reducible to something purely physical. Kant thus distinguishes empirical-substance-dualism, by virtue of which the mind and body would be empirically distinct substances, from transcendental-dualism, according to which the mind-in-itself must be distinguished from the empirically-knowable-mind.

Kant is certainly committed to a transcendental-dualism that implies two irreducible perspectives on mental life. Transcendental anthropology is distinct from empirical anthropology, and insofar as there is an empirical mind, it can be distinguished from its noumenal ground. But substance-dualism is not needed to preserve both a standpoint on the mind-in-itself that is irreducible to empirical descriptions and the possibility of normative claims about human thoughts, feelings, and choices. Even if some metaphysics of mind is needed to ground this distinction between standpoints – something about which contemporary interpreters of Kant sharply disagree – one could draw on transcendental property-dualism according to which the human mind has properties "in-itself" that are irreducible to its empirical properties. Kant's transcendental idealism commits him to some dualism, but not to a distinction between two interacting substances. And in this manner, Kant provides a way to be materialist about the *empirical* mind while reserving a space for normativity and other "from-within" aspects of the mind understood transcendentally.

In discussing the empirical mind, however, Kant argues that because "the soul can perceive itself only through the inner sense" (12: 35) and inner sense is purely temporal while the physical body is always spatial—temporal, the most that physiological explanation could ever do is explain "the matter that makes possible" mental phenomena (12: 35). Mental phenomena as such have a non-spatial character that is irreducible to the physical. The content of an inner experience – a feeling of fear, for example – thus cannot be identical to the content of an observed brain-state. Just as empirical psychology must posit different kinds of mental state to make sense of human mental phenomena, science in general cannot depend upon purely physical causes in making sense of the behavior of living things. Science should use as few principles as possible, but as many as are truly needed to make sense of observed phenomena. Just as Newton legitimately (according to Kant) posited gravitational force to model physical motions, Kant posits psychological forces not reduced to physical ones.

These Kantian arguments need not imply empirical-substance-dualism. The argument based on distinguishing inner from outer sense is a sort of qualia argument, consistent with various accounts of mind–body unity. Kant even does some speculative neuroscience, suggesting chemical processes in "the water of the brain" that might underlie processes of "separating and combining given sensory representations" (12: 34). And the argument from the need for purely psychological laws is empirically contingent and might be falsified given neuroscientific progress. At present, however, optimism that all psychological laws will eventually be translatable into neuro-physiological laws is merely a scientific ideal; and the multiple-realizability of mental states provides reasons for thinking that even the most sophisticated neuroscience will still leave room for properly psychological laws in explaining human thoughts and actions. But this argument, too, does not require a substance-dualism, only an irreducibility of the relevant laws. The same substance can have different powers – as Kant clearly thinks is true of the human soul – and there is no reason that the physical powers of the brain and the mental powers of the mind could not be distinct powers of the same thing (the brain–mind).

In general, Kant's anthropology situates him well vis-a-vis contemporary debates in the philosophy of mind. Kant arguably develops a functionalist account of mental states that need not depend upon any empirical sub-stance-dualisms and can actually contribute to contemporary functionalist accounts (cf. Meerbote 1989, Brook 2004). His argument based on the non-spatial character of inner sense contributes an important variation on the qualia argument. His generally Newtonian approach to science provides a basis for distinguishing psychological and physical laws, one that is appropriately modest about the prospects for neuroscience, not limiting these prospects a priori but also recognizing the still-present need for non-physical laws to fully make sense of human beings. In both respects, Kant's philosophy of mind anticipates important contemporary arguments for an empirical dualism between mind and body. Kant's transcendental idealism, wherein the mind as seen from-within and bound to normative laws is distinguished from the mind as an object of empirical knowledge, further enriches his philosophy of mind. Moreover Kant rightly argues that with respect to normativity, the problem is not eliminativism or materialism but any form of naturalism. Treating the mind as an object of description according to natural laws is insufficient for giving an account of the mind as bound by normative laws. The normativity problem calls for a different sort of solution than the problems of irreducibility and qualia.

Even if Kant's overall account of the human being is compatible with general developments in neuroscience, however, certain neuroscientific findings have been taken to challenge particular Kantian claims about human beings. Many of these findings require only minor modifications of or additions to Kant's psychology, but some recent research suggests pictures of the human mind that seem to challenge some of our (and Kant's) most fundamental conceptions of what it means to be human. A study by Benjamin Libet, for example, has subjects flick their wrists while researchers scan their brain activity with an EEG. Subjects flicked their wrists at will, and Libet found that each wrist-flicking was preceded by a consistent EEG pattern. Libet then asked subjects to look at a simple, rapidly moving clock face and note the position of a dot (equivalent to a clock hand) at the moment they made the conscious decision to flick their wrist. The surprising result is that the EEG pattern that brings about wrist-flicking preceded the conscious decision to flick. As Libet puts the results of his study, "The initiation of the freely voluntary act appears to begin in the brain unconsciously, well before the person consciously knows he wants to act! Is there, then, any role for conscious will in the performance of this voluntary act?" (Libet 1999: 51).[1]

For Kant, however, "conscious decision-making" is an ambiguous phrase that can refer to either an object of inner sense – one's introspection of a particular event of cognition giving rise to a volition – or a transcendental standpoint of evaluating choices "from-within" deliberation. Empirically, Libet's experiment need not raise any red flags, since Kant's empirical dualism is consistent with conscious psychological states being correlated with and even caused by physical states. Explanation in terms of conscious decisions takes place at a different level from explanation in terms of brain-state fluctuations, so what matters in this case is merely that conscious decision takes place, not the timing of that decision relative to the physical changes that underlie it.

The greater threat might seem to be to the transcendental perspective on action, since Libet's experiment makes it look as though brain-states must be the cause of choices rather than vice versa. But for Kant, the priority of free choice over the determinism of the empirical world is not temporal. The suggestion that brain-patterns precede conscious choices seems threatening because we assume that unless our choices come temporally first and determine the structure of the world, we cannot really be responsible for them. This is just the conception of freedom that Kant's transcendental anthropology rejects, by showing that we can be responsible for actions even if, from a scientific perspective, we need to see those actions as the results of prior causes in a deterministic world. It should come as no surprise that scientists looking for causes of human actions eventually find them, since they modify their overarching theories in order to make human behavior fit into the same causal–determinist models as other phenomena. But the fact that scientists can and must continue to refine their theories to develop better and better causal models of human behavior does not change the nature of our transcendental standpoint on human action. From within the standpoint of a deliberating agent, we must still see our actions as the free results of choices that *ground* those actions and are undetermined by physical causes.

Darwinism and Human Evolution

Contemporary neuroscience invites questions about how physical systems such as the human brain arose. As we saw in Chapter 2, Kant rejected contemporaries' attempted naturalistic explanations of basic human pre-dispositions (8: 110). But Darwin's theory of evolution offered a new theoretical framework for answering such questions. The twentieth century saw a "Darwinian synthesis" of Darwin's theory of natural selection and Gregor Mendel's theory of heredity, and the discovery of DNA by Watson and Crick in 1943 further explained the physical bases of human evolution.

The immediate implications of the current biological synthesis between Darwinian natural selection and molecular biology for thinking about human beings are fairly straightforward. Like all life on earth, humans evolved from simpler organisms. Early in the history of our planet, molecules emerged that were capable of replicating themselves with slight variations. Those variations better at self-replication and persistence in the environment increased in number, and at a certain point reached levels of complexity that could warrant the label "life." These self-replicating "organisms" competed for energy and other resources and, through natural selection, those better at replicating in their environments grew in number. The features that distinguish human beings from other animals are features that arose by means of molecular (primarily genetic) mutations preserved through this process of natural selection, whereby variations that add "fitness" – that is, allow survival and reproduction in greater numbers – grow more prevalent in the population. Human animals are well-adapted to our environments because earlier members of our genus that were not well-adapted died and left no offspring. The human brain has the complex structure that it does because this advanced brain allowed ancestral humans to outcompete their closest relatives.

As a tool for making sense of our world and ourselves, evolutionary biology has proven incredibly powerful over the past fifty years in such areas as understanding and diagnosing diseases, preserving endangered species, conducting population studies, and doing forensics. Evolutionary models of human beings also provide a naturalist framework for theorizing about human nature. One can explain central features of human beings by showing how those features could have evolved through natural selection. Given recent work applying evolutionary theory to human beings, there is reason to think that such accounts will be more illuminating than one might have expected. One might even think that the advanced state of human sciences such as evolutionary biology leave little for philosophy but to clarify and systematize "investigations in the natural sciences" (Dennett 2003: 15).

Many worry that any evolutionary approach to human beings will result in a picture of humans as hopelessly selfish animals seeking only to thrive and reproduce in a cut-throat world where "the fittest survive." More generally, some wonder whether central human concerns – morality, art, and even the sciences themselves, not to mention true love and religious experience – can be accounted for by evolutionary theory. Some of these concerns are concerns about naturalism more generally, questions about whether any theory that treats human beings as natural beings can accommodate central aspects of who we are. But some are tied to the particular kind of naturalist explanations offered by evolutionary theory.

In the last thirty years, sophisticated Darwinian accounts of human nature have emerged that move beyond caricatures of evolution as implying that human beings are fundamentally nothing more than clever, selfish primates. The richness of these accounts is impossible to convey in this short chapter, but three central issues – the evolution of altruism, the role of "memes" in evolution, and the nature of human freedom – give a sense of how evolutionary theory is used to make sense of aspects of human beings that might seem to transcend simplistic inferences from descent by natural selection.

Evolutionary theorizing about altruism might seem oxymoronic because many see the claim that everyone is out for themselves as a central premise of evolution. But Darwin's own *Descent of Man* emphasized that human fitness is enhanced through the development of "social instincts" that "lead an animal to take pleasure in the society of its fellows, to feel a certain amount of sympathy for them, and to perform various services for them" (Darwin 1981: 72). As our understanding of the processes of evolution grows, we see cooperative forms of natural selection playing key roles in the development of virtually all life on earth. A first approximation to altruism is present even in the most basic units of life on earth, the "eukaryotes" that consist in mutually dependent descendants of formerly independent organisms. Human cells contain, for example, mitochondria, which do most of the energy-processing in our cells and which have their own DNA, and the vast majority (more than 99 percent!) of the genes in our bodies are in "non-human" micro-organisms living in our guts (Gill et al. 2006). Evolutionary "fitness" is not merely – or primarily – a matter of killing off opponents. It can just as easily be a matter of cooperating in particularly effectively ways (cf. Dennett 1995).

> Similarly in the human case, societies whose members cooperate tend to outperform those that constantly fight, so social affection and cooperation evolve among human beings.
>
> When two tribes of primeval man, living in the same country, came into competition, if the one tribe included ... a greater number of ... sympathetic and faithful members, who were always ready to warn each other of danger, to aid and defend each other, this tribe would without doubt succeed best and conquer the other.
>
> (Darwin 1981: 162)

Darwin's point can be seen from the perspective of genetics. In *The Selfish Gene* (1974), Richard Dawkins helpfully highlights that evolutionary "selfishness" takes place at the level of the genes. This does not mean that there is a gene "for selfishness," but rather that genes code for what best allows the *gene* to survive and replicate (over the long term). Because familial groups share much genetic material, genes tend to survive and propagate insofar as they give rise to instincts to protect one's kin. The "interest" of one's genes might well require that one sacrifice oneself for the sake of a sibling or child who shares copies of those genes. And that will tend to foster altruism at least toward groups to which one is genetically similar. Importantly, there is nothing "selfish" about one's behavior here; genes code for behavior that – from the standpoint of the individual – is *genuinely* altruistic. To these considerations about genetic and kin selection, many add game theoretic accounts of benefits of altruism (when supplemented with retributive tendencies) in the context of repeated "Prisoner's Dilemma" situations (see e.g. Maynard Smith 1982,

Dennett 2003: 147–50). Other contemporary biologists argue that altruism can evolve through group selection in populations of non-genetically related groups formed through "assortative" interactions (Sober and Sloan Wilson 1998: 137–40).

Even if evolutionary theory is not committed to a conception of human beings as thoroughly selfish, however, it may seem ill-equipped to account for the great cultural achievements of human beings, our religious institutions, great works of literature, complex social orders, and scientific knowledge. In recent years, evolutionary theorists developed various theoretical tools for this task, such as the concept of "memes." A meme is a "cultural replicator parallel to [a] gene," or, put another way, a "parasite ... [that] use[s] human brains ... as [its] temporary homes and jump[s] from brain to brain to reproduce" (Dennett 2003: 175). The basic idea behind memes involves applying the general structure of Darwinian selection beyond the specific context of physical–biological entities.[2] Genes are relatively complex molecules capable of mutations that can either enhance or diminish the capacity of the gene to replicate in a particular environment. Self-enhancing mutations produce more gene-copies and the mutated genes spread and persist, while self-diminishing mutations eventually perish. Similarly, memes are relatively complex units of culture; "made of information," memes can be "carried" as contents of mental states or written in a book or stored on a computer or posted on a billboard. Like genes, memes are capable of mutations that can either enhance or diminish the capacity of the meme to replicate in a particular environment. Self-enhancing mutations produce more meme-copies and the mutated memes spread and persist, while self-diminishing mutations eventually perish. Memes can include items as diverse as melodies that get stuck in one's head, corporate logos, mathematical theorems, cooperative strategies, religious doctrines, habits, biases, and artistic techniques. Any possible "unit of culture" is capable of mutation and subject to forces of natural selection. The most successful memes survive.

Just as genes did not exist on earth until a couple billion years ago, sophisticated memes did not exist until about 50,000 years ago, when certain groups of animals – human beings – developed brains sufficiently advanced to develop cultural mechanisms – particularly complex languages – for the transmission of information. At first, the development of linguistic capacity served humans' selfish genes. Humans with brains that could host more memes created communities with more advanced possibilities of cultural transmission that were better able to navigate the world in which they lived. Such communities grew and thrived, while communities with less cultural potential died off. Human brains' abilities to generate, host, and transmit memes grew.

Once human brains became efficient meme-hosts, memes developed on their own. Like parasites, some memes enhance their hosts' fitness (e.g. hygiene techniques), while others do not (birth control techniques). In some cases, memes that inhibit hosts' fitness thereby destroy their potential for replication (Shakers' commitment to universal celibacy). In other cases, memes thrive and replicate even when they do not serve their hosts' genes (birth control, again). And some memes that might enhance hosts' fitness nonetheless are not good at replicating (information about foods' caloric content).

The relative independence of memes from genes provides a Darwinian way of explaining aspects of our lives that can seem mysterious from a narrowly gene-centered point of view: art, religion, poetry, and sciences are all memes or systems of memes. Creativity in these fields is the result of the tendency of memes, in the medium of the human brain, to mutate. Moreover, because memes often include standards for the adoption of future memes, "successful" memes must conform to the standards of the memetic landscape in which they emerge. The general model of memes as structures that mutate and compete for replication and persistence in human brains could explain progress in science; "great works" of art, music and poetry; and the delicate balance of tradition and innovation that characterizes religions and cultures. Recognizing the role of memes even helps make sense of human thirsts for knowledge and art "for their own sakes," since meme-success can be independent of other forms of success.

The combination of more sophisticated thinking about evolutionary theory (as in the case of altruism) with the addition of memes to the evolutionary framework has given rise to Darwinian-naturalistic accounts of human freedom and morality. Not all Darwinian naturalists think that freedom is something worth saving. Explaining human beings in terms of evolution by natural selection, especially with the addition of selfish genes, makes many think that freedom, and even morality, is simply a relic of scientific ignorance (e.g. Pereboom 2001). But the most sophisticated philosophical appropriations of Darwinism have sought to make sense of freedom and morals. Memes provide a first, crucial tool in freeing human beings from genetically programmed behaviors. Just as Kant emphasized the importance of the "higher faculty of desire" – motivation to act on principles rather than mere instincts – Darwinian naturalists can distinguish humans from other animals in that we often act in the interest of memes rather than genes. And meme-motivated action has a very different character than gene-motivated behavior.

> [A]ccess to memes [has] the effect of opening up a world of imagination to human beings that would otherwise be closed off. The salmon swimming upstream to spawn may be wily in a hundred ways, but she cannot even

contemplate the prospect of abandoning her reproductive project and deciding instead to live out her days studying coastal geography. The creation of a panoply of new standpoints is … the most striking product of the [memetic] revolution.

(Dennett 2003: 179)

Already, this is a huge step toward both freedom and morality. Human action takes place in the light of memes, reasons that motivate us insofar as we think about them. And moral systems, complex memetic structures that develop in the context of natural tendencies toward altruism, can present themselves as standpoints that inform our actions.

So far, this shows only that selfish genes and selfish memes can pursue their "own interests" independently of each other. Humans need not serve our genes, since we can also serve our memes. But how can we be "free" of both genes and memes? The answer to these questions is a twenty-first century naturalist version of a key Kantian empirical claim about what distinguishes human beings from animals. For Kant, what "raises him infinitely above all other living beings on earth" is "the fact that the human being can have the 'I' in his representations … Because of this he is a person, and by virtue of the unity of consciousness through all changes that happen to him, one and the same person" (7: 127). In the context of Darwinian naturalism, this "I" is itself a meme, one that has proven particularly adept at self-replication and that opens up a whole new vista of "self"-understanding and "self"-control. There are many possible routes for the formation, development, and persistence of the I-meme, but, however it arose, once human beings have a sense of self, there is no reason that this sense of self must remain motivationally inert. Recall that there were good reasons, from the gene-centered point of view, for the development of memes, but once memes came into the world, they took on a life of their own. In the same way, the emergence of an I-meme in human brains gives rise to a new kind of entity, a "self." And this new entity need not serve the interests of the memes that gave rise to it. Moreover, this new entity sets its own ends. As an entity with a sense of self, it is capable of higher-order desires, reflection on its identity, and even governance of itself by norms – including moral norms – that it "autonomously" endorses. For Darwinian naturalists, this is a sufficient basis for freedom, at least in every sense "worth wanting" (Dennett 1984).

A sufficiently rich Darwinian naturalism thus provides a much better answer to Kant's question than one might expect. Human beings are animals, but not "mere" animals. We are social animals that care about one another, expressing sympathy and compassion for those in need and resentment toward those who harm us. We have a complicated cognitive architecture that makes us hosts to countless "memes," units of culture that mutate and propagate in ways that provide a wide diversity of thoughts, opinions, and practices. Among these memes are moral rules, social and cultural norms, and even that sense of self by virtue of which we regulate our thoughts and behavior in accordance with what we take to be most important. By virtue of our evolutionary history, we have, as Dawkins put it, "the power to defy the selfish genes of our birth." We are animals but also agents, expressions of genes but also self-expressions, homo sapiens but also wise beings-like-us.

In assessing the possible relationship between Kant and contemporary Darwinism, an obvious starting point is Kant's philosophy of biology, one of the central claims of which is "that we can never adequately come to know organized beings ... in accordance with merely mechanical principles of nature ... [so] it would be absurd ... to hope that there may yet arise a Newton who could make comprehensible even the generation of a blade of grass according to natural laws that no intention had ordered" (5: 400). Some 150 years after Darwin laid out a detailed explanation of the origin of species, and fifty years after the birth of the molecular biology that describes precisely how genetic material develops into living things, Kant's despair about a Newton of a blade of grass seems exaggerated. As Ernst Mayr put it, "Darwin ... solved Kant's great puzzle" (Mayr 1988: 58). At the very least, Kant's indifference to and skepticism about scientific explanations of origins has been shown to be misguided.

In other respects, however, Kant's philosophy of biology is presciently anticipatory of present-day Darwinism. Kant's appeal to predispositions was an innovative response to biological debates in which the main protagonists argued either that biology was reducible to physics or that all living things were "preformed" in their earliest ancestors. Kant's middle ground posited that living things are not literally preformed but that explaining them also requires principles that go beyond mere mechanism. Darwinism clearly fits this general model. Evolution by natural selection, though not "teleological" in Kant's sense, is a principle for explanation distinct from the mechanical explanations that dominate physics. Kant was wrong about the specific principles that regulate the practice of biology, but correct that some heuristic principle of a broadly purposive nature is needed. And even if the origins of (human) predispositions are in principle explicable in terms of evolution, Kant was correct that any explanation of biological characteristics depends upon seeing how environmental conditions affect the expression of inherited (and not immediately explicable) "predispositions" for those characteristics.

But what of the further claim that understanding the evolution of human beings (and their predispositions) provides the basis for a sufficient answer to the question "What is the human being?" Did Kant, by ignoring questions of origins, pass over the best and most adequate answer to the question that sums up the whole of philosophy?

I think not. From a Kantian perspective, the question "What is the human being?" can be answered transcendentally, empirically, and pragmatically. Evolutionary biology greatly enriches Kant's empirical anthropology by showing origins of humans' natural predispositions, and accounts of these origins can even help explain the nature of those predispositions. Because empirical anthropology provides empirical insights needed for pragmatic anthropology, revisions and additions to our empirical picture of human beings can enrich or modify pragmatic anthropology. In addition to the many medical uses to which genetics, for instance, has been put, recognizing what makes memes thrive in particular contexts can help us influence others and avoid unwanted manipulation of ourselves. But for Kant, *transcendental* anthropology provides the most fundamental answers to the question "What is the human being?," answers that not only get to the root of who we are but also provide norms to orient pragmatic anthropology. The real dispute between Darwinian naturalism and Kant comes down to whether naturalism gives good reasons to reject Kant's three-fold division of anthropology, his prioritization of transcendental over empirical anthropology, or his transcendental anthropology.

When thinkers like Daniel Dennett insist that philosophy does little more than systematize insights of empirical sciences, it can seem as though Darwinists deny the need for and possibility of transcendental anthropology altogether. But even Dennett recognizes that there are distinct perspectives that one can take on human beings. The "meme-centered" point of view and especially the self's point of view can be explained naturalistically but are not themselves "naturalistic" perspectives. Dawkins, Dennett, and others rightly insist that once reflection and self-image enter the scene, human beings can ask for reasons and reflect normatively on what to think and do. Even memes that do not "enhance our fitness ... may be good for us in other, more important regards (e.g. literacy, music, and art)" (Dennett 2003: 177). Despite initial appearances, there is no dispute between Kant and the most prominent evolutionary naturalists about whether there is a normative perspective "from-within." Kant and Dennett both acknowledge that human beings can be studied as empirical objects in nature, and both recognize that the laws that explain the development of human selves are not identical to the rules that govern those selves from-within.

Nonetheless, Kant and Dennett fundamentally differ about the relative priority of transcendental and empirical anthropology. While Dennett explains transcendental anthropology with an empirical account of its evolution, Kant explains empirical anthropology with a transcendental account of its justificatory basis. Thus Dennett sees "the creation of a panoply of new standpoints" as "the most striking product of the ... [biological] revolution" that gave rise to human organisms (Dennett 2003: 179), while

Kant would see the ability to give an evolutionary account of human cognition as one striking result of applying our causal way of thinking about the world to ourselves. Dennett sees the biological standpoint as, fundamentally, the true standpoint, the "God perspective" (Dennett 2003: 45). Kant sees evolutionary biology as a standpoint of empirical cognition, which gets at one kind of truth, truth about the world-as-we-experience-it. Fundamentally, the difference between Kant and Dennett relates to the status of science as such.

Naturalists like Dennett tend to be strong scientific realists, who take natural science, at least ideally, to describe the truth, the whole truth, and nothing but the truth. Strong scientific realists need not think the current state of science gets everything correct, but insofar as our science fails to tell the (whole) truth, it needs improvement. By contrast, Kant is a limited scientific realist, who takes an ideal science to lay out truth and nothing but truth, but truth only about the world-as-we-can-experience-it. Scientific claims are claims that human beings, given our structure of cognition, should believe about the world.

One reason to favor limited scientific realism relates to Kant's central argument for his anthropological turn. Science operates with assumptions that guide inquiry and restrict the scope of scientific explanation. To some extent, these assumptions are justified by their success. Hypotheses are "confirmed" which bear fruit in terms of predictive or explanatory success. Ultimately, though, even the claim that predictive success is an indicator of truth is a mere assumption. And science operates with numerous heuristics ("look for adaptive advantages of distinctive features" and "as much as possible, explain similar effects by appeal to similar causes") and restrictions ("do not appeal to divine explanations" and "the future cannot cause changes in the past") that are not empirically tested but nonetheless constrain scientific explanation. As Kant argues, some scientific assumptions are impossible for human beings to question. We explain changes in terms of causes and assume that nature is uniform. We might add that when we engage in scientific explanation of the world, we treat hypotheses that are highly predictive as more likely than those without predictive value. But all these standards are rooted in the (transcendental) nature of human cognition; they reflect necessary conditions for humans to understand an empirical world. (A god would not need to appeal to predictive success to confirm hypotheses.)

What are we to make of these assumptions in human science? We could take them as self-evident, but doing so imports dogmatic rationalism into science. We could take them as purely arbitrary, but this undermines any justification for scientific realism. We could simply not worry about them; who doubts, after all, that a theory with predictive success is at least closer to the truth than one that consistently fails to make accurate predictions? This approach makes it psychologically possible to sustain a commitment to strong scientific realism, but provides no justification for that realism. Kant provides a better approach. Given that certain conditions seem to be necessary for humans to experience the world, we can simply take these conditions to be true of the world we experience. This is a pretty strong sort of realism that takes the best scientific theories to be true albeit only of the experienceable world. But while preserving a substantial commitment to scientific knowledge of the world, Kantian scientific realism rejects the God's-eye point of view assumed by strong scientific realists such as Dennett.

In itself, Kantian scientific realism might be *consistent* with strong scientific realism (what Kant would call "*transcendental* realism"); one could simply take on faith that what we experience exhausts all there is. But Kant explains that scientific explanation is merely one perspective human beings take on the world, one constrained by certain basic concepts and methodological assumptions. Humans also make sense of the world from within standpoints of practical and epistemic deliberation. For evolutionary biology to provide a sufficient answer to the question "What is the human being?" it must make sense of these standpoints. Strong scientific realism – the view that science provides the whole truth – depends upon biology providing an adequate *transcendental* anthropology. And evolutionary biology fails at this.

Evolution explains well how various human predispositions evolved. But evolutionary stories fail to reveal the transcendental structure of our faculties of cognition, feeling, and volition. We can tell stories about why humans have cognitive structures that make us think that 2 + 2 = 4, but this neither shows whether "2 + 2 = 4" is actually justified nor reveals the conditions of possibility of such justification. Similarly, even if kin selection and cognitive evolution give rise to propensies to endorse certain ethics-memes, this cannot show whether we are right to endorse those memes, or what the transcendental conditions of possibility of choice are (i.e. what is implied in our taking ourselves to be responsible for something).

When it comes to these sorts of normative claims, evolutionary approaches are notoriously unhelpful. When Dennett notes that memes that are deleterious from the point of view of survival and reproduction "may be good for us in other, more important regards," he says nothing about *why* those other regards are or even may be more important. And when he asks "whether or not morality itself is a feature we should try to preserve in our societies" (Dennett 2003: 279), there is nothing in his evolutionary account that can answer this question. Evolution might explain why art or music *in fact* matters more to us than genetic fitness, but Dennett does not even attempt to show how it can explain what makes certain goods genuinely more important. The reason for this failure is one that Kant rightly emphasizes. When actually trying to figure out what to believe, feel, or do, one looks not for explanatory causes that could predict beliefs or choices but for justificatory reasons for them. Once there are beings capable of reason-guided reflection, those beings take standpoints within which causal explanations are insufficient.[3]

The problem of justification arises for science itself. Evolutionary biology fails to justify the very cognitive practices it employs. Nothing about evolution, even supplemented by memes, shows that beliefs arising through natural selection are justified or true. Evolutionary explanation is *compatible* with an epistemology that could justify knowledge-claims, but evolution is not *sufficient* for such an epistemology. Evolutionary theory must be supplemented by something like Kant's transcendental anthropology, and because this transcendental anthropology provides the conditions of justification of science itself, it is more fundamental than biology. Moreover, even the most sophisticated description of human beings is insufficient to justify adopting any beliefs or choices without reason to use this description in some particular way. Evolutionary biology provides no transcendental anthropology because strong scientific realism is false. Evolutionary biology might tell the truth, but not the whole truth.

In itself, evolutionary biology fails to provide a transcendental anthropology. It also fails to successfully criticize Kant's transcendental anthropology. Dennett has objected, "Kant held that [pure, emotionless] judgments are not only the best sort of moral judgments, they are the only sort of judgments that count as moral judgments at all ... Is this perhaps a case in which holding out for perfection ... conceals the best path?" (Dennett 2003: 213). The question mark is apt, since Dennett provides no reason for thinking that Kant is misguided to "hold out for perfection." How would one answer this question? Not by appealing to evolutionary history, or even the role emotions actually play in most (even all) judgments considered "moral." Rather, one must look at volition from-within, asking what would justify "holding out for perfection" or looking for a better path. And Kant does this reflection. *Groundwork* argues that while human beings in fact act largely from "emotions," when reflecting upon what we ought to do, we see that a commitment to do what one feels like doing is not morally praiseworthy, even if one feels like doing the right thing. Kant might be wrong about this, but if he is, it is because he misread what volition looks like from-within, not because he failed to trace the evolutionary origin of moral judgment.

As in the case of neuroscience, contemporary evolutionary biology enriches our empirical self-conception and provides valuable insights that can be used in pragmatic anthropology. But Kant's transcendental anthropology – or something like it – is necessary to explain the science's conditions of possibility, to guide how empirical knowledge is used, and to justify norms for how humans ought to think, feel, and act.

Contemporary Psychology

The previous sections drew attention to developments in biology with significant impacts for understanding ourselves as human beings. Many recent advances in psychology are rooted in these biological developments. For example, one can make claims about the mental processes involved in various activities through scanning the brain and noting which areas are most active while subjects are engaged in various tasks, and psychologists have used studies of animals to gain insight into the way human brains work. But psychology has also made progress as a science distinct from biology through increasingly sophisticated experimental methodologies that provide evidence for claims about humans' mental lives. Because Kant developed a detailed empirical psychology, it is natural to compare Kant's psychology with contemporary psychological methods and theories. Moreover, as in the case of neuroscience and evolutionary biology, contemporary psychology has been a source for naturalist approaches to human beings. And recently, philosophers have appealed to specific findings in psychology that seem to raise problems for Kant's anthropology. This section starts with a brief Kantian discussion of methods and models within contemporary psychology and then turns to two ways in which contemporary psychology has fed naturalist philosophical accounts of human beings in ways that seem to threaten Kant's epistemology and moral theory.

Contemporary psychology has made considerable strides toward re-appropriating a broadly Kantian approach to the mind. In the mid-twentieth century, behaviorism dominated psychology. Promoted especially by B.F. Skinner, behaviorists assumed that human mental life was reducible to externally observable behaviors. In its most extreme form, the human mind was seen as a mere stimulus–response machine, and psychology was the science of classifying stimuli and responses. Recently, however, psychologists have regained an interest in the mind as such. Partly this has been for experimental reasons; one famous study on rats suggests the reality of "latent learning," where animals make evident that they knew things that were not normally expressed in behavior (Tolman and Hoznik 1930, Rescorla 1991). Partly, the shift away from behaviorism comes from the more obvious fact that even if certain very simple human responses are explicable in terms of innate or conditioned responses to stimuli, to explain even something as simple as why one runs out of a flaming building (see Pinker 1997: 62) or why one looks for one's own car in a parking lot, one must appeal to beliefs and desires. And more complicated aspects of being human seem utterly inexplicable without appealing to mental states. Imagine trying to distinguish, based purely on conditioned responses, between a person who marries for money, another who marries because she does not want to die old and alone, another who remains unmarried to avoid a messy divorce later, and a last who does not marry in order to have a good career. Explanations in terms of mental states are straightforward and predictively successful; those in terms of external inputs and behavioral outputs alone are hopelessly insufficient. Thus the study of mental states has become a mainstay of psychology (again).

For Kant, this shift is welcome. Kant's psychology systematically studied mental states and their inter-relationships. Like contemporary psychologists, Kant explains some behaviors as conditioned responses but appeals to complicated mental states for most behavior. Moreover, like contemporary psychologists, Kant is not content with casual folk psychology but seeks law-like relationships among clearly delineated types of mental states. And this brings out a further important parallel between Kant's psychology and contemporary psychology. Increasingly, psychologists today reject "blank-slate" approaches to human mental life in favor of approaches that look more like Kant's taxonomy of basic powers. As one philosopher of psychology has put it, "one of the major insights of [contemporary psychology] has been the extent to which we depend upon a natural cognitive endowment, which assigns processing tasks to modular structures with quite specific and restricted domains and inputs" (Botterill and Carruthers 1999: 50, cf. Fodor 1983, Pinker 2002). Just as Kant divided the mental into irreducible but interacting "powers" and "faculties" that operate by different causal laws, contemporary psychologists study the mind as a set of interacting "modules" that perform different tasks in bringing about human thoughts and actions. Moreover, like Kant, psychologists distinguish between biological bases for mental modules (Kantian "predispositions") and fully formed mental modules ("powers") that emerge when these bases develop in particular contexts (Botterill and Carruthers 1999: 96).

There are important differences between Kant's basic powers and modern mental modules. Kant's approach involved a metaphysical model of substances interacting by means of powers, while the modern approach sees modules as mental functions rooted in the evolved architecture of the brain. Kant's "powers" were also fairly commonsensical, and one distinguished between them using a broadly introspective approach. And Kantian powers are domain-general, in that a given power covers a wide range of possible contents. (Reasoning about statistics and about friends' reliability are both rooted in "reason.") By contrast, modern modular accounts of the mind assume that most modules are unconscious and can be distinguished by studying developmental evidence, neuro-psychological damage, and even brain-scanning. And domain-specific modular accounts of the mind are increasingly the norm. Thus the lists of mental modules in contemporary psychology look quite different from Kant's taxonomy, including specific modules for perception of color, perception of shape, detection of rhythm, and recognition of other people (Fodor 1983: 47–48).

Kant could accept most of these modifications of his view. While Kant did not draw all the distinctions of contemporary modular psychology, his empirical methodology lends itself to a willingness to admit sub-distinctions within his overall faculty psychology. And many of Kant's most important distinctions, such as his tri-partite conception of mental faculties or his distinction between higher and lower cognition, are vindicated by recent psychological research. The fact that many of these processes are unconscious need not pose intractable problems for Kant's empirical psychology. While there is a philosophical challenge in making sense of what it means for a mental state to be unconscious, Kant already made important steps in this direction. Natural propensities need not be conscious, lower faculties are not conscious in a reflective sense, and Kant was perfectly willing to allow for unconscious physical processes underlying humans' mental states. To make the further move that there could be particular psychological processes that operate like conscious mental states but without consciousness is a step beyond Kant, but not one he would have to reject.

Methodologically, two shifts have occurred over the past 100 years that raise questions about Kant's conception of the nature of empirical psychology. First, Kant insisted in his philosophy of science that psychology "can … never become … a science" (4: 471), but its progress might call this pessimism into question. Second, Kant's empirical anthropology is rooted in introspection, but introspection is regarded with suspicion in contemporary psychology (see, e.g., Bem 1967).

With respect to the first issue – the scientific status of psychology – there is virtually no real disagreement between Kant and contemporary psychologists. Psychology today, as for Kant, is a wholly empirical study of the human mind that aims to lay out the structure and explain the development of human mental structures. Specific thoughts and actions as well as the mind's underlying structures should be explained in accordance with the simplest possible causal laws. On all of these points, Kant's description of psychology fits contemporary practice. But Kant calls this a "natural history of the mind" that is only "science" in a loose sense. For Kant, science strictly speaking must have an a priori foundation, and Kant insists that no such foundation can be found for psychology. As far as contemporary psychologists indicate, Kant is correct. There are two minor ways in which contemporary psychology is more "scientific" than Kant supposed possible. First, psychology has made substantial progress toward grounding psychological explanation in biology. Kant, too, situated psychology in the context of biology, but evolution-informed psychology goes beyond Kant's expectations for the science. Second, Kant insisted that "there can be only so much *proper* science as there is *mathematics* therein" (4: 470) and that "mathematics is not applicable to" psychology (4: 471). But some forms of contemporary psychology are highly mathematical, including statistics to describe, organize, and interpret data and mathematical models of brain activity. This mathematization of psychology is important and unexpected by Kant, even if not the sort of mathematics that confers scientific status in Kant's sense because it does not allow for a priori psychological claims.

With respect to the second issue – introspection – the divergence between Kant and psychology today is more important. While Kant insisted that empirical anthropology "is provided with a content by inner sense" (7: 398, cf. 25: 252, 863–65), contemporary psychologists often disparage "introspection" as an outdated and unscientific approach to studying the mind. Moreover, empirical evidence questions introspection as a methodological tool. The most famous article to this effect concludes that "there may be little or no direct introspective access to higher order cognitive processes" (Nisbett and Wilson 1977: 231). The evidence comes from countless studies in which subjects questioned about the causes of their own beliefs or actions fail to accurately report on these causes. In one such study, subjects were invited to evaluate the quality of various consumer products (four different nightgowns in one iteration of the study, four identical nylon stockings in another). The result was "a pronounced left-to-right position effect," such that the rightmost object in the array was heavily over-chosen. But although the position of the products was clearly a factor in the choices of at least some subjects, "when asked about the reasons for their choices, no subject ever mentioned spontaneously the position of the article … and when asked directly about a possible effect of the position of the article, virtually all subjects denied it" (Nisbett and Wilson 1977: 243–44). Introspection is so unreliable that even when people seem to be accurate about what moves them to a particular judgment, the authors conclude (and have evidence to back up) that this accuracy is based on an inference from behavior and context to internal states, precisely the same sort of inference that would be made by an external observer.

In fact, Kant and contemporary psychology are closer than they seem, even with respect to introspection. Many psychologists continue to depend explicitly upon introspection, and any move away from behaviorism requires at least some appeal to introspection. Even claiming, for example, that "subjects are … unaware of the existence of a stimulus that importantly influenced a response" (Nisbett and Wilson 1977: 231) assumes that the reports (and/or the "worried glances") of subjects are reliable indicators of the subjects' "awareness." But the need for introspection goes deeper insofar as non-behaviorist psychologists take research to have implications for how mental states themselves can be studied. Investigators seeking to explain behavior often think about what would "make sense" of different responses of subjects, but judgments of "making sense" are based on general sorts of introspection, long experience with the sorts of considerations that motivate one to think and act in certain ways (cf. e.g. Nisbett and Wilson 1977: 231, 238, 248). Even if people are often wrong about motives for reactions in particular cases, introspection is still effective and even necessary for discerning what sorts of mental states there are and how, in general, these interact. Insofar as psychologists make claims about mental states as such, they must include at least some appeal to introspective awareness.

Of course, the need to appeal to introspection in this general way does not alleviate the very real problems to which these experiments draw attention. But Kant, too, was acutely aware of these problems. In his *Anthropology*, Kant lists "considerable difficulties" that face any psychology seeking to "trac[e] everything that lies hidden in" the human mind. He specifically mentions both dissembling, where one "does not want to be known as he is" and a sort of embarrassment that make it impossible to show oneself as one really is. And with respect to many mental processes, Kant points out that "when the incentives are active, he does not observe himself, and when he does observe himself, the incentives are at rest" (7: 120–21, 398–99). As with Kant's empirical anthropology in general, contemporary psychological research has provided substantially more specification of and evidence for the difficulties with introspection to which Kant drew attention. But Kant was not so naïve about introspection that he would find this recent psychological research surprising, nor is psychology today capable of doing without at least the general and constantly corrected introspection that Kant put at the heart of empirical anthropology.

Kant's approach to psychology, then, is broadly compatible with contemporary "scientific" psychology. As in the cases of neuroscience and evolutionary biology, philosophers have appropriated psychology in the service of a thoroughgoing naturalism about human beings, one that aims for psychologically informed naturalistic approaches to epistemology and ethics. In general terms, Kant's response to psychological naturalism will be that naturalist assumptions are appropriate for the purposes of studying human beings as empirical objects, but these assumptions cannot adequately make sense of the normative demands implicit within humans' transcendental standpoint. Because this general argument will be similar to his responses to evolutionary and neuroscientific naturalism, the rest of this section focuses on two more particular recent attempts to appropriate insights from empirical psychology to make normative claims about human beings. Showing how Kant might respond to these attempts further highlights the important distinction (and relationship) between transcendental and empirical anthropology.

One arena of contemporary psychological research that has garnered substantial philosophical attention is the so-called "biases and heuristics" research program pioneered by Daniel Kahneman and Amos Tversky. This research program shows striking irrationality in human thinking, even among experts thinking about highly significant but fairly straightforward problems in their field of expertise. It has highlighted pervasive forms of human irrationality, including the "fundamental attribution error" (attributing behavior to character rather than situation), "base-rate neglect," and self-serving bias (the "Lake Wobegon effect"). For one example (base-rate neglect), faculty and students at Harvard Medical School were given the following problem:

> If a test to detect a disease whose prevalence is 1/1000 has a false positive rate of 5% [i.e., 5% of those tested falsely test positive for the disease], what is the chance that a person found to have a positive result actually has the disease ... ?
>
> (Casscells, Schoenberger, and Grayboys 1978, cited in Bishop and Trout 2005: 122)

Almost half of the respondents (and a much higher percentage of non-experts) answer that the chances of having the disease are 95 percent, and only one in five respondents give the correct answer (the chances are actually less than 2 percent).[4] This and similar empirical studies of how humans in fact reason call into question our ability to make good decisions, and such studies have led some epistemologists to argue for radical revisions in how we ought to employ our reasoning ability. Michael Bishop and J.D. Trout use this research to offer a wholesale rejection of what they call "Standard Analytic Epistemology" (Bishop and Trout 2005: 104–18). Among other things, they argue "that it would often be much better if experts, when making high-stakes judgments, ignored most of the evidence, did not try to weigh that evidence, and didn't try to make a judgment based on their long experience" (Bishop and Trout 2005: 25). Because of the unreliability of basic cognitive processes, we should replace those processes with others that are empirically demonstrated to be more reliable.

Contemporary research in psychology is also used in ethics. One prominent use has been "situationist" critiques of character-based ethical theories.[5] Psychological research has increasingly shown the context-sensitivity of human decision-making, and philosophers like John Doris, Gilbert Harman, and Kwame Anthony Appiah use this research to critique character-based ethics: "The experimental record suggests that situational factors are often better predictors of behavior than personal factors ... To put it crudely, people typically lack character" (Doris 2002: 2, cf. Harman 2000: 168, 178). In one particularly dramatic example, students at Princeton seminary were invited to participate in a study of religious vocation. Subjects filled out questionnaires and were instructed to give a verbal presentation on the story of the Good Samaritan (Luke 10: 25–37) in another building. After the questionnaire, subjects were told either they were late, on time, or early for the presentation. Along the way, the subjects passed an (apparently) extremely distressed person. Whether they stopped to help correlated strongly with their level of hurry: only 10 percent of "high hurry" subjects stopped while 63 percent of "low hurry" subjects stopped. Likewise in other cases, circumstances better predict behavior than character. Many philosophers take "situationist psychology" to imply that "[r]ather than striving to develop characters that will determine our behavior in ways substantially independent of circumstance, we should invest more of our energies attending to the features of our environment that influence behavioral outcomes" (Doris 2002: 146).

How would Kant respond to these developments? Starting with the empirical psychology itself, Kant's empirical anthropology is not only compatible with but anticipates both the biases and the heuristics program and situationism. Most of the empirical detail in Kant's account of cognition comes in descriptions of various "prejudices" that explain how people diverge from ideal ways of thinking. Like the biases and heuristics program, Kant characterizes effects of these prejudices and diagnoses their underlying grounds. Of course, the specific principles Kant lays out are different from those discovered recently, but the overall structure of Kant's account – supplementing a logic of ideal thought-processes with detailed empirical studies of systematic divergences from those ideals – is consistent with contemporary developments. Similarly, with respect to human choice and action, Kant insists that firm character is "rare" (7: 292); Kant – like situationists – argues that which principles people act on depends, often in unacknowledged ways, on contingent circumstances and inclinations. Kant's empirical account of action requires refinement given recent situationist research. More actions might be motivated by lower faculties than Kant envisioned, and the ways in which character is affected by circumstances seem to be more complicated than he supposed. But the fundamental structure of Kant's empirical anthropology remains sound.

With respect to both situationism and biases and heuristics, however, Kant's endorsement of contemporary psychological research would be conjoined with vehement rejection of the dominant ways naturalist philosophers make use of that research. This anti-naturalism is clearest for ethics. Whereas ethical naturalists see in situationist psychology a basis for "caution ... about shortcuts like 'character education'" (Appiah 2008: 71) and a reason to "invest ... our energies attending to the features of our environment that influence behavioral outcomes" (Doris 2002: 146), Kant sees situationist psychology as an empirical confirmation of humans' radical evil (see Frierson 2010c).[6] Rather than accommodating demands of morality to the general lack of character among human beings, Kant argues for precisely the opposite emphasis. Since Kant gives good a priori grounds for the moral importance of character, the rarity of character provides a reason to do empirical research on how character can be cultivated and Kant even suggests specific, empirically informed techniques to foster character (see 7: 294). As with much of his pragmatic anthropology, his suggestions are based on limited empirical knowledge. But instead of subordinating moral philosophy to situationist psychology, Kant's approach suggests that rather than using the explanatory salience of situational variables in, for instance, the Princeton seminary case, we should focus on the 10 percent of "high hurry" subjects that stopped, to gain insights that might make it possible to better foster strong character in others. If all that matters morally is maximizing good behavior or consequences, then one might reasonably take situationism to support devoting resources to creating situations conducive to behaving well. But if, as Kant argues, it matters morally whether or not one acts from a good character, then one cannot ignore character even if it is difficult to cultivate.

Similarly, with respect to epistemology, Kant can and does make use of empirical insights into flawed reasoning for the purposes of pragmatic anthropology. The fact that people err in reasoning in predictable and systematic ways gives good reasons to develop techniques for counter-acting these errors and for cultivating reasoning abilities less liable to error. But facts about how people reason cannot set standards for how people ought to reason. One example of such normative divergence can be highlighted by the recent attempt by Bishop and Trout to use empirical studies of human reasoning to justify reasoning strategies such as the use of "statistical prediction rules (SPRs)," simple rules based on a few variables that highly correlate with desired predictions. For example, to figure out whether a married couple will be happy (or at least, report that they are happy), "take the couple's rate of lovemaking and subtract from it their rate of fighting" (Bishop and Trout 2005: 30). Or, to figure out whether a particular patient is neurotic or psychotic, use the "Goldberg Rule," a formula based on the patient's Minnesota Multiphasic Personality Inventory profile. These rules should not be used merely as part of deliberation, but should *trump* considered judgments, even of experts. Thus no matter how well you think you know a couple, you would do better to use the simple "lovemaking-minus-fighting" rule than to judge based on your experience, and no matter how sophisticated a clinician you are, you should use the Goldberg Rule rather than your own careful and detailed assessment of the patient's mental state. The evidence supporting this recommendation is that moderately good SPRs work better than even very good expert opinion: "when tested on a set of 861 patients, the Goldberg Rule had a [success] rate of 70%; clinicians' ... varied from ... 55% to ... 67%" (Bishop and Trout 2005: 89). Relative to judgments based on long experience and careful examination of all available evidence, simple prediction rules take less effort, require fewer facts as inputs, and give more accurate results.

Bishop and Trout recognize that as tidy as these rules look from outside the process of reasoning, it is very difficult to remain faithful to them in practice:

> We understand the temptations of defection. We know what it's like to use a reasoning strategy of proven reliability when it seems to give an answer not warranted by the evidence. It feels like you're about to make an unnecessary error. And maybe you are. But in order to make fewer errors overall, we have to accept that we will sometimes make errors we could have corrected, errors that we recognized as errors but made them nonetheless ... People often lack the discipline to adhere to a superior strategy that doesn't "feel" right. Reasoning in a way that "feels" wrong takes discipline.
>
> (Bishop and Trout 2005: 91)

When thinking about close friends who do not make love much, who fight about substantive issues and end up "stronger for it," who work and play together and have kids that they love and care for, it can seem insane to limit my judgment about their happiness to a simple "lovemaking-minus-fighting" calculus. But Bishop and Trout claim, for a variety of cases like this one, that we precisely *should* ignore the additional experience and evidence that we think is relevant and focus just on the simple formula. From-within, such a strategy can seem irrational, and hence Bishop and Trout say that they "understand" the temptation to defect. But we should resist that temptation so that we will get better epistemic results.

Despite their assurances to the contrary, however, Bishop and Trout's emphasis on "feeling" shows that they do not *really* understand the temptation to defect. The problem is not merely that something feels wrong, but that ignoring evidence violates an epistemic standard to which we hold ourselves from-within. Bishop and Trout suggest revising epistemic standards away from reasoning based on what seems to be good evidence toward reasoning that brings about good effects, whether aletheic (truth-conducing) or otherwise: "The primary aim of epistemology, from our perspective, is to provide *useful*, general advice about reasoning" (Bishop and Trout 2005: 94, emphasis added), where advice is "useful" toward the end of "human well-being" (Bishop and Trout 2005: 94). This pragmatic purpose of knowledge might seem obvious, especially when we add "discovering the truth" as a central aim (Bishop and Trout 2005: 97). But in fact, it is not clear that maximizing true beliefs about practically and theoretically relevant features of the world is or should be our highest epistemic value. Consider Kant's slogan "think for yourself," about which Kant admits

that such thinking will at first lead to more error than simply trusting for-
mulaic thoughts handed down by experts, and cautions that "the danger ...
makes [those starting to think for themselves] timid and usually frightens
them away from any further attempt" (8: 35). But for Kant, *autonomy* of
thought is valuable in itself. Kant does not spend much time *defending*
autonomy as an epistemic value, but one might make an argument here
akin to his argument for the value of moral autonomy. Human beings are
cognitively free precisely because we can weigh evidence for ourselves.
Insofar as we relinquish that capacity, we relinquish our freedom, and, in
an important sense, no longer "think" at all.[7] Much more would need to
be said here to fully defend this "deontological" epistemic standard
against Bishop and Trout's consequentialism. But at least the application of
psychological research on aletheic and practical benefits of certain reasoning
strategies is not *sufficient* to justify those strategies epistemically.

Naturalism and Freedom

This chapter has only scratched the surface of the amazing progress in our
empirical understanding of human beings. From the standpoint of Kant's
empirical psychology, this progress is largely welcome. Kant fully accepted
natural–causal accounts of human cognition and activity. He developed
psychological theories about the nature of various human mental faculties
and conjectured about brain chemistry that made such mental faculties
possible. And while Kant was skeptical about fully understanding either
underlying brain-states or historical causes for basic mental structures,
nothing about his philosophical approach to human beings precludes
such developments. Kant's transcendental philosophy even provides
grounds for insisting upon a thoroughly naturalist account of human
beings within empirical anthropology. At the same time, his pragmatic
anthropology suggests ways of using empirical findings for improving
human lives. But Kant's transcendental anthropology suggests caution in
taking developments in empirical anthropology to imply the sort of
thoroughgoing naturalism that would preclude the need for theorizing
from-within. Empirical knowledge about how humans think or choose
cannot establish normative standards for thoughts and choices. In that sense,
Kant embeds a naturalist approach to science in modesty about science's
scope. Rather than seeing natural sciences as a God's-eye perspective on all
reality, Kant insists that they are human ways of understanding the world
we experience. And these sciences must be supplemented with an account
of human beings that makes sense of normativity. In laying out the relationship between transcendental and empirical anthropology, Kant's philosophy not only solves a pressing problem of the modern age – how to take
both science and values seriously – but also cuts off many egregious

misuses of contemporary scientific theories (to justify sloppy thinking or immoral actions).

So far, however, this chapter has side-stepped a very important point of contention between Kant's philosophy and contemporary sciences: Kant's view that human beings are "transcendentally free," uncaused causes of changes in the world. Many have (rightly) seen that sciences depend upon a more determinist conception of human beings and thus have (wrongly) taken them to disprove Kant's account of freedom. Others have (rightly) recognized the importance of a Kantian conception of freedom for making sense of our lives and thus have (wrongly) tried to find a place for freedom within natural science. Both of these approaches are partially misguided, but they reflect the real urgency of the problem of freedom. Echoing Kant (see Bxxix), the psychologist Steven Pinker has put the problem this way: "Either we dispense with morality as an unscientific superstition, or we find a way to reconcile causation (genetic or otherwise) with responsibility and free will" (Pinker 1997: 55).

Roughly speaking, we can outline four ways of relating freedom and contemporary natural science:

1. *Anti-normative fatalism.* For many, this is the most natural response to insights of natural sciences into the brain-dependence of mental states, the genetic–memetic bases of behavior, and/or psychological determinism. If sciences explain human behavior with natural causes (especially if these causes can be traced to causes pre-existing one's birth), then human beings are not free and hence not responsible for their thoughts or actions (e.g. Pereboom 2001).

   There are several major problems with this view. First, the fact that sciences explain human behavior causally need not imply (as Kant showed in his Third Antinomy, see Chapter 1) that human beings are not free. Second, while scientists *assume* that human behavior can be explained in terms of natural causes, contemporary human sciences are far from succeeding in actually explaining human complexity except in the broadest outlines. Finally, the view is prima facie self-undermining when applied to epistemic norms. If causal determination precludes normative evaluation, then the natural sciences themselves have no legitimate claim to truth.

2. *Indeterminism.* Contemporary physics, unlike the Newtonianism of Kant's day, includes quantum mechanics, which postulates indeterminism in nature. Given the complexity of the brain, quantum indeterminism can significantly affect human thoughts and behavior. Robert Kane has suggested that "physical modeling in the brain" that incorporates "neural network theory, nonlinear thermodynamics, chaos theory, and quantum physics" can "put ... the free will issue into greater dialogue

with developments in the sciences" and provide a scientifically plausible free will that justifies "the power of agents to be the creators ... of their own ends and purposes" (Kane 1996: 17, 4). This indeterminism fits with strong scientific realism, in that sciences exhaust what there is to know about human beings, but because sciences themselves are indeterminist, some human behavior may be as well, which leaves room for freedom.

Unfortunately, this view confuses indeterminism with freedom. Unless I have reason to identify with quantum fluctuations in my brain rather than deterministic processes shaped by my genetic and environmental background, the "ends and purposes" arising from those quantum fluctuations will be no more my own than those arising from deterministic influences. Because self-image is largely shaped by features that are stable or at least consistent with our past personality, changes arising from quantum fluctuations may even be *less* my own than those that are strictly determined. Moreover, since the physical models by which human beings are free posit chaotically complex systems that are only sometimes affected in significant ways by quantum fluctuations, there is no way to know, for any particular end or purpose, whether that end or purpose is really free, which undermines much of the practical value of positing freedom. (It will not be the case, for example, that all cases where one would naturally ascribe moral responsibility will be cases within which relevant quantum fluctuations were present.)

3. *Compatibilism.* Compatibilists, like indeterminists, seek to find freedom within scientific accounts of human beings. But compatibilists do not aim to find freedom in the indeterminism of the natural world. Instead, compatibilists aim to show that mysterious and metaphysical "transcendental" freedom is not the sort of freedom human beings need. To make sense of normativity, moral responsibility, and our sense of ourselves as free, we need only an ability to impact what happens in our lives. If this ability is grounded in genes or brain-states or psychological structures, that is irrelevant. What matters is an ability we can identify with and see as genuinely efficacious. Some sorts of determinism might make it hard or impossible to identify with aspects of our psychological make-up. If we recognize that our inability to focus on our work is genetically programmed or that our fear of spiders is a childhood phobia, we might not think of those aspects of our psychology as really "us." But the mere fact that some aspect of our psychology is determined need not preclude us from identifying with it.

Compatibilism might provide an adequate conception of freedom, and recent philosophical work on freedom provides substantial resources for conceptions of freedom that fit within wholly naturalistic approaches to human beings. In his own transcendental analyses, especially of moral responsibility, Kant argued that morality requires a transcendental freedom that stands above any determination by natural causes. Recent years have seen many attempts to make sense of moral responsibility without assuming transcendental freedom. Such attempts, however, cannot be "naturalist" in the sense of merely "clarify[ing] and unify[ing]" scientific theories (Dennett 2003: 13). Rather than starting with science, figuring out what sort of freedom it allows for, and then arguing that this freedom is sufficient, a compatibilism that would do justice to our from-within sense of moral responsibility must start from-within, look carefully at the presuppositions of our conception of moral responsibility, and then see whether this is compatible with science (see e.g. Frankfurt 1988; Wallace 1994, 2006).

4. *Perspectivism*. The previous three approaches to freedom all fit with strong scientific realism. Throughout this chapter, however, I have emphasized that Kant's contribution to debates about the natural sciences is his perspectivism. By recognizing that science represents one perspective on the world, Kant makes room for other perspectives, including a practical perspective within which freedom plays an important role. Many contemporary natural scientists have adopted a similar view. Dawkins and Dennett point out that human beings are capable of taking a stance toward the world that is not reducible to their genes or memes. Steven Pinker has, more forcefully, insisted that "science and ethics are two self-contained systems played out among the same entities in the world" (Pinker 1997: 45). Perspectivists can thus defend the integrity of an incompatibilist conception of freedom as a concept that, as Pinker puts it, "makes the ethics game playable" (Pinker 1997: 45). For perspectivists of this stripe, compatibilism is wrong in trying to find a notion of freedom that is compatible with our best scientific theories. Freedom is needed within ethics; causation is needed within science. These are two different perspectives.

Importantly, one can prioritize perspectives in different ways. Most natural scientists and naturalist philosophers are *science-first perspectivists*. Pinker is typical here:

> Ethical theory requires idealizations like free, sentient, rational, equivalent agents whose behavior is uncaused, and its conclusions can be sound and useful even though the world, as seen by science, does not really have uncaused events ... [T]he world is close enough to the idealization of free will that moral theory can meaningfully be applied to it.
>
> (Pinker 1997: 55)

In thinking of the world as "close enough" to ethical assumptions, Pinker implicitly assumes that the world "as seen by science" is the real world, and ethics is all right because its assumptions, like those of Euclidean geometry, are not too far off, good enough for practical purposes. But this sort of perspectivism cannot be adequate for normativity. If we are in fact only approximately free, then either the "ethics game" (Pinker's term) requires only approximate freedom to be legitimate (as, for instance, getting good results in structural engineering requires only that the world be approximately Euclidean), or the ethics game, while playable, is a sham. Perhaps Pinker is willing to affirm some sort of idealized uncaused freedom merely in the absence of the well-worked-out compatibilist account that would show that the freedom we really need is actually compatible with science. But if morality really depends upon seeing ourselves as uncaused, it is unclear how a determinist world can be "close enough" to save it, at least in the sense of *justifying* it (as opposed to merely preserving its psychological force).

Instead of a science-first perspectivism, one might adopt a *neutral perspectivism*, as has become increasingly common amongst contemporary Kantians. Christine Korsgaard, for example, argues that the fact that "freedom ... is not a theoretical property which can ... be seen by scientists" will be taken to imply "that ... freedom is not 'real' only if you have defined 'real' as what can be identified by scientists looking at things ... from outside" (Korsgaard 1996b: 96). But there is no reason to do this, since "we need" a from-within practical perspective – and thus freedom – just as much as we need scientific theories, so "neither standpoint is privileged over the other" (Korsgaard 1996a: 173). This approach is considerably more promising because it preserves the insights of science without according science an unjustifiably privileged place in our self-understanding. It thereby avoids the most serious problems of science-first perspectivism.

But Kant (and some contemporary Kantians) offers good reasons to reject even neutral perspectivism in favor of *freedom-first perspectivism*. On this view, the scientific view of the world is subordinate to the view of the world according to which human beings are free. The predominant argument for the priority of this free perspective on human beings within contemporary philosophy is simply that any perspective that claims any sort of justification – even the scientific perspective itself – implicitly appeals at least to the freedom to believe on the basis of normative standards of good evidence. In holding each other and ourselves responsible for our beliefs, whether scientific or otherwise, we treat those beliefs as "up to us" rather than mere effects of empirical causes. But there is no corresponding dependence of normative perspectives upon scientific ones. Once one treats human beings as natural objects, one must explain the capacity for norm-governed thought and action in terms of science, but one can think of oneself and others as norm-governed without committing oneself to a scientific picture of the world.

Kant offers a further reason for freedom-first perspectivism, based on a fundamental difference between the "ethics game" and what we might call the "science game." Humans treat each other as morally responsible, which depends upon seeing each other as free; and we study each other empirically, which depends upon seeing each other as determined by natural causes. So far, the games are parallel; each depends upon a certain assumption as its condition of possibility. But the parallel nature of these assumptions conceals a deeper difference between them. For the ethics game, as we saw above, it is not enough that we seem free, or that we are close enough to being free. In that case, we might still engage in the ethics game, but the game itself would be a sham. For the science game, however, it is not necessary that we really be wholly determined by natural causes. It is enough that human behavior, whatever its ultimate basis, is sufficiently regular to be explained in terms of natural causes. Moreover, as Kant argues in his *Critique of Pure Reason*, the demand for ultimate scientific explanations cannot be met. As one commentator puts it:

> all naturalistic explanations – even the most impressive explanations of some future neuroscience – are conditional explanations. ... In a certain sense they are incomplete, for they can never explain that any natural law should take the form that it does.
>
> (O'Neill 1989: 68)

Science explains regularities in terms of increasingly general laws, but these explanations are always incomplete in a way that leaves room for the sort of freedom Kant defends in his transcendental philosophy. Practically speaking, since the evidence that some empirical cause brings about an action can never be based in a *self-evident* causal law, it always remains open to make an exception of ourselves. Since the science-game does not depend upon a science-first perspective and the ethics game does depend upon a freedom-first perspective, we can and should adopt the freedom-first perspective.

Summary

Where does modern science leave us with respect to Kant's question? We now have a much more sophisticated empirical understanding of human beings, from our complex psychology to the brain-chemistry that makes this psychology possible to the evolutionary origins and genetic bases of our wonderful brains. Kantians can and should embrace the results of the natural sciences into empirical anthropology. And that means, of course, that Kantians can and should embrace the methodological naturalism that makes these sciences possible; humans should be treated as ordinary objects in the natural world and studied according to the best methods of natural science. Kant even provides grounds for embracing a modest scientific realism, in which one takes the methodological assumptions of natural science to be empirically real, that is, to be constitutive of the world we experience.

However, the question "What is the human being?" is not merely a question about the distinctive features of a certain type of natural entity. Answering the question requires thinking not only about how to pick out homo sapiens from amongst other natural objects, but also about how to make sense of ourselves, from-within. And this question from-within is not merely philosophical but also practical, a matter of asking what to do with our lives, what to think, and what to find pleasure in. For those questions, naturalism is insufficient. But Kant's philosophical framework not only includes an empirical realism according to which science is true of the empirical world, but also a transcendental idealism that insists that science is only one perspective, that there is more to the world-in-itself than what is captured in the empirically knowable world. In Pinker's terms, Kant's justification of the science-game allows for a realism sufficiently robust to allow us to pursue and benefit from science, but it mitigates that realism just enough to make room for freedom. Moreover, precisely because Kant engages in both the empirical-science-game and the normativity games of epistemology, ethics, and aesthetics, he provides a better model for answering the question "What is the human being?" than modern naturalism. Kant justifies the fundamental normative standards of epistemology, ethics, and aesthetics independent of the natural sciences; but he is still able to use the results of those natural sciences in the context of a pragmatic anthropology that thinks about how we, as empirically knowable human beings, can best promote ways of thinking, acting, and feeling that conform to our ideals.

Further Reading

Contemporary philosophy of mind is a major philosophical subfield, so the best introductions are edited anthologies (e.g. Heil or Chalmers) of key articles. Botterill and Carruthers gives a helpful overview of philosophy of psychology, and Chalmers is one of the most influential contemporary views.

George Botterill and Peter Carruthers, *The Philosophy of Psychology* (Cambridge: Cambridge University Press, 1999)

David Chalmers, *The Conscious Mind: In Search of a Fundamental Theory* (Oxford: Oxford University Press, 1996)

David Chalmers (ed.), *Philosophy of Mind: Classic and Contemporary Readings* (Oxford: Oxford University Press, 2002)

John Heil, *Philosophy of Mind: A Guide and Anthology* (Oxford: Oxford University Press, 2004)

Wilson helped reinvigorate evolutionary approaches to the human being, and Dawkins and Dennett further elaborate this approach. Aunger provides an excellent discussion and critique of memetics from various perspectives. Pinker provides an evolutionary psychologist's perspective on the issues in this chapter. Fodor specifically responds to Pinker. Sober and Wilson provide an excellent and detailed analysis of the evolution of altruism, with an emphasis on defending the role of group selection. Kitcher provides a very detailed corrective to excessive sociobiological pretentions. For works closer to Darwin, see Chapter 6.

Robert Aunger (ed.), *Darwinizing Culture: The Status of Memetics as a Science* (Oxford: Oxford University Press, 2000)
Richard Dawkins, *The Selfish Gene* (Oxford: Oxford University Press, 1976)
Daniel Dennett, *Freedom Evolves* (New York: Penguin, 2004)
Jerry Fodor, *The Mind Doesn't Work that Way* (Cambridge, MA: MIT Press, 2000)
Philip Kitcher, *Vaulting Ambition: Sociobiology and the Quest for Human Nature* (Cambridge, MA: MIT Press, 1985)
Steven Pinker, *How the Mind Works* (New York: W.W. Norton, 1997)
Elliot Sober and David Sloan Wilson, *Unto Others: The Evolution and Psychology of Unselfish Behavior* (Cambridge, MA: MIT Press, 1998)
E.O. Wilson, *Sociobiology* (Cambridge, MA: Belknap Press, 1975).

Contemporary philosophy abounds with appropriations of contemporary research in psychology. For a readable introduction to the role of psychological research in philosophical ethics, see Appiah. For focused discussion of situationism, see Doris. For discussion of the research program of Kahnman and Tversky, see Bishop and Trout and Kahneman's own articulation of the significance of that research program. For various discussions of the importance of research in psychology for moral issues, see Sinnott-Armstrong (2007).

Kwame Anthony Appiah, *Experiments in Ethics* (Cambridge, MA: Harvard University Press, 2008)
Michael Bishop and J.D. Trout, *Epistemology and the Psychology of Human Judgment* (Oxford: Oxford University Press, 2004)
John Doris, *Lack of Character: Personality and Moral Behavior* (Cambridge: Cambridge University Press, 2002)
Daniel Kahneman, *Thinking Fast and Slow* (New York: Farrar, Straus and Giroux, 2011)
Walter Sinnott-Armstrong (ed.) *Moral Psychology* (3 volumes, Cambridge, MA: MIT Press, 2007)

8 Historicism and Human Diversity

> Perhaps the time is at hand when it will be comprehended again and again how little used to be sufficient to furnish the cornerstone for such sublime and unconditional philosophers' edifices as the dogmatists have built so far: any old popular superstition from time immemorial (like the soul superstition, which, in the form of the subject and ego superstition, has not even yet ceased to do mischief); some play on words, perhaps, a seduction by grammar, or an audacious generalization of some very narrow, very personal, very human, all too human, facts.
>
> Friedrich Nietzsche, *Beyond Good and Evil* (Preface)

> It seemed to me that, for the moment, the essential task was to free the history of thought from ... transcendental narcissism.
>
> Michel Foucault, *The Archaeology of Knowledge* (Foucault 1982: 203)

Kant's lifetime saw a rise in the consciousness of human beings as historical beings. The seventeenth and eighteenth centuries had been a period of rejecting contingent, tradition-bound ideologies of the Middle Ages, but the Enlightenment alternative was not taken as just another tradition. Instead, Enlightenment philosophers saw themselves as replacing historical traditions with ahistorical truths grounded in reason and experience. Kant, too, laid out necessary and universal transcendental structures of human thought and action, stripped free of anything merely historical. At the same time, however, Kant was attuned to human historicity and even emphasized the historicity of Enlightenment itself (cf. Foucault 1984: 32–50). Kant's students (Herder) and followers (Reinhold) further emphasized this point. By the time of Hegel and Marx, the idea that humans' fundamental ways of thinking about and acting within the world differ from culture to culture and change from one historical epoch to another had become commonplace. Today, this emphasis on human variety pervades disciplines of history, sociology, anthropology, cultural studies, and even parts of psychology and literary theory.

But the notion of "historicity" is ambiguous. In its most mundane sense, the claim that human beings are historical is one that (virtually) no one would deny. Humans age and change. We live in communities with varied and changing cultures. But historicism is generally not limited to this mundane historicity. In Chapter 6, we saw two importantly different sorts of historicism. One, represented by Hegel and Marx, emphasized the necessity of historical change. The other, represented by Nietzsche, used historicity and diversity to emphasize the contingency of particular modes of thought and forms of life. For both sets of historicists, humans' historical nature is not limited to external studies of changing individuals and cultures. Over history and across cultures, human beings differ in how they see the world. In Kantian terms, *transcendental* anthropology is historicized and localized. Any transcendental analysis justifies only "the morality [or other norms] of their environment, their class, their church, the spirit of their time, their climate and part of the world" (Nietzsche 1966: 97). In the rest of this chapter, "historicism" refers to what we might call a "transcendental historicism" that treats humans' from-within, normative perspectives as historically conditioned.

This historicism has become a mainstay of our world. In its most facile form, it manifests itself in trite relativisms that only refer to what is true-for-me or good-to-me. Such relativists generally think that diversity of human ways of thinking establishes that no particular perspective on the world can be right. Relativism is often confused with tolerance, as though the most respectful stance to take toward different times and cultures is to recognize that their beliefs and values were true for them, just as one's own beliefs and values are true for oneself. At the end of this chapter, I return to this simplistic but all-too-common relativism, but for the bulk of this chapter, I focus on three significant and more nuanced historicists.

I start with the rise of historicism regarding natural sciences, focusing on Thomas Kuhn, through whom the concepts of a "paradigm" and a "paradigm shift" have become commonplace. Kuhn and post-Kuhnian philosophy of science are important because they seem to undermine not only strong scientific realism but also Kant's own modest realism about natural science. If natural sciences are historically conditioned, it becomes hard to see how one can talk about *the* empirical world or take Kantian categories of experience to have strict universality. From Kuhn, I turn to Foucault. Like Kuhn, Foucault questions basic aspects of Kant's transcendental framework, but Foucault focuses on the problematic and historically contingent notion of "the human being" as such. In particular, Foucault historicizes both the general framework of Kantian anthropology – what Foucault calls "man" as an "empirico-transcendental doublet" (Foucault 1973: 319) – and the conception of human agency underlying Kant's moral theory. Finally, I turn to the contemporary discipline of cultural anthropology, where human diversity – rather than historicism as such – provides a perspective within which the supposed universality of Kant's anthropology is questioned.

Historicism and Natural Science

The roots of historicism in the natural sciences lay in mid-nineteeth-century developments within mathematics. Mathematicians such as Lobachevsky, Poincaré, and Reimann began thinking of basic geometrical axioms – such as that parallel lines never meet – not as intuitively obvious truths about space but as "conventions." Mathematicians began exploring non-Euclidian geometries within which familiar geometrical claims – such as that the sum of the interior angles of a triangle is 180 degrees – no longer hold true. In itself, this development in mathematics was important since it suggested a human capacity to think about worlds with structures very different from our own. But Euclid's axioms were still generally taken to define the true nature of space. Mathematicians might think about worlds where parallel lines touch, but these were just mathematical fantasies.

Then Einstein argued that the world itself was non-Euclidean. Straight lines can cross themselves, parallel lines touch, and the interior angles of triangles are not 180 degrees. At the same time, other radical changes were happening in physical sciences. Quantum mechanics challenged basic notions such as the continuity of time, determinacy of space, and principle of causation. Within quantum mechanics, time no longer passes in a continual stream but in little jumps, or quanta. Objects are not located in particular spaces but smeared out in waves of probability. And events in the world are not universally explicable in terms of causes and effects. Some things happen, literally, by chance. Euclid's space was replaced by Einstein's, his deterministic world by rolls of the dice.

As philosophers increasingly sought to come to terms with these and similar developments in science, the Kantian model of science as built on a priori synthetic claims about any possible experience seemed increasingly implausible. In a classic paper, W.V.O. Quine (1951) argued against the distinction between synthetic and analytic claims and the possibility of any knowledge that could not be changed in the light of experience. If Euclidean geometry could be abandoned for relativity theory and determinism for quantum mechanics, then "no statement is immune to revision"; any claim is open to empirical challenge, including "even ... logical law[s]" such as the law of the excluded middle or the principle of non-contradiction (Quine 1951: 40). "The totality of our so-called knowledge or beliefs, from the most casual matters of geography and history to the profoundest laws of atomic physics or even of pure mathematics and logic, is a man-made fabric which impinges on experience only along the edges," such that while experience can lead to revisions in our web of belief, "No particular experiences are linked with any particular statements in the interior of the field, except indirectly through considerations of equilibrium affecting the field as a whole" (Quine 1951: 40).

Quine's account of knowledge set the stage for Thomas Kuhn's historical turn in philosophy of science. Kuhn's *Structure of Scientific Revolutions* rejected dominant models of scientific progress within which old illusions give rise to more and more accurate scientific theories and the scientific method measures hypotheses against empirical evidence, rejecting theories that fail to be confirmed. Against this conception of science, Kuhn argues both that the "scientific method" does not consist in the attempt to falsify hypotheses and the rejection of those that fail to measure up to empirical data and that "scientific revolutions" are not unambiguous forms of progress. Kuhn distinguishes between what he calls "normal science," "extraordinary science," and "scientific revolutions." Normal science, what most practicing scientists generally engage in, consists of "puzzle-solving." This science takes place within a "paradigm," a "constellation of beliefs, values, techniques, and so on shared by the members of a given [scientific] community" (Kuhn 1996: 174) that supplies "a criterion for choosing problems that ... can be assumed to have solutions" (Kuhn 1996: 37). The paradigm resists falsification by empirical data. Scientists often are unable even to see data that contradicts the paradigm – the paradigm structures "the perceptual process itself" (Kuhn 1996: 62). Even if scientists perceive contradicting data, they initially interpret it in ways that preserve the paradigm itself. Finally, if they are unable to explain the troubling data, scientists generally move to other areas of research rather than reject theories. As Kuhn put it, "Paradigms are not corrigible by normal science at all" (Kuhn 1996: 122).

Sometimes, however, empirical findings that conflict with scientific paradigms – "anomalies" – are sufficiently disturbing to provoke "extraordinary science," examining the anomaly in greater detail and seeking to explain it within the broad contours of one's paradigm. Generally, anomalies are resolved with only slight changes to the dominant paradigm. Sometimes, however, an anomaly is sufficiently problematic, or an alternative paradigm sufficiently attractive, to prompt a crisis and eventually a "scientific revolution." This transition from an old paradigm to a new one "is far from a cumulative process," more like a "gestalt switch" than a refinement of the old paradigm (Kuhn 1996: 86). One sees science in a new light; theories and even data of the old paradigm are often not even translatable into the new one. Kuhn points out, for example, that whereas many today think of Einstein's physics as a refinement of Newton's, within which Newtonian physics is merely an approximation, in fact "Einstein's theory can be accepted only with the recognition that Newton's was wrong" (Kuhn 1996: 100) and even the most basic "variables and parameters" in each's theory – the variables referring to "time, mass, etc." – have different meanings in the two theories. The "fundamental structural elements of which the universe … is composed" are different; the apparent similarity of Einstein's laws of motion at slow speeds to Newton's laws is merely superficial (Kuhn 1996: 101–2). Similarly, any true scientific revolution changes the whole "conceptual network through which scientists view the world" (Kuhn 1996: 102). Put another way, both deeply Kantian and deeply historicist, "after a revolution, scientists are responding to a different world," or, even more radically, "when paradigms change, the world itself changes with them" (Kuhn 1996: 111).

Scientific revolutions do not simply replace a falsified theory with one that fits all the empirical evidence. Often, in fact, new paradigms fit available evidence worse than old ones. Because previous evidence was collected in order to confirm the old paradigm, the new paradigm often has a very difficult time making sense of it. Kuhn points out that Copernicus's astronomy did not predict the motions of planets any better than Ptolemy's, Lavoisier's revolution that paved the way for modern chemistry "deprive[ed] chemistry of some actual and much potential explanatory power" (Kuhn 1996: 107, cf. 131), and "the striking quantitative success of both Plank's radiation law and the Bohr atom quickly persuaded many physicists to adopt them even though, viewing physical science as a whole, these contributions created many more problems than they solved" (Kuhn 1996: 154). What new paradigms bring is not primarily better ways of handling old evidence but new ways of looking at the world, new criteria for success in science, new assumptions about what sorts of empirical problems are worth investigating, new ways of interpreting empirical data, new experimental techniques, and even new criteria for deciding amongst competing theories. Whereas "progress" makes sense "during periods of normal science" where a paradigm provides accepted standards, it makes no sense for measuring shifts between paradigms: "a decision [between competing paradigms] can only be made on faith" (Kuhn 1996: 158). But then "[w]e may … have to relinquish the notion, explicit or implicit, that changes of paradigm carry scientists and those who learn from them closer and closer to the truth" (Kuhn 1996: 170, but cf. Kuhn 1977).

Kuhn developed his notion of paradigm shifts primarily within the philosophy of natural sciences, and his overall theory has led to a wide growth in investigations of historical and social conditions that shape scientific theory and practice. Thus sociologists of science offer detailed studies of social, cultural, and psychological factors that shape scientific developments. At their most extreme, historicist studies defend the social construction of "scientific facts" (see Latour and Woolgar 1986, Pickering 1984). Feminist philosophers of science show how the male-dominance of science skews collection and interpretation of data

(Longino 1990, Okruhlik 1995). Kuhn's concept of "paradigm shift" has filtered into culture more generally, resulting in historicist conceptions of knowledge according to which experiences, practices and our world itself are constituted by paradigms that change and can differ between different groups of people. What the world looks like from-within, including the most basic norms for how one evaluates one's beliefs, is historically conditioned.

This Kuhnian historicism is, in some respects, strikingly Kantian. Like Kant, Kuhn suggests that human experience is structured by forms of cognition that precede that experience. With his claim that different scientists inhabit different worlds, Kuhn even endorses something like Kant's Copernican turn (Kuhn 1996: 110). With Kant, moreover, Kuhn gives reasons to reject strong scientific realism by showing how science results from presuppositions human beings bring to analysis of the world. Scientific theories, whether about atoms or human nature, are constructed in the context of prior commitments. While this need not wholly undermine the "rationality" of science nor even some sort of scientific "objectivity" (see Kuhn 1977), it calls into question the strong scientific realism implicit in philosophical naturalism. Kuhn goes further in this respect than Kant, claiming that "the notion of a match between the ontology of a theory and its 'real' counterpart in nature … seems … illusive in principle" (Kuhn 1996: 206, cf. also McMullin 1993).

But Kuhn historicizes and relativizes Kant's Copernican turn. Paradigms that are "a priori" in the sense that they structure one's experience of the world are not necessarily "a priori" in the stronger sense of being unrevisable in the light of further empirical research (or even, as has been emphasized by post-Kuhnian sociology of science, of changing social conditions). What scientific theorizing looks like from-within is determined in part by historically contingent facts. This raises the prospect that transcendental forms of cognition that Kant argues to be conditions of possibility of any human experience might merely be historically local paradigms. For Kant, the idea of data that could contradict transcendental categories or forms of intuition was literally not-humanly-thinkable. For Kuhn, such data is not only thinkable but actual. The history of science shows that even apparently necessary claims are abandoned in scientific revolutions that radically restructure our whole approach to our world.

As a vague and general point, this assertion of historical contingency need not be fatal to Kant's transcendental anthropology. Kant's account of empirical concepts leaves room for the development of concepts that shape one's experience of the world, even when these concepts are themselves ultimately rooted not in the necessary structure of human cognition as such but in the contingent ways human beings respond to particular experiences. Kant's accounts of prejudice further suggest a framework for thinking about cognitive structures that are contingent but nonetheless "a priori" in that they shape how we experience the world. Kant's theory of biology comes even closer to Kuhn; experience of natural organisms justifies an a priori principle for further empirical investigation. And Kant's philosophy of history provides bases for thinking that human perspectives on the world can change. Thus Kant could allow that, *in addition to a priori and universal structures of human cognition*, there are also historically contingent mental structures that shape our experience.

Unfortunately, historicist philosophy of science does not let Kant off that easily. First, the details of Kuhn's history of science suggest that the particular structures Kant assumed to be a priori are not. For Kant, space, time, causation, and a continuum of degrees of sensible properties are among the most fundamental a priori conditions of the possibility of any human experience. By virtue of the aprioricity of space, we can know that (Euclidean) geometry applies to the empirical world. By virtue of the principle of causation, we can know a priori that every alteration has a cause that determined it to occur. But relativity theory seems to require rejecting Euclidean space, and Einstein's notion of "space-time" is inconsistent with Kant's careful distinction between space and time. Meanwhile, dominant interpretations of quantum mechanics imply that deterministic causation is not universal, that alterations occur probabilistically, the result, at least in part, of random chance. Thus the specific positive metaphysical claims of Kant's transcendental anthropology of cognition seem to be rejected by the best science of our day.

But the problem is even deeper. Precisely because Kant's transcendental anthropology of cognition did such a good job picking out the best candidates for the most basic presuppositions of human experience, if even these presuppositions are historically conditioned, there seems little hope for *any* truly universal structure of human cognition. All categories by means of which we make sense of the world seem open to revision. The fact that some philosophers suggest rejecting the principle of identity (a = a) and even the principle of non-contradiction in order to better make sense of contemporary physics drives this point home even more forcefully. Not only the details of Kant's transcendental anthropology but even the very idea that there could be a universally human transcendental structure of cognition seem vulnerable to historicist critique.

Historicism and the Human Sciences: Foucault

While the history of natural science contributes important historicist dimensions to understanding human cognition, more radical historicisms have emerged in those sciences devoted to studying human beings as such. The hero of this brand of historicism is Michel Foucault, whose detailed historical analyses of key concepts and practices employed in human self-understanding threaten the universality of not only Kantian cognitive categories but also his whole transcendental anthropology. By historically analyzing ways of thinking, Foucault challenges Kant's universalism, and a central proposal of Foucault's work is the historically conditioned nature of human subjectivity itself. Foucault aims to show the historical emergence and contingency of precisely the conception of the human being that lies at the heart of Kant's anthropology.

Foucault's historicist approach avoids blanket theoretical claims about human historicity. Claiming that "human thinking is always historically-bound," like relativist claims that "all truths are relative," is self-undermining, a purportedly absolute truth that all truths are relative. But Foucault neither assumes an omniscient posture nor makes such over-arching pronouncements. Instead, while recognizing and even embracing the historical-situatedness of his own work, Foucault "analyzes specific rationalities" (Foucault 1982: 210), studying particular developments in structures of human knowledge and society. Thus Foucault's first major work, *A History of Madness* (1961), traces the origin of our concept of "mental illness," showing how "mental disease, with the meanings we now give it, is made possible" (Foucault 1988: 270, Foucault 1961/2006: 504). Foucault's *History of Sexuality* shows, among other things, how sexual categories and even basic structures of ethical life shift from ancient Greece to Christian Europe to the present. By emphasizing detailed studies of particular cases – the "gray, meticulous, and patiently documentary ... accumulation of source material" (Foucault 1984: 76) – Foucault eschews appeals to timeless truths without making absolute claims about the impossibility of such truths. He models historicist thinking while avoiding dogmatic theoretical relativism. Thus Foucault's threat to Kant is not as a competing theory, but a historicist way of thinking that provides an alternative to Kant's anthropology and depicts that anthropology as historically local rather than universal.

For Foucault, the "accumulation of source material" is neither a way of tracing the factual flow of history nor a way of describing historical "progress." Instead, like Kuhn, Foucault emphasizes the historicity of basic structures of human thought and action. Foucault's approach is "deliberately both historical and critical, ... concerned ... with determining the conditions of possibility of" particular forms of experience (Foucault 1994: xix). This historical method includes two key components: "archeology" and "genealogy." The former describes a "historical a priori," an "episteme" or "epistemological field" that defines "conditions of possibility" of knowledge in a particular historical epoch (Foucault 1969/1982: 127). Whereas Kant's a priori categories of experience are purportedly universal, formal structures of any possible human cognition, Foucault's historical a priori is "not a condition of validity ... , but a condition for the reality of statements," describing historically contingent conditions structuring what is thought at any given time. To this archaeological excavation of historical epistemological fields, Foucault adds a genealogical component that traces how different fields arise and change, appropriate and dominate one another. It is "the history of morals, ideals, and metaphysical concepts" (Foucault 1984: 86).[1] Consistent with both Kuhnian historiography and Nietzschean genealogy, Foucault's histories emphasize contingency and complexity in historical changes and reject "progress" toward some supra-historical ideal.

Foucault (unlike Kuhn) explains the emergence, modification, and reinterpretation of various epistemic fields in terms of power or domination. While Kuhnian paradigms are relatively benign structures of thought, and Kantian categories are necessary conditions that function to empower humans to know the world, Foucaultian epistemes are moves in a "hazardous play of dominations" (Foucault 1984: 83, cf. Foucault 1977: 27). This is not the simplistic claim that people often advance agendas by trying to get others to think like them. Foucault's approach to power does not center on its use by some human agents to dominate and control others, but on systems of knowledge and action that constrain and enable further knowing and acting (Foucault 1977: 27–28, 1984: 150). Foucault focuses on social and institutional forces that are both "made up" of human actions and also "determine the forms and possible domains" of human thought and action. Thus, for example, "a certain way of rendering men docile and useful ... required the involvement of definite relations of knowledge ... [and thereby] ... made the human sciences historically possible" (Foucault 1977: 305). Power structures of modern society shifted from emphasizing the king's absolute power over subjects to punishing free and equal citizens and then to establishing "normality" in a population. The present "carceral society" that seeks "docile and useful" human bodies depends upon knowledge of human beings as subject-objects capable of (self-)control/responsibility and allows for techniques of observation that make the construction of this sort of knowledge possible. This does not mean that "human sciences emerged from the prison" (Foucault 1977: 305); Foucault is not claiming some sort of plot on the part of political leaders to set up empirical human sciences in order to better control subjects. Rather, he emphasizes a power–knowledge *system* that requires both certain forms of domination and certain forms of knowledge (Foucault 1990: 95, 1980: 203).

This de-centering of the subject as locus of power and knowledge arises from Foucault's historicizing of the very notion of a human "subject." For Foucault, the subject itself is a recent historical emergence, a part of our present episteme, and one the contingency of which Foucault aims to reveal. Foucault's work as a whole is a "history of the different modes by which, in our culture, human beings are made subjects" (Foucault 1982: 208).

While revealing the contingency of this conception of the human as subject-object, Foucault refuses simply to adopt the episteme he analyzes. Instead, his genealogical methodology effects new ways of studying power and knowledge that do not depend upon "the human" as subject.

Foucault's historical a priori is thus much more radical than Kuhn's because Foucault calls into question the whole idea of the thinking subject as locus of cognition/knowledge.

> [Genealogy] needed to be something more than the simple relativization of the ... phenomenological[2] subject. I don't believe the problem can be solved by historicizing the subject ..., fabricating a subject that evolves through the course of history. One has ... to arrive at ... what I would call genealogy, that is, a form of history which can account for the constitution of knowledge, discourses, domains of objects, etc., without having to make reference to a subject which is either transcendental in relation to the field of events or runs in its empty sameness throughout the course of history.
>
> (Foucault 1984: 58–59)

Foucault's historical a priori is not a subjective from-within perspective that changes through different historical conditions. For Foucault, neither knowledge nor the a priori is primarily "within" subjects. Knowledge is part of a knowledge–power structure that constrains and includes human actions; the "subject" that is the focus of Kant's transcendental anthropology is, for Foucault, a recent innovation of our present knowledge–power complex, an innovation wrapped up with domination in the service of docile normalcy, an innovation that – in theory but especially in historical practice – Foucault seeks to resist and reinterpret. By describing how "we constitute ourselves as subjects of knowledge" (Foucault 1983: 237), Foucault de-privileges Kant's "transcendental" perspective, reinterpreting it as a contingent perspective created by historically local power relations (Foucault 1973: 310, 322).

The human "subject" Foucault describes is not merely Kant's transcendental anthropos, but the whole "empirico-transcendental doublet" that seemingly characterizes Kant's anthropology as a whole. For Foucault, Kant inaugurated a shift from a Classical conception of thinking-as-representation to a view of human cognition as something that orders the world in terms of its *own* nature. But for Foucault, this shift leads to a problem, since "man appears in his ambiguous position as an object of [empirical] knowledge and as a subject which knows." In its nineteenth- and twentieth-century forms, this ambiguous position leads to an "analytic of finitude," where thinkers aim to show how "man's being will be able to provide a foundation in their own positivity for all those forms that indicate to him that he is not infinite" (Foucault 1973: 312, 315). In the end, Foucault argues that this analytic is irresolvable, that the nineteenth and twentieth centuries represent a series of failed attempts to analyze the human being as "a being such that knowledge will be attained in him of what makes all knowledge possible" (Foucault 1973: 318, see also 322). The result is an intellectual culture that

> produces, surreptitiously and in advance, the confusion of the empirical and the transcendental ... [a]nd so we find philosophy falling asleep once more ... , this time not in the sleep of Dogmatism but that of Anthropology [where a]ll empirical knowledge, provided it concerns man, can serve as a possible philosophical field in which the foundation of knowledge, the definition of its limits, and, in the end, the truth of truth must be discovered.
>
> (Foucault 1973: 341)

Foucault thus suggests a shift away from "man" as object of anthropological investigation toward a "Nietzschean ... promise of the superman," a refusal – "with a philosophical laugh" – to give in to the myth of "man" (Foucault 1973: 342–43).

This genealogy of "man" challenges virtually every aspect of Kant's anthropology. Archeological and genealogical investigations of how empirical human sciences are caught up in systems of domination and control reveal the contingency and potential dangers of these sciences. These analyses challenge naturalist attempts to use empirical sciences to answer the question "What is the human being?," but they also call into question Kant's own empirical (and pragmatic) anthropology, which, like its more contemporary forms, depends upon classification and observation in the service of normalization and control. Moreover, Foucault's genealogical treatments of how "we constitute ourselves as moral agents" (Foucault 1983: 237) aim to show that the way we (and Kant) think of ethics is historically local. While Kant's transcendental anthropology of volition starts from the "fact" of moral obligation, Foucault claims that "[N]obody is obliged in classical ethics" (Foucault 1983: 240). If moral responsibility itself is merely an aspect of modern European knowledge–power, Kant's moral philosophy merely answers the question "What ought I – as an eighteenth-century modern man – do?" and his "anthropology" is really just a study of human beings living within a particular, contingent system of knowledge–power. The moral law is "universal" only in representing a particularly modern-European ambition to subordinate all diversity and particularity to a single overarching system of normalcy. And "autonomy" is really just how observational systems of the modern world seek to impose power through creating self-disciplining human beings. For Foucault, "Kant introduces one more way in our tradition whereby the self is not merely given but is constituted in relationship to itself as subject" (Foucault 1983: 252).

Even Kant's question "What is the human being?" is suspect: "the notion of human nature seems to me mainly to have played the role of ... designating certain types of discourse" (Foucault 1984: 4). "[M]an, as a primary reality with its own density, as the difficult object and sovereign subject of all possible knowledge" is a recent innovation, something with "no place" even in the Classical era of Descartes, much less in ancient or medieval forms of life (Foucault 1973: 310). Even if the question could make sense, Kant's answer to it is, at best, the careful analysis of a particular eighteenth-century episteme that plays a role in our self-conceptions. But unlike Kant's "Conjectures on the Beginning of Human History" that depict the emergence of a from-within perspective that is now, for all intents and purposes, the necessary structure of human beings as such, Foucault's "genealogy of the subject" aims to disclose the contingency of human subjectivity as it emerged in our culture in order to open up possibilities for revision:

> The target now is not to discover what we are, but to refuse what we are ... We have to promote new forms of subjectivity through refusal of {the} kind of individuality which has been imposed on us for several centuries.
>
> (Foucault 1982: 216)

Rather than transcendental justification of "the" structure of subjectivity through analysis of its conditions of possibility, Foucault offers a genealogy of the emergence of our distinctive forms of subjectivity in order to refuse those forms. Summing up his relationship with Kant, Foucault explains,

> If the Kantian question was that of knowing what limits knowledge has to renounce transgressing, it seems to me that the critical question today has to be turned back into a positive one: in what is given to us as universal, necessary, obligatory, what place is occupied by whatever is singular, contingent, and the product of arbitrary constraints? The point is, in brief, to transform the critique conducted in the form of necessary limitation into a practical critique that takes the form of a possible transgression.
>
> This entails an obvious consequence: that criticism is no longer going to be practiced in the search for formal structures with universal value, but rather as a historical investigation into the events that have led us to constitute ourselves and to recognize ourselves as subjects of what we are doing, thinking, saying. In that sense, this criticism is not transcendental, and its goal is not that of making a metaphysics possible: it is genealogical in its design and archaeological in its method.
>
> Archaeological – and not transcendental – in the sense that it will not seek to identify the universal structures of all knowledge or of all possible moral action, but will seek to treat the instances of discourse that articulate

what we think, say, and do as so many historical events. And this critique will be genealogical in the sense that it will not deduce from the form of what we are what it is impossible for us to do and to know, but it will separate out, from the contingency that has made us what we are, the possibility of no longer being, doing, or thinking what we are, do, or think. It is not seeking to make possible a metaphysics that has finally become a science; it is seeking to give new impetus, as far and wide as possible, to the undefined work of freedom.

(Foucault 1984: 45–46)

Cultural Diversity

Historicism is one form of a general trend toward emphasizing human diversity. For historicists, there is no uniform answer to the question "What is the human being?" because human beings change. But even at any given time, humanity includes substantial diversity based on sex or gender, race or ethnicity, and culture. In Chapter 5, we discussed Kant's (over)attentiveness to such distinctions and looked at contemporary responses to Kant's accounts of sex, gender, race, and ethnicity. This section focuses on the important role that increased awareness of cultural difference plays in conceptions of "the" human being today. Recognizing and appreciating distinct human cultures is not new, but increased globalization has made diversity more obvious, important, and endangered than ever.

Increased awareness of human diversity brings both practical and philosophical challenges. Like historicism, awareness of diversity threatens Kant's anthropology with relativism. If some cultures do not ascribe moral responsibility to one another, or do not see morality as universal, that would call into question Kant's moral philosophy. If some cultures do not understand the world in terms of necessary causal interactions between spatial–temporal objects, that would threaten his epistemology. Kant's empirical anthropology, with its tidy classification of human mental states, is based upon the introspection and limited observations of a man who never went more than ninety miles from home. Today one might wonder whether there really are empirically universal characteristics of human nature. Even Kant's conception of "unsocial sociability" driving human progress might seem incompatible with the existence of relatively peaceful and stable cultures.

Practically, increased interactions require discerning what responsibilities we have with respect to those from other cultures. For Kant, enlightenment arises through the vibrant exchange of ideas aiming toward the truth. But this truth-orientation is also an orientation toward agreement, or conformity. As "multiculturalism" and "pluralism" have come to be taken as goods in their own right, one might question Kant's emphasis on agreement. Might it not be better to allow, protect, and even promote widely divergent conceptions of reality amongst different human groups (e.g. by protecting dying languages)? Morally, we might ask how respect for others should manifest itself in interactions with those from other cultures. For example, if women in a particular culture are mistreated or abused, should "we" refrain from interfering out of respect for the culture or should we intervene out of respect for the woman? Or is there some other option? Politically, problems of diversity are acute. Kant used his claim that no political order is fully just until it becomes part of a global federation of states to argue against unjust colonization of other peoples (8: 357–60, 6: 353). But he also recognized that his own theory of universal consent is susceptible to an all-too-common "Jesuitism" that would "ask whether ... we should not be authorized to found colonies, by force if need be, in order to establish a civil union ... and bring these human beings (savages) into a rightful condition" (6: 266). As many today promote visions of "liberal empire" (Arneil 2007: 302), these problems are particularly urgent.

One popular way of reacting to human diversity is to embrace cultural relativism about truth, virtue, and beauty. As in the case of historicism, there are both methodological and substantive versions of this relativism. Methodologically, at least a limited relativism has become a norm among cultural anthropologists. In studying other cultures, anthropologists typically focus on discerning the practices, presuppositions, and values of a particular culture without aiming to assess the value of those practices in terms of supposedly absolute standards. Clifford Geertz makes explicit the "relativist bent" that is "in some sense implicit in the field as such" (Geertz 2000: 44). And Ruth Benedict, in her classic *Patterns of Culture* (Benedict 1934/2005), explains:

> To the anthropologist, our customs and those of a New Guinea tribe are two possible social schemes for dealing with a common problem, and insofar as he remains an anthropologist he is bound to avoid any weighing of one in favor of the other.
>
> (Benedict 1934/2005: 1)

Methodologically, the relativist bent of anthropologists commits them to a different project from that of philosophers or even many psychologists. Rather than trying to figure out the best way of dealing with various problems that might arise in societies, anthropologists observe and seek to understand how other cultures respond to those problems. To avoid projecting one's values onto other cultures and to remain sensitive to their nuances, some sort of relativism – at least in the negative sense of refraining as much as possible from evaluating other cultures in terms of one's own – has proven immensely valuable for understanding human diversity.

Substantive relativism takes this relativist bent further, claiming that basic concepts of truth and value *are* culture-relative, and not merely in that what people *find* true and valuable is largely culture-bound, but that truth and value are *in fact* culturally relative. Methodological relativism refrains from asking ultimate questions about Truth or Goodness. Substantive relativism claims that there are no (universal) answers to those questions, that "morality differs in every society, and is a convenient term for socially approved habits" (Benedict 1934). Geertz suggests how anthropological research promotes this substantive relativism:

> One cannot read too long about Nayar matriliny, Aztec sacrifice, the Hopi verb, or the convolutions of the hominid transition and not begin at least to consider the possibility that, to quote Montaigne ..., "each man calls barbarism whatever is not his own practice ... for we have no other criterion of reason than the example and idea of the opinions and customs of the country we live in." That notion, whatever its problems, and however more delicately expressed, is not likely to go away unless anthropology does.
>
> (Geertz 2000: 44–45)

As much as Geertz and Benedict see substantive relativism as a consequence of anthropological study, however, it does not follow logically from the fact of human diversity, nor from the methodological relativism that enhances our understanding of that diversity. It would be perfectly sensible to recognize that human beings hold different beliefs about physics, for example, or to study different cultures' mathematical systems without evaluating their soundness, while still affirming that, for instance, projectiles really do travel on parabolic paths and spells cannot transform lead into gold. Similarly, it would be perfectly sensible to recognize that human beings have different moral values regulating interactions, while still affirming that, for example, value systems that endorse slavery or malicious deception are wrong.

In its most blatant form, substantive relativism is self-defeating. Benedict rightly notes that "recognition of cultural relativity carries with it its own values," and while these values "need not be those of [prior] absolutist philosophies" (Benedict 1934/2005: 278), they are just as absolutist as those. In fact, substantive relativism is particularly parochial; while some other cultures may endorse epistemic and moral relativism, the particular forms of relativism dominant today emerged only in the context of moral and anthropological developments in "the West" in the past hundred years. Substantive relativism of this dogmatic sort is just as ethnocentric and absolutist as any other substantive dogma.

There are, however, less dogmatic sorts of relativism that still go beyond the merely methodological relativism of contemporary anthropology. Anthropological study, like Foucault's and Kuhn's historical studies, can show that from-within perspectives Kant took for granted are less universal than he supposed. Citing his own pioneering work in cultural anthropology, Geertz notes,

> [T]he constructivism of Thomas Kuhn and ... Foucault ... suddenly made a concern with meaning-making an acceptable pre-occupation for a scholar to have [and] they provided the ... speculative instruments to make the existence of someone who saw human beings as, quoting myself ... "suspended in webs of meaning they themselves have spun" a good deal easier ... [In] Bali, ... I tried to show that kinship, village form, the traditional state, ... and, most infamously, the cockfight could be read as ... enacted statements of ... particular ways of being in the world.
>
> (Geertz 2000: 17)

For Geertz, "The whole point of this ... approach to culture is ... to aid us in gaining access to the conceptual world in which our subjects live so that we can, in some extended sense of the term, converse with them" (Geertz 1973: 24). In that context, "descriptions of Berber, Jewish, or French culture must be cast in terms of the constructions we imagine Berbers, Jews, or Frenchman to place upon what they live through" (Geertz 1973: 15), and one comes to see one's own "ideas [and] values ... [as] cultural products" (Geertz 1973: 50). Entering others' "worlds" inhibits Kant's kind of transcendental anthropology, not because of a dogmatic assertion that there are no universals, but simply because we come to see new possibilities – and hence new "conditions of possibility." One need not deny a universal point of view to make one's own point of view seem provincial. And a transcendental analysis of a provincial and contingent point of view falls short of the anthropology in which Kant was so interested.

As in the case of historicism, with this *general* objection come *specific* points of comparison between what Kant took to be universal aspects of human nature and what anthropologists find in other cultures. For example, Ruth Benedict describes the Dobu of the South Pacific in ways particularly problematic for Kant's moral philosophy:

> The Dobuan is dour, prudish, and passionate, consumed with jealousy and suspicion and resentment. Every moment of prosperity he conceives himself to have wrung from a malicious world by a conflict in which he has worsted an opponent. The good man is the one who has many such conflicts to his credit, as anyone can see from the fact that he has survived with a measure

of prosperity. It is taken for granted that he has thieved, killed children and his close associates by sorcery, cheated whenever he dared. [T]heft and adultery are the object of the valued charms of the valued men of the community.

(Benedict 1934/2005: 168–69)

The general claim that moral norms differ between cultures is troubling, but the *details* of these differences seem to pose particular problems. Whatever Dobuans mean by "good," they cannot refer to one who acts only on maxims that can be willed to be universal. A "good" person, on Benedict's reconstruction of the Dobu, acts on maxims that precisely *cannot* be universalized, exploiting his fellows for personal benefit. Any "transcendental anthropology of volition" for the Dobu will, it seems, have to look very different from Kant's.

Along with this undoing of Kant's universalist anthropology, many of those interested in human diversity add an ethical and pragmatic "relativist bent." Geertz, for example, largely accepts the point that substantive relativism is self-undermining. But he takes this precisely as a reason not to worry about objecting to it. As he puts it, "The image of vast numbers of anthropology readers running around in so cosmopolitan a frame of mind as to have no views as to what is and isn't true, or good, or beautiful, seems to me largely a fantasy" (Geertz 2000: 46). By contrast, however, the thought of lots of Kantians running around interpreting everyone in terms of their own prejudices about knowledge, goodness, and even beauty is one worthy of genuine concern. Thus rather than a Kantian, *universalist* anthropology, we need "connoisseur[s] ... of alien turns of mind," of whom "the connoisseur par excellence ... has been the ethnographer, dramatizing oddness, extolling diversity, and breathing broadmindedness" (Geertz 2000: 82–83).

Alongside undermining Kantian naïveté about the universality of one's own perspective, many add an ethical sense that "provincialism ... [is a] more real concern [than relativism]" (Geertz 2000: 46). This broadminded love of diversity leads to a new vision for answering the question "What is the human being?"

> [W]hat men are, above all other things, is various. It is in understanding that variousness – its range, its nature, its basis, and its implications – that we shall come to construct a concept of human nature that, more than a statistical shadow and less than a primitive dream, has both substance and truth ... To be human here is thus not to be Everyman; it is to be a particular kind of man, and of course men differ ... [I]t is in a systematic review and analysis of [different ways of being human] – of the Plain's Indian's bravura, the Hindu's obsessiveness, the Frenchman's rationalism, the Berber's anarchism, the American's optimism – that we shall find out what it is, or can be, to be a man.
>
> (Geertz 1973: 52–53)[3]

Even without going as far as substantive relativism, contemporary cultural anthropology – and its spin-offs into cultural studies, postcolonial studies, gender studies, and studies of diversity in all its forms – invites a shift in perspective. Just as historicists resist univocal, trans-historical notions of "human being," cultural anthropologists object to a cross-cultural conception of *the* human being, replacing it with a rich variety of human ways of being.

Kantian Responses to Historicism

Kuhn, Foucault, Benedict, and Geertz all draw attention to seemingly fundamental human differences that would not only reflect empirical variations but also affect how humans see and live in their worlds. They threaten not only Kant's empirical claims, but his transcendental anthropology. While the claims of each thinker require specific responses, contemporary Kantians might use three general strategies of response: offering Kant-inspired objections to historicism, partially absorbing and reinterpreting specific historicist claims, and/or developing distinctively Kantian versions of historicism.

Kantian Objections to Historicism

One response to historicist challenges would be for Kant to maintain the basic tenets of his transcendental anthropology and challenge specific historical–cultural claims that seem to threaten those tenets. Such Kantians would refuse to give up the central claims that all human volition involves awareness of the moral law and all human cognition involves spatial–temporal intuition and a priori categories such as causation. Despite challenges posed by scientific developments, one could deny that relativity theory and quantum mechanics, as generally interpreted, provide actual cognition of the world. Any contradiction between Kant's transcendental anthropology and Einstein's physics would be bad news for Einstein, not for Kant. With respect to Foucault and Geertz, Kantians might simply deny that these figures properly interpret human history or diverse cultures, or they might deny that the interpretations really represent counter-examples to Kant's transcendental anthropology.

Such strong objections to historicist claims are not wholly unjustified. Regarding developments in science, Kant's arguments for the apriority of our forms of cognition were based on conditions for arriving at genuine empirical *understandings* of the world. And it is not clear that modern scientific theories are literally understandable in their non-Kantian forms. The mathematics of relativity theory and quantum mechanics does not conflict with Kant's a priori structures of human cognition. Kant never claimed that it would be impossible to *think about* what would follow from rejecting one or more of Euclid's axioms, only that it would be impossible to actually cognize such a world, that is, to fill in one's concepts with intuitions of objects. When "explaining" objects quantum mechanically or relativistically, scientists notoriously turn to metaphor and analogy, suggesting that literal understandings of modern physics are not yet available. Kantians might reasonably insist on intuitive comprehensibility as a constraint on scientific realism, and Kant himself proposes a similar approach against those in his day (and ours!) who assume the existence of a vacuum.

> Nearly all natural philosophers, since they perceive a great difference in the quantity of matter of different sorts in the same volume ... infer that this volume ... must be empty in all matter, although to be sure in different amounts. But ... their inference rest[s] solely on a metaphysical presupposition ... for they assume that the *real* in space ... is *everywhere one and the same* and can be differentiated only according to its ... amount. Against this presupposition, ... I oppose a transcendental proof, which, to be sure, will not explain the variation in the filling of space, but which still will entirely obviate the alleged necessity of the presupposition ... which has the merit of at least granting the understanding the freedom to think of this difference in another way.
>
> (A173–74/B215–16)

The details of this particular debate are unnecessary here; the general point is that Kant willingly set his transcendental proof against decrees of "nearly all natural philosophers" even when unable to explain the phenomena their theories purported to explain. Similarly, Kantians today might insist that quantum mechanics and relativity theory cannot be adequate explanations of the world, since they are inconsistent with our forms of intuition and thus literally incomprehensible as applied to objects. They can still be good models for prediction, but not for understanding, and rejecting scientific realism here may even "have the merit" of encouraging work in new directions in physics. Akin to Einstein's early critique of quantum mechanics, we might see Kant as insisting that the fact that scientists have not *found* deterministic laws does not imply that there *are* no deterministic laws. Kant might even point out that appeals to sub-atomic quantum states and bendable space–time that cannot be literally understood as we understand objects of experience reflect a 21st-century version of the classic metaphysical temptation to turn to things-in-themselves – thinkable but non-intuitable psuedo-objects – as a shortcut for explaining the empirical world.

Similarly, both Foucaultian genealogy and Geertzian anthropology are susceptible to Kantian objections. One Kantian response would involve an attitude toward cultural difference that many ascribe to Kant, conceding cultural diversity while maintaining transcendental anthropology by insisting that some peoples and cultures are not "human" in the fullest sense. If a particular group conceives of decision-making *purely* in categories of beauty (as Foucault suggests for the ancient Greeks) or prudence (as Benedict suggests for the people of Dobu), Kantians might just say that such people lack a fully developed predisposition to personality and, in that sense, are not really "human." Whether or not this would warrant treating them with disrespect would remain an open question, but it would be a way of saving Kant's *philosophical* account from anthropological challenge. As offensive as the approach sounds, there is some degree to which it is unavoidable. We see the world through our own eyes and our own values, and while our perspective might change through understanding others, if relativist cultural anthropologists are right, there would be no single perspective that all groups share. But since we do decide what to believe and how to act, we will, at least in practice, think and act in accordance with norms we think best, and we will thereby at least implicitly view other groups as seeing through the wrong eyes. Even the relativist bent shared by Benedict, Geertz, and Foucault is a particular bent not shared by many other cultures. Insofar as "What is the human being?" is a *normative* question about how *best* to be human, it is inevitable, if we know enough about human diversity, to see some forms of diversity as failures to live up to what it means to be a human in the fullest sense.

But there are other, better, Kantian objections to Foucault and Geertz. One important move for the Kantian will be to distinguish between *particular* knowledge- or value-claims and the overall *structure* of knowledge- or value-claims. Even if other cultures, for example, disagree about what causes particular kinds of changes, they may still agree on the notion of temporal succession (and thereby on some shared conception of causation). Even if cultures disagree about, say, cannibalism, they might still adhere to general conceptions of respect for others. And even if – as in Benedict's account of the Dobu – some cultures do not even believe in anything that could be called Kantian respect, they might still adhere to a sense of "goodness" as something that would be "good" for anyone. Thus one of Benedict's Dobuans might say that *anyone* who successfully exploits and abuses others is "good." And in such a case, Kant might be able to run transcendental arguments to show that built into this conception of goodness is a standard at variance with the particular ethical prescriptions of Benedict's Dobu.

Kant also could rightly insist upon a difference between from-within standpoints of evaluation and deliberation and people's actual customs and practices. Kant admits that human beings are "radically evil" and even that this evil manifests itself in corrupting societies such that "someone already counts as good when his evil is common to a class" (6: 33). Given variable conditions, human inclinations and prejudices develop in different ways, with correspondingly different manifestations of immorality in different cultures. Thus just as the Dobu might excuse the immorality of adultery or witchcraft and praise its prudence, those on Wall Street might excuse the immorality of competitive "sharp practice" and praise the returns brought home to shareholders. In neither case are these forms of praise reflections of a different moral code; they just reflect ordinary ways in which social forms of radical evil corrupt strict applications of the moral law.

Finally, Kant might rightly point out that much perceived variation amongst cultures could be due to a *pre*judgment or inclination toward novelty, one widely shared by the sorts of people that typically become anthropologists and (Foucaultian) historians. Kant emphasizes,

> from a multiplicity of descriptions of countries one can prove, if one wants to, that Americans, Tibetans, and other genuine Mongolian peoples have no beard, but also, if it suits you better, that all of them are by nature bearded ... ; that Americans and Negroes are each a race, sunk beneath the remaining of the human species in their mental predispositions, but on the other side by just as apparent records that as regards their natural predispositions, they are to be estimated equal to every other inhabitant of the world; so it remains to the choice of the philosopher whether he wants to assume differences in nature or wants to judge everything in accordance with the principle "Everything is as it is with us."
>
> (8: 62)

A certain relativistic bent – and often even an Orientalizing fascination with the exotic (see Said 1979, Obeyesekere 1993 and 2005) – is not only a natural *result* of anthropological study, but a sort of dispositional and methodological *presupposition* of certain kinds of anthropological investigation (including, alas, Kant's). Likewise, Foucault's genealogical and archeological projects, as much as they seem to provide evidence of the historical emergence of frameworks of thought and action, ultimately *presuppose* a historicist approach to structures of human knowledge–power. In his *Anthropology*, Kant points out that "without ... a plan ... all acquired knowledge [of the world] can yield nothing more than fragmentary groping around and no science," and for Kant, this plan requires that *"General* knowledge always precede *local* knowledge," that is, that one has a sense of the human being in general before studying local variations (7: 120). Whether or not one agrees with *this* methodological prescription, it is worth noting that anthropologists studying the world with this sort of Kantian methodology may come to very different conclusions from those who *begin* with a more relativistic bent. There is reason for at least some skepticism about the empirical findings – and their interpretations – offered by the more relativistically inclined anthropologists amongst us.

Thus whereas Foucault focuses on the *emergence* of contemporary notions of subjectivity, a Kantian historicist might instead look for Kantian conceptions of subjectivity in historical periods when Foucault denies them and in cultural contexts where contemporary anthropologists claim not to find them. Where Foucault claims that "nobody is obliged in classical ethics," Kant might claim that classical notions of "beautiful existence" are taken, even in ancient Greece, as "to-be-chosen" in ways that correspond to categorical "obligation."[4] Historical ways of describing subjectivity would be merely different "formulae" for common underlying transcendental structures that Kant elucidates in terms of "obligation," "freedom," and "autonomy." It is worth emphasizing here that Kant's moral anthropology and conception of subjectivity were at variance even with what one may have discovered – as an anthropologist or historian – about *his own time*. Kant emphasizes the independence of conscience from religion, the importance of adhering to strict principles, the extent to which morals must be carefully distinguished from the pursuit of happiness. Kant saw these claims as *implicit* in the volitional structure of his compatriots (and human beings in general), but all of them could have been occluded in historical or anthropological studies of his culture.

This skepticism, of course, can lead to a different way of doing anthropology, and only time would tell whether this Kantian cultural anthropology would hold up to empirical facts on the ground. There are, however, promising hints that an anthropology that leaves more room for human universals – especially of the rational variety in which Kant would be most interested – may be more fruitful than anthropologists like Benedict and Geertz suggest (see e.g. Bok 2002, Pinker 1992, Tsing 2005). Perhaps the most famous example in recent anthropology is the debate between two pre-eminent contemporary anthropologists – Gananath Obeyesekere and Marshall Sahlins – regarding the Hawaiians' reception of Captain Cook. While Sahlins undertook that study largely with the "relativist bent" of a European interested in the exotic and developed a picture of native Hawaiians that makes them seem very different from Europeans then and now, Obeysekere went into the study with a skepticism about the nature of European anthropological and "myth-making" practices and called into question exoticizing descriptions of the reception of Cook shared by modern anthropologists and ultimately even Hawaiians themselves.[5] Equally important is the work of anthropologists like Anna Tsing, whose study of "engaged universals" and the ways that "universals are effective within particular historical conjunctures that give them content and force" represents a Geertz-informed cultural anthropology that takes universals seriously without denying their problematic features in concrete practice (Tsing 2005: 8, see Abu-Lughod 1999).

To take a less famous and more pointed example, Susanne Kuehling has recently published a book-length study of the Dobu people in which she makes clear not only the profound limitations of the original field research on which Benedict relied (by an anthropologist who consulted *one* Dobuan for one month and wrote with "the imperial attitude of his time" (Kuehling 2005: 14)) but also how "Benedict's travesty" (Kuehling 2005: 136) warped even that "vastly oversimplified" account to portray an "even darker" picture of the Dobu "as an extreme example of human moral possibilities" (Kuehling 2005: 16), a "characterization ... that bears no resemblance to [the] Dobu" experienced by Kuehling over the course of several years of intense fieldwork. In sharp contrast to the "inverted morality" portrayed by Benedict, Kuehling highlights the Dobu's "egalitarian ethic" (Kuehling 2005: 117) and emphasizes that among the Dobu an "ethics of respect, self-discipline, and generosity are the keys to appropriate behavior" (Kuehling 2005: 69). Of course, Kuehling's own account, which highlights the "ethics of exchange" as a framework for understanding the Dobu, does not show that they share the general presuppositions of Kant's moral anthropology, but she goes into her study with a different agenda, with a different "general knowledge," and thus Kant would be unsurprised that she neither looks for nor finds a Kantian "predisposition to personality." What she clearly illustrates, however, is the importance of taking *any* anthropological "counter-examples" to Kantian transcendental anthropology with a grain of salt. She thus justifies, at least provisionally, an unwillingness to take as given the "observations" and "facts" of anthropologists who go into the field with deeply non- or even anti-Kantian presuppositional frameworks.

Partial Accommodation

A second approach to dealing with historicism would involve giving up specific a priori structures, such as Euclidean space, Newtonian deterministic causation, or specific formulations of the categorical imperative, but preserving more general a priori structures, roughly corresponding to Kant's. Just as contemporary psychology requires revising details of Kant's empirical anthropology but not his overall framework, historicist or anthropological studies might require revising details of Kant's transcendental anthropology. Alternatively, one might limit the *scope* of Kant's a priori structures, insisting that they underlie ordinary experience but not scientific or moral theorizing.

This sort of accommodation is a plausible and significant Kantian approach to historicism. With respect to relativity theory, for example, Henrik Lorentz already developed an "empirically equivalent" alternative to Einsteinian special relativity theory that preserves an "essentially classical spatio-temporal structure" (Friedman 2001: 87). And the probabilistic causation of quantum mechanics already fits with a slightly modified version of Kant's approach to causation. For Kant, the fundamental role of causation is to preserve the directionality of time. Kant assumed that the only causal principle by which one could order the world requires that given effects necessarily follow causes according to deterministic rules. With quantum mechanical causation, succeeding states follow initial states according to probabilistic rules. While giving up determinism would be an important shift, it would not require relinquishing the basic structure of succeeding states following from previous ones according to rules.

One might imagine further accommodation, such that one ends up with increasingly thin a priori structures of cognition. Kuhn himself argues for some form of this approach, defending general epistemic virtues such as accuracy, consistency, simplicity, and fruitfulness as general characteristics of any good scientific theory (Kuhn 1977). Similarly, Kant might argue that whatever particular structures human beings use to interpret their world, they make use of certain a priori principles to guide empirical cognition. This strategy could be extended to variations in conceptions of the world discovered by anthropologists. While other cultures may allow for witchcraft, cycles of time, or radically different approaches to understanding the world, one might still find common basic structures underlying them all. Even something like Foucault's analysis of earlier forms of subjectivity might leave structures – say, some general notion of normativity or basic distinction between a from-within and an objective perspective – that are common to different, historically local ways of conceptualizing these structures.

Beyond changing particular claims while keeping more general ones, an important sort of accommodation, especially in the scientific context, would concede historicism about scientific cognition while preserving Kant's transcendental anthropology for ordinary cognition. Even if scientists now think of the world as involving probabilistic causation and non-Euclidean space, ordinary human experience is universally and ahistorically based on Kant's a priori cognitive structures. Especially conjoined with a deprivileging of scientific cognition, such accommodation preserves a substantial role for Kant's transcendental anthropology of cognition while leaving science subject to historicism. One might do something similar with other cultures, arguing that, say, religious or mythical beliefs might violate Kant's categories of experience while everyday interactions would still be governed by them.

Historicized Kant, Kantian Historicism

Accommodation might go so far that nothing is left of Kant's distinctive transcendental anthropology. Even the most basic cognitive and volitional values might be exposed as historically contingent. In this context, one might simply need to concede that Kant's transcendental anthropology must be replaced by a historicist one. Even a wholesale acceptance of historicism, however, need not completely reject insights from Kant's transcendental anthropology. For example, Michael Friedman has defended a "modified version of a Kantian philosophy of science" centered on the concept of a "relativized yet still constitutive a priori" (Friedman 2001: 71). Friedman embraces the historical contingency of cognitive structures while sustaining a commitment to seeing these structures as constitutive of (our understanding of) our world. For Friedman, even a relativized a priori is an important contribution to contemporary philosophy of science in that it implies, against Quine's holistic "fabric" of knowledge, that knowledge has a structure with "fundamental asymmetries," such that within any (scientific) body of knowledge, there are "necessary pre-suppositions constituting the conditions of possibility of the properly empirical parts" (Friedman 2001: 35, 37). Even if every aspect of human knowledge is in principle revisable in the light of further experience, there is a fundamental distinction between the ways in which specific empirical laws and the relativized a priori structures of cognition are revisable. Even when fully historicized, Kant's general transcendental approach contributes to understanding human beings. Arguably, it is even Kant's transcendental anthropology of cognition that makes Kuhnian historicism possible. Without Kant, one might be able to trace, as Quine does, the evolution of different ways of thinking about the world. But one would be unable to see, as Kuhn does, the way that historically changing ways of looking at the world structure and constrain human experience itself.

In the context of Foucault, too, completely accepting historicism would require a radical reorientiation of Kant's anthropology but need not require rejecting it entirely. Importantly, a strategy like Friedman's – that concedes the historicity of a priori structures – would not constitute a sufficient concession to Foucault, since Foucault historicizes the whole notion of a priori structures of an individual subject. In the case of Foucault, at least, fully historicizing Kant would essentially require replacing Kant with Foucault. Arguably, however, this replacement remains within the general sphere of Kant. Foucault read Kant's "What is Enlightenment?" as a proto-historicist work (see Foucault 1984: 32–50), and Foucault's intellectual career began with his effort to struggle through problems in Kant's *Anthropology* (see Foucault 2008). Arguably, Foucault is a sort of radically historicized Kant, and in that sense, Foucault himself models what a "Kantian–Foucaultian" might look like.

Finally, even a complete Kantian concession to cultural relativism could be interesting and important. Kantian distinctions – particularly between transcendental and empirical anthropology – can help cultural anthropologists more effectively study other cultures. It is one thing to describe how people act and even the way they use normative language, and quite another to investigate how thoughts and actions appear from-within. The latter task is more difficult than the former for an "outsider," and if the from-within perspectives of others are radically incommensurable with our own, it may be impossible. But clarifying the distinction will force anthropologists to direct attention in more precise ways. Moreover, even within transcendental anthropology, there is an important distinction between first-order normative claims and the elucidation of conditions of possibility for those claims. For example, it is one thing to say, from-within, that the boat is moving downstream; it is another to show – as Kant claims to do – that a condition of possibility of the legitimacy of such judgments is a category of causality. The investigation of transcendental conditions of possibility of "alien" ways of thinking and valuing could be an exciting Kantian philosophical anthropology (here using "anthropology" in something like its contemporary sense), a development of *different* transcendental anthropologies (here using "anthropology" in something like its Kantian sense).

The Problem of Normativity

In various ways, historians, historicist philosophers, and anthropologists challenge Kant's anthropology. The last section looked at a series of approaches that Kantians can use to respond to these challenges while preserving, to varying degrees, a distinctively "Kantian" approach to historical and cultural diversity. But regardless of which of these approaches one adopts, there arises a further important question, one that mere *descriptions* of human difference and historical change cannot answer: What are the implications of human differences for how we, here and now, *should* think, feel, and act? As *descriptions* of human difference and historical change, historicist and anthropological accounts are challenging and illuminating. But in themselves, they do not tell us what to *do* with these descriptions.

In his *Birth of the Clinic*, Foucault highlights this problem: his method "is concerned – *outside of all prescriptive intent* – with determining the conditions of possibility of medical experience in modern times" (Foucault 1994: xix, emphasis added). In their study of Foucault, Hubert Dreyfus and Paul Rabinow add, with respect to Foucault's self-proclaimed goal of "seeking to give new impetus ... to the undefined work of freedom" (Foucault 1984: 45–46) by resisting the "docile normalcy" of carceral society,

> What is wrong with carceral society? Genealogy undermines a stance which opposes it on the grounds of natural law or human dignity ... Genealogy also undermines opposing carceral society on the basis of subjective preferences and intuitions ... What are the resources which enable us to sustain a critical stance?
>
> (Dreyfus and Rabinow 1982: 206)[6]

The same point could be made with respect to Kuhn. If categories and practices of modern science are recent and revisable paradigms, what should we do? Should we oppose normal science and try to think of what is truly necessary? Should we simply embrace a scientific process that may be leading us down a misguided path? Similarly, Benedict and Geertz argue that our moral and epistemic values may not be shared by other cultures. If this is true, should we abandon those values? Should we adopt the values of the Dobu? (If so, whose Dobu?)

These questions remind us that there is, in fact, a from-within, norm-governed perspective. And they remind us that empirical descriptions, whether natural–scientific or historical, cannot answer normative questions. Foucault, Kuhn, and Benedict show that the fact that one holds a particular normative standard can be explained in terms of historical and cultural conditions. But when I, or you, or Foucault or Benedict, decide whether or not to apply a standard, even one that has been revealed as historically local, we cannot merely think about that standard in historicist or culturally relativist terms. While Foucault's histories or Geertz's ethnographies broaden our sense of possible ways of thinking and acting, they cannot in the end tell us how to decide, within that range, what to think or do.

One response to this predicament – Kant's – is to look again, from-within, at the ever-better-understood world in which we live. As we gain new insights into other time periods and other cultures, we can ask ourselves transcendental questions about those insights themselves: what are the conditions of possibility of historical knowledge? How is it possible that we are able to know such things about other cultures? What are the limits of such knowledge-claims? For Kant, the answers to these questions will *include* his general conditions of possibility for knowledge (space, time, causality, etc.), and will likely include other more specific conditions of possibility (in the way in which biological knowledge requires assuming purposiveness). We can go further, developing our transcendental anthropology of volition in the light of new insights about other cultures. What sorts of obligations might one have toward people with different moral norms? What are the conditions of possibility of mutual respect across cultural difference? What are my duties toward diverse others, especially as I come into greater contact with them? And while these questions, for Kant, involve various new subsidiary moral principles, they all require application of the universal moral law.

Summary

Historicism and cultural anthropology present detailed accounts of human diversity. Kuhn shows how scientific progress effects changes in paradigms that might otherwise seem to be fixed and transcendental conditions of possibility of empirical cognition. By depicting their emergence as historically contingent ways of conceiving of human beings, Foucault challenges Kant's moral theory, his conception of human subjectivity, and his "transcendental-empirical" account of the human being as a whole. And Benedict, Geertz, cultural anthropologists more generally, and a whole range of disciplines focused on human diversity challenge the purported universality of Kant's anthropological claims. To all of these thinkers, Kant has a variety of available responses, ranging from counter-objections such as insisting that there simply is not as much real diversity as they suggest, to accommodations that allow for some deep variations but within a framework that is still in some respects universal, to a complete but still Kantian historicism that preserves important Kantian insights about the nature of transcendental perspective but historicizes and relativizing this "a priori." All historicisms, however, face a problem when it comes to putting their insights to use. Human beings must decide what to think and do, and knowing that our frameworks for making these decisions are historically or culturally contingent does not directly tell us what to make of this knowledge. Thus there remains, from-within, a need for some normative framework for dealing with diversity.

One might, of course, seek normative frameworks other than Kant's. In Chapter 10, we look at several responses that preserve the basic notion that there are norms that can and should govern our thought and action from-within, but that vary regarding the universality and foundations of those norms. One might also – like Nietzsche – take diversity as a basis for liberation into a creativity that rises above present values. The lesson of historicism and cultural diversity, one might think, is that we should stop *looking* for absolute standards "out there," and start *making* cognitive and volitional standards for ourselves. In its most influential modern form, this emphasis expresses itself in existentialism, to which we now turn.

Further Reading

The best works to read for getting a sense of Kuhn, Foucault, and Geertz are works by those authors themselves. *Structure* is Kuhn's classic work and Kuhn 2000 collects many important papers that trace later developments of that view. Nickles is a good collection of essays on Kuhn's thought with helpful references for further study.

Thomas Kuhn, *The Structure of Scientific Revolutions* (Chicago: University of Chicago Press, 1996)

Thomas Kuhn, *The Road Since Structure* (ed. James Conant and John Haugeland, Chicago: University of Chicago Press, 2000)

Thomas Nickles (ed.) *Thomas Kuhn* (Cambridge: Cambridge University Press, 2002)

The Order of Things is the published work in which Foucault most directly engages with Kant, but the set of essays included in *The Foucault Reader* gives a better overview of his philosophy. Dreyfus and Rabinow, which includes two important essays by Foucault, is a good scholarly overview of Foucault's thought. Gutting is a great short overview of Foucault, and Han helpfully situates Foucault vis-à-vis Kant.

Hubert Dreyfus and Paul Rabinow, *Michel Foucault: Beyond Structuralism and Hermeneutics* (Chicago: University of Chicago Press, 1983)

Michel Foucault, *The Order of Things* (New York: Vintage, 1994)

Michel Foucault, *The Foucault Reader* (ed. Paul Rabinow, New York: Vintage, 1984)

Gary Gutting, *Foucault: A Very Short Introduction* (Oxford: Oxford University Press, 2005)

Béatrice Han, *Foucault's Critical Project: Between the Transcendental and the Historical* (Stanford: Stanford University Press, 2002)

Interpretation of Culture is Geertz's classic articulation of his approach to cultural anthropology, while *Available Light* is a more recent set of reflections on philosophical issues with contemporary anthropology. Benedict and Kuehling provide two sharply contrasting descriptions of the Dobu. Tsing provides an excellent example of recent trends in cultural anthropology that take universality and interconnections between cultures seriously while still remaining broadly Geertzian in terms of several key issues in this chapter.

Ruth Benedict, *Patterns of Culture* (New York: Mariner Books, 1934/2005).

Clifford Geertz, *The Interpretation of Cultures* (New York: Basic Books, 1973)

Clifford Geertz, *Available Light: Anthropological Reflections on Philosophical Topics* (Princeton: Princeton University Press, 2000)

Susanne Kuehling, *Dobu: Ethics of Exchange on a Massim Island* (Honolulu: University of Hawaii Press, 2005)

Anna Tsing, *Friction: An Ethnography of Global Connection* (Princeton: Princeton University Press, 2005)

9   Existentialism

In a 1966 review for the journal *L'Arc*, Jean-Paul Sartre – who would become a pre-eminent voice of existentialism – criticized Foucault's *On the Order of Things*:

> What do we find in *The Order of Things*? Certainly not an archaeology of human sciences. Archaeology ... studies a style that had been designed and implemented by men. This style could thereafter present itself as a natural state, taking the allure of something given. It is nonetheless the result of a practice, the development of which the archaeologist traces. What Foucault offers is ... a geology: ... Each layer defines the conditions of possibility of a certain type of thought that triumphs for a certain period. But Foucault does not tell us what is most interesting: how every thought is built from these conditions, nor how people pass from one thought to another. This would require the intervention of praxis, thus history, and this is precisely what he refuses ... [H]e replaces the cinema with the magic lantern, the movement with a succession of static states.
>
> (Sartre 1966)[1]

Historicists like Foucault rightly pointed out the role of a "historical a priori" that shapes how human beings think and act. Like historicists, Sartre insists that humans see the world in historically contingent paradigms or "styles." But to Sartre, Foucault – along with other historicists and even naturalists – fails to recognize how human freedom effects world-changing paradigm shifts. Where historicists and naturalists see humans primarily as products of historical or natural forces, Sartre insists that even history and biology themselves, insofar as they are significant, are products of humans' responses to their situations. "[M]an ... causes a world to be discovered" (Sartre 1956: 59) and sciences are just "ways in which human beings behave" and "neither the sole nor the most immediate kind" (Heidegger 1953: 11). Paradigms – scientific or otherwise – are expressions of human freedom.

Alongside naturalism and historicism, the past century has seen the birth and development of an "existentialism" that emphasizes seeing oneself as free but finite, confronting a world of possibilities. Like cultural or historical relativists, existentialists deny any universal answer to "What is the human being?" But existentialists contrast universal human nature not with locally defined traits but with "subjectivity," the idea that "Man is nothing else but what he makes of himself" (Sartre 1993: 13, 15). The name "existentialism" was first used by Gabriel Marcel to describe the circle that emerged around Sartre and Simone de Beauvoir in Paris in the 1940s (de Beauvoir 1987: 45–46, Cooper 1990: 1). Martin Heidegger set the stage for modern existentialism by using Kierkegaard's concept of "existence" to develop an "existential analysis" (Heidegger 1953: 13, 42) of what Heidegger calls "Da-sein," an existential analytic that Heidegger calls "*the* a priori which must be visible if the question 'What is human being?' is to be discussed philosophically" (Heidegger 1953: 42). For Heidegger, "The 'essence' of Da-sein lies in its existence" (Heidegger 1953: 42), but Heidegger contrasts this existence with the "Being of beings" like tables and chairs: "The characteristics to be found in [Dasein] are thus not objectively present 'attributes' of an objectively present being which has such and such an 'outward appearance,' but rather possible ways for it to be, and only this" (Heidegger 1953: 42).[2] Following Heidegger, Sartre insists that "existence precedes essence" (Sartre 1993: 13) to resist any human "nature" or "concept" (Sartre 1993: 30, 15). What we do – our "existence" – defines who, and what, we are. The question "What is the human being?" shifts from being about an object – the human being – to being about an adverb: how should we humanly be?

Existentialism explicitly draws from Kant and is the most Kantian contemporary approach discussed thus far. Like Kant, existentialists emphasize human freedom and finitude and focus on being human from-within[3] rather than on humans as objects. But existentialists radicalize and modify these Kantian themes in important ways that challenge Kant's conception of the human being. First, while Kant's transcendental analyses of human beings from-within focus on three faculties that are taken to be fundamentally distinct, self-consciously reflective, and highly structured by norms, existentialists aim to analyze what they take to be a more fundamental, primordial "Being-in-the-world" that does not admit of Kant's sharp distinctions between faculties nor his prioritization of the highly structured norm-governed forms of human experience. Second, where Kant defends freedom-as-autonomy subject to a moral law, Sartre insists upon "absolute freedom" that outstrips any "book of ethics" (Sartre 1993: 25, cf. Kierkegaard 2006). Third, existentialists' emphasis on absolute freedom brings an ideal of "authenticity," a way of being within which submission of freedom to universalizable laws looks like inauthentic enslavement to "the they" or a form of "bad faith" in which one pretends that some law arises "necessarily." Finally, existentialism emphasizes the role of others in different ways from Kant, and recently new approaches – most notably by Derrida and Levinas – have shifted from a first-personal ("ontological") existentialism toward an emphasis on the radical and primordial heteronomy required by one's interactions with "alterity," or the "Other."[4]

Being-in-the-World

Unlike Kant, existentialists emphasize being-in-the-world. For Heidegger, the "being which we ourselves in each case are" is not merely "Sein," or "Being," but Da-sein, or Being-there. Human being is always situated in a particular context. Whereas Kant generally treats the from-within perspective as a "view from nowhere" (albeit a distinctively human one),[5] existentialists emphasize that human existence is always existence with specific, concrete projects and possibilities. Take Kant's examples from his discussion of causation: the house and boat (see Chapter 1, p. 17). Kant imagines how disinterested, barely embodied observers collect subjective perceptions of house-states or boat-states into objective cognitions. But he does not consider where the knower finds herself, nor why she seeks to cognize these objects. Kant's knower could be anyone anywhere with no particular stakes in the situations she surveys. Existentialists, by contrast, emphasize that human being is not disembodied contemplation, but being that always finds itself already "there," always "in-the-world." The person surveying the house is located some distance from it and surveys it for some reason, and everything about the house (its perceived "distance," the detail with which one perceives it, etc.) is affected by one's purposes in surveying it. Because human being is "being-in-the-world" rather than being-from-nowhere, human thoughts and actions are not separate from context. Sartre describes this as our "facticity" (Sartre 1956 passim, cf. 617, 669) and Heidegger as what he calls "thrownness" or our "thrown possibility" into "definite possibilities" (Heidegger 1953: 144).

One implication of this conception of being-in-the-world is the rejection of several dualisms permeating Kant's philosophy, including that between subject and object (which Sartre describes as "useless and disastrous" (Sartre 1956: 318)) and between "practical" and "theoretical" realms. For example, Heidegger criticizes Kant's epistemology (and that of the whole Western tradition) for focusing on "conspicuous" or "merely objectively present" things (Heidegger 1953: 71, 73). We initially and for the most part encounter "handy" objects:

> The closest kind of association {with things in the world} is not mere perceptual cognition, but, rather, a handling, using, and taking care of things which has its own kind of knowledge ... To expose what is merely objectively

present, cognition must first penetrate beyond things at hand being taken care of. Handiness is the ontological categorial definition of beings as they are "in themselves."

(Heidegger 1953: 67, 71)

Kant's house and boat are not first objects to be surveyed, but places to live or vehicles for travel on the river. The objectivizing reflection Kant takes as fundamental is actually a highly derivative form of knowing that abstracts from lived knowledge of the world of handy objects that always already have meaning in the context of Da-sein's being-in-the-world. Thus Heidegger attends to experiences of hammering (Heidegger 1953: 69), and Sartre existentially describes phenomena as diverse as sexual attraction, shame, smoking a cigarette, and giving in to fatigue during a mountain-climb (Sartre 1956: 497f., 350f., 73, 584f.).

In challenging Kant's emphasis on "objective" cognition, existentialists destabilize Kant's limited scientific realism. One might think understanding human being as "being-in-the-world" would privilege natural sciences, but it implies precisely the opposite. Being-in-the-world is not an objective, scientifically studiable attribute; humans are not like trees or spoons, "in-the-world" as being spatially located objects. "Being-in-the-world" is a way we are from-within that collapses Kantian (and modern scientific) distinctions between knowing, feeling, and acting and thereby undermines sciences' supposed "objectivity." Heidegger and Sartre both show how a purportedly "objective" perspective arises for specific purposes: "Even the disinterested attitude of a scientist ... is the *assumption* of a disinterested position with regard to the object and hence one conduct among others" (Sartre 1956: 613).

Kant need not deny that natural sciences are limited, nor even that there are non-objective perspectives humans take on the world, but for Kant, sciences do provide our best account of the empirical world. But existentialists describe science as merely *one* "way in which human beings behave" (Heidegger 1953: 11), and not even a "primordial" one; any object of experience "is always already a thing at hand ... and precisely not 'initially' merely objectively present 'world-stuff'" (Heidegger 1953: 85, see also 8–9). As Sartre puts it,

I can establish that the warm water appears cold to me when I put my hand in it after having first plunged my hand in hot water. But this establishment which we pompously call "the law of relativity of sensations" has nothing to do with sensations. Actually we are dealing with a quality of the object which is revealed to me: the warm water is cold when I submerge my heated hand in it. A comparison of this objective quality of the water to equally objective information which the thermometer gives me simply reveals to me a contradiction. This contradiction motivates on my part a free

> choice of true objectivity. I shall give the name subjectivity to the objectivity which I have not chosen.
>
> (Sartre 1956: 412)

Where Kant privileges the scientific standpoint as the correct and normatively required standpoint for understanding the world, Sartre sees merely incompatible objectivity-claims. If anything, existentialists' emphasis on being-in-the-world suggests that the immediate awareness of the water as cold is more important, while science is secondary, derived, and, in its theory-ladenness, no less personal. As Heidegger puts it with respect to space and time,

> An "objectively" long path can be shorter than an "objectively" much shorter path which is perhaps an "onerous one" … When there is a prior orientation toward [scientific] "nature" and the "objectively" measured distances of things, one is inclined to consider such interpretations … "subjective." However, that is a "subjectivity" which perhaps discovers what is most real about the "reality" of the world.
>
> (Heidegger 1953: 106)

While Kuhn's scientific historicism calls into question Kant's transcendental analysis of scientific knowing, existentialists show that Kant's analyses fail to reflect ordinary, lived, human experience.

Most basically, this existentialist critique draws attention to the priority of handy things over theoretical "objects." But existentialists' critiques cut deeper as they get more specific, such as in existentialist reinterpretations of time. Heidegger's *Being and Time* restores a focus on lived time and points out that, within lived experience, time does not appear as what Kant called "objective succession." Within Kantian "time," basic temporal categories of past, present, and future are merely derived relations between the times in which events take place and the temporal location of oneself. The categories of "past, present, and future" are all-too-commonly used in a sense derived from the broadly Kantian, "vulgar … derivative … [and] inauthentic" conception of objective time, where these are merely objectively locatable time-slices that include different moments. But Heidegger develops a notion of "temporality" as "the unified phenomenon of the future that makes present in the process of having-been" (Heidegger 1953: 300). Heidegger's complex terminology draws attention to our lived experience of temporality. From-within, the "present" is not a particular moment between past and future moments, but a projecting toward possibilities, a projecting that is always in the process of having-been-in-the-world. The future is not first and foremost an objective time that will come to be present later, but a set of possibilities toward which one aims.

The past is not first and foremost a set of events that previously occurred, but what is given about one's situation, what one can (re)interpret but not "change." And the present is not a moment that happens to occur between past and future but is one's existence itself, that way of being from the past into the future. Within our lived experience of the world, the heat-death of the universe is not an event in our future nor the Big Bang an event in our past; these moments do not show up in "our" time at all. And the derision that "will" be directed toward me as a result of the obnoxious (e)mail I overhastily sent is as much a part of my "past" as the event of sending it. I act toward my future possibilities in the light of an embarrassment or defensiveness that reflects the fact that this derision has occurred, even though, in terms of "objective" time, the recipient of my mail "will" not open it until later. What Kant isolates as "time" is thus not the lived temporality of human being but a highly derived sense of "objective" time, a sort of "time" that is important for objective, scientific knowledge, but not the primordial temporality of Da-sein. Similar existential reinterpretations offered for basic Kantian categories like space, causality, or substantiality highlight the distance of Kant's transcendental anthropology of cognition from the ordinary ways of cognizing objects in which humans initially and for the most part engage. The "experience" of Kant's first *Critique* is artificial, scientific objectivizing of the empirical world.

In responding to this existential critique, Kant need not claim that most or even any of our lived experience is reducible to merely objective knowledge disconnected from feelings and purposes. And Kant can certainly admit that cognitions of objects employ purposive and affective concepts (such as "hammer," "too heavy," or "fearsome"). In fact, Kant's *Anthropology* accommodates an integrated world-cognition that anticipates existentialist claims about lived experience. To take one mundane example, Kant notes that "German miles (which are not ... indicated with milestones ...) always become shorter the nearer we are to a capital (e.g., Berlin), and longer the farther we are from one (in Pomerania)" (7: 234). Kant's epistemological focus on objective spatial and temporal relations does not preclude his awareness of and attention to the *non*-"objective," ordinary, lived experiences of human beings. But for Kant, any cognition, whether related to feelings and volitions or not, includes an element directed toward objects as such:

> there is always a great difference between representations belonging to cog-
> nition, insofar as they are related merely to the object and the unity of
> the consciousness of it, and their objective relation where, considered as at
> the same time the cause of the reality of this object, they are assigned to the
> faculty of desire, and, finally, their relation merely to the subject, where
> they are ... {related} to the feeling of pleasure.
>
> (20: 206)

Even if most relations with objects include all three components – mere cognition, desire, and pleasure or pain – there is still, for Kant, a distinction between these components of lived experience.

As a first step toward defending this claim, we might note that modern science, and even ordinary "objective" judging, at least *seems* to fit Kant's description of "cognition" as such. Even if many aspects of science have practical ambitions in view, much so-called "pure" science seeks merely to explain our world accurately. Even sciences like evolutionary biology and modern chemistry are defended first and foremost as accurate representations of the world, not practical tools for medicine or industry. Many important scientific debates and even the ambition for scientific progress itself seem best explained in terms of scientists' striving to accurately describe the world. Relatedly, scientific knowledge – and "objective" knowledge more generally – at least *seems* less subjective, less tied to the particular situations or tendencies of individual knowers, than the average, everyday experience on which Heidegger and Sartre focus. In that sense, objectivity seems to get at something important about how the world is independent of our particular relations to it. Finally, some sort of objective awareness of objects seems to be implicated even in our ordinary lived experience. Hammers are handy when I want to pound a nail only because they are solid, etc., and because, in some sense, I cognize them this way.

We can put these points in terms of Sartre's example of immersing one's hand in water. It is true that in *some* sense I can "give the name subjectivity to the objectivity which I have not chosen" (Sartre 1956: 412). And it is even true that the *felt* temperature of the water, rather than the temperature on a thermometer, is often our primary engagement with water. But it is not arbitrary to describe the relatively high temperature on the submerged thermometer as "objective" and the perception of the water as cold by my hot hand as "subjective." The former, but not the latter, remains constant as long as the condition of the water remains constant, while the latter is subject to wild fluctuations based on *my* present condition. Partly for this reason, the former, but not the latter, is something that I can share with others. And an explanation of why water that is "really" warm "seems" cold to my hand can be much more straightforward than an attempt to explain why water that is "really" cold "seems" warm to the thermometer.

We can better develop this Kantian response by comparing this optimistic sketch of science with Heidegger's treatment of how "something at hand with which we have to do ... turns into something 'about which' the statement that points it out is made" (Heidegger 1953: 147). Heidegger rejects the picture of science as merely "keeping our distance from handling" or "merely looking at beings ... [by] *abstain{ing}* from any kind of use," arguing instead that one must come to "look ... *at* the thing encountered in a 'new' way, as something objectively present" (Heidegger 1953: 357, 361). This process involves two important components. First, an initially handy and inconspicuous object becomes "unusable" and thus "conspicuous" (Heidegger 1953: 73). When the hammer we use is "too heavy" or a table leg breaks, we come to see "the character of objective presence in what is at hand." That is, we come to see the hammer or table as something that "just lies there," something that, even when handy, "is always also objectively present with this or that appearance" (Heidegger 1953: 73). Second, the conspicuous attention provoked by things' unusability can become privileged when we begin to make "statements" about such things, and especially when we seek *uniformity* of judging.

> {B}y and *for* this way of looking what is at hand is veiled as something at hand ... [and] forced back to the uniform level of what is merely objectively present ... This leveling down of the primordial "as" of circumspect interpretation to the as of the determination of objective presence is the specialty of the statement. Only in this way does it gain the possibility of a pointing something out in a way that we can sheerly look at it.
>
> (Heidegger 1953: 158)

For Kant, this analysis of science's origin captures an important distinction between scientific objectivity and ordinary engagement with handy objects. "Leveling down" of possibilities toward "uniformity" is another way of saying that the scientific project is that form of human engagement with the world in which we seek an understanding that can in principle be shared by all others, regardless of contingent circumstances or particular practical goals. This striving for uniformity explains why the thermometer seemingly gives a more "accurate" measure of temperature than the hand; it gives a measure that is more *uniform*. By analogy with Kant's practical philosophy, we might see science itself as a search for universalizable cognitions. As with the categorical imperative, we "veil" particular projects in order to construct "uniform" judgments. In so doing, we "level down" the world but also thereby *create* a world we can share. Kant models cognition on *judgment*, and both Kant and Heidegger see that emphasizing cognitions we can *say* brings an emphasis on *shareable* cognitions and thereby a uniformity that is particularly "objective."

For Heidegger, this objective cognition is a subsidiary and artificial[6] way of looking at what is "primordially" at hand (Heidegger 1953: 158).[7] Even for Heidegger, when one seeks objective knowledge, one constructs the objective world precisely *as* a privileged world treated as already-there before our projects. For Heidegger, it is constructed in this way by us, for particular reasons, and subsequent to the breakdown of our handy world, so in those senses it is secondary. And it is constructed only by veiling the handiness of the handy world, so in that sense its priority is illusory. But Kant and Heidegger agree that when we think of the world objectively, we think of it as having a sort of priority. What Kant shows is how to access this world as a world that exists independent of our practical engagement with it, that exists "objectively." In our engagement with the world as a world for us to "know," we employ a priori concepts that *justify* everyday objective judgments as well as those of math and science, even if these concepts are limited to the objectively knowable world.

In the end, even if lived human experience does not conform to the sort of "objective" cognition Kant emphasizes, Kant's account provides transcendental conditions of possibility for a sphere of humans' being-in-the-world connected in particularly important ways with our efforts to find consensus amongst human beings and our need to provide *justifications* for beliefs about "conspicuous" objects. Moreover, there is at least some reason to think that this sort of objective cognition is a fundamental constitutive element even of the lived experience on which Heidegger focuses (especially insofar as there is a normative dimension to that lived experience). And privileging scientific objectivity has, at the very least, provided human beings with a self-understanding that, as indicated in Chapter 7, is already improving human lives.

Existential Freedom

Existentialists share Kant's conviction that freedom is central to being human: "Freedom is identical with my existence" (Sartre 1956: 572), so "human freedom precedes essence in man and makes it possible" (Sartre 1956: 60); "Da-sein is … how it is its possibility" (Heidegger 1953: 143). But existentialists see freedom as at once more bound than Kantian freedom, since freedom is always "in-the-world," and more *absolute* than Kant's, since unbound by given, universal *laws* of freedom.

Existentialist freedom is seemingly more limited than Kant's because choice is "choice *in the world*" (Sartre 1956: 617). Being-in-the-world involves being always already "thrown" into "definite possibilities" (Heidegger 1953: 144). Sartre describes this as "the paradox of freedom: there is freedom only in a situation, and there is a situation only through freedom" (Sartre 1956: 629, cf. Sartre 1993: 23, Heidegger 1953: 299–300), such that "I am absolutely free and absolutely responsible for my situation. But I am never free except in situation" (Sartre 1956: 653). Existentialists thus "reject Kant's 'choice of intelligible character'" (Sartre 1956: 617), juxtaposing their emphasis on situated freedom with Kant's timeless, situation-less free will "independent of all empirical conditions" (5: 29, see also A539/B567).

In fact, however, Kant's own emphasis on free *finitude* also emphasizes situatedness. Within epistemology, Kant along with existentialists insists that human cognition involves application of concepts to intuitions of *given* objects; spontaneity of cognition is about how we *respond* to a *given* world. And regarding human *choice*, Kantian freedom comes through subjecting to the moral law maxims that are formulated in terms of interests and situations in which we initially and for the most part simply find ourselves. One only has freedom to refrain from false promising when in situations where one is inclined to falsely promise, such as when needing money one is unable to repay. Kant's life of freedom is a life of constraining maxims that emerge from one's situation. Because the moral law is timeless, there is something timeless about human freedom, but this law is applied to contexts that are as situated as Sartre's.

The more pressing challenge to Kant's conception of freedom is the converse of the first. Where existentialists' emphasis on being-in-the-world leads to rejecting what they (wrongly) see as an overly *un*constrained sense of "intelligible" freedom, their emphasis on "absolute freedom" (Sartre 1956: 653) leads them to reject *constraints* Kant identifies as intrinsic to freedom: "Freedom has no essence" (Sartre 1956: 566). Within the epistemic realm, this means that existentialists reject Kant's prescription of categories and forms of intuition to "spontaneous" human understanding. Our knowing is part of a being-in-the-world for which we are responsible, a being-in-the-world that is always situated but never forced – neither by the world itself nor by any "nature" or "transcendental structures" – to interpret that world in any given way.

> The world by means of its very articulation refers to us exactly the image of what we are ... [T]he world necessarily appears to us as we are. In fact it is by surpassing the world toward ourselves that we make it appear such as it is. We choose the world, not in its contexture as in itself but in its meaning, by choosing ourselves.
>
> (Sartre 1956: 596)

> Being is what it is; it cannot possess in itself the determination "this one" ... it is the presence of the for-itself which causes the existence of a "this" rather than a "that" ... Negativity as original transcendence [i.e., freedom] is not determined in terms of a this; it causes a this to exist.
>
> (Sartre 1956: 249, see also 264)

The world we know and experience is structured by our free orientation toward it, by our projects and priorities. Against existentialists' conception of "freedom as the foundation of all essences" (Sartre 1956: 567), Kant's insistence that human knowers have fixed cognitive constraints like space, time, and causality looks like merely veiled essentialism. For existentialists who insist that "'There is' truth only insofar as Dasein is" (Heidegger 1953: 226) and "the rise of man ... causes a world to be discovered" (Sartre 1956: 59), absolute freedom precludes any transcendental anthropology that would prescribe fixed cognitive categories to humans' world.

Absolute freedom also precludes Kant's limitation of the freedom of *choice* by any fixed and determinate moral law. Sartre illustrates this freedom with the case of a student:

> [H]is father was on bad terms with his mother, and, moreover, was inclined to be a [Nazi] collaborationist; his older brother had been killed in the German offensive of 1940, and the young man ... wanted to avenge him. His mother lived alone with him, very much upset by the half-treason of her husband and the death of her older son; the boy was her only consolation.
>
> The boy was faced with the choice of leaving for England and joining the Free French Forces – that is, leaving his mother behind – or remaining with his mother and helping her to carry on. He was fully aware that the woman lived only for him and that his going off ... would plunge her into despair. He was also aware that every act that he did for his mother's sake was a sure thing, in the sense that it was helping her to carry on, whereas every effort he made toward going off and fighting was an uncertain move which might run aground and prove completely useless ... [H]e was faced with two very different kinds of action: one, concrete, immediate, but concerning only one individual; the other concerned an incomparably vaster group, a national collectivity, but for that very reason was dubious, and might be interrupted en route. And, at the same time, he was wavering between two kinds of ethics. On the one hand, an ethics of sympathy, of personal devotion; on the other, a broader ethics, but one whose efficacy was more dubious. He had to choose between the two.
>
> Who could help him choose? ... No book of ethics can tell him. The Kantian ethics says, "Never treat any person as a means, but as an end." Very well, if I stay with my mother, I'll treat her as an end and not as a means; but by virtue of this very fact, I'm running the risk of treating the people around me, who are fighting, as means; and, conversely, if I go to join those who are fighting, I'll be treating them as an end, and ... risk treating my mother as a means. If values are vague, and if they are always too broad for the concrete and specific case that we are considering, the only thing left for us is to trust our instincts. That's what this young man tried to do; and when I saw him, he said, "In the end, feeling is what counts. I ought to choose whichever pushes me in one direction. If I feel that I love my mother enough to sacrifice everything else for her – my desire for vengeance, for action, for adventure – then I'll stay with her. If, on the contrary, I feel that my love for my mother isn't enough, I'll leave."
>
> (Sartre 1993: 24–26)

For Sartre, "causes and motives have meaning only inside a projected ensemble which ... is ultimately myself as transcendence" (Sartre 1956: 564). Any particular choice is "unjustifiable ... , not deriving from any prior reality" (Sartre 1956: 598). In retrospect, we may construe actions in terms of ethical codes that require them, but those codes' salience is the consequence, not cause or even antecedent normative constraint, of free choices.

Similarly, Heidegger discusses Kant's "fact of reason" as a "fact ... always and only given by us to ourselves" and argues against understanding this fact with "any formula or ... value held up before us" (Heidegger 2002: 201). The fact of pure reason is given only in our "resolve to pure willing or against this," where pure willing is "to be in the mode of self-responsibility, to answer only to the essence of one's self" (Heidegger 2002: 201). Unsurprisingly, "conscience" for Heidegger is not an implicit understanding of a possibly articulable moral law (as in Kant), but rather an invitation to a "resolution" that has no articulable form: "to what does Da-sein resolve itself in resoluteness? On what is it to resolve? Only the resolution itself can answer this ... The indefiniteness that characterizes every factically projected potentiality-of-being of Da-sein belongs necessarily to resoluteness" (Heidegger 1953: 298).[8]

One final way in which existentialists radicalize Kant's conception of freedom arises from their rejection of Kant's distinctions between cognition, feeling, and volition. Although Kant discusses understandings' spontaneity and the freedom of aesthetic pleasure, volitional freedom is distinguished from and prioritized over these other freedoms. But existentialists pull together freedoms of thought, feeling, and choice into a single, free projection toward one's possibilities. Thus while Kant insists we cannot be held directly responsible for emotions because they are not under our direct control (see 5: 83), Sartre seeks an "existential psychoanalysis" that ascribes all thoughts, feelings, and deliberate choices to an "original choice" or "fundamental project" (Sartre 1956: 728, 729), "the free project of the unique person" (Sartre 1956: 782).[9]

> [Existential] psychoanalysis must ... understand someday why Pierre likes oranges and has a horror of water, why he gladly eats tomatoes and has a horror of beans.
>
> (Sartre 1956: 770)

> [T]astes do not remain irreducible givens; if one knows how to question them, they reveal to us the fundamental projects of the person. Down to even our alimentary preferences they all have a meaning.
>
> (Sartre 1956: 783)

Ultimately, then, existentialists propose a freedom that is absolute both in *quality* (unconstrained by antecedent norms) and in *scope* (applicable to all aspects of a person). Freedom, while always taking place within situation, is the ultimate basis not merely of choices for or against the moral law, but even of basic desires, immediate sensory attention, and apparently uncontrolled "passions" or "moods."

Angst and Authenticity

Existentialists' conception of absolute freedom is intricately linked with their attention to the attitude of "angst" and an ideal of authenticity. The rejection of Kant's distinction between cognition, feeling, and volition fostered attentiveness to the disclosive function of moods and emotions, among which *Angst* (anxiety) pre-eminently discloses humans' absolute freedom. Angst is like fear, but whereas fear is directed toward some threat to one's being, Angst focuses on "being-in-the-world as such," and in particular the world as "the possibility of things" in relation to "the ownmost individualized being [the 'being-possible'] of Da-sein" (Heidegger 1953: 187, 265). Sartre explains this point with the example of walking along a narrow precipice. One can be afraid of the precipice: it "presents itself to me as to be avoided; it represents a danger of death" (Sartre 1956: 66). But one experiences Angst in relation to oneself and the ever present "possibility ... to throw myself over the precipice" (Sartre 1956: 67). Not only is such a course of action wholly up to me, "our choice—i.e., ourselves—[i]s unjustifiable"; "nothing, absolutely nothing, justifies me in adopting this or that particular value" (Sartre 1956: 598, 76). The mid-career professional's angst-filled "midlife crisis" arises from recognizing that no past choices or commitments justify present actions. In angst, even the world itself "has the character of complete insignificance" (Heidegger 1953: 186); in recognizing that the world is meaningful only through one's own unjustified and unjustifiable being-in-the-world, one experiences the disorientation of freedom.[10]

Of course, existential Angst is not the prevailing mood governing most of our lives: "'real' Angst is rare" (Heidegger 1953: 190). The professional facing mid-life crisis leaps into work more firmly, buys a sports car, and/ or has a fling with a co-worker. The hiker along the precipice briefly entertains leaping, but quickly recalls obligations to family or pleasures with friends and focuses on hiking. Most of us, most of the time, evade angst by focusing on concrete tasks that we assume as given, doing "what must be done," "what is expected," or "what I feel like." Faced with absolute freedom, the typical response, one that for Sartre is all-too-common and for Heidegger is inevitable, is to flee from one's "ownmost possibilities" into something more comfortable. Heidegger describes this flight as "inauthenticity" (Heidegger 1953), Sartre as "bad faith" (Sartre 1956: 711).

Bad faith is the denial of the fundamental existential insight that "I am not what I am" (Sartre 1956: 108). "What I am" refers to my facticity or being-in-the-world, the way existentialism limits freedom. Freedom starts in a situation defined by choices already made, a past already lived, roles in which we find ourselves. "I am not" refers to the always present absolute freedom. Whatever "I" am in my facticity – a father, a writer, a lover of chocolate, a philosopher – I am not that facticity. I can choose to accept or reject any particular role, desire, or past. By taking up my situation, my past, my roles in terms of different future possibilities, I define the facticity that "I" am, and thus I am not reducible to any given facticity. Bad faith denies one or another of the aspects of this "I am not what I am." We might take, as an example, someone who avoids socializing and is frequently shy or awkward in social situations.[11] Such a person might say of herself, perhaps in response to criticism, "I'm not shy."

> She would actually be right if she understood the phrase, "I am not shy" in the sense of "I am not what I am." That is, if she declared to herself, "to the extent that a pattern of conduct is defined as the conduct of someone who is shy, and to the extent that I have adopted this conduct, I am shy. But to the extent that human reality can not be finally defined by patterns of conduct, I am not shy." [But insofar as] ... she lays claim to "not being shy" in the sense in which this table is not an inkwell, she is in bad faith.
>
> (Sartre 1956: 108)

When the girl says "I am not shy" in order to deny her facticity, she speaks in bad faith; but were she to say "I am not shy" in order to deny that she *is* her facticity, she would speak truly. Alternatively, our shy character might affirm, "I am shy." Here, too, this is true only in that "I am not what I am." This self-understanding is authentic only insofar as she understands shyness as something for which she is responsible, something up to her. Insofar as she claims to "be shy" in the sense that the table "is a table," she is, again, in bad faith. In each case, she ignores either her facticity, supposing that freedom takes place without situation, or her freedom from her facticity, supposing that previous patterns of behavior wholly determine who she is. Both poles are forms of denying absolute freedom, which transcends situation.

Rather than living in bad faith, one can and should live in good faith, "authentically" or "sincerely." Authentic living requires (only) recognizing one's choices as one's own, taking up one's situation in light of the free projection of possibilities: "One may choose anything if it is on the grounds of free involvement" (Sartre 1993: 47–48). But choosing really freely, and really involvedly, is not as straightforward as it sounds. One must, as Heidegger puts it, heed the "call of conscience" that *"summon{s}* Dasein to its ownmost potentiality-of-being-a-self"* (Heidegger 1953: 269). Like Kant's, this summons is adverbial rather than action- or object-focused, but it is more radically adverbial than Kant's. We cannot "define *what is spoken*" in this call of conscience, since "the call does not say anything ... 'Nothing' is called *to* the self ... , but it is summoned to itself, ... to its ownmost potentiality-of-being," so "what the call discloses ... gets interpreted in different ways in individual Da-sein" (Heidegger 1953: 273–74). Heeding conscience "brings the self back from the loud idle chatter of the they's common sense" (Heidegger 1953: 296). But conscience cannot replace this chatter with another principle, which would become another chatter; heeding conscience is not a matter of doing "the right thing," but of authentically realizing potentialities that are one's *own*.

In a sense, there is nothing "wrong" with bad faith or inauthenticity. Sartre criticizes the term authenticity as "dubious and insincere because of [its] implicit moral content" (Sartre 1956: 680), and Heidegger resists "moralizing critique" because terms like inauthenticity "do not express any negative value judgment" but merely refer to how "Da-sein is initially and for the most part" (Heidegger 1953: 167, 175, cf. 42–43). Because nothing constrains freedom, existentialists propose no *standards* of authenticity that one "must" or "ought to" live up to. But without moralistically requiring us to live up to certain standards, Sartre and Heidegger *invite* us to live differently. In that sense, there is some admonition to authenticity in Heidegger, some reproach of bad faith in Sartre. "Da-sein bears witness to a possible authenticity of its existence ... [and] demands it of itself" and "conscience ... summons Da-sein to existence, to its ownmost [and thus authentic] potentiality-of-being-a-self" (Heidegger 1953: 266–67, 294). And Sartre "bring[s] moral judgment to bear" on one's existential situation:

> [T]here is ... dishonesty if I choose to state that certain values exist prior to me ... Suppose someone says to me, "What if I want to be dishonest?" I'll answer, "There's no reason for you not to be, but I'm saying that that's what you are, and that the strictly coherent attitude is that of honesty."
>
> (Sartre 1993: 45)

Those in bad faith deceive themselves about their freedom to define their own values, and even while recognizing that bad faith is always possibile, Sartre (and Heidegger) call their readers to something more. But Sartre's reference to "coherence" gets at something deeper about the strategies of Sartre and Heidegger (and Nietzsche and Kierkegaard). By drawing attention to the possibility of authenticity, Sartre and Heidegger show how "the attitude of refusal and flight which remains possible is despite itself the free assumption of what it is fleeing" (Sartre 1956: 680). Reading Sartre and Heidegger makes it impossible to continue in bad faith just as before.[12] In his proto-existentialist *Sickness unto Death*, Kierkegaard takes readers from unreflective everyday inauthenticity through a process of self-awareness that ends with either "demonic" inauthenticity that "rebel[s] against all existence" (Kierkegaard 1989: 104–5) or a breakthrough into authenticity (or "faith"). Similarly, Sartre and Heidegger push readers toward recognizing their freedom, in the context of which even bad faith takes on a more "authentic" character, since it is deliberately chosen in defiance of freedom. In that sense, at least, witnessing the possibility of authenticity is a sort of call to authenticity. Existentialism, by repeatedly bearing this witness, continually issues this call.

This call can be a serious challenge to Kant. Both Kant's privileging of objective knowledge and his emphasis on the moral law as the law of freedom seem, from an existentialist standpoint, to be forms of inauthenticity. Heidegger notes that Kantian objective knowing is a "leveling down" that "force[s] back" what is at hand "to the uniform level of what is merely objective" (Heidegger 1953: 158). Nietzsche, with more vitriol, criticizes herd mentalities that prefer shareable or "common" truths over "secret gardens" (Nietzsche 1967: 17) one cultivates for oneself. Kant offers transcendental conditions of possibility of thinking-just-like-everyone-else and acting-just-like-everyone-else. In a move that would be comic were it not so tragic, Kant even seeks transcendental conditions of possibility of universal judgments about beautiful objects, finding universality even in humans' only truly *"free* satisfaction" (5: 210). Against Kant's attempts to justify necessary and universal standards of thought, feeling, and choice, the existentialist ideal is a call to authentically think, feel, choose, and *be* for oneself.

To some extent, Kant endorses existentialists' ideal of authenticity. Kant's "What is Enlightenment?" famously begins with the claim that "Enlightenment is the human being's emergence from his self-incurred ... inability to make use of his own understanding without direction from another" and Kant mocks those who "have a book that understands for me, a spiritual advisor who has a conscience for me ... and so forth" (8: 35). "Character," so fundamental to Kant's moral and empirical anthropology, "consists precisely in originality in the way of thinking. He who has character derives his conduct from a source that he has opened by himself" (7: 293). And autonomy, which is central to Kant's transcendental anthropology, is based on the fundamental principle that "the human being ... is subject *only to laws given by himself* and ... is bound only to act in conformity with his own will" (4: 432). Kant accepts and even emphasizes the fundamental existential commitment to one's *ownmost* possibility, to an authenticity that refuses to see its choices as those of a generic "human being."

But this emphasis is combined, in Kant, with a commitment to *universality*. "What is Enlightenment?," while defending "one's *own* understanding" (8: 35), insists that only a "*public* use of one's reason" brings enlightenment (8: 35, 37). One with character is neither an "imitator" nor "an *eccentric*" (7: 293). And autonomously binding, self-given laws must be "still universal" (4: 432). Kant's emphasis on autonomy and thinking for oneself is *not* an emphasis on *uniqueness*. One's ownmost possibility does not set one apart from others; it is a possibility one shares with others. And Kant vehemently protests against various "egoisms" that take one's own beliefs, feelings, or volitions to be sufficient without testing them against "other men's insights," which Kant calls the "touchstone of the understanding" (24: 178, cf. 5: 294, 7: 128–29).

Moreover, Kantian autonomy has a positive structure. Following certain determinate and universal laws is necessary in order to truly pursue one's ownmost possibilities. Against existentialism, Kant defends a single categorical imperative by which all authentic agents must govern themselves. This a priori imperative might seem to override one's freedom, but for Kant, subjection to the moral law is precisely the condition of possibility of freedom and thus of *any* authentic engagement with the world. The fact that this law is the same *for everyone* seems to make Kantian morality a paradigmatic "herd morality," a morality of "the they" rather than a truly authentic expression of one's *ownmost* possibilities. But it is important to recall that existentialist authenticity is not as much about what one does as about how one does it. And for Kant, as for existentialists, one ought not obey the moral law simply because others are doing so, nor simply because Kant says one should, nor even because it is a law of God. One ought obey the moral law because it is the law of one's own will. Thus even if the moral law is identical to the law of "the they," the Kantian moral agent obeys it *as* a law of her own will. She obeys this law authentically. Moreover, Kant is well aware that particular judgments of particular societies – of "the they" – can be at odds with the moral law. The fact that Kant's ideal moral (and even epistemic) standards are normatively universal (in that they ought to hold for all people) does not mean that they are universal "norms" in the sense of actually being embraced by "the they." By providing (universal) conditions of justification from-within for individual agents, Kantian autonomy even supplies emboldening resources to stand up authentically against one's society's "norms."

In their appeals to authenticity and warnings about succumbing to "bad faith" or "herd mentality," existentialists rightly highlight concerns that can be missed by a Kantian focus on autonomy. Despite Kant's insistence on autonomy as *self*-governance, it can become merely a stale formula by which one lives. Kantians should follow existentialists in emphasizing the importance of obeying the moral law *as one's own law*, a law that, although necessary, is nonetheless freely self-imposed. But Kant, in return, can enrich existentialism by highlighting that authenticity cannot be merely a matter of asserting uniqueness or constantly reinventing oneself. To say, as Sartre's student said about joining the Resistance, "In the end, feeling is what counts" (Sartre 1993: 25), is a far cry from authenticity. *True* authenticity comes, as Kant insists, from *autonomy*, from governing oneself in accordance with laws one can see as truly coming from one's *self*, laws that will, by virtue of being *laws* and thereby susceptible to justification, be universal.

Moreover, within the broad universal laws by which we govern ourselves, Kant admits the importance of individuality. The moral law is not as *radically* adverbial as existential authenticity; it implies some content, such as that we must avoid false promises and promote the perfection and happiness of self and others. But it is still a *formal* law within which lie many possible ways of being moral, and thus room for particular expressions of one's "ownmost" possibilities. Authentic actions that are universalizable in principle (and hence moral) can still express one's uniqueness. Sartre's example illustrates this point particularly well. Sartre rightly notes, for the student deciding whether to join the French Resistance, that Kant's ethics does not tell him whether to join or to stay with his mother. But Sartre is wrong about the *reason* Kant's ethics fails. As Sartre sees it, one violates one's moral responsibilities whatever one does, treating either "the people around me who are fighting" or "my mother as a means" (Sartre 1993: 25–26). But the "problem" is quite the opposite. The relevant duties (to mother or Resistance) are imperfect. One must respond to imperfect duties, but one is not strictly required to fulfill any particular ones. Thus the student can be autonomous whichever option he chooses. This does not mean that "authenticity" is *all* that matters. The moral law restricts the *range* of choices. He cannot deceive his mother for the sake of her feelings, telling her he is going to a desk job when really going to the front. He cannot pledge to join the Resistance and then back out when the going gets tough. He cannot join the Nazis. But within the limits he ought to impose on himself, there is room to decide his particular destiny.

Even here, Kant can learn from existentialism. Although Kant's empirical account of human beings includes a wide range of propensities and inclinations, his from-within treatment of volition tends to see all choice as essentially just a matter of how one prioritizes self-love vis-à-vis duty. Existentialists show that particulars are significant not merely as ways to pursue happiness or do one's duty. When choosing *amongst* morally acceptable ends, Kant's emphasis on happiness (both one's own and others') and perfection (especially one's own) insufficiently recognizes the importance of manifesting freedom even in not-strictly-moral choices. Choosing particular paths in life comes to define who we take ourselves to be, and even if only morality matters "without qualification," particular concerns can be much more closely tied to our self-conceptions than their merely moral dimensions suggest. Existentialism shows that much of what makes human life worth living cannot be reduced to formulae, that one must make choices about what to think, feel, and do that cannot be dictated by rules. Insofar as one chooses what to think, feel, and do entirely in accordance with rules, one is blind to something in oneself that transcends those rules. This attention to what cannot be reduced to rules, categories of the understanding, or publically accessible language and concepts reflects a genuine contribution of broadly existentialist approaches to the self, one that Kantians should take seriously.

Kant also has important things to teach existentialists. Even if universal rules are limiting, one must still think and act in the world. And knowing merely that rules underdetermine thoughts and choices does not help one make choices. By providing a priori rules for genuinely free thought and action, Kant's philosophy meets problems real thinkers and choosers face. And Kant's transcendental analysis of volition helpfully reveals a fundamental difference in urgency between two sorts of choices. As important as it might seem – and really be – to choose the right partner(s) in love, the right career(s), and the right balance of work, deep relationships, and raw pleasures, these choices are less important than choices about whether to do what is right or to forgo moral requirements for other ends. Kant rightly claims that even within the structure of morality, there is important room for choice. One's imperfect duties to perfect talents and promote others' welfare do not dictate whether to become a concert pianist, a subsistence farmer, a work-a-day paralegal with a vibrant social life, a stay-at-home parent, or a professional philosopher. What one chooses will have immense impact on one's sense of oneself and the quality of one's life. But Kant insists that *all* lives constructed in the context of an overall commitment to duty are good without limitation; any such life constitutes the supreme good for human being, irrespective of its specific form. And while this realization does not eliminate the angst that can be faced by those making difficult life decisions, it puts those decisions in a larger context that can alleviate paralyzing despair or haughty hubris about one's chosen path.

In the end, Kant can and should embrace much of the existential "ideal" of authenticity while offering a valuable antidote to the cult of authenticity prevalent today. Autonomy, like authenticity, involves governing oneself, refusing to let one's decisions be dictated by the "they," making choices with awareness of one's own freedom. And for all of the content (albeit formal) that Kant gives his conception of autonomy, Kant – like existentialists – insists that merely following the categorical imperative is insufficient to be autonomous; one must do what is right autonomous*ly*, must will universally and respect others *because one legislates this law to oneself*. For Kant, one who does what is morally required because it is required by God, one's society, one's ultimate happiness, or for any reason other than as a form of *self-command*, does not act autonomously and thus does not really do what is morally required. In that sense, Kant's ethics of autonomy *is* an ethics of authenticity. Kant can and should enrich his account with a greater emphasis on choosing authentically, in a way that is genuinely responsive to who one takes oneself to be, in every area of life, even when morality is not specifically at issue. But for Kant, authenticity is limited; one is *truly* authentic only insofar as one acts morally. And choosing morally well is the only authenticity that matters *unqualifiedly*. But these limitations, far from weakening Kant's overall account, make Kantian existentialism more realistic, more just, and more effectively action-guiding than its more extreme contemporary counterparts.

Heteronomous Existentialism

Before closing this chapter, I turn to one last approach to the human being that fits, albeit broadly, within the existentialist tradition: the "heteronomous existentialism" (my term) of Emmanuel Levinas (and, in different ways, the late Heidegger, Jacques Derrida, and others). Shortly after Sartre published "Existentialism is a Humanism" (1946, cf. Sartre 1993), which became the classic statement of modern existentialism, Heidegger rejected the label "existentialist" and distanced himself from Sartre in his own "Letter on Humanism" (1947), in which he shifts from an emphasis on Da-sein back to the question of "Being" and de-emphasizes the role of the human subject. There Heidegger rejects the Sartrean view that "the essential worth of man ... consists in his being the substance of beings as the 'Subject' among them" and emphasizes "thinking" as a form of "letting" oneself "be claimed by Being" (Heidegger 1977: 234, 218, cf. Sartre 1993: 50):

> Man is ... "thrown" from Being itself into the truth of Being ... in order that beings might appear in the light of Being as the beings they are. Man does not decide whether and how beings appear, whether and how God and the gods or history and nature come forward into the clearing of Being ... [F]or man it is ever a question of finding what is fitting in his essence that corresponds to such destiny.
>
> (Heidegger 1977: 234)

This emphasis on "man" as fundamentally *responsive* is taken up, in different ways, in various figures in late twentieth-century philosophy, most notably in an explicit emphasis in Emmanuel Levinas (1906–95) on "heteronomy" vis-à-vis the "face" of "the Other." Thus far, I have neglected the role of others (or "the Other") in existentialism. Both Sartre and (early) Heidegger thematized our existence in relation to others, albeit in different ways, and heteronomous existentialism can best be understood in contrast with their approaches.

For Heidegger, the primary existential orientation toward others is "Mit-sein" or Being-with. Heidegger argues that "the 'subject' of every-dayness ... is precisely not I myself ... 'others' are always already there with us in Being-in-the-world" (Heidegger 1953: 114–16). Just as who one is is a matter of how one exists in and toward concrete situations in which one finds oneself, so one's situation is always one of being "with" others. Unlike handy objects, others are not there for us, but are those *with whom* we use objects. Working with a hammer puts the hammer to use for one's purposes; working with another person involves working alongside her, sharing purposes with her, seeing the world through common eyes.

Similarly, Sartre recognizes that others are not simply things-in-the-world defined by one's projects, but for Sartre, our primary orientation toward others is "being-*for*-others" rather than "being-with-others." Sartre describes, for instance, how our (freely adopted) jealousy might lead us to "look through a keyhole" and thereby make the keyhole something handy, something "to be looked through" that "exists [in this way] only in relation to a free project of my possibilities" (Sartre 1956: 347–48). In this situation, even the person I spy on is merely an object of my activity whose meaning is given by my jealousy.

> But all of a sudden I hear footsteps in the hall. Someone is looking at me! What does this mean? It means that I am suddenly affected in my being and that essential modifications appear in my structure ... I now exist as myself ... I see myself because somebody sees me ... my freedom escapes me in order to become a given object ... The Other has to make my being-for-him be insofar as he has to be his being. Thus each of my free conducts engages me in a new environment where the very stuff of my being is the unpredictable freedom of another. Yet by my shame I claim as mine that freedom of another.
>
> (Sartre 1956: 349–51)

In feeling ashamed at the look of another, I "am" for the other. And for Sartre, this is not merely a matter of being seen as an object, since it is precisely my freedom (or "transcendence") that, in my shame, I feel as being objectified by the other: "my transcendence becomes for whoever makes himself a witness of it ... a purely established transcendence, a given-transcendence" (Sartre 1956: 352). Sartrean being-for-others reduces one's freedom itself into a mere object.[13]

For both Heidegger and Sartre, others (or the Other, or "the they") threaten authentic existence. For Sartre, insofar as I merely accept the Other's judgment of me, relinquishing my being-for-itself into a being-for-another, I fail to acknowledge that "I am [in my freedom] not what I am [for-others]." While "I am responsible for the very existence of the Other" (Sartre 1956: 382), since only by my freely taken up projects do I feel ashamed and thereby give the look meaning as a look, giving the look this meaning nonetheless relegates my meaning to the Other. To avoid being objectified, I can turn back on the one looking at me, objectifying and thereby disempowering the other: "One must either transcend the Other or allow oneself to be transcended by him. The essence of the relations between consciousnesses is ... conflict" (Sartre 1956: 555). Or, more concisely, "hell is other people" (Sartre 1989: 45). Even in Heidegger, being-with threatens authenticity.

> [In] being-with ..., as everyday being-with-one-another, Da-sein stands in subservience to the others. It itself is not; the others have taken its being away from it. The everyday possibilities of being of Da-sein are at the disposal of the whims of the others ... What is decisive is only the inconspicuous domination by others that Da-sein as being-with has already taken over unawares ... [B]eing-with-one-another as such creates averageness. It is an existential character of the they.
>
> (Heidegger 1953: 126–27)

"The they," for Heidegger, is the "subject" that replaces the "I" in Da-sein's everyday activities. Human being as being-with-others is always open to losing unique being-toward-possibilities and instead merely thinking and doing what everyone thinks and does. I might engage in various activities because they are activities that "one in my position" should be doing, in a sense letting "them" – that is, the diffuse, widespread, and internalized expectation of those with whom one exists – make existential choices for me. "Being-with-one-another" thus "level[s] down all possibilities of being" and "takes the responsibility of Da-sein away from it" (Heidegger 1953: 127, but cf. Heidegger 1953: 298 for an account of authentic being with others).

Levinas revalues Sartre's account of the look by prioritizing being-for-another over being-for-itself through a turn from (Heideggerian) "ontology" to "ethics." But Levinasian ethics is not Kantian, not an effort to discern universal moral principles by which all ought to conduct themselves. Instead, Levinasian ethics is a "total passivity," a "calling into question of my spontaneity in the presence of the Other" (Levinas 1969: 88, 43). This "passivity more passive ... than any passivity" is the "passivity of the 'for-another,'" a passivity "in which no reference, positive or negative, to a prior will enters" (Levinas 1998a: 50–51). The "Other" here is the "face" of the "neighbor" (Levinas 1997: 92, Levinas 1969: 194f.)

For Levinas, the sensible expression that opens this new dimension is "the face." What is "appresented"[14] in the face of the other is not some*thing*, but "unicity and alterity," the wholly unique and wholly other.

> The face resists possession, resists my powers ... The face, still a thing among things, breaks through the form that nevertheless delimits it. This means concretely, the face speaks to me and thereby invites me to a relation incommensurate with a power exercised, be it enjoyment or knowledge. And yet this new dimension opens in the sensible appearance of the face ... The face at the limit of holiness ... is thus still in a sense exposed to powers.
> (Levinas 1969: 197–98)

When "the face speaks," she ceases to be merely an object to categorize in terms of my projects and possibilities. I am addressed *by* the other and thereby made responsible for the other. Neither I nor the other are "objects" in the traditional sense. The other is a subject by and for whom I can be held to account, and "I" am one to whom speech is addressed.

Importantly, for Levinas, the Other who addresses me is neither merely a concrete other with determinate qualities one can recognize and accommodate nor a universal "humanity" that requires respect. Levinas's Other outstrips conceptualization. The very attempt to "understand" the other is a way of trying to reduce the Other to the Same, and thereby to make oneself, one's own subjectivity, the center of the universe. Levinasian "ethics" thus cannot be a matter of laying out fundamental moral principles, but only a recurring provocation to see the infinite Otherness of this face, a clearing away of distracting "categories" that prevent such seeing.

For Levinas, moreover, encountering the Other is not merely one way that I relate to my world. "I" come to be only through responsibility to the absolutely Other: "[T]he identity of the subject comes from the impossibility of escaping responsibility" (Levinas 1997: 120). "Responsibility preced[es] freedom" (Levinas 1997: 94, see also 119, 121) and thus "cannot have begun in my commitment, in my decision" (Levinas 1997: 117). Against both Sartre and Kant, Levinas argues,

> Existence is not in reality condemned to freedom, but it is invested as freedom ... To philosophize is to trace freedom back to what lies before it ... Knowledge as a critique, as a tracing back to what precedes freedom, can arise only in a being that has an origin prior to its origin—that is created ... The presence of the Other, a privileged heteronomy, does not clash with freedom but invests it. The shame for oneself, the presence of and desire for the other are not the negation of knowing: knowing is their very articulation. The essence

of reason consists not in securing for man a foundation and powers, but in calling him into question and in inviting him to justice.

(Levinas 1969: 84–85, 88)

One is free only in response to responsibility toward the Other.[15] The absolutely free Sartrean subjectivity that rises above given codes or laws *proceeds from* a heteronomy of absolute responsibility. Because the Other is infinitely Other, no set codes or principles can be sufficient for guiding one's responsibility, so one is absolutely free (Levinas 1997: 23). This emphasis on the impossibility of subsuming responsibility under fixed categories of reason marks a sharp contrast from the Kantian attempt to derive a "formula" of morality from the conditions of possibility of moral responsibility as such. Levinas's rejection of such a formula follows from his thinking about the radical Otherness of the Other, and as in the case of Sartre and Heidegger's rejection of similar formulae, responding to the Other is not a matter of doing any particular thing, but of having a certain attitude, of doing whatever one does with a sense of responsibility before something infinitely other to and for whom one is infinitely responsible.

Levinas's *heteronomous* existentialism that sees the self as constituted by a response to an inscrutable but vulnerable other challenges the Kantian primacy of autonomy as a source of practical and epistemic norms. For Kant, as for Levinas, one is justified in seeing oneself as a free subject only through recognizing one's *responsibility*. But Kantian responsibility is *autonomous*, relatively *determinate*, and *universal*. Kant's insistence that "the human being … is subject *only to laws given by himself but still universal* and … he is bound only to act in conformity with his own will" (4: 432) could not be further from Levinas's equally vehement insistence that in the experience of responsibility, "no form, no capacity preexisted in me to espouse the imperative and make it my own. Not being able to treat the law as a law I myself have given myself is just in what the sense of alterity consists" (Levinas 1998a: xvii).

Kant's paradigm "feeling" of responsibility for others is "respect," which precludes undermining others' wills (e.g. not deceiving, enslaving, or "killing") and requires promoting their "happiness," where happiness is both "indeterminate" (4: 418) and – as indicated by Kant's empirical anthropology – highly individual. In these senses, Kant agrees with Levinas about the dangers of reducing the "Other" to the "Same." Human self-conceit tends to enforce our own identities by imposing them on others, denying that others are unique individuals with their own goals and projects. Responsibility for the Other, for Kant as for Levinas, requires respecting others *in their uniqueness*. But for Kant it is by virtue of others' free capacity for choice that *they* – rather than, say, their instincts – are able to impose obligations. Thus Kant reverses Levinas's "privileged heteronomy" in what we might see as Kant's transcendental conditions of possibility of the "face." Kant (re)prioritizes autonomy first in that it is by *taking* the other to be an Other that she has a face (for me), and second, in that the basis for taking the other to be Other requires seeing her as sharing in common with oneself at least the ability to choose freely, to be an I that can impose responsibilities on a you. In that sense, the "Other" is, as Levinas fears but Kant does not, reduced to an order of the Same. It is by virtue of recognizing another as being the Same (sharing one's free rational agency) that others can be "Others" (now in a Kantian rather than strictly Levinasian sense) to whom one can be responsible.[16]

By this Kantian standard, universal rules of justice need not be *totalizing* and thereby *violent* forms of interaction. When one seeks community with multiple others governed by mutual respect, this *does* require subjecting individuality – one's own and that of others – to universal norms, but it does *not* require the elimination of individuality in the face of those norms. Kant explains that "pure practical reason merely *infringes upon* self-love [promotion of one's particular ends] … [b]ut it *strikes down* self-conceit [unconditional presumption in favor of one's particular ends]" (5: 73). In a Levinasian context, we might make use of a similar distinction with respect to others. In requiring respect for every other Other, practical reason *infringes upon* responsibilities to a particular Other but *strikes down* the absolute responsibility implied by Levinasian heteronomous existentialism.

Put this way, it becomes clear how Levinas's philosophy helpfully draws attention to a dangerous risk of Kant's (and many other) ethics. Recognizing common humanity and appreciating others' specific features creates the risk of *reducing* personhood to shared humanity or those features. Kant, of course, insists that respect for others involves respecting and promoting individual projects and ends, but emphasizing general principles for dealing with all others can have the effect, as Levinas rightly realizes, of helping one complacently accept injustices against particular others, even against the immediate neighbor, that one ought to remedy.

At the same time, Kant valuably protects against enthusiastic excesses of heteronomous existentialism. For Kant, the Other – every Other – *does* elicit infinite responsibility. One must, if necessary, sacrifice every finite interest for the sake of one's unconditional obligations. But one's obligations to any particular Other are not infinite in extent; one has specific, mostly negative responsibilities (not to deceive or torture) and general but "wide" positive responsibilities (to meet others' needs). The former are sufficiently specific that one can usually meet them merely by conducting one's behavior within certain limits. The latter, as "wide" duties, "leave room for free choice in … complying with" one's duties (6: 390). Kant's general point, against both Sartre and Levinas, is that one is not (morally) responsible for one's whole world, nor *wholly* responsible for the Other with whom one is faced. One might think that Levinas is surely correct, that one should never succumb to the moral complacency of thinking that one has done "what one can" or "what one must" for another in need. Kant agrees that moral complacency is a real danger, an especially important danger given the self-deception implicit in humans' radical evil. But Kant sees an equal danger in a "moral enthusiasm" or "moral fanaticism" that extols extraordinary moral demands but ignores the importance of ordinary duties.[17] After offering an interpretation of the commandment "Love God above all, and your neighbor as yourself" (5: 83), Kant adds:

> This consideration is intended not so much to bring clear concepts to the evangelical commandment just cited in order to reduce *religious enthusiasm* [or superstition, *Schwärmerei*] ... but to determine accurately the moral disposition directly, in regard to our duties toward human beings ... and to check, or where possible prevent, a *merely moral* enthusiasm which infects many people. The moral level on which a human being ... stands is respect for the moral law ... By exhortation to actions as noble, sublime, and magnanimous, minds are attuned to nothing but moral enthusiasm and exaggerated self-conceit ... they produce in this way a frivolous, high-flown, fantastic cast of mind, flattering themselves with a spontaneous goodness of heart ... and thereby forgetting their obligation ... If enthusiasm in the most general sense is an overstepping of the bounds of human reason ..., then moral enthusiasm is such an overstepping of the bounds that practical pure reason sets to humanity ... If this is so, then not only novelists and sentimental educators ... but sometimes even philosophers ... have ushered in moral enthusiasm instead of a sober but wise moral discipline.
>
> (5: 84–86)

As with "novelists and sentimental educators," when Levinas and others emphasize "infinite" ethical demands to the absolutely Other in such a way that one could never, even in principle, fulfill them (or even articulate what they are!), they risk promoting an even greater moral complacency than Kant's "sober but wise moral discipline." What seem to be intense ethical admonitions turn out to be frivolous and fantastic justifications for self-conceit.

This final Kantian critique of Levinas can also be put in terms of a more general problem with existentialist conceptions of freedom, or the absolute, or the infinite. Once freedom or the Other is distinguished from any conception that allows for discerning determinate paths of action or determinate obligations toward others, it becomes unclear what kind of normative guidance these views provide. The diversity of practical prescriptions for action amongst existentialists – from Sartre's Marxism to the Nazism of Heidegger and de Man to Levinas's emphasis on brute human suffering – only reinforces the sense that existentialism, for whatever depth of insight it might provide about the human condition, ultimately fails to answer urgent questions about how to live and think. In one sense, this is precisely the point. Sartre sees any attempt to "find answers" to these questions as a form of bad faith, and Levinas sees the attempt to discern *determinate* ways of interacting with "others" as a sort of violence against them. But the failure of existentialism to provide normative guidance, like the similar failures of naturalism and historicism, leaves us with a need for further philosophical reflection on the human being. To that, we now turn.

Summary

Existentialism provides a contemporary account of human being that emphasizes human freedom and finitude and focuses on being human from-within, but existentialists' versions of this account radicalize Kant's through their emphasis on "being-in-the-world," their absolute freedom that supersedes all norms, and their ideal of "authenticity." Heteronomous existentialism departs even further from Kant, emphasizing a "total passivity" before the "Other," a "privileged heteronomy" fundamental to human being. Kant can and should draw important lessons from existentialists. Without giving up the importance of objective knowing, Kant can and does acknowledge that most human engagement with the world involves integrated complexes of cognition, feeling, and desire. And without allowing that freedom supersedes all norms, Kant can and should endorse existentialists' emphasis on human freedom and the importance of authenticity, even in spheres of life that are not governed by antecedent norms. And while refusing to give up the determinacy of obligations toward others, Kant should appreciate what Levinas points out as the dangers of violence toward others involved in reducing them to pre-determined categories.

Further Reading

Sartre's classic statement of existentialism is *Being and Nothingness*, but the selections collected in Sartre 1957 are a more manageable introduction. *Being in Time* is Heidegger's extremely difficult magnum opus. Krell provides a slightly more accessible set of readings that includes Heidegger's later writings. Heidegger 1990 is his most direct engagement with Kant. A good overview of existentialism can be found in Cooper. Kaufman and Solomon provide excellent collections of existentialist primary sources going back to nineteenth-century sources.

David Cooper, *Existentialism: A Reconstruction* (Oxford: Wiley-Blackwell, 1999)

Martin Heidegger, *Kant and the Problem of Metaphysics* (trans. Richard Taft, Bloomington: Indiana University Press, 1990)

Martin Heidegger, *Basic Writings* (ed. David Krell, New York: Harper-Collins, 1977, 1993)

Martin Heidegger, *Being and Time* (trans. Joan Stambaugh, Albany, NY: SUNY, 1996)

Walter Kaufman (ed.), *Existentialism: From Dostoyevsky to Sartre* (New York: Penguin Books, 1989)

Jean-Paul Sartre, *Being and Nothingness* (trans. Hazel Barnes, New York: Citadel Press, 1956)

Jean-Paul Sartre, *Existentialism and Human Emotions* (New York: Citadel Press, 1957)

Jean-Paul Sartre, *Nausea* (trans. Lloyd Alexander, New York: New Directions Press, 1959)

Robert Solomon (ed.), *Existentialism* (Oxford: Oxford University Press, 2005)

For heteronomous existentialism in particular, Levinas and to a lesser extent Derrida are the most important primary sources, but both are very difficult texts. Critchley provides a helpful and readable introduction to the ethics underlying both thinkers.

Simon Critchley, *The Ethics of Deconstruction* (Purdue, IN: Purdue University Press, 1999)

Jacques Derrida, *The Gift of Death* (trans. David Wills, Chicago: University of Chicago Press, 1996)

Emmanuel Levinas, *Emmanuel Levinas: Philosophical Writings* (ed. A. Peperzak, S. Critchley, and R. Bernasconi, Bloomington: Indiana University Press, 2008)

Emmanuel Levinas, *The Humanism of the Other* (trans. Nidra Poller, Urbana: University of Illinois Press, 2005)

10 Normativity

The approaches to human beings in the previous three chapters foundered on problems of normativity. Biology and psychology explain how the human mind as an empirical object works. History and the study of diversity show wide variations amongst human beings. And existentialism's emphasis on freedom drives home the difficulty of determining any fixed human "nature." Nonetheless, normative issues – what we *ought* to think, feel, or do – remain. Insofar as human sciences (whether biology or history or anthropology) purport to provide anything like knowledge, they appeal to epistemic standards. Moreover, as forms of life, the practice of these sciences involves appeal to volitional standards. Even those not directly involved in these scientific and philosophical developments need to decide what to make of them. And as reflective thinkers, feelers, and actors, we find ourselves needing to decide how to think, feel, and choose. As existentialists rightly show, even refusal to see oneself as needing to make such decisions is an exercise of freedom, albeit in bad faith.

Unfortunately, none of these developments provide, in themselves, the tools for deciding how to think, feel, and act. Even if evolutionary biology shows how humans evolved to care about one another, this does not in itself tell whether such caring is to be fostered or resisted. Even if historical analyses show how modern physics overturned Newtonian paradigms, how modern moral categories emerged, or even how human beings became "subjects," historical analysis alone cannot tell whether to believe the claims of physics, embrace current moral categories, affirm subjectivity, or reject such developments. Comparison of different ways of thinking can reveal contingency, but cannot tell whether this contingency should be embraced as delightful pluralism, rejected as tribal ethnocentrism, or treated in some different way. And existentialism's emphasis on freedom and authenticity calls universal standards into such suspicion that it (intentionally) fails to guide the decisions whose omnipresence it reveals.

As we saw in Chapter 1, Kant's transcendental anthropology provides a normative framework for answering questions about what to think, feel, and do. Kant's purely formal normativity leaves room for individual thoughts and choices to be influenced by historically evolving cultures and biological capacities/tendencies while still being incorporated into normative frameworks that are at once authentically one's own and genuinely universal. But there are rich normative alternatives to Kant, many informed by increasingly rich conceptions of human beings. In fact, as natural and human sciences split from "philosophy" to form their own disciplines, many philosophers focused on normative issues that sciences are incapable of answering.

To summarize all of contemporary normative theory in a single chapter is impossible, so I focus on just five recent and important approaches. Except the first, all take seriously the problems posed by naturalism, existentialism, and human diversity. I first discuss intuitionism, a cluster of philosophical approaches that dominated much twentieth-century philosophy. I then turn to Rorty's pragmatism and MacIntyre's emphasis on narrative and tradition, two provocative recent approaches to normativity that seriously address naturalism, historicism, and existentialism. The last two approaches – Habermas's communicative ethics and Korsgaard's constructivism – are the most influential contemporary appropriations of Kant. Both incorporate substantial elements of naturalism, historicism, and existentialism while remaining recognizably and self-consciously Kantian. They thus exemplify how Kant might be updated for the twenty-first century.

Phenomenology and Intuitionism

We start our grand tour of contemporary philosophy with two early twentieth-century thinkers whose general approaches, though not always explicitly invoked, still dominate much contemporary philosophical theorizing: Edmund Husserl (1859–1938) and G.E. Moore (1873–1958). Both thinkers used "intuitions" to discern philosophical truth, and both left extensive legacies on contemporary philosophy, Husserl as father of contemporary "Continental" philosophy and Moore, along with Russell and Frege, a father of contemporary "analytic" philosophy. One result is that much contemporary philosophical work is unabashedly intuition-driven.

Husserl's phenomenology represented an early attempt to reinvigorate philosophy in the face of rising "psychologism" by focusing on the search for "essences." Husserl sees "the question of philosophy's relation to the natural and humanistic [i.e. historical] sciences" as a central issue and aims to establish philosophy "as a rigorous science" without falling into scientific naturalism (Husserl 1965: 72). Against the neo-Kantianism that dominated German philosophy in the early twentieth century and preached "back to Kant," Husserl proposes that philosophers go "back to the things themselves" (Husserl 1965: 96–97), where the "things" at which

Husserl aimed are not individual objects but *essences*: "Pure phenomenology as science ... can only be essence investigation" (Husserl 1965: 116, cf. Husserl 1983: 8, 65–66). While natural and human sciences study relations between particular things, they can never make the necessary and universal claims about things that constitute claims about something's *essence*. And while Kant focuses on merely *formal* structures of experience, Husserl insists on a "material" a priori that goes far beyond Kant's own transcendental philosophy: "nature with all its thing-like contents certainly also has its a priori" (Husserl 2001: 43). For instance, we can know a priori that "colors" cannot literally be heard based on the insight that being entirely visual is essential to color.

One accesses essences through what Husserl calls "eidetic seeing" or "essential intuiton" (Husserl 1965: 110, 1983: 8–9). Such intuitions, properly understood, provide a "foundation free of doubt" (Husserl 1965: 76) for philosophical progress.[1] While "intuition" is infallible as a foundation, its reliability depends upon remaining *"within the limits in which it is presented there"* (Husserl 1983: 44). Husserl thus insists that one focus on "phenomena" as presented to consciousness, which requires "a general reversal of that 'natural attitude' in which everyday life as a whole as well as the positive sciences operate. In [this natural attitude] the world is for us the self-evidently existing universe of realities which are continuously before us in unquestioned givenness" (Husserl 1981: 27b). Husserl describes this "reversal" of the natural attitude as an *"epoche,"* a "bracketing" of ordinary assumptions about the world to focus specifically on what is immediately present in intuition. By bracketing assumptions about individual objects, one effects an "all-embracing transition from the factual to the essential form, the *eidos*" (Husserl 1981: 25b). One way of doing this is through "imaginative variation," where "the phenomenological actual fact ... serves only as an example and as the foundation for a free but intuitive variation ... [wherein] the theoretical eye directs itself to the necessarily enduring invariant in the variation" (Husserl 1981: 25b). Rather than descriptively asking how people become aware of colors, one takes the experience of a particular color as occasion for "free but intuitive variation" whereby one gets "knowledge which will have validity far beyond the psychologist's own particular psychic experience" (Husserl 1981: 25b, 23b).[2]

At this level of generality, Husserl's phenomenology can be applied to anything: tones, colors, material objects, and so on. But Husserlian phenomenology focuses on the essence of *consciousness* in its various forms (perception, recollection, valuing, etc.) to "advance toward a descriptive knowledge of the totality of mental processes, toward a comprehensive type of a life of the psyche" (Husserl 1981: 23b, see also Husserl 1983: 67ff.). From this methodology and focus, Husserl developed an elaborate phenomenology of consciousness. His most important eidetic insight was the recognition that consciousness is essentially "intentional," in that it "intends," or is directed toward, particular objects. That is, consciousness in all its forms is consciousness *of* (perception *of*, valuing *of*, willing *of*, etc). From this, Husserl distinguishes what he calls "noesis" and "noema," referring (respectively) to the "intentive mental process" by which an object is intended in a particular way (e.g. perceiving of a cup) and the objects as objects of consciousness (cup as perceived). (Because the natural attitude is bracketed, even "imaginary" objects are noema, in the sense that one's imagining *of* a unicorn has an object just as much as one's perception of a cup.)[3] Both Husserl's general methodology and his specific claims have been appropriated and critiqued by an ongoing phenomenological tradition that aims to discern essential structures of consciousness through an examination of them from-within that brackets scientific–naturalistic assumptions that interfere with attending to consciousness. Existentialism is the most prominent contemporary representative of this phenomenological tradition.

G.E. Moore operated within a very different philosophical climate from Husserl but articulated views that are similar in important respects. Moore's most famous philosophical position is his attempted "Proof of the Existence of the External World." Moore offers a "perfectly rigorous" proof of the external world:

> How? By holding up my two hands, and saying, as I make a certain gesture with the right hand, "Here is one hand", and adding, as I make a certain gesture with the left, "and here is another."
>
> (Moore 1959: 146)

Moore raises the obvious objection, that he does not really "know" that his hands exist, and responds,

> How absurd it would be to suggest that I did not know it, but only believed it, and that perhaps it was not the case! You might as well suggest that I do not know that I am now standing up and talking – that perhaps after all I'm not, and that it's not quite certain that I am!
>
> (Moore 1959: 146)

There is no "proof" of Moore's "Here is one hand" and "Here is the another," but, Moore argues, it is unnecessary to *prove* these premises, as long as one *knows* them. "I can know things, which I cannot prove; and among things which I certainly did know, even if (as I think) I could not prove them, were the premises of my two proofs" (Moore 1959: 148). Strictly speaking, Moore does not describe these known-but-not-proven premises as "intuitions," and he is better understood here as a common-sense philosopher than an "intuitionist" strictly speaking.[4] But this proof captures Moore's spirit of basing philosophy on obviously true claims and contributes to a broader intuitionism.

Moore's worked-out philosophical intuitionism comes in ethics. Moore accuses attempts to explain the good of a "naturalistic fallacy," which, in its most common form, involves identifying "good" with some natural property such as pleasure. For any definition, it remains an "open question" whether "pleasure (or whatever it may be [that one identifies with the good]) [is] after all good." And one "can easily satisfy himself that [in asking this question] he is not merely wondering whether pleasure is pleasant" (Moore 1913: 16). With Kant, it seems coherent to ask, "Is acting only on universalizable maxims good?" and this question is quite unlike "Are universalizable maxims universalizable?" Countless people answer the former question with a resounding "No" when considering such tricky cases as the Nazi at the door. For Moore, even debate about such cases suggests that "'good' denotes a simple and indefinable quality," much like basic perceptual qualities such as "yellow" (Moore 1913: 10).

Because goodness is simple and indefinable, Moore turns to intuition[5] to discover which states of affairs have "goodness": "[we] must consider what things are such that, if they existed by themselves, in absolute isolation, we should yet judge their existence to be good" (Moore 1913: 187). Like Husserl, Moore emphasizes imaginative variation to focus intuition:

> [I]f we place before ourselves the question: Is consciousness of pleasure the sole good? The answer must be: No ... [W]e isolate consciousness of pleasure [and] ask: Suppose we were conscious of pleasure only, and of nothing else, not even that we *were* conscious, would that state of things ... be very desirable? No one, I think, can suppose it so.
>
> (Moore 1913: 95)

The question "What ought I to do?" reduces to "What kind of things ought to exist for their own sakes?" and "What things are related as causes to that which is good in itself?" (Moore 1913: viii, 146). The first is answered via intuitions that certain states of affairs have the simple and indefinable property of goodness; the second via ordinary, scientific causal reasoning. Thus intuitions form the core of Moore's account of volitional normativity.

Neither Husserlian phenomenology nor Moorean intuitionism are particularly popular today. Both Moore and Husserl suffered philosophical attacks from former students – Heidegger in the case of Husserl, Wittgenstein in the case of Moore – attacks that affect how phenomenology and intuitionism have been appropriated today. In both cases, these attacks targeted (among other things) how Moore and Husserl sought *unrevisable* conclusions based on *isolating* particular intuitions, and both Heidegger and Wittgenstein rejected the broadly *foundationalist* philosophical program shared by Husserl and Moore. Most contemporary philosophers follow Heidegger and Wittgenstein in giving up basing indubitable philosophical systems on intuitions.

However, important features of these thinkers' approaches are widely shared within epistemology, moral philosophy, and metaphysics. Phenomenological appeals to what is evident through careful attention is evident in existentialist phenomenologies of Heidegger, Sartre, and Levinas. And analytic normative theorizing uses intuition in epistemology and moral theory, especially among philosophers who aim to avoid or supplement scientific naturalism and who have neither concern for historicism nor sympathy with existentialism.

One place where the appeal to intuition has been particularly prominent is "analytic epistemology," wherein "a priori theorizing about the nature, conditions, and extent of human knowledge, rationality, and justification" is the primary alternative to naturalism (Sosa 2009: 103). The most discussed problem within twentieth-century analytic epistemology is based on intuitions about "knowledge." A dominant account of knowledge posited that knowledge is "justified, true belief" (e.g. Chisholm 1957: 16). But in 1963, in "Is Justified True Belief Knowledge?," Edmund Gettier proposed two cases (many more would follow) that "show" that knowledge cannot merely be justified true belief. For example,

> Smith has strong evidence ... [that] Jones owns a Ford ... [and infers that] (h) "Either Jones owns a Ford, or Brown is in Barcelona." Smith is ... completely justified in believing [this] proposition [since it follows from the claim that Jones owns a Ford]. But imagine now that ... Jones does *not* own a Ford, ... [and], by the sheerest coincidence, and entirely unknown to Smith, ... [Barcelona] happens really to be the place where Brown is. If these two conditions hold, then Smith does *not* know that (h) is true, even though (*i*) (h) is true, (*ii*) Smith does believe that (h) is true, and (*iii*) Smith is justified in believing that (h) is true.
>
> (Gettier 1963: 123)

This sort of epistemology involves imaginatively varying conditions to better intuit the essence of something, in this case "knowledge." The conviction that this case is not real knowledge is based on epistemologists' intuitions. If one thinks Smith *does* know (h), there seems little reason to challenge the conception of knowledge as justified true belief, and thus little sense in much contemporary epistemology, which responds to Gettier-style counter-examples to various definitions of knowledge.

The general style of argument for analytic epistemologists is, as in the case of Husserl and Moore, intuition-driven. Just as Husserl sought to discern "essences" by means of imaginative variation, contemporary analytic epistemologists continually form and refine accounts of belief, knowledge, justification, and so on based on intuitions formed about countless examples and counter-examples. The goal is to get to universal and necessary (a priori) claims about *the* nature of knowledge, belief, and so on; and thus (in ways that are increasingly suspect (see Sosa 2009)) to get an answer to the question of what one ought to believe.

Similarly, within contemporary moral philosophy, much work is done by moral intuitions.[6] "Moral intuitionism" of the Moorean sort is largely rejected by contemporary moral philosophers, who, if they are not Kantians, prefer various kinds of "utilitarianism" or "virtue ethics." But within all these major approaches to ethics, moral intuitions play major roles. Kantians make use of intuitions both in establishing key starting points (such as the claim that moral claims must be universal) and, often, in discerning what sorts of maxims can actually be willed universally. Utilitarians often appeal to intuition to justify their principle of utility. Mill's claim that happiness is the only good is based on a series of intuitions that in everything else we want, we ultimately want happiness. Virtue ethicists appeal to intuitions either about particular "thick" ethical notions (courage, temperance, etc.) or about what constitutes human flourishing. Finally, even insofar as epistemology or moral philosophy shift from using intuitions for *foundational* roles, intuitions are still *accommodated* through *coherence* or *reflective equilibrium*.[7] Almost all contemporary ethical theory appeals, at least implicitly, to a process of "reflective equilibrium" whereby moral theories are susceptible to criticism when they diverge too significantly from ordinary moral intuitions. Thus, famously, divergence between moral intuitions about lying to a murderer at the door and Kant's rigorist adherence to truth-telling is taken as a serious challenge to Kant's moral theory.

Recently, intuitionism in philosophy has been criticized from at least two perspectives. First, it is criticized by (broadly existentialist) critics who simply ask why one should take the fact that something *seems* true to mean that it *is* true, those, that is, who recognize that in general one is capable of standing back from intuitions and asking about them, "But is this *really* true?" Christine Korsgaard, for example, points out that intuitionists fail to answer normative problems precisely when they are most acute: "if someone falls into doubt about whether obligations really exist, it doesn't help to say, 'ah, but indeed they do. They are *real* things.' Just now he doesn't see it, and herein lies his problem" (Korsgaard 1996b: 38). Human beings can – and often must – ask themselves whether values that seem to matter really *do* matter, and intuitionists who say, "Think carefully and it'll be obvious" fail to address the situation of *not* finding the value of values obvious. Second, naturalists, historicists, and those who emphasize human diversity point out that intuitions are largely cultural. As ways of discerning the nature of "truth" or what we "ought" to do or believe, it seems unreasonable to favor our (contingent) intuitions over those of people with other backgrounds. Even for more coherentist approaches, the "garbage-in-garbage-out" objection claims that if one's initial intuitions are misguided or historico-culturally contingent, one will reach only misguided or historically local equilibriums that give little grounds for believing one has discovered any supra-historical normativity. For these critics, intuitionist epistemologists and moral philosophers really offer only a highly local "anthropology" that specifies carefully taught (and selected for) prejudices of a small tribe of mostly wealthy, mostly white, mostly male philosophers in English-speaking universities in the twentieth and early twenty-first centuries. As Stephen Stich dramatically put it, "the best reaction to the High-S[ocio]E[conomic]S[tatus], Western philosophy professor who tries to draw normative conclusions from the facts about 'our' intuitions is to ask: What do you mean 'we'?" (Weinberg et al. 2008: 40, see also Appiah 2009, Knobe and Nichols 2008).

Kant's philosophical approach helps address both sets of concerns. Regarding naturalist and historicist critiques, one can appeal to the difference between transcendental and empirical perspectives, or between linguistic analysis and intuitions about the realities to which one's words apply. Moreover, while there is considerable historical and cultural divergence with respect to certain intuitions, there is considerably less divergence with respect to others, such as the experience of an objective world and the presence of some moral constraints. Finally, the naturalist and historicist claims that seem to call intuitions into question are based to some degree on intuitions. Without some reason to view scientific methodology as reliable, no such studies can call intuitions into question. To *some* degree at least, one must take one's own sense of what counts as justification for granted if one takes historicist or naturalist objections seriously. Depending upon the results of such studies, one may have to give up confidence in *some* intuitions, but one cannot give up confidence in *all* without giving up the studies themselves.

With respect to more existentialist concerns, Kant might rightly point out that "standing back" from intuitions is always a *normative* standing back, that is, a way of asking whether one *should* remain committed to what one finds oneself committed to. And normatively standing back depends upon standards for normative evaluation, so that one cannot stand back from intuitions without having or at least seeking some basis for evaluating them. This does not mean that one can evaluate intuitions only based upon other intuitions one already has. In that sense, *intuitionism* may turn out to be the wrong way to go about developing a normative theory. But it does imply that *some* sort of normativity is necessary; in the absence of other candidates, this would require evaluating some intuitions based on others.

As these responses suggest, however, Kant's philosophy differs in important ways from contemporary appeals to intuition. Kant's transcendental anthropology appeals only to very general intuitions such as the existence of obligations, the fact that we experience an objective world, and the impossibility of imagining this world non-spatially. Kant's own defense of the categorical imperative, for instance, does not depend upon intuitive awareness of that particular moral law, nor even a process of reflective endorsement whereby the law is confirmed by its conformity with our moral intuitions. *Kant's* argument is — or at least aims to be — that if we have *any* moral intuitions at all, that is, any sense that we are obligated to do anything, then we are committed to a sort of moral responsibility, the condition of possibility of which is that we are bound by this particular moral law. Thus Kant avoids brute appeals to particular intuitions while still providing some place for intuitions of the most general sort.

"Cheerful Ethnocentrism"

Ordinary people as well as philosophers continue to use intuitions to decide what to think and do and what theories of knowledge and action to adopt, but the historical and cultural variability of intuitions and the seeming impossibility of any truly universal, foundationalist philosophical system have led to alternative approaches to normativity. One such approach accepts that one's intuitions are simply one possible set of intuitions among others but embraces them nonetheless. One of the most important and interesting contemporary approaches along these lines is a form of neopragmatism espoused by Richard Rorty.

We can understand Rorty's position as a generalization of the Kuhnian, historicist claims that "normal science" is characterized by norms intrinsic to a particular paradigm and that there are no supra-paradigmatic standards for evaluating paradigm shifts. For Rorty, every "language game" is governed by norms for the use of words within that game, and in that sense, every ordinary use of language is akin to the practice of "normal science." Rather than a specifically "epistemic" normativity that would ask "What should I believe?," Rorty focuses on a more linguistic normativity that asks, "What should I *say*?" (which will include such things as saying to oneself, "I believe such and such"). And the answer to that question is local. Language-games include their own norms, and one should generally say only what is consistent with the internal norms of one's game. Normativity is a matter of "criterion-governed sentences within language games" (Rorty 1988: 5). Within certain religious or poetic language-games, one can say, "Phoebus rounded the earth in his flaming chariot." Within ordinary language of daily life and weather channels, it makes sense to say, "Tomorrow, the sun will set at 7:13 p.m." And in the language-game of introductory astronomy, it makes sense to say, "The earth lies at a distance of 150 million kilometers from the sun, orbiting it at 100,000 kilometers per second, and spinning with one rotation every 23.93 hours." For all these cases, criteria of correctness are *internal* to the particular language-game.

One can, of course, ask whether one ought to adopt a particular language-game. If one chooses to use a particular term – say, "spinster," "heretic," "homophobe," "quark," or "essence" – one is governed by norms intrinsic to the language-games of which they are a part. But if one asks whether to use these terms at all, we seem to need norms that transcend particular language-games, norms for choosing which vocabulary best tracks reality. Rorty resists this move: "the world does not tell us which language games to play ... Philosophy ... makes itself ridiculous when it steps forward at such junctures and says that it will find neutral ground on which to adjudicate the issue" (Rorty 1988: 5, 51). One's choice of vocabulary, too, is ultimately local, though in a different sense. We should "treat alternate vocabularies ... like alternative tools" (Rorty 1988: 11). In such a context,

> We will not be inclined to ask questions like "what is the place of consciousness in a world of molecules?" ... "what is the place of value in a world of fact?" ... "What is the relation between the solid table of common sense and the unsolid table of microphysics?" ... "Merely philosophical" questions, like [the] question about the relation between the two tables, are attempts to stir up a fictitious theoretical quarrel between vocabularies which have proved capable of peaceful coexistence.
>
> (Rorty 1988: 10–11)

Choice of vocabularies/language-games/paradigms is local in that one chooses one's vocabulary *for a purpose*. For heightening devotion, use religious–poetic descriptions of the sun. For determining when to go to the beach to enjoy the sunset, use the weather channel. And for determining when (and at what speed) to launch a satellite, use scientific description. Emphasis on vocabularies' *utility* makes Rorty's philosophy a sort of "pragmatism." What we say and think should help us get things done.

But Rorty's norms are "local" in another sense, since he rejects any neutral practical ground as much as any epistemic master vocabulary. If we could determine a priori what "should be done," we might determine what to say and think based on some categorical imperative of action. (For example, if we could know that religious devotion is dangerous superstition, we could justifiably send religious language to the scrap-heap, or, perhaps better, use it to new ends.) But for Rorty, norms about what to *do* are internal to particular language-games and the particular forms of life that support them.

> I do not think there are any plain moral facts out there in the world, nor any truths independent of language, nor any neutral ground on which to stand and argue that either torture or kindness are preferable to the other.
>
> (Rorty 1988: 173)

For Rorty, then, normativity is local both because norms are intrinsic to particular language-games and because choices of language-games are tied to locally relevant conceptions of a good life. The result is what Rorty calls a "cheerful ethnocentrism," according to which "What counts as being a decent human being is relative to historical circumstance, a matter of transient consensus about what attitudes are normal and what practices are just or unjust" (Brandom 2000: 20, Rorty 1988: 189).

One might think that recognizing one's values as historically contingent would undermine commitment to them, but for Rorty, "belief can still regulate action, can still be thought worth dying for, among people quite aware that this belief is caused by nothing deeper than contingent historical circumstance" (Rorty 1988: 189). Rorty's pragmatism alleviates the need for indubitable and final justifications. Once we stop using language of objectivity and "absolute" truth, we need not take beliefs' contingency as undermining them. Commitment to any particular value will depend upon one's particular projects, the value of which will, in turn, depend upon other values. As Rorty puts it, "*We* have to start from where *we* are" (Rorty 1988: 198). Ethnocentrism need not be a "relativist" undermining of commitment to beliefs and values, but can be a "cheerful" acceptance of them.

Especially when cheerful, however, ethnocentrism can seem like a vice to avoid. For one thing, "cheerful ethnocentrism" suggests stale conservatism of beliefs and values. If norms are intrinsic to forms of life, they might seem immune to whole-hearted revision. If one could justify stasis because one finally figured out what the world is *really* like or what a good human life *really* is, stasis might not be so bad. But cheerful ethnocentrism offers no such assurance and so seems unjustifiably stagnant. Moreover, "ethnocentrism" can lead to ignorance about and intolerance toward others; at worst, without non-local bases for reasoned agreement, ethnocentrism in our pluralist and interconnected world seems to invite imperialism and oppression.

To Rorty's great credit, he takes on these concerns and emphasizes both creativity (or "irony") and tolerance ("liberalism"). Rorty's "irony" manifests itself particularly poignantly in his rejection of philosophical intuitionism. One might expect a cheerful ethnocentrist to embrace the prevailing intuitions of his "ethnos," but Rorty does not:

> the claim that an "adequate" philosophical doctrine must make room for our intuitions is a reactionary slogan, one which begs the question at hand ... What is described as such a consciousness is simply a disposition to use the language of our ancestors ... Unless we suffer from what Derrida calls "Heideggerian nostalgia," we shall not think of our intuitions as more than platitudes, more than the habitual use of a certain repertoire of terms, more than old tools which as yet have no replacements.
>
> (Rorty 1988: 22)

While admitting that intuitions, *for now*, are "tools that have no replacements," Rorty rejects both Heideggerian nostalgia for originary insights and Moorean conservatism that takes present intuitions as eternal truths. Instead, he opts for a Nietzschean optimism that hopes for new intuitions in a better and brighter future we make for ourselves. This future is partly social, in that new terms and visions can become shared intuitions. But Rorty also endorses a personal ideal of irony represented by poets who transcend norms and tools (linguistic and otherwise) of their societies. (Rorty reads Derrida as a poet of this sort.) Ironists in this sense are existentialists par excellence who actualize freedom through creatively reinterpreting and thereby superseding currently dominant "intuitions." Rather than stale conservatism, cheerfully ironic ethnocentrism supports radical and playful revisions of dominant norms and intuitions in the service of personal authenticity.

But irony alone does little to alleviate ethical concerns about intolerance and imperialism. A willingness to violate, transcend, and reinterpret the values of one's culture need not imply any greater tolerance for others' values and often leads to the opposite. Rorty is aware that "attempts at [authenticity], our private obsessions with the achievement of a certain sort of perfection, may make us oblivious to the pain and humiliation we are causing" (Rorty 1988: 141). Unlike Kant, Rorty sees nothing that links "duties to self and duties to others" (Rorty 1988: 141); no a priori principle that shows *true* creativity requires allowing others space to be creative in turn; irony's conditions of possibility do not require respect for others. But, Rorty insists, commitment to respecting others need be no less forceful for lack of an a priori principle (see Rorty 1988: 189). Rorty's *liberal* irony brings two commitments that mitigate free-for-all creativity. First, "liberals are the people who think that cruelty is the worst thing we do" (Rorty 1988: xv), even if "[t]here is no neutral, non-circular way to *defend* the liberal's claim that cruelty is the worst thing we do" (Rorty 1988: 196). As a liberal, Rorty is sensitive to cruel acts and attitudes. And Rorty insists that ironic creativity *rather* than transcendental justification is needed to be a better liberal. One committed to being less cruel needs greater sensitivity to various forms of cruelty, not an assurance that we are right to avoid these. Cultivating this sensitivity requires revisions of perspective. When Foucault shows how "humane" prison conditions dehumanize, when Nabokov shows the cruelty of pursuing personal fulfillment against social norms, and when Levinas shows how systems of "justice" impose de-facing categories on others, attention is drawn to forms of cruelty often obscured by philosophical argument. Ironic overcoming of philosophical "objectivity" and "justification" contributes to better liberalism.

Another element of Rorty's liberalism further alleviates concerns with oppression and complacency. While rejecting "objectivity" and Kantian "universality," Rorty proposes an ironic–liberal ideal of "solidarity." Solidarity includes "the imaginative ability to see strange people as fellow sufferers" (Rorty 1988: xvi), so it helps avoid cruelty. And solidarity gives new meaning to "objectivity":

> For pragmatists, the desire for objectivity is not the desire to escape the limitations of one's community, but simply the desire for as much intersubjective agreement as possible, to extend the reference of "us" as far as we can.
>
> (Rorty 1990: 23)

Rather than conforming beliefs to a "real world," liberal ironists alleviate negative connotations of "ethnocentrism" by aiming for more and more diverse epistemic, social, and political communities:

> What takes the curse off ethnocentrism is … that it is the ethnocentrism of a "we" ("we liberals") which is dedicated to enlarging itself, to creating an ever larger and more variegated *ethnos*. It is the "we" of a people who have been brought up to distrust ethnocentrism.
>
> (Rorty 1988: 198)

Rorty is not an ethnocentrist who excludes other people and their points of view out of hand, but one who seeks to *include* them in an ever-broadening, peaceful, and multifaceted perspective.

Much is appealing in Rorty's cheerful ethnocentrism.[8] From-within, we have no choice but to take ourselves as we are. Even when we incorporate new perspectives, we take them seriously by, in some way, making them our own. Any problems for given presuppositions appeal to other presuppositions. Ethnocentrism is right as far as it goes, and it might be as far as we can go. If so, then I share Rorty's desire for a liberal, compassionate, and tolerant ethnocentrism. But Rorty's positive arguments for local norms are much stronger than his negative arguments against universal ones. There may be hope for normativity that is more robust, less ethnocentric, and more "objective" than Rorty's.

And we – at least many of us, at least some of the time – *need* something more than what Rorty provides. Rorty's liberal irony provides little guidance to one genuinely concerned about what to do or believe. Even if already engaged in language-games with their own internal norms, I can wonder whether I *should* think and act in the light of these norms. Rorty writes approvingly of Freud, who "does not ask us to choose" between the "merely moral man" and the "poet" because he "does not think we have a faculty which can make such choices" (Rorty 1988: 35). But from-within, we often *must* make such choices. Even if I already accept that "cruelty is the worst thing one can do" and endorse a personal ethic of creativity, I can raise questions about the legitimacy of these ideals. Rorty's way of dealing with this existential possibility is to focus on particulars, to look at specific and local reasons for preferring one ideal over another. His solution is simply to "get over it," to stop reflecting too much. There is no need to ask questions about whether what I ultimately care about most is *worth* caring about; and Rorty proposes revising philosophical and even everyday language to make such questions increasingly difficult to ask.

For Kant, however, human beings are always able to ask such questions, and "enlightenment" or "autonomy" precisely consists in refusing to let these questions be silenced, refusing to let oneself simply absorb others' categories and values. Even if (as Foucault and Rorty suggest) this ideal of autonomy is historically local, it is one "we" share. Rorty-the-ironist agrees with his Romantic and Nietzschean predecessors that the autonomy worth caring about does not depend upon universal standards. And he offers examples, in his own writing and those of his ironist heroes, of creativity arising from being set free from these standards. But this absence of standards and Rorty's cheerful ethnocentrism leave one open to the question, which Kant claims is inevitable and which Rorty has not yet cured, of whether ironic play and liberal hope are really worth it after all. Rorty fails to fully answer the normative question in the way that it shows up, or at least can show up, to human beings.

Moreover, today's world is increasingly pluralist. Rorty is right that one great merit of liberal societies is "our" desire to be inclusive and fair to those marginalized by "us." But he underestimates the extent to which this ideal, even if only "our" ideal, commits us to non-ethnocentric ways of arbitrating between diverse forms of life. Rorty often portrays this arbitration as fundamentally *political*, and there is a pressing political problem of how to respect those whose values differ fundamentally from one's own. But there is also a more *personal* problem for modern liberal individuals, the problem of how to decide what *I* should believe or do in the light of contact with communities who hold incompatible visions of the world and the good life. In the modern world, one cannot simply assume the vocabulary of one's birth. Before becoming cheerfully ethnocentric, one needs to decide which ethnos (or better, ethnoi) to make one's own.

Local Normativity, Narrative Unity, and Tradition(s)

Given that our world includes multiple incompatible sets of norms, we require some way of arbitrating between them. Intuitionists affirm norms that emerge on reflection as obviously or intuitively right. Cheerful ethnocentrism accepts evaluative structures without suggesting that those in other cultures would rationally accept them. Both approaches risk underplaying diversity of norms and the extent to which, for many people, this diversity is internalized. In the final two sections, we look at broadly Kantian approaches that seek to construct universalist orders that can have priority over intuitions, values, and language-games of particular cultures. Before turning to those Kantian approaches, this chapter looks at a non-universalist approach that emphasizes that norms of human deliberation are not primarily logical or foundationalist but *narrative*. Our exemplar of this approach, Alasdair MacIntyre, shares many of Rorty's claims about normativity's local character. But MacIntyre reveals an underlying normativity in the notion of "narrative unity" with tradition and develops an account of "the rationality of traditions" that, without providing a "master vocabulary" or "view from nowhere," still can justify one tradition (and hence language-game) over another. MacIntyre thereby provides more general normative claims than *mere* cheerful ethnocentrism, without requiring absolute and universal principles that rise above all contingent and particular human communities.

For MacIntyre, individual choices have a narrative structure: "Narrative history ... [is] the basic and essential genre for the characterization of human actions" (MacIntyre 1984: 208), so one makes an action, statement, or choice "intelligible by finding its place in a narrative" (MacIntyre 1984: 210). Narrative does not merely make sense of *others*: it is also essential for the intelligibility of thought and choice "to agents themselves" (MacIntyre 1984: 208, cf. 212). One decides which language-games to play, which purposes to pursue, what kind of beliefs to hold or actions to take, in terms of an overall life-narrative. "To ask, 'what is the good for me?' is to ask how best I might live out that unity ['of a narrative embodied in a single life'] and bring it completion. To ask, 'What is the good for man?' is to ask what all answers to the former question must have in common" (MacIntyre 1984: 218–19).

This approach captures much day-to-day experience of the normative character of choice. As existentialists recognized, decisions about life involve incorporating one's past into a projected future; they have a narrative structure. One looks back, seeing roles and responsibilities one has taken on, and thinks about how present and future actions can "complete" one's life so far. This explains the sense of being "trapped" in a "dead-end" career, relationship, or habit. When it is difficult to envision a coherent story that goes from what one has been toward any complete life one would find worth living, one is at a "dead-end."

Life's narrative structure has two features essential to narrative normativity. First, a "crucial characteristic of all lived narratives" is "a certain teleological [goal-oriented] character" (MacIntyre 1984: 215). Second, one's life-narrative is interconnected with one's community. Not only does one depend upon that community for support in living one's life, but also "we approach our own circumstances as bearers of a particular social identity" (MacIntyre 1984: 220).

> I can only answer the question, "What am I to do?" if I can answer the prior question, "Of what story or stories do I find myself a part?" We enter human society, that is, with one or more imputed ... roles.
>
> (MacIntyre 1984: 216)

Neither the child whose immigrant parents worked to send him to college nor the fourth-generation child of a long line of Marines can construct a personal narrative according to which he just falls into plumbing as a career. If he chooses to be a plumber, it will be a form of rejecting or radically reinterpreting a role his parents' goals and sacrifices prepared. We find ourselves, first as children (and siblings), then as students, friends, spouses, workers of particular kinds, and so on, in a host of social roles. These roles are defined by one's community, and while one can appropriate, revise, or reject them, one cannot construct one's personal narrative independent of them. In that sense, "We are never more (and sometimes less) than the co-authors of our own narratives" (MacIntyre 1984: 213). "What ought I to do?" quickly becomes "How should I balance family responsibilities (as child/spouse/parent) with teaching responsibilities (as professor)?"

While individuals choose in the light of stories constructed around roles within a community, communities too have stories, so "the story of my life is always embedded in the story of those communities from which I derive my identity ... I find myself part of a history ..., one of the bearers of a tradition" (MacIntyre 1984: 221). Just as one sees individual choices teleologically, as about how to complete the life that one has lived, one sees these choices also as about how to be part of one's community's progress toward goods that make sense within that community's narrative:

> All reasoning takes place within the context of some traditional mode of thought, transcending through criticism and invention the limitations of what had hitherto been reasoned in that tradition ... A living tradition then is an historically extended, socially embodied argument, and an argument precisely in part about the goods which constitute the tradition.
>
> (MacIntyre 1984: 222)

So far, this sounds like Rortian ethnocentrism with a narrative twist. And MacIntyre, like Rorty, rejects any "neutral tradition-independent standard of a rationally justifiable kind to which we may appeal" in "decid[ing] between rival and mutually exclusive claims ... [T]here is ... only the practical-rationality-of-this-or-that-tradition and the justice-of-this-or-that-tradition" (MacIntyre 1988: 329, 346).

But MacIntyre differs from Rorty in two fundamental respects. One, shared by many cheerful ethnocentrists who reject Rorty's extreme pragmatism, is that MacIntyre sees an important role for "truth" within tradition-guided enquiry. Where Rorty sees "the idea of Truth as something to be pursued for its own sake" as "the central theme" of a *particular* tradition beginning with Plato and, he hopes, ending with himself (Rorty 1990: 21), MacIntyre sees the pursuit of Truth as intrinsic to *any* tradition of enquiry: "implicit in the rationality of [tradition-constituted] enquiry there is indeed a conception of final truth" (MacIntyre 1988: 360). Thus "every tradition, whether it recognizes the fact or not, confronts the possibility that at some future time it will fall into a state of epistemological crisis," such that "that particular tradition's claims to truth can ... no longer be sustained" (MacIntyre 1988: 364).

This leads to a second difference: although MacIntyre rejects "neutral standards," he develops a theory of traditions' rationality that allows for a supra-traditional evaluative framework that can "answer relativism" in ways Rorty is uninterested in:

> The grounds for an answer to relativism and perspectivism are to be found, not in any theory of rationality as yet explicitly articulated and advanced within one or more of the traditions ..., but rather with a theory embodied in and presupposed by their practices of enquiry, yet never fully spelled out ... The rationality of a tradition-constituted and tradition-constitutive enquiry is ... a matter of the kind of progress which it makes.
>
> (MacIntyre 1988: 354)

Two senses of "rationality of traditions" are at play here. *Within* each tradition are necessary standards of rationality: "traditions possess measures to evaluate their own progress or lack of it, even if such measures necessarily are framed in terms of and presuppose the truth of those central theses to which the tradition gives allegiance" (MacIntyre 1988: 167). But between traditions, meta-standards operate that, while never fully articulable because any articulation would be tradition-bound, can be seen particularly in historical evolutions of and confrontations between traditions. MacIntyre focuses on what he calls a "dialectical" rationality within and between traditions:

> The kind of justification that [first principles within a tradition] receive is at once dialectical and historical. They are justified insofar as in the history of this tradition they have, by surviving the process of dialectical questioning, vindicated themselves as superior to their historical predecessors.
>
> (MacIntyre 1988: 360)

In describing this vindication, MacIntyre explains,

> [P]rotagonists of each tradition ... ask whether the alternative and rival tradition may not be able to provide resources to characterize and to explain the failing and defects of their own tradition more adequately than they, using the resources of that tradition, have been able to do.
>
> (MacIntyre 1988: 167)

For example, MacIntyre explains why Aquinas's philosophy rightly superseded its predecessors:

> What justifies [Aquinas's] representation of the order of things over against its Averroist, Neoplatonist, and Augustinian rivals is its ability to identify, to explain, and to transcend their limitations and defects, while preserving from them everything that survives dialectical questioning in a way which those rivals are unable from their philosophical resources to provide any counterpart.
>
> (MacIntyre 1988: 172, see also 175–76)

This dialectical norm of tradition development steers clear of mere ethnocentrism without articulating specific principles of rationality to which all traditions must subscribe.

For Kant, MacIntyre's emphasis on narrative unity and finding one's place in the tradition can be entirely welcome. Especially in his account of evil, Kant recommends seeing one's life as a narrative (of moral progress), and he can accommodate the need for thoughts and actions to be consistent with the values of our tradition even while pushing them forward. Kant might rightly object to the vagueness of mere "narrative unity," especially given Kant's specific suggestions for bringing life to coherent unity through cultivating a character that unifies consistent principles into a moral whole. MacIntyre's "narrative unity" is also insufficiently autonomous, allowing for primarily passive relationships to substantive values one adopts from one's tradition. Moreover, while MacIntyre's insistence upon "truth" and his supra-traditional evaluative framework improve on Rorty's cheerful ethnocentrism, this framework is too amorphous and arbitrary to sustain the from-within needs of twenty-first-century thinkers and actors who find themselves only loosely tied even to their own traditions.

MacIntyre's approach is strongest where it is most Kantian. Overlaying his treatment of narrative and tradition, MacIntyre emphasizes a set of "virtues" that "find their point and purpose not only in ... sustaining the form of an individual life ... but also in sustaining those traditions which provide both practices and individual lives with their necessary historical context" (MacIntyre 1984: 223). While MacIntyre specifically contrasts these "virtues" to any "a set of ... maxims which may provide our practical inferences with major premises" (MacIntyre 1984: 223), they are universally required as necessary conditions for the possibilities of narratively unifying life and rationally developing tradition. They are general conditions – albeit character traits rather than moral principles – of the possibility of normativity.

Habermas and Communicative Rationality

Contemporary neo-Kantians incorporate many insights of previously discussed approaches but retain emphases on universality and autonomy. The rest of this chapter focuses on the two most important contemporary neo-Kantian (moral) philosophers: Jürgen Habermas and Christine Korsgaard.

Habermas offers a Kantian version of MacIntyre's "rationality of traditions." Like MacIntyre and Rorty, Habermas recognizes rationality embedded in particular cultural traditions and admits that many life decisions occur in the context of cultural roles and norms. Like MacIntyre and against Rorty, Habermas also insists that traditions of enquiry embody a commitment to "truth" that appeals to something supratraditional that functions as a regulative ideal and describes a dialectical and historical process for the context of conflicting traditions (cf. MacIntyre 1988: 360, Habermas 1993: 96–105, 1990: 4–5, 87). But Habermas argues that this dialectical process involves universal and necessary norms of interaction that can be articulated and defended. Habermas thereby aims to reconstruct Kantian moral philosophy as a "discourse ethics" or "theory of communicative action" that articulates universal norms arising within and governing concrete efforts of members of different traditions to come to agreement.

Habermas describes his view as a Kantian (re)appropriation of Hegel's insight that normativity and rationality are fundamentally public and social. In Habermas's hands, Hegel's social rationality gives rise to an "intersubjective interpretation of the categorical imperative" (Habermas 1993: 1). On this view,

> Controversial questions of normative validity can be thematized only from the first person plural perspective, that is, ... "by us": for normative validity claims are contingent on "our" recognition.
>
> (Habermas 1993: 49)

Thus, "it becomes imperative to submit all norms to a public, discursive, generalization test that necessitates reciprocal perspective taking" (Habermas 1993: 64). The need to develop norms within (and subject to) public discourse "ground[s] the moral principle in the normative content of our practice of argumentation" (Habermas 1993: 30) and thereby generates "the distinctive idea of an ethics of discourse":

> Only those norms can claim to be valid that meet (or could meet) with the approval of all affected in their capacity *as participants in a rational discourse.*
>
> (Habermas 1990: 66, see Habermas 1993: 31–32, 50)

In itself, this procedural principle has no content, but discourse ethics articulates further principles constitutive of genuinely rational discourse. A rational discourse, or a truly "communicative" interaction, aims for "truth ... rightness ... truthfulness" and ultimately mutual, rational motivation, as opposed to mere "strategic action" where "one actor seeks [merely] to *influence* the behavior of another," say through manipulation, deceit, or coercion. Norms such as "openness, equal rights, truthfulness and the absence of coercion" partially constitute communicative action (Habermas 1993: 32). Rather than a moral theory laying out what individuals ought to choose, Habermas's ethics of discourse elucidates standards governing how communities seeking norms together ought to speak with one another. From these standards, Habermas provides a further discourse ethics in various provisional and fallible normative claims that emerge *from* ethically conducted discourses.

Throughout, Habermas insists on "actual participation [in] ... real discourse" (Habermas 1990: 67–68, cf. Habermas 1993: 51). One cannot *simply* analyze conditions of possibility of communicative action as an "ideal ... isolated subject" (Habermas 1993: 48): "no norm ... can be justified ... privately in the solitary monologue of the soul with itself" (Habermas 1993: 64, cf. Habermas 1990: 65–67). This gives rise to an important Habermasian "fallibilism" (Habermas 1993: 38). Because "the social world ... is *historical*" (Habermas 1993: 39), norms that seem justified in particular historico-social contexts may no longer be justified later. Not only do "those affected" by a norm change, one might *think* a norm "could meet" with approval by all affected only to find, in the course of *actual discourse*, that it cannot. Without succumbing to quasi-relativist historicism, Habermas allows that the communicative process whereby human beings form universal norms is subject to imperfections of real, historical, dialogues. Habermas is recognizably Kantian in his emphasis on universality, but he replaces an isolated individual assessing beliefs and choices with a *community* discoursing about them. Thereby Habermas, more than Kant, recognizes the important cultural and historical dimensions of cognition and moral reflection.

Habermas further alters Kant by blurring boundaries between transcendental, empirical, and pragmatic anthropology and thereby developing a more naturalist conception of norms and a more value-loaded empirical psychology than Kant's. Habermas "situate[es] reason" by "detranscendentalizing" both "the subject of knowledge" (Habermas 2008: 25) and the "acting subject" (Habermas 2008: 40), who are "dislodged from the kingdom of intelligible beings into the linguistically articulated lifeworld of socialized subjects" (Habermas 2008: 40, cf. 30, 34). Actual communication in a real world of embodied and socialized human beings gives rise to epistemic and moral norms and thereby to the objective world within which human beings find themselves and the moral demands to which they are subject. What for Kant were a priori transcendental conditions of possibility of cognition and volition become, for Habermas, standards emerging from concrete acts of communication.

While rooting transcendental anthropology in the empirical–social world, Habermas also insists that empirical investigations of human beings cannot be isolated from moral norms. For Habermas, the cognitive psychology of Lawrence Kohlberg exemplifies an "empirical theory" "dependent on the philosophical theories it employs" that therefore provides "indirect testing" for the (broadly Kantian) normative theories underlying it (Habermas 1993: 115, 1990: 117). Kohlberg's research program posits stages of moral (and cognitive) development, where "universal ethical principles" mark the highest stage. Given the interdependence between normative assumptions about what constitutes a higher stage of development and the empirical claims to which Kohlberg's model gives rise, Kohlberg's success (partly) justifies a (more-or-less) Kantian conception of moral ideals.[9] The interweaving of normative and empirical is like Kant's pragmatic anthropology in seeking empirical work relevant to achieving moral and cognitive ideals, but Habermas's reading of Kohlberg makes the empirical and transcendental interdependent rather than complementary. Thus empirical research can challenge or confirm transcendental ideals, rather than merely showing strategies for better achieving them.

Another important difference between Habermas and Kant relates to the criticism – shared by Hegel, MacIntyre, and existentialists – that Kant's dichotomy between morality and self-love fails to recognize important roles that *non*-moral life-choices play in human self-conceptions. In response, Habermas adds Hegel's notion of the ethical to Kant's dichotomy between morality and prudence:

> The question "what should I do?" takes on a pragmatic, an ethical, or a moral meaning depending upon how it is conceived ... The rational consideration of an important value decision that affects the whole course of one's life is ... different [from both pragmatic and moral considerations. It] involves hermeneutical clarification of an individual's self-understanding and ... questions of a ... not-failed life. The terminus ad quem of a corresponding ethical-existential discourse is advice concerning the correct conduct of life and the realization of a personal life project. Moral judgment ... is something different. It serves to clarify legitimate behavioral expectations in response to interpersonal conflicts resulting from the disruption of our orderly coexistence by conflicts of interests.
>
> (Habermas 1993: 8–9)

Habermas preserves Kant's emphasis on the importance of moral judgments, but he also recognizes the important role of decisions affecting whether one's life as a whole fails or succeeds in *non*-moral, existential terms. Even for these decisions, however, "there is room for discourse because here too the steps in argumentation should ... be comprehensible in intersubjective terms. The individual attains reflective distance from his own life history only within the horizon of forms of life that he shares with others and that themselves constitute the context for different individual life projects" (Habermas 1993: 11). Habermas adds MacIntyre's emphasis on shared forms of life to existentialist authenticity while rejecting MacIntyre's conflation of moral and ethical. *Ethical* values, which are always rooted in particular social and cultural traditions but can also be highly individual, are distinct from *moral* norms, which "must detach themselves from the concrete contents of the plurality of attitudes ... that now manifest themselves" to be "grounded solely in an abstract social identity that is henceforth circumscribed only by the status of membership in *some* society, not in this or that particular society" (Habermas 1993: 47). Habermas, like Kant but with a greater awareness of the not-merely-pragmatic importance of non-moral choices, advocates a "morally justified pluralism of life projects and life-forms" (Habermas 1993: 75). And he adds that as pluralism grows and thereby "the sphere of questions that can be answered rationally from the moral point of view shrinks ..., finding a solution to these few more sharply focused [moral] questions becomes all the more critical to coexistence" (Habermas 1993: 91).

Given developments in understanding human beings over the last two centuries, Habermas's communicative ethics has important advantages over Kant's anthropology. His moderate naturalism provides for jettisoning what many see as needless metaphysical baggage from Kant. And his appropriation of Kohlberg provides an important way of relating empirical psychology and normativity. His fallibilism accommodates historicism without succumbing to it, and his category of "ethical-existential" highlights the importance of historically-culturally-individually-local norms without losing something like Kant's category of moral norms. Finally, Habermas's sociopolitical approach to Kant makes it possible to appropriate Kant's emphasis on morality in contexts where it seems most important – arbitrating interpersonal and intercultural conflicts – while leaving decisions about how to lead one's life open to a broader range of influences.

But Habermas's differences from Kant bring disadvantages. His naturalism compromises the sharp dichotomy between transcendental and empirical anthropology that enabled Kant to maintain commitment to strong norms of thought and action in the light of naturalist and historicist threats. And the accommodation to existentialist and MacIntyrean approaches to "ethics" opens Habermas to some of the vagueness, indeterminacy, and potential heteronomy of MacIntyre's account of narrative unity. (Where MacIntyre replaces Kantian *morality* with ethics, however, Habermas's ethics only supplements Kant's *hedonism*, which is already vague, indeterminate, and heteronomous.) Perhaps most importantly, Habermas's resistance to allowing the determination of moral norms to take place in individuals, while it has important advantages, also makes his theory less helpful than Kant's for the from-within perspective of individuals seeking to discern what to think and do in non-ideal conditions, where we simply cannot engage in the requisite discussions but must nonetheless decide how to live.

Korsgaard and the sources of normativity

Like Habermas, Christine Korsgaard is a contemporary Kantian responding to challenges of naturalism, historicism, diversity, existentialism, and alternative normative approaches that have emerged over the past 200 years. Korsgaard has directly commented on Kant (see especially Korsgaard 1996a), but her most important work is her Kant*ian* normative theory, laid out in *The Sources of Normativity* (1996b). Like Kant, Korsgaard insists that respect for humanity is a "categorical imperative," that this imperative normatively binds all human agents, that freedom is a condition of possibility of morality and responsibility, and that human deeds are both free (in something like Kant's sense) and causally determined. But Korsgaard's

Kantianism differs from Kant's in three key respects: human freedom's relation to natural necessity, how morality's normative status is justified, and the importance of contingent "practical identities" in human life. In these areas, Korsgaard's Kantianism accommodates and responds to recent developments in answering Kant's question.

Korsgaard avoids metaphysically loaded construals of Kant's theory of freedom. She interprets transcendental idealism not as two metaphysically distinct worlds, a phenomenal world of causally determined appearances and a noumenal world including freedom, but as two distinct standpoints, a scientific one that sees the world as a set of causally determined interactions amongst objects and a practical one from which one views oneself as a free agent effecting changes in the world.

> Determinism is no threat to freedom ... The freedom discovered in reflection is not a theoretical property which can also be seen by scientists considering the agent's deliberations third-personally and from outside. It is from within the deliberative perspective that we see our desires as providing suggestions which we may take or leave. You will say that this means that our freedom is not "real" only if you have defined the "real" as what can be identified by scientists looking at things third-personally and from outside.
>
> (Korsgaard 1996b: 96)

In itself, this is no "departure" from Kant; it articulates the importance of the from-within perspective on which this book has focused. But unlike Kant, Korsgaard tends to see these two standpoints as non-hierarchically arranged; even when mentioning Kant's "priority of the practical," Korsgaard more often emphasizes that "neither standpoint is privileged over the other – each has its own territory" (Korsgaard 1996a: 173). Korsgaard defends what we called in Chapter 7 "neutral" rather than "freedom-first" perspectivism. This difference marks a minor *departure* from Kant, but is a metaphysically deflationary *reading* that seeks to maintain as much of Kant's transcendental idealism as possible while keeping his metaphysics as naturalistic and this-worldly as possible.

The next two points need to be taken together, since Korsgaard's defense of the importance of morality depends upon her account of practical identities. The most basic difference between the arguments of Korsgaard and Kant can be seen in Korsgaard's broadly *existentialist* starting point. Her 2009 book *Self-Constitution* begins with a direct allusion to Sartre: "Human beings are condemned to choice and action" (Korsgaard 2009: 1, cf. Sartre 1956: 568).

> The human mind is ... essentially reflective ... And this sets us a problem no other animal has. It is the problem of the normative. For our capacity to

turn our attention onto our own mental activities is also a capacity to distance ourselves from them, and to call them into question ... The reflective mind cannot settle for perception and desire, not just as such. It needs a *reason*. Otherwise, at least as long as it reflects, it cannot commit itself to go forward.

(Korsgaard 1996b: 92–93)

For Sartre, this problem leads to existential angst, humans' recognition that they are utterly responsible for their actions. From within, human beings seek reasons for what we believe and do, which sets us a problem. This problem of reflection, in fact, has haunted each of the last three chapters because, on their own, naturalism, historicism, and even existentialism fail to *address* reflective human beings; they fail to give us *reasons*.

For Kant, humans' from-within stance is not *merely* existential; there is a "fact of reason" that "forces itself upon us" (5: 31) to make us immediately aware of our *moral* responsibility, a *categorical imperative*. The normative pull of morality is something *given*, the conditions of possibility for which Kant seeks (and finds pre-eminently in freedom), but morality is not something that he needs to, or even can, "prove." But Korsgaard, partly in response to new skepticisms introduced by Nietzsche and his historicist and existentialist heirs, seeks to show that morality's normative force is built into the merely reflective existential situation of human beings. She rehabilitates an earlier argument from Kant's *Groundwork* that emphasizes how "to every rational being having a will we must necessarily lend the idea of freedom also, under which it acts" (4: 448), and she argues that Kant is the ultimate conclusion of something like Sartre's search for an existentialist ethics (Sartre 1947–48).

Korsgaard starts by arguing that human freedom involves searching for justified *reasons*. Human beings must choose, and choose in the light of what we take to be good reasons. The key question is whether we are "*justified* in according [special] importance to morality" (Korsgaard 1996b: 13). And the answer must *address* one who finds herself in a situation where morality requires significant sacrifices, where one genuinely wonders whether to accord it overwhelming weight. Korsgaard critiques classic ways of explaining morality's normative force, including accounts similar to intuitionism (Korsgaard 1996b: 33–34) and cheerful ethnocentrism (Korsgaard 1996b: 88–89). In all these cases, reflection does not proceed far enough. When one has an intuition of an action's rightness, one can ask why one should care so much about that intuition. When one finds oneself – as Rorty does – caring deeply about cruelty, one can ask whether this concern for cruelty is *justified*. And while this question might be dismissed in academic discussions, it cannot be dismissed by one facing real conflicts between moral obligations and other deeply held interests.

Like intuitionists and even Rorty, Korsgaard begins by arguing that what it takes for an action to be justified is that it survives careful consideration, what she calls "reflective endorsement" (Korsgaard 1996b: 49ff.). Unlike intuitionists, however, Korsgaard's existentialist Kantianism sees values as *constructed* by human beings; we impose and create values *autonomously*. But unlike Rortian ironic liberalism, Korsgaard emphasizes the constraints within which values are imposed, the first of which brings her closer to MacIntyre. For Korsgaard, reasons arise from "practical identities," "description[s] under which you value yourself and find your life to be worth living" (Korsgaard 1996b: 101). These identities can be, and typically are, rooted in contingent historical situations and local communities. I might value myself as a father, teacher, liberal, wine enthusiast, United States citizen, human rights advocate, philosopher, mountain-climber, or/and friend. All these identities give life meaning, but only some are so important that I would find life worthless without them. In various contexts, one or more identities provide reasons to act in particular ways. Often, they conflict.

The introduction of practical identities enriches Kant's picture of obligation to help meet concerns raised by existentialists, historicists, and communitarians. Where Kant emphasizes a dichotomy between inclinations and duty, Korsgaard recognizes that humans define themselves in terms of wide varieties of "obligations" that are neither moral nor mere inclination. This ennobles non-moral choices (like existentialists) and moves toward MacIntyre's emphasis on tradition and sociocultural context. For Korsgaard, cultural and historical contexts do not *determine* identities under which we value ourselves. (One's identity as a child, for instance, cannot be biologically determined, since one can always choose not to *value* oneself under the description of "child.") But most of our daily decisions involve reasons rooted in *socially, culturally, and historically constructed* identities. When I value myself as a "citizen of the United States," I embrace – perhaps in a mitigated way and/or with desire to change historic conceptions of citizenship – an identity constructed by others over hundreds of years. Korsgaard's "practical identities" flesh out her broadly Kantian anthropology to incorporate both existentialists' sense that non-moral choices are intensely important and historicist and traditionalist emphases on historico-cultural context.

For Korsgaard, however, reflection is not limited to consideration of reasons for action in the context of particular practical identities. One can and should also reflect on practical identities themselves.

> The activity of reflection has rules of its own, rules which ... are constitutive of it. And one of them ... is the rule that we should never stop reflecting until we have reached a satisfactory answer, one that admits of no further questioning. It is the rule, in Kant's language, that we should seek the unconditioned.
>
> (Korsgaard 1996b: 257–58)

Korsgaard's Kantian insistence on pushing reflection until we get to an "unconditioned" is widely contested. Existentialists despair of ever getting a "satisfactory answer," while historicists, ethnocentrists, and traditionalists like MacIntyre insist that any such answer is always historically conditioned. But for Korsgaard, no historically conditioned answer can satisfy, since one can always ask, "But why value this particular tradition?" And while one might feign cheerful ethnocentrism, such cheerfulness fails to address reflection's demands. Fortunately, however, against historicist and existentialist pessimisms, it *is* possible to reach an unconditioned, a practical identity about which it no longer makes sense to ask, "But why should I value that?" This identity is one's humanity. Korsgaard's concise argument for this claim is worth quoting in full.

> I have argued that human consciousness has a reflective structure that sets us normative problems. It is because of this that we require reasons for action, a conception of the right and the good. To act from such a conception is in turn to have a practical conception of your identity, a conception under which you value yourselves and find your life to be worth living and your actions to be worth undertaking. That conception is normative for you and in certain cases it can obligate you, for if you do not allow yourself to be governed by any conception of your identity then you will have no reason to act or live. So a human being is an animal who needs a practical conception of her own identity, a conception of who she is which is normative for her.
>
> But you are a human being and so if you believe my argument you can now see that that is *your* identity. You are an animal of the sort I have just described. And that is not merely a contingent conception of your identity, which you have constructed or chosen for yourself, or could conceivably reject. It is simply the truth. It is because we are such animals that our practical identities are normative for us, and, once you see this, you must take this more fundamental identity, being such an animal, to be normative as well. You must value your own humanity if you are to value anything at all.
>
> Why? Because now that you see that your need to have a normative conception of yourself comes from your human identity, you can query the importance of that identity. Your humanity requires you to conform to some of your practical identities, and you can question this requirement just as you do any other. Does it really matter whether we act as humanity requires, whether we find some ways of identifying ourselves and stand by them? But in this case, you have no option but to say yes. Since you are human you *must* take something to be normative, that is, some conception of practical identity must be normative for you. If you had no normative conception of your identity, you could have no reasons for action, and because your consciousness is reflective, you could then not act at all. Since

you cannot act without reasons and your humanity is the source of your reasons, you must value your humanity if you are to act at all.

It follows from this argument that human beings are valuable. Enlightenment morality is true.

(Korsgaard 1996b: 122–23)

On its own, this argument does not establish the legitimacy of Kant's formulation of the moral law because while it gives a reason to value *one's own* humanity, this need not imply valuing the humanity of others. So Korsgaard takes up a point implicit in Kant, but which she draws from Wittgenstein, the point that normative categories are necessarily social. There can be neither private language nor private values. Language makes it possible for others to intrude into our reflection and give us candidate reasons for action: "If I call out your name, I make you stop in your tracks ... Now you cannot proceed as you did before ... you can proceed, but not as you did before" (Korsgaard 1996b: 140). Korsgaard's point is that other people simply *are* capable of obligating us, of requiring us to take them seriously and endorse or reject their needs and sufferings as (candidate) reasons for action. When we honestly reflect about these reasons, we see that we ought to endorse them, at least sometimes, just as we endorse our own desires, at least sometimes: "[I]f you are a law ... insofar as you are just human, just *someone*, then the humanity of others is also a law ... In hearing your words as *words*, I acknowledge that you are *someone*," and thus entitled to some degree of respect (Korsgaard 1996b: 143).

There are further nuances and details of Korsgaard's argument, but already it should be clear how Korsgaard is genuinely Kantian, but modifying Kant in the light of nineteenth- and twentieth-century developments. Her argumentative strategy is at once thinner and more substantive than Kant's. It is thinner in that it starts from mere choice, rather than choice already aware of moral obligations. For Kant a being – though not a "human" being – could be an *agent* without any capacity for being a *moral* agent (see *Religion* 6: 26n), so Kant appeals to a "fact of reason" to show how human deliberators are aware of moral demands. Korsgaard, writing after Nietzsche questioned moral universality and after Sartre highlighted humans' universal plight as free beings, reverses Kant's argument to move *from* practical freedom *to* moral obligation. But Korsgaard's argument is also more substantive than Kant's in recognizing that human beings are not pulled merely between a pleasure principle of self-love and a moral principle of duty. Humans are governed by diverse arrays of practical identities. *Moral* obligation – commitment to our identity *as human beings* – is one sort of obligation. And while Korsgaard argues that this sort of obligation is pre-eminently important, she does so by highlighting its role as underpinning other, contingent practical identities. This move ascribes to choices of particular identities – of friends, lovers, occupations, hobbies, and so on – something of the dignity ascribed to them by existentialists. And it equally importantly gives crucial place in human formation to contingent identities we endorse but do not strictly "choose," identities that come to us from our cultural and historical contexts.

Korsgaard's neo-Kantianism is not without its problems. Some issues arise in the details of her argument, such as how one moves from the necessity to value one's humanity to according it special or privileged value. Other issues are more general. The overly symmetrical account of the relationship between freedom and natural necessity downplay important Kantian insights about the priority of the practical, and Korsgaard's reading of Kant precludes possible metaphysical implications of that priority. Korsgaard is also focused almost entirely on moral normativity and so contributes little to understanding epistemological, metaphysical, or aesthetic norms. Moreover, while her view *accommodates* significant historicist and naturalist insights, she does little to incorporate these into her account of the human being. Nonetheless, Korsgaard's philosophy overall provides for a naturalist, historically sensitive, existential Kantianism. Where Habermas combines these elements in a social way, Korsgaard does so at the level of individuals making choices in their own lives. Together they provide a pair of Kant*ian* answers that address human agents asking themselves Kant's philosophical but also deeply practical question, "What is the human being?"

Summary

The problem of normativity haunted naturalism, historicism, and existentialism, but Kant's approach to normativity is not the only philosophical account. Various forms of *intuitionism* – Husserl's phenomenology, Moore's common-sense intuitionism, or various more recent intuitionisms – attempt to solve normative problems by appealing to humans' intuitions. While some level of appeal to intuition may be necessary for any normative theory, most intuitionist approaches appeal too much to intuitions that are too specific and/or contingent to provide for a universally compelling theory. One might give up on any kind of universality and hold to a *cheerful ethnocentrism* that simply accepts one's own convictions as one's own but none-the-less-true for all that. If this ethnocentrism is the best we can do, then we should, with Kant and Rorty, be the most liberal and broad-minded ethnocentrists we can be. But there is reason to think that some norms can be defended in a way that is less locally specific than Rorty's ethnocentrism implies. At the very least, MacIntyre's notions of *narrative unity*, the *rationality of traditions*, and *virtues* provide resources for arbitrating amongst competing tradition-bound normative frameworks.

The neo-Kantian approaches of Habermas and Korsgaard go further, giving universal bases for normative claims. Habermas's discourse ethics grounds universal norms in the conditions for reasoned discourse, while Korsgaard defends a universal obligation to respect humanity in oneself and others by appealing to a human identity that unconditionally should be endorsed on reflection. Both Habermas and Korsgaard incorporate key insights from naturalism, historicism, and existentialism, and thereby present updated Kantian anthropologies that must be taken seriously today.

Further Reading

Normative theorizing dominates much contemporary philosophy. Husserl 1965 and Moore 1968 are the best places to start for exploring their philosophies. Murphy and Bishop 2009 includes important criticisms of intuitions and a vigorous defense (in a chapter by Sosa) of intuitions in philosophy. Rorty 1998 provides a clear and succinct formulation of Rorty's pragmatism, and Brandom (2000) includes several important commentaries and criticisms of Rorty's view (including one by Habermas). MacIntyre 1984 lays out his basic ethical framework, including his discussion of narrative unity and the virtues. MacIntyre 1988 discusses the rationality of traditions. Korsgaard 1996 is the most Kantian formulation of her overall moral theory and includes four essays by critics (and a response). Korsgaard 2009 is a more recent formulation of her account. Habermas's corpus is massive, but Habermas 1990 and 1993 provide good introductions to his thought. Finally, Herman and Wood offer two other important neo-Kantian approaches to moral philosophy.

Robert Brandom (ed.), *Rorty and his Critics* (Oxford: Blackwell, 2000)

Jürgen Habermas, *Moral Consciousness and Communicative Action* (trans. C. Lenhardt and S.W. Nicholsen, Cambridge, MA: MIT Press, 1990)

Jürgen Habermas, *Justification and Application* (trans. C.P. Cronin, Cambridge, MA: MIT Press, 1993)

Barbara Herman, *The Practice of Moral Judgment* (Cambridge, MA: Harvard University Press, 1993)

Barbara Herman, *Moral Literacy* (Cambridge, MA: Harvard University Press, 2007)

John Horton and Susan Mendus (eds.), *After MacIntyre: Critical Perspectives in the Work of Alasdair MacIntyre* (Notre Dame, IN: University of Notre Dame Press, 1995)

Edmund Husserl, *Phenomenology and the Crisis of Philosophy* (trans. Q. Lauer, New York: Harper and Row, 1965)

Edmund Husserl, *Ideas Pertaining to a Pure Phenomenology and to Phenomenological Philosophy* (trans. F. Kersten, The Hague: Martinus Nijhoff Publishers, 1983)

Christine Korsgaard, *The Sources of Normativity* (Cambridge: Cambridge University Press, 1996)

Christine Korsgaard, *Self-Constitution: Agency, Identity, and Integrity* (Oxford: Oxford University Press, 2009)

Alasdair MacIntyre, *After Virtue* (Notre Dame, IN: University of Notre Dame Press, 1984)

Alasdair MacIntyre, *Whose Justice, Which Rationality* (Notre Dame, IN: University of Notre Dame Press, 1988)

G.E. Moore, *Principia Ethica* (reprint, Buffalo: Prometheus Books, 1968)

Dominic Murphy and Michael Bishop (eds.), *Stich and His Critics* (Hoboken, NJ: Wiley-Blackwell, 2009)

Richard Rorty, *Contingency, Irony, Solidarity* (Cambridge: Cambridge University Press, 1998)

Allen Wood, *Kantian Ethics* (Cambridge: Cambridge University Press, 2007)

Conclusion

What is the human being? For Kant, human beings are free but finite thinkers, feelers, and choosers, capable of being investigated transcendentally, empirically, and pragmatically. Transcendental anthropology outlines the norms that govern cognition, (aesthetic) feeling, and volition and describes the conditions of possibility for these norms, most notably transcendental freedom for norms of volition and a "Copernican turn" whereby the world itself, rather than something that stands apart from human thinking, necessarily conforms to our structures of cognition. Empirical anthropology describes what can be known about human beings by studying them scientifically, and it depicts human beings as organisms with complex sets of predispositions, organized in terms of higher and lower faculties of cognition (including sensibility, imagination, and reason), feeling (of pleasure and displeasure), and desire (including instincts, inclinations, and character). In describing how human beings in fact think, feel, and act, Kant's empirical psychology enriches our understanding of what gives rise to particular beliefs, feelings, and volitions. Among other things, this shows just how complex human happiness is, requiring the satisfaction of various instincts, inclinations, and principled commitments that are susceptible in various degrees of cultivation and control. And Kant's empirical anthropology rightly highlights that there are important differences between human beings, even if he gets wrong precisely what those differences are and how they should be explained. But while distinguishing them in their foundations and methodology, Kant does not leave his transcendental and empirical anthropologies separate. Once he defends the norms governing human beings and describes the way we actually are, he can apply these insights together. The first result of this is the unfortunate recognition that human beings are radically evil. We can see empirically that we act in certain ways, and we can judge normatively that these actions are ascribable to freely chosen evil. But further results of the joint application of transcendental and empirical anthropologies are more positive, first in the recognition that human history is a history of progress, but more importantly in the development of various empirically informed techniques for improving the functioning of all human capacities toward the ends of greater autonomy, happiness, and virtue. This "pragmatic" anthropology marks the culmination of Kant's account of human being and satisfies his desire to turn his "researcher" inclinations to defend human dignity and improve human lives.

Developments in philosophy and human sciences over the past 200 years have called into question many of the details of Kant's treatment of the human being. His despair about explaining the origins of human predispositions or the neurological bases of human mental states has largely been shown to be unjustified. The specifics of his empirical psychology require considerable filling in and some important revisions. His conception of the fixed, transcendental structures of human thought and action may be less fixed and less universal than he thought. And even if many of the structures Kant emphasized are genuinely universal, his general conception of human faculties as governing how we see the world and our options in it should be supplemented with some notion of a "historical a priori" that reflects the important role of community and tradition in shaping the worlds of human beings in different contexts. Kant's emphasis on norm-governed freedom can and should be supplemented by a more forceful emphasis on authenticity, one that expands the range of life-shaping, free choices beyond those specifically governed by antecedent norms to include those that are part of shaping the unique individual that each of us is.

All of these changes are possible without a fundamental revision of Kant's emphasis on human beings as free and finite thinkers, feelers, and choosers. And many details of Kant's account, as we have seen throughout this book, provide important resources for enriching our understanding of ourselves even in the context of 200 years of further reflection. His specific claims about the importance of character, the distinctions between mind and body, or the role of unsocial sociability in human history, remain plausible even if not unchallenged claims that should be taken seriously today. But the most important Kantian insight for today is the importance of human beings as free beings governed by norms to which they *ought* to adhere. Kant unashamedly, and rightly, puts human autonomy at the center of his transcendental anthropology. His philosophy as a whole shows how even the most sophisticated, causally governed empirical anthropology does not preclude the recognition that freedom must be prioritized over any causal account of human actions. His transcendental anthropology shows that human cognition, feeling, and volition is – when properly studied from within – free. But this same transcendental anthropology emphasizes that this freedom is a norm-governed one. Naturalism, historicism, existentialism, and even many normative approaches today fail to provide any adequate account of human being from within because they fail to provide for the conditions of possibility of living a life governed by the norms that make us human.

There is, of course, much more to be said in response to Kant's question. This book has focused on cognitive and volitional aspects of the human being, often neglecting feeling in general and aesthetic feeling in particular, despite the importance of feeling for Kant's conception of the human being[1] and within contemporary understandings of the human being, where aesthetics remains a central subfield within philosophy and emotions an increasingly important one.[2] Kant's emphasis on human evil and human progress also deserves reassessment in the light of the past two centuries, which have seen genocides, world wars, and terrorism but also the partial realization of Kant's dreams for a League of Nations and widening cosmopolitan ethical attitudes. This book has also largely ignored any role for theological conceptions of human beings, despite the role of God, immortality, and grace in Kant's anthropology and the enduring importance of such conceptions for many people in the world. And there are a host of practical issues about defining the human being, including the ethics of cloning and abortion, the status of stem cells and cyborgs, the nature of psychopaths and the severely disabled, and the extent to which certain animals (cetaceans, elephants, other primates) might warrant being considered "human" in an ethical sense. This book should help address these issues, but they have not been discussed explicitly, and many may raise important challenges for various conceptions of "the human being" outlined here. What I have done in this book, however, is to provide a framework for understanding the human being in terms of Kant's philosophy and the most important developments in thinking about this issue over the past 200 years. My hope, like Kant's, is that this framework can support continued reflection on what remains "the greatest concern of the human being," that is, "to know how properly to fulfill his station in creation, and to rightly understand what one must be in order to be a human being" (20: 41).

Notes

Introduction

1 Throughout this quotation and the following one, I've changed "man" and "men" to "the human being" or "human beings."

2 Excepting the *Critique of Pure Reason*, references to Kant's works are cited by volume: page number of *Kant's Gesammelte Schriften*. 1900–. Ed. The Royal Prussian (later German) Academy of Sciences. Berlin: Georg Reimer (later Walter de Gruyter). References to *The Critique of Pure Reason* are made to the pagination in the first (A) and second (B) German editions of that work. Throughout, translations are taken from *The Cambridge Edition of the Works of Immanuel Kant*, Ed. Paul Guyer and Allen Wood, Cambridge University Press, 1992–.

1 Kant's Transcendental Anthropology

1 The first four columns are taken directly from Kant's own work, though I have edited them and modified the terminology a bit. I have added the final two columns to show the connection with Kant's writings and his central questions. As with most of Kant's tidy charts, this one hides many complications (for instance, Kant typically identifies his question "What may I hope?" with his writings on religion and not directly with the *Critique of Judgment*), but it is helpful for a general overview.

2 For discussion, see Grier forthcoming, Allison 1983, Ameriks 1982a and 2003, Guyer 1987, Kitcher 1993, and Longuenesse 1997.

3 Another important discussion is Kant's critique of rational psychology in his *Paralogisms of Pure Reason*. For discussion of these Paralogisms and Kant's philosophy of mind more generally, see Ameriks 1982a, Brook 1994, and Kitcher 1993.

4 For discussion of this shift, see Ameriks 2003: 161–92.

5 For a defense of the claim that they are not significantly related, see MacFarland 1974. For a detailed reading of the *Critique of Judgment* as a coherent whole, see Zuckert 2007.

6 Ultimately, answering this question depends upon Kant's philosophy of religion and history as well (see 11: 429), but the *Critique of Judgment* provides an important starting point.

7 Cf. Allison 2001, Ginsborg 1997, Guyer 1979, and Zuckert 2007.

2 Kant's Empirical Anthropology

1 Even with intoxicants, Kant's reference to the propensity of "savages" is more likely an assertion of the *universality* of this propensity than a limitation of it to a particular group. Kant's view seems best captured by his claim in a lecture on anthropology that "Human beings across the whole world have a propensity to drink [alcohol]" (25: 1112).

2 This passage is typically, and rightly, used to analyze the practical perspective from which we are transcendentally free vis-à-vis all of our actions. Kant's specific language in this passage confirms that he primarily has this transcendentally free power of choice in mind, rather than the

specifically empirical faculty of choice. But the claim about acting on the basis of maxims here has an empirical correlate, as this section will show.

3 See Allison 1990, Beck 1960, Grenberg 2005, McCarty 1993 and 1994, and Reath 1989.

3 Kant on Human Evil and Human History

1 For discussion of more specifically religious aspects of Kant's justification of moral hope, see Quinn 1984 and 1990, Mariña 1997, Michaelson 1990, Frierson 2003, 2007b, and 2010b.

2 For further discussion of the possibility of moral progress in history, see Anderson-Gold 2001, Cohen 2009, Frierson 2003, Kleingeld 1995 and 1999, Louden 2000, Wood 1999, Yovel 1980.

4 Kant on Human Diversity

1 See Frierson 2009a and 2009b, Shell 1996: 268–305.

2 In this context, Kant's note at 15: 758–65 on "mistakes" or "failings" (*Fehler*) associated with different temperaments is an excellent example of working through the challenges that those with different temperaments will particularly have to face in living a good and happy life. My reading of Kant here differs importantly from that recently offered by Mark Larrimore. I disagree with Larrimore's claims that a phlegmatic temperament "is a duty" (Larrimore 2001: 284) and that phlegma should be identified with apathy. Phlegma is a temperament that is *like* apathy and that makes it particularly easy to develop true moral character (which includes apathy), but I take Kant's repeated claim that phlegma can do what philosophy or wisdom does *without real philosophy or wisdom* to be an important *warning* to the phlegmatic. Whereas a sanguine person who lives life according to principles can and should regard that as a moral accomplishment, the phlegmatic one should not.

3 Throughout his discussion of sex differences, Kant assumes heterosexuality and conflates what we would now call sex differences and gender differences.

4 For specific treatments of Kant's accounts of marriage and women's citizenship, see Denis 2007, Mendus 1992, and Shell 1996.

5 I also do not discuss Kant's important comments about Jews (see especially 6: 125ff.); some, but not all, of the present discussion is relevant to assessing these comments. While his views have been seen as important precursors of later German anti-Semitism, they would take the present discussion too far afield because Kant sees the Jews primarily through a cultural and religious rather than a racial lens.

6 Kant taught a course in Physical Geography for decades (more than any other single course), and, like his lectures on anthropology, student transcripts of these lectures were circulated during Kant's days. Until recently, the main form in which these lectures have been available to Kant scholars has been in an edition put together by Kant's student Friedrich Theodor Rink, likely based on notes from two different courses and included in volume 9 of Kant's works. Volume 26 of Kant's works (published partly in 2009 and partly forthcoming) will include many more versions of student notes from Kant's Physical Geography course.

7 The remarks at 25: 843, while not wholly reliable because based on lecture notes, are perhaps the most disturbing. There Kant not only sets up an implicit hierarchy of races, but adds that "Negros are not capable of any further civilization ... The Indians and Chinese seem to be static in perfection, for their history books show that they do not know more now than they have long known" (25: 843). For both Africans and Asians, Kant alludes to character traits that are not merely physical (civilization and learning) and suggests not only that these races are inferior to whites, but also that they cannot ever improve.

8 In eighteenth-century biology, the technical term "degenerate" lacked many of the negative connotations we associate with it today.

9 Kant's unpublished writings are less clear. In notes written during the 1780s, Kant seems to accept the notion that "Americans and negroes cannot govern themselves. Thus [they] are good only as slaves" (15: 878). But Kant's notes for his *Perpetual Peace* include condemnations of slavery – especially the enslavements of non-whites by whites – that are even more impassioned and detailed than those in his published writings (see Kleingeld 2007: 15).

5 Kant's Pragmatic Anthropology

1 For a detailed defense, see Frierson 2003. Consistent with his empirical anthropology, Kant's pragmatic anthropology treats human beings as "free" in the sense that they have faculties of desire capable of acting for the sake of ends and a *higher* faculty of desire capable of acting from principles (cf. Cohen 2009). But what makes the anthropology *pragmatic* is not the way humans are treated teleologically–biologically rather than mechanically, but the fact that Kant emphasizes those aspects of human nature that free human beings can *use*.

6 Hegel, Marx, Darwin, Nietzsche, and Freud

1 For discussion of these developments, see Ameriks 2000, Beiser 1993 and 2002, Bowie 1993 and 2003, diGiovanni and Harris 1985, Sassen 2000, and Snow 1996.
2 For a similar critique of both Kant and Hegel, see Marx's letter to the *New-York Daily Tribune*, February 17–18, 1853 (available at http://www.marxists.org/archive/marx/works/1853/02/18.htm). There Marx explains that "From the point of view of abstract right, there is only one theory of punishment which recognizes human dignity in the abstract, and that is the theory of Kant, especially in the more rigid formula given to it by Hegel," but goes on to describe this merely *abstract* conception of human dignity as a "specious ... transcendental sanction [for] the rules of existing society," a "delusion [that] substitute[s] for the individual with his real motives, with multifarious social circumstances pressing upon him, the abstraction of 'free-will'."
3 See the aptly titled *Marx after Marxism* (Rockmore 2002).
4 See the subtitle to *Beyond Good and Evil: Prelude to a Philosophy of the Future*.
5 This account is different from Freud's early theory in two important respects. In his early work, Freud had not yet distinguished between the ego and the super-ego, and he had identified the ego with consciousness and what he would later term the id with unconscious processes. For his most detailed discussions of this shift, see Freud 1923/1960 and Freud 1933/1964 (chapter 31).

7 Scientific Naturalism

1 Wegner 2003 (pp. 52f.) expands on Libet's neuroscientific findings to argue for "the illusion of conscious will." For compelling (but not particularly Kantian) criticisms of Libet (and Wegner), see Mele 2006: 30–38 and Dennett 2003: 227–58. In this chapter, I focus on distinctively Kantian critiques of the widespread overuse of Libet's research to support overblown philosophical conclusions.
2 Meme theory is not without its critics within the philosophy of science. See, for example, Kitcher 1985, Kronfelder 2011. For a recent, rigorous, and accessible treatment of cultural selection processes, see Richerson and Boyd 2005. And for a collection of papers on various sides of the issue, see Aunger 2000.
3 For an insightful, early version of this objection (directed against E.O. Wilson), see Kitcher 1985: 417–34.
4 Most people reason that since the false positive is 5 percent, the 95 percent of positive tests must be true. The correct answer is given by reasoning as follows: For every 1000 people, 50 (5 percent) will falsely test positive and one will truly test positive. Thus there will be 51 people who test positive, one of whom actually has the disease. That is, the chance that the person actually has the disease is slightly less than 2 percent.
5 Recently, Joshua Green has also used contemporary neuroscience to argue that deontological moral theories (like Kant's) mistake post hoc justifications of emotional reactions for moral reasoning (see Green 2007). For general critiques of Green, see Berker 2009 and Klein 2011. For a Kantian response, see Frierson (in process).
6 It is particularly striking that Appiah, who is otherwise quite aware of problems with these inferences from situationist psychology (see Appiah 2008: 49), nonetheless endorses the fallacious

inference from the claim that situation often affects behavior to the claim that "experimental psychology shows that people *cannot* have ... character traits" (Appiah 2008: 47, emphasis added, see also Appiah 2008:69–71) and thus endorses Harman's proposal to "put less emphasis on moral education and on character building and more emphasis on trying to arrange social institutions so that human beings are not placed in situations in which they will act badly" (Harman quoted in Appiah 2008: 71).

7 We can see this if we think about how we might evaluate epistemic failure. If one weighs all the evidence and makes a judgment in accordance with one's best estimate of where the evidence falls, one's epistemic merit (or demerit) will be genuinely one's own. But if one simply applies a Statistical Prediction Rule, and that rule turns out to be misguided (even *systematically* misguided), it is not really *my* epistemic mistake. It is the mistake of the rule.

8 Historicism and Human Diversity

1 Foucault scholars often distinguish between a period within which archeology is Foucault's primary method of history (beginning with *History of Madness* and ending with *The Order of Things* and *The Archeology of Knowledge*) and a period within which genealogy dominates his approach (in *Discipline and Punish* and *The History of Sexuality*). But although Foucault does not explicitly articulate genealogy as governing his approach until "Nietzsche, Genealogy, History" (1971) elements of both methods are evident through his work. The shift between early and later works is primarily one of emphasis.

2 Foucault says "phenomenological" here to target Husserl and Heidegger, but he makes similar points about Kantian "transcendental" subjects (Foucault 1969/1982: 128).

3 Geertz adds that this "series of tags" is one that "I should not like to have to defend" and, further, that "we must ... descend in detail, past the misleading tags, past the metaphysical types, past the empty similarities to grasp firmly the essential character of not only the various cultures but the various sorts of individuals within each culture, if we wish to encounter humanity face to face" (Geertz 1973: 53).

4 Kant's ethics, in fact, is often referred to as "deontological," from the *Greek* term "*dei*," which refers to that which is binding or what it behooves one to do, as in the Iliad's "ti de *dei* polemizemenai ... Argeious" ("why do the Argives *have to* fight?") (II.9.337).

5 A full discussion of this debate would go far beyond the scope of this book. For a clear overview with further references, see Borofsky and Kane 1997.

6 Foucault seems to recognize that history provides no guide here: "The historian's essential role ... [is to provide] a topological and geological survey of the battlefield ... But as for saying, 'Here is what you must do!,' certainly not" (Foucault 1980: 62).

9 Existentialism

1 At the time of the review, Foucault had not yet articulated his "genealogical" method, which arguably comes closer – though not close enough – to what Sartre sought.

2 In order to think about human being without slipping into traditional–objective forms of thought, Heidegger employs new vocabularies of philosophical analysis, including not only Da-sein rather than "human being" but also a distinction between "ontical" and "ontological" analysis and distinctions between characteristics of Dasein (called "existentials") and "categories" of objects, and then whole sets of existential categories such as "being-in-space" or "being-toward-death."

3 The from-within emphasis in existentialism has its most immediate roots in early twentieth-century "phenomenology," which will be discussed in the next chapter. But this emphasis ultimately traces to Kant and post-Kantian philosophers such as J.G. Fichte (who also radicalized these Kantian themes), along with post-Idealist thinkers like Kierkegaard, Nietzsche, and Dostoveysky.

4 The emphasis in this chapter is on the existentialisms of the early Heidegger, early Sartre, and Levinas. Existentialism is a much richer and more diverse approach than I can do justice to in this

short chapter. A fuller discussion would include attention to Jaspers, Camus, Merleau-Ponty, the later (Marxist) Sartre, Derrida, Unamono, and many others, not to mention historical antecedents, most notably Kierkegaard and Nietzsche.

5 See Nagel 1986, but cf. Hanna 2006.

6 Heidegger also sees this sort of knowing as inauthentic, a more general "*leveling down* of all possibilities of being" that "takes the responsibility of Da-sein away from it" (Heidegger 1953: 127). The importance of authenticity will be clearer later in this chapter.

7 Heidegger finds oblique confessions of the priority of this primordial and holistic "as" in Kant's *Critique*, particularly Kant's allusion to the imagination as a "common root" of concepts and intuitions (Heidegger 1997: 103).

8 Despite his metaphysical critique that Kant's transcendental freedom of the will is a "rape and perversion of logic" (Nietzsche 1966: 28), Nietzsche's proposal to go "beyond good and evil" (Nietzsche 1966) towards "your true nature [that] lies ... immeasurably high above you" (Nietzsche 1997:129) fits well with Sartre's and Heidegger's existentialism. See too Kierkegaard's "teleological suspension of the ethical" in the name of an inarticulable and unjustifiable "absolute duty" (Kierkegaard 2006).

9 This emphasis on choice can easily be misread (see e.g. Merleau-Ponty 1945) if one forgets that Sartre rejects distinctions between cognition, feeling, and volition. The free "choice" Sartre references here is elsewhere called a "passion" (Sartre 1956: 797), and Sartre insists that "the will, far from being the unique or at least the privileged manifestation of freedom, actually ... must presuppose the foundation of an original freedom" (Sartre 1956: 571).

10 For Heidegger, but not for Sartre, the revelation of possibilities as one's ownmost is pre-eminently accessible through what he calls "being-toward-death," and thus "being-toward-death," for Heidegger, "is essentially Angst" (Heidegger 1953: 266, cf. Sartre 1956: 683).

11 Sartre gives, as an example, a "homosexual" (who he also refers to as a "paederast," Sartre 1956: 107–8) but we could envision any character who is ashamed of past behavior or of his or her desires, preferences, etc. In the following quotation, I've modified the gender of the character and the relevant characteristic (from pederasty to shyness).

12 Or, better, this is impossible while reading (and reflecting on) Sartre and Heidegger. As Sartre, Heidegger, and especially Kierkegaard point out, it is remarkably easy, even immediately after being struck with the angst of one's freedom, to throw oneself back into the distractions of everyday life.

13 While I have focused on examples of actually present others, both Heidegger and Sartre emphasize that being-with or being-for-another "existentially determines Da-sein even when another is not factically present" (Heidegger 1953: 120, cf. Sartre 1956: 370, 373).

14 Levinas borrows the concept "appresentation" (Levinas 1997:166) from Husserl, who used it to describe how even when only a single facet of an object is directly presented, the whole is perceived because its not-directly-seen aspects are "appresented."

15 As his reference to "knowing" makes clear, for Levinas even knowing is merely an articulated response to an encounter with the face of an Other.

16 For a contemporary, broadly Kantian working out of this "second person standpoint," see Darwall 2006.

17 For an example of this sort of exaggerated moral enthusiasm, consider this passage from Derrida's *Gift of Death*:

As soon as I enter into a relation with the other ..., I know that I can respond only by sacrificing ethics, that is, by sacrificing whatever obliges me to also respond, in the same way, in the same instant, to all the others ... By preferring my work, simply by giving it my time and attention, by preferring my activity as a citizen or as a professorial and professional philosopher, writing and speaking here in a public language ..., I am perhaps fulfilling my duty. But I am sacrificing and betraying at every moment all my other obligations: my obligations to other others whom I know or don't know, the billions of my fellows (without mentioning the animals ...), my fellows who are dying of starvation or sickness. I betray my fidelity or my obligations to other citizens, to whose who don't speak my language and to whom I neither speak nor respond.

(Derrida 1996: 68–69)

10 Normativity

1 Though see Husserl 1983: 212, where Husserl admits the possibility of "errors" in phenomenology, but then proposes "weeding out errors by measuring them against intuition."
2 By bracketing the natural attitude, one considers possibilities not in terms of possible realization *in the objective world* but in terms of the essence of color as such. Even if, scientifically speaking, color is impossible without "energy," one can eidetically distinguish between colors and various interpretations of energy (as possible work, possible heat, etc.) by imaginatively considering a possible experience of color independent of any energy-effects.
3 For discussion of noesis and noema, see Husserl 1983: 205ff.
4 Moore is also very far from *Husserlian* intuitionism because he assumes the natural attitude and uses common sense to make substantive existential claims (not mere claims about essences and certainly not claims limited to a phenomenology of consciousness).
5 Moore elsewhere argues that "intuitionism is mistaken" (Moore 1913: 148), but he has in mind intuitionism about particular duties rather than about the good.
6 See Frazier 1998, Jones 2005, Sinnott-Armstrong 1992, Sturgeon 2002.
7 For the classic discussion of reflective equilibrium, see Rawls 1971: 20. For recent discussions of coherentism, Brink 1989, Sayre-McCord 1996, and Timmons 1999.
8 For other cheerfully ethnocentric philosophical approaches, see Blackburn 1998 and Timmons 1999.
9 The converse also applies. Thus Carol Gilligan's criticism of Kohlberg's developmental model (e.g. Gilligan 1982) would challenge the fruitfulness of Kohlberg's empirical research program *and* its broadly Kantian underpinnings, a point not missed by feminist philosophers who use Gilligan to argue against Kant's moral theory (e.g. Noddings 1984).

Conclusion

1 Recall Kant's claim that "beauty is valid only for human beings ...; the good is valid for every rational being in general" (5: 210).
2 One philosopher recently claimed, "No aspect of our mental life is more important to the quality and meaning of our existence than emotions" (deSousa 2010: 1).

Bibliography

Excepting the *Critique of Pure Reason*, references to Kant's works are cited by volume: page number of *Kant's Gesammelte Schriften*, 1900–, Ed. The Royal Prussian (later German) Academy of Sciences. Berlin: Georg Reimer (later Walter de Gruyter). References to *The Critique of Pure Reason* are made to the pagination in the first (A) and second (B) German editions of that work. Throughout, translations are taken from *The Cambridge Edition of the Works of Immanuel Kant*, Ed. Paul Guyer and Allen Wood, Cambridge University Press, 1992–.

Abu-Lughod, L. (1999) "The Interpretations of Culture(s) after Television" in Sherry Ortner (ed.) *The Fate of Culture: Geertz and Beyond*, Berkeley, CA: University of California Press.

Allison, H. (1983) *Kant's Transcendental Idealism: An Interpretation and Defense*, New Haven, CT: Yale University Press.

——(1990) *Kant's Theory of Freedom*, Cambridge: Cambridge University Press.

——(2001) "Ethics, Evil, and Anthropology in Kant: Remarks on Allen Wood's *Kant's Ethical Thought*," *Ethics* 111: 594–613.

Ameriks, K. (1982a, 2nd edn. 2000) *Kant's Theory of Mind*, Oxford: Oxford University Press.

——(1982b), "Recent Work on Kant's Theoretical Philosophy," *American Philosophical Quarterly* 19: 1–24.

——(1982c) "How to Save Kant's Deduction of Taste," *Journal of Value Inquiry*, 16: 295–302 (reprinted in Ameriks 2003: 285–307).

——(2000) *Kant and the Fate of Autonomy: Problems in the Appropriation of the Critical Philosophy*, Cambridge: Cambridge University Press.

——(2003) *Interpreting Kant's Critiques*, Oxford: Oxford University Press.

Anderson-Gold, S. (2001) *Unnecessary Evil*, Albany, NY: SUNY Press.

Appiah, K. (2008) *Experiments in Ethics*, Cambridge, MA: Harvard University Press.

——(2009) "Experimental Moral Psychology," *Daedelus* 138: 92–102.

Arneil, B. (2007) "Citizenship Studies," *Global Citizenship and Empire*, 11: 301–28.

Augustine (1961) *Confessions* (trans. R. S. Pine-Coffin), New York: Penguin Classics.

Aunger, R. (ed.) (2000) *Darwinizing Culture: The Status of Memetics as a Science*, Oxford: Oxford University Press.

Beck, L.W. (1960) *A Commentary on Kant's* Critique of Practical Reason, Chicago: University of Chicago Press.

Beiser, F. (1993) *The Fate of Reason: German Philosophy from Kant to Fichte*, Cambridge, MA: Harvard University Press.

——(2002) *German Idealism: The Struggle Against Subjectivism 1781–1801*, Boston: Harvard University Press.

Bem, D.J. (1967) "Self-perception: An Alternative Interpretation of Cognitive Dissonance Phenomena," *Psychological Review* 74: 183–200.

Benedict, R. (1934/2005) *Patterns of Culture*, New York: Mariner Books.

——(1934) "Anthropology and the Abnormal," *Journal of General Psychology* 10: 59–82.

Berker, Selim (2009) "The Normative Insignificance of Neuroscience," *Philosophy and Public Affairs* 37: 293–329.

Bernasconi, R. (2001) "Who Invented the Concept of Race?" in R. Bernasconi (ed.) *Race*, Oxford: Blackwell, pp. 11–36.

——(2002) "Kant as an Unfamiliar Source of Racism" in J. Ward and T. Lott (eds.) *Philosophers on Race: Critical Essays*, Oxford: Blackwell.

Bishop, M. and Trout, J.D. (2005) *Epistemology and the Psychology of Human Judgment*, Oxford: Oxford University Press.

Blackburn, S. (1998) *Ruling Passions*, Oxford: Oxford University Press.

Block, N. (1980) "What is Functionalism?" in Ned Block (ed.) *Readings in Philosophy of Psychology* vol 1., Cambridge, MA: Harvard University Press, pp. 171–84.

Bok, S. (2002) *Common Values*, Colombia, MO: University of Missouri Press.

Borofsky, R. and Kane, H. (1997) "Cook, Lono, Obeyesekere, and Sahlins" (with replies by Obeyesekere and Sahlins), *Current Anthropology*, 38: 255–82.

Botterill, G. and Carruthers, P. (1999) *The Philosophy of Psychology*, Cambridge: Cambridge University Press.

Bowie, A. (1993) *Schelling and Modern European Philosophy: An Introduction*, Abingdon: Routledge.

——(2003) *Introduction to German Philosophy: From Kant to Habermas*, Cambridge: Polity Press.

Boxill, B. and Hill Jr., T. (2001) "Kant and Race" in B. Boxill (ed.) *Race and Racism*, Oxford: Oxford University Press, pp. 448–71.

Brandom, R. (ed.) (2000) *Rorty and His Critics*, Oxford: Blackwell.

Brink, D. (1989) *Moral Realism and the Foundations of Ethics*, Cambridge: Cambridge University Press.

Brook, A. (1994) *Kant and the Mind*, Cambridge: Cambridge University Press.

——(2004) "Kant, Cognitive Science, and Contemporary Neo-Kantianism," *Journal of Consciousness Studies* 11: 1–25.

Casscells, W., Schoenberger, A., and Grayboys, T. (1978) "Interpretation by Physicians of Clinical Laboratory Results," *New England Journal of Medicine* 299: 999–1001.

Chisholm, R. (1957) *Perceiving: A Philosophical Study*, Ithaca, NY: Cornell University Press.

Churchland, P. (1984) *Matter and Consciousness*, Cambridge, MA: MIT Press.

Cohen, A. (2008) "The Ultimate Kantian Experience: Kant on Dinner Parties," *History of Philosophy Quarterly* 25: 315–36.

——(2009) *Kant and the Human Sciences: Biology, Anthropology, and History*, London: Palgrave Macmillan.

Cooper, D. (1990) *Existentialism: A Reconstruction*, Hoboken, NJ: Wiley-Blackwell.

Damasio, A. (1994) *Descartes' Error: Emotion, Reason, and the Human Brain*, New York: Penguin.

Darwall, S. (2006) *The Second-Person Standpoint: Morality, Respect, and Accountability*, Cambridge, MA: Harvard University Press.

Darwin, C. (1859/1982) *The Origin of Species* (ed. J. W. Burrow) New York: Penguin Classics.

——(1871/1902) *The Descent of Man*, New York: American Home Library Company. (Available on googlebooks.)

——(1981) *The Descent of Man, and Selection in Relation to Sex* (ed. J.T. Bonner and R. May), Princeton, NJ: Princeton University Press.

——(1987) *Charles Darwin's Notebooks* (ed. P. Barrett, P. Gautrey, S. Herbert, D. Kohn, and S. Smith), Ithaca, NY: Cornell University Press.

Dawkins, R. (1976) *The Selfish Gene*, Oxford: Oxford University Press.

de Beauvoir, S. (1987) *Force of Circumstance*, New York: Penguin.

Dean, R. (2006) *The Value of Humanity in Kant's Moral Theory*, Oxford: Oxford University Press.

Denis, L. (2007) "From Friendship to Marriage: Revising Kant," *Philosophy and Phenomenological Research* 63: 1–28.

Dennett, D. (1984) *Elbow Room: The Varieties of Free Will Worth Wanting*, Cambridge, MA: MIT Press.

——(1991) *Consciousness Explained*, New York: Back Bay Books.

——(1995) *Darwin's Dangerous Idea*, New York: Simon and Schuster.

——(2003) *Freedom Evolves*, New York: Penguin.

Derrida, J. (1996) *The Gift of Death* (trans. D. Wills), Chicago: University of Chicago Press.

deSousa, R. (2010) "Emotion," Stanford Encyclopedia of Philosophy, http:// plato.stanford.edu/entries/emotion/ (accessed January 2012).

diGiovanni, G. and Harris, H.S. (eds.) (1985) *Between Kant and Hegel: Texts in the Development of Post-Kantian Idealism*, Indianapolis: Hackett.

Doris, J. (2002) *Lack of Character: Personality and Moral Behavior*, Cambridge: Cambridge University Press.

Dreyfus, H. and Rabinow, P. (1982) *Michel Foucault: Beyond Structuralism and Hermeneutics*, Chicago: University of Chicago Press.

Eze, E. (1994) "The Colour of Reason: The Idea of 'Race' in Kant's Anthropology" in K.M. Faull (ed.) *Anthropology and the German Enlightenment*, Lewisburg, PA: Bucknell University Press.

Fichte, J.G. (1993) *Fichte: Early Philosophical Writings* (ed. D. Breazeale), Ithaca, NY: Cornell University Press.

——(1994) *Introductions to the Wissenschaftslehre* (ed. D. Breazeale), Indianapolis: Hackett.

Fodor, J. (1968) "The Appeal to Tacit Knowledge in Psychological Explanation," *Journal of Philosophy* 65: 627–40.

——(1983) *Modularity of Mind: An Essay on Faculty Psychology*, Cambridge, MA: MIT Press.

Foucault, M. (1961/2006) *A History of Madness* (ed. J. Khalfa, trans. J. Murphy), London: Routledge.

——(1969/1982) *The Archeology of Knowledge* (trans. A.M. Sheridan Smith), New York: Vintage.

——(1973) *The Order of Things*, New York: Vintage.

——(1977) *Discipline and Punish* (trans. A.M. Sheridan Smith), New York: Pantheon.

——(1980) *Power/Knowledge: Selected Interviews and Writings* (ed. C. Gordon), New York: Pantheon Books.

——(1982) "The Subject and Power" in H. Dreyfus and P. Rabinow (eds.) *Michel Foucault: Beyond Structuralism and Hermeneutics*, Chicago: University of Chicago Press.

——(1983) "On the Genealogy of Ethics: An Overview of a Work in Progress" in H. Dreyfus and P. Rabinow (eds.) *Michel Foucault: Beyond Structuralism and Hermeneutics* (2nd edn.), Chicago: University of Chicago Press.

——(1984) *The Foucault Reader* (ed. P. Rabinow), New York: Vintage.

——(1988) *Madness and Civilization* (trans. R. Howard), New York: Vintage.

——(1990) *The History of Sexuality, vol. 1* (trans. R. Hurley), New York: Vintage.

——(1994) *The Birth of the Clinic* (trans. A.M. Sheridan Smith), New York: Vintage.

——(2002) *The Archaeology of Knowledge* (trans. A. Sheridan), London: Routledge.

——(2008) *Introduction to Kant's Anthropology* (trans. R. Nigro and K. Briggs), Los Angeles: Semiotext(e).

Frankfurt, H. (1988) *The Importance of What We Care About*, Cambridge: Cambridge University Press.

Frazier, R.L. (1998) "Intuitionism in Ethics" in E. Craig (ed.) *The Routledge Encyclopedia of Philosophy*, London: Routledge.

Freud, S. (1900/1965) *On the Interpretation of Dreams* (trans. James Strachey), New York: Avon Books.

——(1901/1960) *The Psychopathology of Everyday Life*, New York: W.W. Norton.

——(1920/1963) *Introductory Lectures on Psychoanalysis* (trans. James Strachey), New York: W.W. Norton.

——(1920/1961) *Beyond the Pleasure Principle* (trans. James Strachey), New York: W.W. Norton.

——(1923/1960) *The Ego and the Id*, (trans. James Strachey), New York: W.W. Norton.

——(1927/1961) *The Future of an Illusion* (trans. James Strachey), New York: W. W. Norton.

——(1933/1964) *New Introductory Lectures on Psychoanalysis* (trans. James Strachey), New York: W.W. Norton.

Friedman, M. (2001) *Dynamics of Reason*, Stanford, CA: CLSI Publications.

Frierson, P. (2003) *Freedom and Anthropology in Kant's Moral Philosophy*, Cambridge: Cambridge University Press.

——(2005) "The Moral Importance of Politeness in Kant's Anthropology," *Kantian Review* 9: 105–27.

——(2006) "Character and Evil in Kant's Anthropology," *Journal of the History of Philosophy* 44: 623–44.

——(2007a) "Review of Richard Dean, *The Value of Humanity in Kant's Moral Theory*," *Notre Dame Philosophical Reviews*, http://ndpr.nd.edu/review.cfm?id=9364.

——(2007b) "Providence and Divine Mercy in Kant's Ethical Cosmopolitanism," *Faith and Philosophy* 24: 143–63.

——(2008) "Empirical Psychology, Common Sense, and Kant's Empirical Markers for Moral Responsibility," *Studies in the History and Philosophy of Science* 39: 473–82.

——(2009a) "Kant on Mental Disorder 1: An Overview," *History of Psychiatry* 20: 267–89.

——(2009b) "Kant on Mental Disorder 2: Philosophical Implications of Kant's Account," *History of Psychiatry* 20: 290–310.

——(2010a) "Two Standpoints and the Problem of Moral Anthropology" in Benjamin Libscomb and James Krueger (eds.) *Kant's Moral Metaphysics*, Berlin: deGruyter.

——(2010b) "Rational Faith: God, Immortality, and Grace" in W. Dudley and K. Engelhard (eds.) *Kant: Key Concepts*, Durham, UK: Acumen Publishing.

——(2010c) "Kantian Moral Pessimism" in S. Anderson-Gold and P. Muchnik (eds.) *Kant's Anatomy of Evil*, Cambridge: Cambridge University Press.

——(in process) "The Open Secret of Kant's Soul."

Geertz, C. (1973) *The Interpretation of Cultures*, New York: Basic Books.

——(2000) *Available Light: Anthropological Reflections on Philosophical Topics*, Princeton, NJ: Princeton University Press.

Gettier, E. (1963) "Is Justified True Belief Knowledge?," *Analysis* 23: 121–23.

Gill, S. et al. (2006) "Metagenomic Analysis of the Human Distal Gut Microbiome," *Science* 312: 1355–59.

Gilligan, C. (1982) *In a Different Voice: Psychological Theory and Women's Development*, Cambridge, MA: Harvard University Press.

Ginet, C. (1990) *On Action*, Cambridge: Cambridge University Press.

——(1997) "Freedom, Responsibility, and Agency," *Journal of Ethics: An International Philosophical Review* 1: 85–98.

Ginsborg, H. (1997) "Lawfulness without a Law: Kant on the Free Play of Imagination and Understanding," *Philosophical Topics* 25: 37–81.

Goodenough, W. (1970) *Description and Comparison in Cultural Anthropology*, Chicago: Aldine.

Gouax, Charles (1972) "Kant's View on the Nature of Empirical Psychology," *Journal of the History of the Behavioural Sciences* 8: 237–42.

Gould, S.J. (1981) *The Mismeasure of Man*, New York: W.W. Norton.

Greene, J.D. (2007) "The Secret Joke of Kant's Soul" in W. Sinnott-Armstrong (ed.) *Moral Psychology, Vol. 3: The Neuroscience of Morality: Emotion, Disease, and Development*, Cambridge, MA: MIT Press.

Grenberg, J. (2005) *Kant and the Ethics of Humility*, Cambridge: Cambridge University Press.

Grier, Michelle (forthcoming) *Kant's Questions: What Can I Know?*, Oxford: Routledge.

Gutting, G. (1989) *Michel Foucault's Archeology of Scientific Reason*, Cambridge: Cambridge University Press.

——(2001) *French Philosophy in the Twentieth Century*, Cambridge: Cambridge University Press.

Guyer, P. (1979) *Kant and the Claims of Taste*, Cambridge: Cambridge University Press.

——(1987) *Kant and the Claims of Knowledge*, Cambridge: Cambridge University Press.

Habermas, J. (1990) *Moral Consciousness and Communicative Action* (trans. C. Lenhardt and S.W. Nicholsen), Cambridge, MA: MIT Press.

——(1993) *Justification and Application* (trans. C.P. Cronin), Cambridge, MA: MIT Press.

——(2008) *Between Naturalism and Religion*, Cambridge: Polity.

Hanna, R. (2006) *Kant, Science, and Human Nature*, Oxford: Oxford University Press.

Harman, G. (2000) *Explaining Value and Other Essays in Moral Philosophy*, Oxford: Clarendon.

Hatfield, G. (1990) *The Natural and the Normative: Theories of Spatial Perception from Kant to Helmholtz*, Cambridge, MA: MIT Press.

Hegel, G.W.F. (1979) *The Phenomenology of Spirit* (ed. A.V. Miller), Oxford: Oxford University Press.

——(1991) *The Philosophy of Right* (ed. Allen Wood), Cambridge: Cambridge University Press.

Heidegger, M. (1953) *Sein und Zeit*, Tübingen: Max Niemeyer Verlag (trans. by J. Staumbaugh as *Being and Time*, Albany, NY: SUNY Press, 1996).

——(1977) *Basic Writings* (ed. and trans. D.F. Krell), New York: HarperCollins.

——(1982) *The Basic Problems of Phenomenology* (trans. A. Hofstadter), Indianapolis: Indiana University Press.

——(1985) *Schelling's Treatise on the Essence of Human Freedom* (trans. Joan Staumbaugh), Athens, OH: Ohio University Press.

——(1997) *Kant and the Problem of Metaphysics* (trans. R. Taft), Indianapolis: Indiana University Press.

——(2002) *The Essence of Human Freedom: An Introduction to Philosophy* (trans. T. Sadler), London: Continuum.

——(2009) *Basic Concepts of Aristotelian Philosophy* (trans. R. Metcalf and M. Tanzer), Indianapolis: Indiana University Press.

Herder, J.G. (2002) *Philosophical Writings* (ed. M. Forster), Cambridge: Cambridge University Press.

Herman, B. (1993) *The Practice of Moral Judgment*, Cambridge, MA: Harvard University Press.

Horton, J. and Mendus, S. (eds.) (1995) *After MacIntyre: Critical Perspectives in the Work of Alasdair MacIntyre*, South Bend, IN: University of Notre Dame Press.

Husserl, E. (1965) *Phenomenology and the Crisis of Philosophy* (trans. Q. Lauer), New York: Harper and Row.

——(1975) *The Paris Lectures* (trans. P. Koestenbaum and S.J. Bartlett), Dordrecht: Kluwer Academic Publishers.

——(1981) *Shorter Works* (ed. P. McCormick and F.A. Elliston), South Bend, IN: University of Notre Dame Press.

——(1983) *Ideas Pertaining to a Pure Phenomenology and to Phenomenological Philosophy* (trans. F. Kersten), The Hague: Martinus Nijhoff Publishers.

——(2001) *Logical Investigations* (trans. J.N. Findlay, ed. M. Dummett), London: Routledge.

Jones, K. (2005) "Moral Epistemology" in F. Jackson and M. Smith (eds.) *The Oxford Handbook of Contemporary Philosophy*, Oxford: Oxford University Press.

Kamtekar, R. (2003) "Situationism and Virtue Ethics on the Content of Our Character," *Ethics* 114: 458–91.

Kane, R. (1996) *The Significance of Free Will*, New York: Oxford University Press.

——(2002) "Free Will: New Directions for an Ancient Problem" in Robert Kane (ed.) *Free Will*, Malden: Blackwell Publishers.

Kierkegaard, S. (1989) *Sickness Unto Death* (trans. A. Hannay), London: Penguin.

——(2006) *Fear and Trembling* (ed. C.S. Evans and trans. S. Walsh), Cambridge: Cambridge University Press.

Kim, J. (1988) "What is Naturalized Epistemology?" in James E. Tomberlin (ed.) *Philosophical Perspectives 2*, Atascadero, CA: Ridgeview.

Kitcher, P. (1985) *Vaulting Ambition: Sociobiology and the Quest for Human Nature*, Cambridge, MA: The MIT Press.

Kitcher, P. (1993) *Kant's Transcendental Psychology*, Oxford: Oxford University Press.

Klein, C. (2011) "The Dual Track Theory of Moral Decision-Making: A Critique of the Neuroimaging Evidence," *Neuroethics* 4: 143–62.

Kleingeld, P. (1993) "The Problematic Status of Gender-Neutral Language in the History of Philosophy: The Case of Kant," *Philosophical Forum* 25: 134–50.

——(1995) *Fortschritt und Vernuft: Zur Geschichtsphilosophie Kants*, Würzburg: Königshausen & Neumann.

——(1999) "Kant, History, and the Idea of Moral Development," *History of Philosophy Quarterly* 16: 59–80.

——(2007) "Kant's Second Thoughts on Race," *The Philosophical Quarterly* 57: 1–20.

Knobe, J. and Nichols, S. (eds.) (2008) *Experimental Philosophy*, Oxford: Oxford University Press.

Korsgaard, C. (1996a) *Creating the Kingdom of Ends*, Cambridge: Cambridge University Press.

——(1996b) *The Sources of Normativity*, Cambridge: Cambridge University Press.

——(2004) *Fellow Creatures: Kantian Ethics and Our Duties to Animals*, Tanner Lectures, http: //www.people.fas.harvard.edu/~korsgaar/CMK.Fellow-Creatures.pdf (accessed September 15, 2010).

——(2009) *Self-Constitution: Agency, Identity, and Integrity*, Oxford: Oxford University Press.

Kramer, P. (2006) *Freud: Inventor of the Modern Mind*, London: HarperCollins.

Kronfeldner, M. (2011) *Darwinian Creativity and Memetics*, Durham, UK: Acumen.

Kuehling, S. (2005) *Dobu: Ethics of Exchange on a Massim Island*, Honolulu: University of Hawaii Press.

Kuhn, T. (1977) "Objectivity, Value Judgment, and Theory Choice," in *The Essential Tension*, Chicago: University of Chicago Press.

——(1996) *The Structure of Scientific Revolutions*, Chicago: University of Chicago Press.

Larrimore, M. (1999) "Sublime Waste: Kant on the Destiny of the 'Races" in C. Wilson (ed.) *Civilization and Oppression*, Calgary: Calgary University Press.

——(2001) "Substitutes for Wisdom: Kant's Practical Thought and the Tradition of the Temperaments," *Journal of the History of Philosophy* 39: 259–88.

Latour, B. and Woolgar, S. (1986) *Laboratory Life: The Construction of Scientific Facts*, Princeton, NJ: Princeton University Press.

Levinas, E. (1969) *Totality and Infinity: An Essay on Exteriority* (trans. A. Lingis), Pittsburgh: Dusquesne University Press.

——(1997) *Basic Philosophical Writings* (ed. A. Peperzak, S. Critchley, and R. Bernasconi), Indianapolis: Indiana University Press.

——(1998a) *Otherwise than Being, or Beyond Essence* (trans. A. Lingis), Pittsburgh: Dusquesne University Press.

——(1998b) *Entre Nous* (trans. M.B. Smith and B. Harshay), New York: Columbia University Press.

Libet, B. (1999) "Do We Have a Free Will?" in Benjamin Libet, Anthony Freedom, and Keith Sutherland (eds.) *The Volitional Brain*, Thorverton, UK: Imprint Academic.

Longino, H. (1990) *Science as Social Knowledge: Values and Objectivity in Scientific Knowledge*, Princeton, NJ: Princeton University Press.

Longuenesse, B. (1997) *Kant and the Capacity to Judge*, Princeton, NJ: Princeton University Press.

Louden, R. (2000) *Kant's Impure Ethics*, Oxford: Oxford University Press.

McCarty, R. (1993) "Kantian Moral Motivation and the Feeling of Respect," *Journal of the History of Philosophy* 31: 421–35.

——(1994) "Motivation and Moral Choice in Kant's Theory of Rational Agency," *Kant-Studien* 85: 15–31.

MacFarland, J.D. (1974) "The Bogus Unity of the Kantian Philosophy" in Pierre Laberge, Francois Duchesneau, and Bryan E. Momssey (eds.) *Proceedings of the Ottawa Congress on Kant in the Anglo-American and Continental Traditions*, Ottawa: University of Ottawa Press.

MacIntyre, A. (1984) *After Virtue*, South Bend, IN: University of Notre Dame Press.

——(1988) *Whose Justice? Which Rationality?*, South Bend, IN: University of Notre Dame Press.

——(1990) *Three Rival Versions of Moral Inquiry: Encyclopedia, Genealogy, and Tradition*, South Bend, IN: University of Notre Dame Press.

McMullin, E. (1993) "Rationality and Paradigm Change in Science" in P. Horwich (ed.) *World Changes: Thomas Kuhn and the Nature of Science*, Cambridge, MA: MIT Press.

Mariña, J. (1997) "Kant on Grace: A Reply to his Critics," *Religious Studies* 33: 379–400.

Marx, K. (1963) *Karl Marx: Early Writings* (trans. and ed. T.B. Bottomore), New York: McGraw Hill.

——(1970) *The German Ideology* (ed. and trans. C. Arthur), New York: International Publishers.

——(1977) *Capital, vol. 1* (trans. B. Fowkes), New York: Vintage Books.

——(1994) *Karl Marx: Selected Writings* (ed. L.H. Simon), Indianapolis: Hackett.

——(1997) *Writings of the Young Marx on Philosophy and Society* (ed. Loyd David Easton and Kurt H. Guddat), Indianapolis: Hackett.

Maynard Smith, J. (1982) *Evolution and the Theory of Game*, Cambridge: Cambridge University Press.

Mayr, E. (1988) *Towards a New Philosophy of Biology: Observations of an Evolutionist*, Cambridge, MA: Harvard University Press.

Meerbote, R. (1989) "Kant's Functionalism" in J.C. Smith (ed.) *Historical Foundations of Cognitive Science*, Dordrecht: Reidel.

Mele, A. (2006) *Free Will and Luck*, Oxford: Oxford University Press.

Mendus, S. (1992) "Kant: An Honest but Narrow-minded Bourgeois?" in H. Williams (ed.), *Essays on Kant's Political Philosophy*, Chicago: University of Chicago Press.

Merleau-Ponty, M. (1945) *Phénoménologie de la Perception*, Paris: Gallimard.

Michaelson Jr., G.E. (1990) *Fallen Freedom: Kant on Radical Evil and Moral Regeneration*, Cambridge: Cambridge University Press.

Moore, G.E. (1913) *Principia Ethica*, Buffalo: Prometheus Books (1968 reprint).

——(1959) *Philosophical Papers*, London: Allen and Unwin.

Munzel, G.F. (1999) *Kant's Conception of Moral Character: The "Critical" Link of Morality, Anthropology, and Reflective Judgment*, Chicago: University of Chicago Press.

Murphy, D. and Bishop, M. (eds.) (2009) *Stich and His Critics*, Hoboken, NJ: Wiley-Blackwell.

Nagel, T. (1974) "What is it Like to be a Bat?," *Philosophical Review*, 83: 435–56.

——(1986) *The View from Nowhere*, Oxford: Oxford University Press.

Nietzsche, F. (1966) *Beyond Good and Evil* (ed. and trans. W. Kaufman), New York: Random House.

——(1967) *On the Genealogy of Morals and Ecce Homo* (ed. and trans W. Kaufman), New York: Random House.

——(1974) *The Gay Science* (ed. and trans. W. Kaufman), New York: Random House.

——(1978) *Thus Spake Zarathustra* (ed. and trans W. Kaufman), New York: Penguin.

——(1997) *Untimely Meditations* (ed. D. Breazeale), Cambridge: Cambridge University Press.

Nisbett, R.E. and Wilson, T.D. (1977) "Telling More than We Can Know: Verbal Reports on Mental Processes," *Psychological Review* 84: 231–59.

Noddings, N. (1984) *Caring: A Feminist Approach to Ethics and Moral Education*, Berkeley, CA: University of California Press.

Noe, A. (2009) *Out of Our Heads: Why You are Not Your Brain, and Other Lessons from the Biology of Consciousness*, New York: Hill & Wang.

Obeyesekere, G. (1993) *The Apotheosis of Captain Cook*, Princeton, NJ: Princeton University Press.

——(2005) *Cannibal Talk: The Man-Eating Myth and Human Sacrifice in the South Seas*, Berkeley, CA: University of California Press.

Okruhlik, K. "Gender Bias in the Biological and Social Sciences," *Canadian Journal of Philosophy*, supplementary volume.

O'Neill, O. (1989) *Constructions of Reason: Explorations of Kant's Practical Philosophy*, Cambridge: Cambridge University Press.

Overbye, D. (2007) "Free Will: Now You Have It, Now you Don't," *The New York Times*, January 2.

Pereboom, D. (2001) *Living Without Free Will*, Cambridge: Cambridge University Press.

Pickering, A. (1984) *Constructing Quarks: A Sociological History of Particle Physics*, Chicago: University of Chicago Press.

Pinker, S. (1997) *How the Mind Works*, New York: W.W. Norton.

——(2002) *The Blank Slate: The Modern Denial of Human Nature*, New York: Viking.

——(2007) *The Stuff of Thought: Language as a Window into Human Nature*, New York: Viking.

Plantinga, A. (1996) "Darwin, Mind, and Meaning," *Books and Culture* (May/June), http://www.veritas-ucsb.org/library/plantinga/Dennett.html (accessed March 2, 2009).

Popper, K. (1972) *Objective Knowledge: An Evolutionary Approach*, Oxford: Clarendon Press.

Putnam, H. (1967) "The 'Innateness' Hypothesis," *Synthese* 17: 12–22 (reprinted as "The Nature of Mental States" in H. Putnam, *Mind, Language, and Reality*, Cambridge: Cambridge University Press, 1975.

Quine, W.V.O. (1951) "Two Dogmas of Empiricism," *Philosophical Review* 60: 20–43.

Quinn, P.L. (1984) "Original Sin, Radical Evil, and Moral Identity," *Faith and Philosophy* 1: 188–202.

——(1990) "Saving Faith from Kant's Remarkable Antinomy," *Faith and Philosophy* 7: 418–34.

Rawls, J. (1971) *A Theory of Justice*, Cambridge, MA: Harvard University Press.

Reath, A. (1989) "Kant's Theory of Moral Sensibility: Respect for the Moral Law and the Influence of Inclination," *Kant-Studien* 80: 284–302.

Reinhold, K.L. (2006) *Letters on the Kantian Philosophy* (ed. Karl Ameriks, trans. James Hebbeler), Cambridge: Cambridge University Press.

Rescorla, R.A. (1991) "Associative Relations in Instrumental Learning," *Quarterly Journal of Experimental Psychology* 43b: 1–23.

Richerson, P.J. and Boyd, R. (2005) *Not by Genes Alone: How Culture Transformed Human Evolution*, Chicago: University of Chicago Press.

Rockmore, T. (2002) *Marx after Marxism*, Hoboken, NJ: Wiley-Blackwell.

Rorty, R. (1988) *Contingency, Irony, Solidarity*, Cambridge: Cambridge University Press.

——(1990) *Objectivity, Relativism, and Truth (Philosophical Papers, vol. 1)*, Cambridge: Cambridge University Press.

——(2000) "Universality and Truth" in R. Brandom (ed.) *Rorty and His Critics*, Oxford: Blackwell.

Rumsey, J. (1989) "The Development of Character in Kantian Moral Theory," *Journal of the History of Philosophy* 27: 247–65.

——(1997) "Revisions of Agency in Kant's Moral Theory" in R. Schott (ed.) *Feminist Interpretations of Immanuel* Kant, Pennsylvania: The Pennsylvania University Press.

Said, E. (1979) *Orientalism*, New York: Vintage.

Sartre, J.-P. (1938) *La Nausée*, Paris: Éditions Gallimard.

——(1947–48/1992), *Notebooks for an Ethics* (trans. D. Pellauer), Chicago: University of Chicago Press.

——(1956) *Being and Nothingness* (trans. H. Barnes), New York: Simon and Schuster.

——(1966) "Review of *The Order of Things*," *L'Arc* 30: 87–96 (reprinted in *Michel Foucault: Critical Assessments* (ed. B. Smart), London: Routledge, 1994).

——(1989) *No Exit and Three Other Plays*, New York: Vintage Press.

——(1993) *Existentialism and the Human Emotions*, New York: Carol Publishing Group.

Sassen, B. (2000) *Kant's Early Critics*, Cambridge: Cambridge University Press.

Sayre-McCord, G. (1996) "Coherentist Epistemology and Moral Theory" in W. Sinnott-Armstrong and M. Timmons (eds.) *Moral Knowledge? New Readings in Moral Epistemology*, Oxford: Oxford University Press.

Schmidt, J. (1996) *What is Enlightenment? 18th Century Questions and 20th Century Answers*, Berkeley, CA: University of California Press.

Schott, R.M. (1993) *Cognition and Eros: A Critique of the Kantian Paradigm*, University Park, PA: Penn State Press.

——(ed.) (1997) *Feminist Interpretations of Immanuel Kant*, University Park, PA: Penn State Press.

Schwartz, S. and Bilsky, W. (1990) "Toward a Theory of the Universal Content and Structure of Values: Extensions and Cross-Cultural Replications," *Journal of Personality and Social Psychology* 58: 878–91.

Shell, S.M. (1996) *The Embodiment of Reason*, Chicago: University of Chicago Press.

——(2003) "Kant's 'True Economy of Human Nature': Rousseau, Count Verri, and the Problem of Happiness" in P. Kain and B. Jacobs (eds.) *Essays on Kant's Anthropology*, Cambridge: Cambridge University Press.

Sidgwick, H. (1901) *The Methods of Ethics*, London: Macmillan & Co.

Sinnott-Armstrong, W. (1992) "Intuitionism" in L. Becker (ed.) *The Encyclopedia of Ethics*, New York: Garland.

Snow, D. (1996) *Schelling and the End of Idealism*, Albany, NY: State University of New York Press.

Sober, E. and Sloan Wilson, D. (1998) *Unto Others: The Evolution and Psychology of Unselfish Behavior*, Cambridge, MA: MIT Press.

Sosa, E. (2009) "A Defense of the Use of Intuitions in Philosophy" in D. Murphy and M. Bishop (eds.) *Stich and His Critics*, Hoboken, NJ: Wiley-Blackwell.

Sperber, D. (1982) "Apparently Irrational Beliefs" in M. Hollis and S. Lukes (eds.) *Rationality and Relativism*, Cambridge, MA: MIT Press.

Spiro, M. (1987) *Culture and Human Nature*, Chicago: University of Chicago Press.

Sturgeon, N. (2002) "Ethical Intuitionism and Ethical Naturalism" in P. Stratton-Lake (ed.) *Ethical Intuitionism: Re-evaluations,* Oxford: Clarendon.

Timmons, M. (1999) *Morality Without Foundations: A Defense of Ethical Contextualism*, Oxford: Oxford University Press.

Tolman, E.C. and Hoznik, C.H. (1930). "Introduction and Removal of Reward, and Maze Performance in Rats," *University of California Publications in Psychology* 4: 257–75.

Tsing, A. (2005) *Friction: An Ethnography of Global Connection*, Princeton, NJ: Princeton University Press.

Tye. M. (2007) "Qualia" (revised entry), *The Stanford Encyclopedia of Philosophy*, http://plato.stanford.edu/entries/qualia/ (accessed June 2010).

Valenstein, E.S. (1986) *Great and Desperate Cures*, New York, Basic Books.

van Cleve, J. (1999) *Problems from Kant*, Oxford: Oxford University Press.

vanInwagen, P. (1986) *An Essay on Free Will*, Oxford: Oxford University Press.

Wallace, R.J. (1994) *Responsibility and the Moral Sentiments*, Cambridge, MA: Harvard University Press.

——(2006) *Normativity and the Will: Essays on Moral Psychology and Practical Reason*, New York: Oxford University Press.

Watkins, E. (2005) *Kant and the Metaphysics of Causality*, Cambridge: Cambridge University Press.

Wegner, D. (2003) *The Illusion of Conscious Will*, Cambridge, MA: The MIT Press.

Weinberg, J., Nichols, S., and Stich, S. (2008) "Normativity and Epistemic Intuitions" in J. Knobe and S. Nichols (eds.) *Experimental Philosophy*, Oxford: Oxford University Press.

Westphal, K. (2005) *Kant's Transcendental Proof of Realism*, Cambridge: Cambridge University Press.

Wilson, C. (1998) "Savagery and the Supersensible: Kant's Universalism in Historical Context," *History of European Ideas* 24: 315–30.

Wilson, E.O. (1978/2004) *Sociobiology*, Cambridge, MA: Belknap Press.

Wilson, H. (2006) *Kant's Pragmatic Anthropology: Its Origin, Meaning, and Critical Significance*, Albany, NY: SUNY Press.

Wood, A. (1984) "Kant's Compatibilism" in Allen Wood (ed.) *Self and Nature in Kant's Philosophy*, Ithaca, NY: Cornell University Press.

——(1999) *Kant's Ethical Thought*, Cambridge: Cambridge University Press.

Wundt, W. (1912) *An Introduction to Psychology* (trans. by Rudolph Pintner), London: George Allen and Unwin.

Yovel, Y. (1980) *Kant and the Philosophy of History*, Princeton, NJ: Princeton University Press.

Zammitto, J. (2002) *Kant, Herder, and the Birth of Anthropology*, Chicago: University of Chicago Press.

Zuckert, R. (2007) *Kant on Beauty and Biology: An Interpretation of the Critique of Judgment*, Cambridge: Cambridge University Press.

Index

Note: page numbers in **bold** refer to tables; page numbers in *italics* refer to figures.